MENU PLANNING

some other AVI books

Food Service

FOOD SANITATION   *Guthrie*
WORK ANALYSIS AND DESIGN IN FOOD SERVICE   *Kazarian*
MEAT HANDBOOK, 3RD EDITION   *Levie*
PRACTICAL BAKING, 2ND EDITION   *Sultan*
CONVENIENCE AND FAST FOOD HANDBOOK   *Thorner*
FOOD BEVERAGE SERVICE HANDBOOK   *Thorner and Herzberg*

Nutrition and Biochemistry

MILESTONES IN NUTRITION   *Goldblith and Joslyn*
NUTRITIONAL EVALUATION OF FOOD PROCESSING   *Harris and Von Loesecke*
PROTEINS AS HUMAN FOOD   *Lawrie*
PROGRESS IN HUMAN NUTRITION, VOL. 1   *Margen*
SULPHUR IN NUTRITION   *Muth and Oldfield*
SELENIUM IN BIOMEDICINE   *Muth, Oldfield and Weswig*
FOOD ENZYMES   *Schultz*
PROTEINS AND THEIR REACTIONS   *Schultz and Anglemier*
CARBOHYDRATES AND THEIR ROLES   *Schultz, Cain and Wrolstad*
CHEMISTRY AND PHYSIOLOGY OF FLAVORS   *Schultz, Day and Libbey*
LIPIDS AND THEIR OXIDATION   *Schultz, Day and Sinnhuber*
PROBIOTICS   *Sperti*

Food Science and Technology

ATTACK ON STARVATION   *Desrosier*
SAFETY OF FOODS   *Graham*
PRINCIPLES OF PACKAGE DEVELOPMENT   *Griffin and Sacharow*
COLOR OF FOODS   *Mackinney and Little*
BAKERY TECHNOLOGY AND ENGINEERING, 2ND EDITION   *Matz*
CEREAL TECHNOLOGY   *Matz*
FOOD TEXTURE   *Matz*
CHOCOLATE, COCOA AND CONFECTIONERY   *Minifie*
FOOD SCIENCE, 2ND EDITION   *Potter*
PRACTICAL FOOD MICROBIOLOGY, 2ND EDITION   *Weiser, Mountney and Gould*

Food and Field Crops Technology

ICE CREAM, 2ND EDITION   *Arbuckle*
FLUID MILK INDUSTRY, 3RD EDITION   *Henderson*
CEREAL SCIENCE   *Matz*
COMMERCIAL CHICKEN PRODUCTION MANUAL   *North*
HANDLING, TRANSPORTATION, STORAGE OF FRUITS AND VEGETABLES, VOL. 1   *Ryall and Lipton*
TREE FRUIT PRODUCTION, 2ND EDITION   *Teskey and Shoemaker*
FUNDAMENTALS OF DAIRY CHEMISTRY   *Webb and Johnson*
BYPRODUCTS FROM MILK, 2ND EDITION   *Webb and Whittier*

MENU PLANNING

By ELEANOR F. ECKSTEIN, Ph.D.

Professor of Home Economics,
Department of Home Economics,
Mississippi State College for Women,
Columbus, Mississippi

Formerly, Assistant Professor of
Food Management,
Department of Nutritional Sciences,
University of California,
Berkeley, California

WESTPORT, CONNECTICUT
THE AVI PUBLISHING COMPANY, INC.
1973

Dedication

This book is dedicated to students in Dietetics, past, present, and future who desire to (a) understand the expected effects of using alternate menu planning strategies and (b) develop skills in monitoring responses to the current menu, assessing menu effectiveness, and planning a more appropriate menu, when called for.

ELEANOR F. ECKSTEIN

Preface

Menu planning is an art that one customarily learns by a costly heuristic or trial and error process. Standard textbooks commonly devote a chapter to the topic, providing some descriptive information and a few samples of menu format. But no systematic or comprehensive treatment of the topic has been available for training or as a reference.

During the 1920's, 1930's and 1940's, institutional food service units were relatively uncomplicated and the pace was slower. Menu planning was learned by experience; a few general rules covering aesthetics and the particular limitations of the specific situation sufficed.

During the 1950's and 1960's, the average size of institutional food service units increased and effective menu planning became a complex challenge. The institutional consumer group became more heterogeneous, reflecting increased mobility; also, more sophisticated expectations became evident. With inflation and sharply rising labor costs resulting in a cost/price squeeze, minimization of production costs became imperative. And, with all this complexity came a work speedup for the food service manager. Moreover, each segment of the institutional food service industry developed according to the needs of its consumer group; accordingly, different philosophies and strategies in menu planning became appropriate.

Until recently, when the educational pendulum swung from the applied to the academic treatment of subject matter, most students developed sufficient skill for entry-level positions. Moreover, the student population was relatively homogeneous (WASP) which simplified the teaching problem. However, with the open door admission policy of many state universities, the student-mix is more heterogeneous, reflecting the economic and ethnic composition of the community. Because of differences in frame of reference, concepts, and priorities, it is difficult for students from non-WASP backgrounds to write "acceptable" menus unless the criteria for item selection are made explicit. Bases for cultural judgment also must be identified.

Until now, a well-trained menu planner could probably cope with the complexity. But, as one attempts to meet the needs of diverse ethnic groups, schedule production tightly for maximum utilization of labor and equipment time, and predict costs accurately, the probability of success diminishes. The computer can be programmed to make the routine decisions in menu planning. However, the criteria for item selection must be explicit and complete or comparable quality menus will not be obtained. For these reasons, premises and hypotheses concerning the consumer group and its needs, labor and equipment scheduling, and numerous other management considerations must be identified and integrated into a theoretical framework that explains the process of item selection and facilitates further research in the subject.

To the extent possible, this book reviews what is known about the bases for item selection and it integrates supporting concepts from related disciplines. It is offered as a first attempt to provide the necessary theoretical framework necessary to development of a rational decision-making process.

February 10, 1973   ELEANOR F. ECKSTEIN
                                             Berkeley, California

Acknowledgements

The author wishes to gratefully acknowledge the support and advice from colleagues and friends that made development of this manuscript possible:

Dr. Maynard A. Joslyn, Professor Emeritus, University of California, Berkeley, who, seeing a need for a textbook on menu planning encouraged the author and gave frequent advice in its preparation.

Miss Nina Gramowich, Administrative Research Dietitian, UCSF Medical Center, who reviewed the entire manuscript for clarity and made numerous suggestions.

Mr. Jacob Rosenthal, President of The Culinary Institute of America, who reviewed the chapter on restaurant menu planning.

Miss Linda Tom and Mr. Wayne D. Wong, who as student representatives of the intended audience, reviewed the manuscript for (a) readability, (b) clarity, relevance, and completeness of concepts, and (c) functionality as a reference; and who suggested the inclusion of the section on the foodways of various subgroups of the American population.

Miss Margaret Yamagami, secretary, who typed the manuscript and corrected inadvertant inconsistencies in format and style.

Mrs. Nancy Moore who prepared the figures for publication.

ELEANOR F. ECKSTEIN

Contents

MECHANICS OF MENU PLANNING

CHAPTER 1

Introduction to Menu Planning

The major objective of a food service organization is to set up a situation in which prospective consumers are induced to consume food items containing needed nutrients in satisfactory quantities. In this regard, the primary function of the menu is either to (a) list the items that will be served or (b) list the alternate items available from which one may select items likely to satisfy one's individual needs (aesthetic, quantitative, nutritive, etc.) at variable prices.

The term "menu planning," as commonly used, refers to a biphasic process which consists of determining (a) *which* items are to be served and (b) *when* they are to be served. Using manual methods, both phases are integrated. Structural requirements define the number of meal components that must be included and alternate patterns if any. Common practice defines item suitability for a given meal component. Items are selected randomly from the recipe pool and are tested for suitability for a particular position on the menu according to implicit criteria. Ordinarily, the repetition frequency for each item and category of items is random and is not explicitly controlled except that unpopular items may not be served more often than once in X days and popular items should be included once in Y days. Using computer methods, both phases may be separate or combined. Moreover, items are selected according to explicitly defined criteria.

The particular list of items that makes up the specific menu determines the number of portions that will be consumed (which varies with the acceptability of the particular item) and, therefore, the quantity to be prepared. The derived production demand, in turn, generates from the recipe quantitative and qualitative requirements for (a) raw materials and, hence, purchasing and inventory systems; (b) facilities and equipment; (c) preparation and service personnel; and (d) food service management activities. The importance of the menu results from its central position in the overall planning process.

CONTEMPORARY PROBLEMS

Bigness and complexity are salient characteristics of contemporary food service units. The average size of an institutional food service is increasing in

order to serve more people and maintain acceptable cost ratios (Cassidy *et al.*
1969). Hospitals often serve 500-800 patients and college residence halls often
serve 1000-2000 students; centralized production units for multiunit operations
produce thousands of meals.

Typically, bigness and complexity result in an increased need for information
and in reduced flexibility. Informational requirements increase because the
consumer group is usually more heterogeneous which changes the pattern of
item consumption. This increases the risk of overproducing some item and
underproducing others. Collection and analysis of preference data are needed to
develop predictors for item demand and, hence, production requirements, costs,
and nutritive intake. Flexibility is reduced because (a) substitution of menu
items is nearly impossible when a large quantity is required and (b) workers cannot or will not adjust to wide variations in workload. Need for specialized skills
and/or equipment requires that data on production requirements be available
in order to efficiently utilize worker time and equipment capacities. Thus, in
order to cope with these realities of bigness and complexity, systematic methods
of menu planning are necessary.

UNIVERSAL CONSIDERATIONS

The menu selection varies considerably among the various types of institutional food service units. Subsequent chapters will discuss differences among
the types of food service that necessitate special considerations in menu planning. However, a number of universal considerations have been listed by West
et al. (1966); these include:

(a) Knowledge of the people to be served: nutritional requirements, food
habits, and the number of people per meal period.
(b) Conditions of preparation and service: availability of equipment and its
arrangement in terms of efficiency; personnel—schedules, skills, and
abilities; budget; style of service.
(c) Outside influences: season, climate, availability of foods.
(d) Food combinations: variety in texture, color, flavor, form or shape, consistency, temperature, satiety value, preparation method.

Subsequent chapters will develop these considerations in great detail.

UNIVERSAL PROBLEMS

Difficulty in systematically evaluating the implications of the complex universal considerations, given the usual pressure of time and cost, has resulted in a
number of universal problems. These include, but are not limited to:

(a) Cultural and/or religious subgroup dissatisfaction with the selection
offered.
(b) Worker dissatisfaction due to variable and/or excessive workload.

(c) Monotonous repetition of some items, although the recipe file contains numerous acceptable items.

(d) Pairs of alternate items that do not improve the choice (forced choice between two unacceptable items is common).

(e) Nutritional balance on paper which is achieved by including liver and/or other rich but unacceptable sources of critical nutrients.

(f) Combinations that are aesthetically poor.

The implications of these problems as related to nonconsumption and production problems will be discussed in chapters 2, 3, and 4.

COMPUTERIZATION

Bigness and complexity created a demand for more systematic methods of menu planning. A review of the menu planning process revealed it as a series of accept-reject decisions based on separate but similar criteria. This led to the recent development of computerized methods for making the routine decisions (Balintfy 1966; Eckstein 1967).

In order to develop or select a computerized system for planning menus, the ramifications of the menu planning process must be completely understood. This book discusses the relevant aspects for each of the major types of institutional food service units. Content is divided into four sections as follows:

(a) Considerations (philosophical and practical).

(b) Mechanics of menu planning.

(c) Specific considerations for each major type of institution.

(d) Computer applications.

The concepts presented in these four sections should facilitate communications among administrators, dietitians, and programmers and should enable these groups to develop responsive menu planning systems that more nearly meet the needs of consumers, workers, and management.

BIBLIOGRAPHY

BALINTFY, J. L. 1966. Linear programming models for menu planning. *In* Hospital Industrial Engineering: A Guide to the Improvement of Hospital Management Systems, H. B. Smalley, and J. R. Freeman (Editors). Van Nostrand Reinhold Co., New York.

CASSIDY, R. J., NEJELSKI, L., and ZACCARELLI, H. (Editors) 1969. Selected research abstracts of published and unpublished reports pertaining to the food service industry including recommendations for research needs. Food Res. Center Catholic Institutions Bull. *ARS 52-46*.

ECKSTEIN, E. F. 1967. Menu planning by computer: the random approach. J. Am. Dietet. Assoc. *51*, 529–533.

WEST, B. B., WOOD, L., and HARGER, V. F. 1966. Food Service in Institutions, 4th Edition. John Wiley & Sons, New York.

CHAPTER 2

Consumer Considerations from the Management Perspective

In order to plan menus that will maximize consumption (that is, *by consumers in the aggregate over time*) a thorough understanding of the basic needs of consumers is required. The discussion of needs will be divided into (a) basic needs, (b) needs of captive consumers, (c) food habits and preferences, (d) nutritional needs, (e) need for variety, and (f) need for reasonable costs. Each topic will be discussed in turn.

COMMON HUMAN NEEDS

According to Maslow (1968), basic human needs can be arranged in a hierarchy from low to high as follows: (a) physiological needs, (b) safety needs, (c) love needs, (d) esteem needs, and (e) need for self-actualization. Each of these will be considered briefly as it relates to menu planning. Maslow (1943) wrote[1]:

Undoubtedly ... physiological needs are the most pre-potent of all needs. What this means specifically is that in the human being who is missing everything in life in an extreme fashion, it is most likely that the major motivation would be the physiological needs rather than any others. A person who is lacking food, safety, love, and esteem would most probably hunger for food more strongly than for anything else.

If all the needs are unsatisfied, and the organism is then dominated by the physiological needs, all other needs may become simply non-existent or be pushed into the background.... For the man who is extremely and dangerously hungry, no other interest exists but food. He dreams food, he remembers food, he thinks about food, he emotes only about food, he perceives only food and wants only food.

Another peculiar characteristic of the human organism when it is dominated by a certain need is that the whole philosophy of the future tends also to change. For our chronically and extremely hungry man, Utopia can be defined very simply as a place where there is plenty of food. He tends to think that, if only he is guaranteed food for the rest of his life, he will be perfectly happy and will never want anything more. Life itself tends to be defined in terms of eating. Anything else will be defined as unimportant....

... It is quite true that man lives by bread alone—when there is no bread. But what happens to man's desires when there *is* plenty of bread and when his belly is chronically filled?

At once other (and "higher") needs emerge, and these, rather than physiological hungers, dominate the organism. And when these in turn are satisfied, again new (and still "higher") needs emerge and so on. This is what we mean by

---

[1] Maslow (1943). Copyright by the American Psychological Association, and reproduced by permission.

saying that the basic human needs are organized into a hierarchy of relative prepotency.

One main implication of this phrasing is that gratification becomes as important a concept as deprivation in motivation theory, for it releases the organism from the domination of a relatively more physiological need, permitting thereby the emergence of other more social goals. The physiological needs, along with their partial goals, when chronically gratified, cease to exist as active determinants or organizers of behavior. They now exist only in a potential fashion in the sense that they may emerge again to dominate the organism if they are thwarted. The organism is dominated and its behavior organized only by unsatisfied needs. If hunger is satisfied, it becomes unimportant in the current dynamics of the individual.

Physiological needs are individual but are planned for in terms of the modal need of the group based on age, sex, and activity. The appropriate Recommended Dietary Allowances (Table 2.1) are the usual standards for assessing adequacy (National Research Council–National Academy of Sciences 1968).

To meet physiological needs, menu selections should be planned so that the most likely combinations will meet physiological needs. Inclusion of unacceptable but rich sources of nutrients only balances the menus on paper.

When physiological needs have been satisfied the safety needs take precedance. Safety needs are associated with security. It is known that people generally fear the unknown, hence they are reluctant to try new foods (Townsend 1928). Numerous preference studies have indicated that unknown items are usually marked disliked. A knowledge of the food habits of the specific population enables the menu planner to restrict variety, i.e., content of the recipe pool, to acceptable items.

When the physiological and safety needs are sufficiently gratified, love or belongingness needs predominate. This is particularly noticeable with teenagers who are apt to consume the currently accepted foods rather than those required physiologically. Intermittent fads involving selected foods appeal to those who are insecure in personal relationships; these fads will have important though transient effects on the demands for standard items.

When all of these needs have been fairly well satisfied, the need for esteem as expressed by prestige, recognition, or attention surfaces. The most common method of catering to this need is through use of unfamiliar and/or foreign menu terms. Items that are served with a flaming flourish at the table or are specially arranged and decorated also gratify this need. The need for independence and freedom are two additional facets of the need for esteem. Consumers gratify this need in making personal selections from among alternate menu items; a forced choice between unacceptable alternates is inherently frustrating. Dissatisfaction resulting from use of a set menu, i.e., no choice or limited choice, is in part due to thwarting of this need.

The highest need, that of self-actualization or the tendency to meet one's potential is ordinarily not gratified by menu selections. There is some evidence

TABLE 2.1

RECOMMENDED DAILY DIETARY ALLOWANCES (REVISED 1968)[1]

Designed for the Maintenance of Good Nutrition of Practically All Healthy People in the United States

Age[2] (Yr) From–Up To	Weight (Kg)	Weight (Lb)	Height (Cm)	Height (In.)	Protein (Gm)	Kcal	Vitamin A Activity (IU)	Vitamin D (IU)	Vitamin E Activity (IU)	Ascorbic Acid (Mg)	Folacin[3] (Mg)	Niacin (Mg Equiv)[4]	Riboflavin (Mg)	Thiamin (Mg)	Vitamin B6 (Mg)	Vitamin B12 (µg)	Calcium (Gm)	Phosphorus (Gm)	Iodine (µg)	Iron (Mg)	Magnesium (Mg)
Infants																					
0–1/6	4	9	55	22	kg × 2.2[5]	kg × 120	1,500	400	5	35	0.05	5	0.4	0.2	0.2	1.0	0.4	0.2	25	6	40
1/6–1/2	7	15	63	25	kg × 2.0[5]	kg × 110	1,500	400	5	35	0.05	7	0.5	0.4	0.3	1.5	0.5	0.4	40	10	60
1/2–1	9	20	72	28	kg × 1.8[5]	kg × 100	1,500	400	5	35	0.1	8	0.6	0.5	0.4	2.0	0.6	0.5	45	15	70
Children																					
1–2	12	26	81	32	25	1,100	2,000	400	10	40	0.1	8	0.6	0.6	0.5	2.0	0.7	0.7	55	15	100
2–3	14	31	91	36	25	1,250	2,000	400	10	40	0.2	8	0.7	0.6	0.6	2.5	0.8	0.8	60	15	150
3–4	16	35	100	39	30	1,400	2,500	400	10	40	0.2	9	0.8	0.7	0.7	3	0.8	0.8	70	10	200
4–6	19	42	110	43	30	1,600	2,500	400	10	40	0.2	11	0.9	0.8	0.9	4	0.8	0.8	80	10	200
6–8	23	51	121	48	35	2,000	3,500	400	15	40	0.2	13	1.1	1.0	1.0	4	0.9	0.9	100	10	250
8–10	28	62	131	52	40	2,200	3,500	400	15	40	0.3	15	1.2	1.1	1.2	5	1.0	1.0	110	10	250
Males																					
10–12	35	77	140	55	45	2,500	4,500	400	20	40	0.4	17	1.3	1.3	1.4	5	1.2	1.2	125	10	300
12–14	43	95	151	59	50	2,700	5,000	400	20	45	0.4	18	1.4	1.4	1.6	5	1.4	1.4	135	18	350
14–18	59	130	170	67	60	3,000	5,000	400	25	55	0.4	20	1.5	1.5	1.8	5	1.4	1.4	150	18	400
18–22	67	147	175	69	60	2,800	5,000	400	30	60	0.4	18	1.6	1.4	2.0	5	0.8	0.8	140	10	400
22–35	70	154	175	69	65	2,800	5,000	—	30	60	0.4	18	1.7	1.4	2.0	5	0.8	0.8	140	10	350
35–55	70	154	173	68	65	2,600	5,000	—	30	60	0.4	17	1.7	1.3	2.0	5	0.8	0.8	125	10	350
55–75+	70	154	171	67	65	2,400	5,000	—	30	60	0.4	14	1.7	1.2	2.0	6	0.8	0.8	110	10	350
Females																					
10–12	35	77	142	56	50	2,250	4,500	400	20	40	0.4	15	1.3	1.1	1.4	5	1.2	1.2	110	18	300
12–14	44	97	154	61	50	2,300	5,000	400	20	45	0.4	15	1.4	1.2	1.6	5	1.3	1.3	115	18	350
14–16	52	114	157	62	55	2,400	5,000	400	25	50	0.4	16	1.4	1.2	1.8	5	1.3	1.3	120	18	350
16–18	54	119	160	63	55	2,300	5,000	400	25	50	0.4	15	1.5	1.2	2.0	5	1.3	1.3	115	18	350
18–22	58	128	163	64	55	2,000	5,000	400	25	55	0.4	13	1.5	1.0	2.0	5	0.8	0.8	100	18	350
22–35	58	128	163	64	55	2,000	5,000	—	25	55	0.4	13	1.5	1.0	2.0	5	0.8	0.8	100	18	300
35–55	58	128	160	63	55	1,850	5,000	—	25	55	0.4	13	1.5	1.0	2.0	6	0.8	0.8	90	18	300
55–75+	58	128	157	62	55	1,700	5,000	—	25	60	0.4	13	1.5	1.0	2.0	6	0.8	0.8	80	10	300
Pregnancy					65	+200	6,000	400	30	60	0.8	15	1.8	+0.1	2.5	8	+0.4	+0.4	125	18	450
Lactation					75	+1,000	8,000	400	30	60	0.5	20	2.0	+0.5	2.5	6	+0.5	+0.5	150	18	450

Source: Food and Nutrition Board, National Academy of Sciences—National Research Council.

[1] The allowance levels are intended to cover individual variations among most normal persons as they live in the United States under usual environmental stresses. The recommended allowances can be attained with a variety of common foods, providing other nutrients for which human requirements have been less well defined.

[2] Entries on lines for age range 22–35 yr represent the reference man and woman at age 22. All other entries represent allowances for the midpoint of the specified age range.

[3] The folacin allowances refer to dietary sources as determined by *Lactobacillus casei* assay. Pure forms of folacin may be effective in doses less than ¼ of the RDA.

[4] Niacin equivalents include dietary sources of the vitamin itself plus 1 mg equivalent for each 60 mg of dietary tryptophan.

[5] Assumes protein equivalent to human milk. For proteins not 100% utilized factors should be increased proportionately.

that variety and aesthetic considerations relate to satisfaction of this need (Wagner 1966).

Generally, hierarchical order correlates with order of precedence in satisfying the basic needs. Thus, in the less developed countries where millions lack sufficient calories or protein, restricted menus are satisfactory as most consumers are primarily motivated to satisfy their physiological needs which are so dominant that other needs are inhibited. Whereas, in affluent America a majority of consumers are concerned with satisfaction of high order needs. As we shall see later, this concept is important in selecting an appropriate computer menu planning model.

THE "CAPTIVE" CONSUMER

The institutional consumer is generally regarded as a "captive" consumer because he does not usually have the alternative of purchasing a meal elsewhere. Because the consumer has no option, the institution is responsible for providing acceptable, nutritious meals.

Captive groups are of two types: short-term and long-term. The typical example of the short-term type is the hospital patient. Patient stay averages about five days but all meals to be consumed must be provided. Although menu choice is desirable, the repetition interval can be short so the menu variety requirement is reduced. A cycle menu, which is a planned sequence of menus that is repeated at regular intervals, is the simplest means of reducing the menu planning task.

Long-term captive consumers characteristically consume institutional meals for months or years. Acceptable variety is necessary to prevent the dissatisfactions resulting from monotony. A cycle menu can be used but a longer sequence is required, usually 3-5 weeks. A different cycle for each season improves acceptability of the cycle menu.

FOOD HABITS, PREFERENCES, AND CONSUMPTION

In addition to the basic needs which are common to all consumers, the menu planner must recognize dominant eating patterns of the group in order to predict consumption. *Food habits* are the practices[2] and associated attitudes that predetermine what, when, why, and how a person will eat, given preferred alternatives. Food habits of individuals are determined by an interaction of environmental, physical, and psychological factors with previous food experience. Contributing factors include age, sex, race, religion, economic status, area of residence, social status, physiological needs, and psychological needs, associations, and compensations (Cussler and deGive 1952; de Garine 1970).

The traditional concept of the institutional consumer group assumed homogeneity; a set menu with one item per meal component was common. Con-

---

[2]Practice (according to Webster's Dictionary): to do or perform often, customarily or habitually. Suggests an act or method followed with regularity and usually through choice.

temporary American society is extremely mobile and includes diverse ethnic, cultural, social, religious, and economic groups. Institutional populations generally reflect the heterogeneity of society; as the size of the institutional population increases so does the problem of selecting menu items "acceptable-to-all." A selective menu with several choices per meal component provides the greatest opportunity for meeting the needs of the various subgroups.[3]

During the 1960's, various ethnic groups forced food managers to become aware of the need to plan menus that meet the needs of population subgroups. When "ethnic foods" are served intermittently, charges of tokenism result. Since members of the subgroups must eat every day in order to supply necessary nutrients, ethnic foods and/or standard items commonly consumed by the subgroup must be included as alternate items for each meal component of every meal.

In recent years the counter-culture has become a significant subgroup. A knowledge of the various types of vegetarian diets is necessary in order to plan acceptable menus. Section 4 on Foodways of American Subgroup Cultures contains detailed information pertaining to various population subgroups.

Intermittently, studies of food habits are conducted to update information. Food habits are usually reported by a consumer who checks a yes–no dichotomy. Food habit studies usually include: (a) meals usually or often skipped, (b) heaviness of the meal desired, (c) categories of food or meal components disliked, and (d) number of snacks consumed.

Food habits often determine food preferences; together they provide the best predictor of consumption. Food habits are personal but are summarized for a specific consumer group by a measure of typicality.

Food preferences are *affective* statements which express degree of liking for a food item (Pilgrim 1957). Food preferences are related to food habits in the following way: people usually prefer foods they consume customarily. Given a choice, most people will select familiar foods that have been personally assigned an informal rating. Moreover, most people instinctively respond to "not tried" items with dislike (Pilgrim 1961).

Two types of food preference ratings may be obtained for each food item; one an index of item popularity, the other an index of combination preference. The first identifies the rank of the item compared to other food items in its category, e.g., apple pie ranks above gooseberry pie. The second index indicates, for example, that apples are customarily served with pork and chicken rather than beef and fish. This index is difficult to develop in precise mathematical terms but it is a major part of the experienced judgment of the menu planner.

---

[3]Within each type of food service, the consumer group is relatively homogeneous with respect to at least one factor. Assumptions based on the homogeneity and problems associated with the relevant categories of heterogeneity will be discussed in the chapters relating to the specific types of food service.

Some recent work by Moskowitz (1972) using the method of magnitude estimation to develop points in psychological space shows promise of providing a means of replacing an intuitive method with a systematic one (see Fig. 2.1).

Population surveys of food preference usually employ the hedonic scale (Fig. 2.2) or a scale similar to the Food Action Rating Scale (FACT) (Fig. 2.3). The hedonic scale is used to rate foods along a nine-point continuum from "like

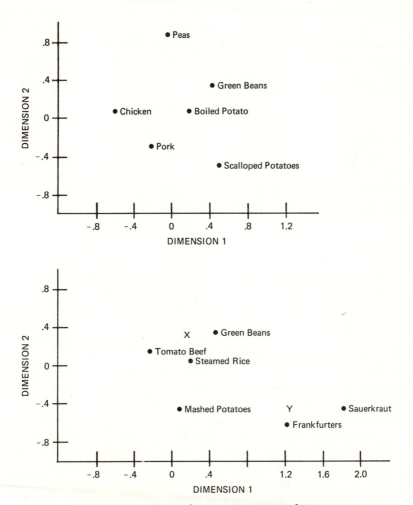

FIG. 2.1. PLOT OF AGGREGATE[1] AND SEGREGATE[2] (X AND Y) COMBINATIONS USING MULTIDIMENSIONAL SCALING; RATINGS WERE OBTAINED BY MAGNITUDE ESTIMATION[3]

[1] Aggregate: each meat is compatible with each vegetable or potato. [2] Segregate: each triplet belongs with itself only. [3] Data supplied by Howard Moskowitz, U.S. Army Natick Laboratories, Natick, Mass.

9	8	7	6	5	4	3	2	1
like extremely	like very much	like moderately	like slightly	neither like nor dislike	dislike slightly	dislike moderately	dislike very much	dislike extremely

1. Orange Juice, Instant	9 8 7 6 5 4 3 2 1	51. Cream of Mushroom Soup	9 8 7 6 5 4 3 2 1
2. Grape Juice	9 8 7 6 5 4 3 2 1	52. Lemon-Lime Soda	9 8 7 6 5 4 3 2 1
3. Whole Wheat Bread	9 8 7 6 5 4 3 2 1	53. Turnip Greens	9 8 7 6 5 4 3 2 1
4. Butterscotch Sauce	9 8 7 6 5 4 3 2 1	54. Roast Beef	9 8 7 6 5 4 3 2 1
5. Chocolate Cream Cake	9 8 7 6 5 4 3 2 1	55. Hominy Grits	9 8 7 6 5 4 3 2 1
6. Manhattan Clam Chowder	9 8 7 6 5 4 3 2 1	56. Molasses Cookies	9 8 7 6 5 4 3 2 1
7. Jellied Fruit Salad	9 8 7 6 5 4 3 2 1	57. Tea	9 8 7 6 5 4 3 2 1
8. Hamburger	9 8 7 6 5 4 3 2 1	58. Mincemeat Pie	9 8 7 6 5 4 3 2 1
9. Strawberry Shortcake	9 8 7 6 5 4 3 2 1	59. Chili Macaroni	9 8 7 6 5 4 3 2 1
10. Bananas	9 8 7 6 5 4 3 2 1	60. Bean Soup	9 8 7 6 5 4 3 2 1
11. Lemon Chiffon Pie	9 8 7 6 5 4 3 2 1	61. Pears (Fresh)	9 8 7 6 5 4 3 2 1
12. Cream of Potato Soup	9 8 7 6 5 4 3 2 1	62. Cranberry Sauce	9 8 7 6 5 4 3 2 1
13. Creamed Style Corn	9 8 7 6 5 4 3 2 1	63. Mixed Vegetables	9 8 7 6 5 4 3 2 1
14. Danish Pastry	9 8 7 6 5 4 3 2 1	64. Lemon Pudding Sauce	9 8 7 6 5 4 3 2 1
15. Mixed Sweet Pickles	9 8 7 6 5 4 3 2 1	65. Baked Macaroni & Cheese	9 8 7 6 5 4 3 2 1
16. Lamb Roast	9 8 7 6 5 4 3 2 1	66. Carrot Sticks	9 8 7 6 5 4 3 2 1
17. Sugar Cookies	9 8 7 6 5 4 3 2 1	67. Fruit Punch	9 8 7 6 5 4 3 2 1
18. Green Beans	9 8 7 6 5 4 3 2 1	68. Salmon	9 8 7 6 5 4 3 2 1
19. Caesar Salad Dressing	9 8 7 6 5 4 3 2 1	69. Peach Crisp	9 8 7 6 5 4 3 2 1
20. Beef Barley Soup	9 8 7 6 5 4 3 2 1	70. Corn on the Cob	9 8 7 6 5 4 3 2 1

FIG. 2.2. EXCERPT FROM FOOD PREFERENCE SURVEY FORM—PART 2, SAMPLE HEDONIC SCALE RATINGS

extremely" through "neither like nor dislike" to "dislike extremely" (Peryam and Pilgrim 1957). The FACT scale points are action statements related to desired frequency of consumption, e.g., ham, once in three days; beef, everyday; etc. (Schutz 1965). This is effective for major items, but yields meaningless data for items such as nuts, toppings, and condiments since compatibility with major items determines acceptability (Table 2.2).

Group approximations for preferences are obtained as mean ratings for individual items or combinations. A stratified random sampling pattern assures inclusion of the preferences of major subgroups. However, mean ratings are valid only if the population is relatively homogeneous. If the population is heterogeneous with large groups who rate foods significantly different from the group-as-a-whole, multimodal distributions will be obtained (Fig. 2.4). These cannot be represented by a mean; if the frequency of serving an item is tied to the mean, the item will be served too frequently.

Because institutional populations are mobile, preference ratings will vary with the preferences of the current group. Hence, a continous sampling is necessary to monitor changes and maintain acceptability of the menus.

Breakfast habits and preferences are particularly stable for most individuals but vary widely among individuals. Preferred items and combinations are those customarily consumed everyday. The typical menu reported by some investiga-

	BREAKFAST		MID-DAY		EVENING MEAL		NEVER
	days per week	weeks per month	days per week	weeks per month	days per week	weeks per month	
1. Orange Juice, Instant	1 2 3 4 5 6 7	1 2 3 4	1 2 3 4 5 6 7	1 2 3 4	1 2 3 4 5 6 7	1 2 3 4	—
2. Grape Juice	1 2 3 4 5 6 7	1 2 3 4	1 2 3 4 5 6 7	1 2 3 4	1 2 3 4 5 6 7	1 2 3 4	—
3. Whole Wheat Bread	1 2 3 4 5 6 7	1 2 3 4	1 2 3 4 5 6 7	1 2 3 4	1 2 3 4 5 6 7	1 2 3 4	—
4. Butterscotch Sauce	1 2 3 4 5 6 7	1 2 3 4	1 2 3 4 5 6 7	1 2 3 4	1 2 3 4 5 6 7	1 2 3 4	—
5. Chocolate Cream Cake	1 2 3 4 5 6 7	1 2 3 4	1 2 3 4 5 6 7	1 2 3 4	1 2 3 4 5 6 7	1 2 3 4	—
6. Manhattan Clam Chowder	1 2 3 4 5 6 7	1 2 3 4	1 2 3 4 5 6 7	1 2 3 4	1 2 3 4 5 6 7	1 2 3 4	—
7. Jellied Fruit Salad	1 2 3 4 5 6 7	1 2 3 4	1 2 3 4 5 6 7	1 2 3 4	1 2 3 4 5 6 7	1 2 3 4	—
8. Hamburger	1 2 3 4 5 6 7	1 2 3 4	1 2 3 4 5 6 7	1 2 3 4	1 2 3 4 5 6 7	1 2 3 4	—
9. Strawberry Shortcake	1 2 3 4 5 6 7	1 2 3 4	1 2 3 4 5 6 7	1 2 3 4	1 2 3 4 5 6 7	1 2 3 4	—
10. Bananas	1 2 3 4 5 6 7	1 2 3 4	1 2 3 4 5 6 7	1 2 3 4	1 2 3 4 5 6 7	1 2 3 4	—
11. Lemon Chiffon Pie	1 2 3 4 5 6 7	1 2 3 4	1 2 3 4 5 6 7	1 2 3 4	1 2 3 4 5 6 7	1 2 3 4	—
12. Cream of Potato Soup	1 2 3 4 5 6 7	1 2 3 4	1 2 3 4 5 6 7	1 2 3 4	1 2 3 4 5 6 7	1 2 3 4	—
13. Creamed Style Corn	1 2 3 4 5 6 7	1 2 3 4	1 2 3 4 5 6 7	1 2 3 4	1 2 3 4 5 6 7	1 2 3 4	—
14. Danish Pastry	1 2 3 4 5 6 7	1 2 3 4	1 2 3 4 5 6 7	1 2 3 4	1 2 3 4 5 6 7	1 2 3 4	—
15. Mixed Sweet Pickles	1 2 3 4 5 6 7	1 2 3 4	1 2 3 4 5 6 7	1 2 3 4	1 2 3 4 5 6 7	1 2 3 4	—
16. Lamb Roast	1 2 3 4 5 6 7	1 2 3 4	1 2 3 4 5 6 7	1 2 3 4	1 2 3 4 5 6 7	1 2 3 4	—
17. Sugar Cookies	1 2 3 4 5 6 7	1 2 3 4	1 2 3 4 5 6 7	1 2 3 4	1 2 3 4 5 6 7	1 2 3 4	—
18. Green Beans	1 2 3 4 5 6 7	1 2 3 4	1 2 3 4 5 6 7	1 2 3 4	1 2 3 4 5 6 7	1 2 3 4	—
19. Caesar Salad Dressing	1 2 3 4 5 6 7	1 2 3 4	1 2 3 4 5 6 7	1 2 3 4	1 2 3 4 5 6 7	1 2 3 4	—
20. Beef Barley Soup	1 2 3 4 5 6 7	1 2 3 4	1 2 3 4 5 6 7	1 2 3 4	1 2 3 4 5 6 7	1 2 3 4	—

FIG. 2.3. EXCERPT FROM FOOD PREFERENCE SURVEY FORM—PART 1, SAMPLE FOOD ACTION RATING SCALE

tors (Eppright 1947; Kennedy 1952) is a composite of favorite items from a population with undefined subgroups and is not really acceptable to the group as a whole. Rotation of a series of composite menus probably does not really improve satisfaction unless customary items happen to be included. The obvious

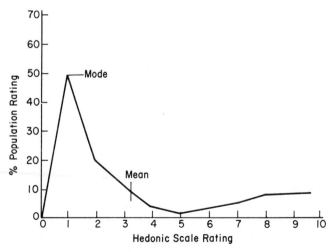

FIG. 2.4. TYPICAL RATING PATTERN FOR LIVER

TABLE 2.2

SAMPLE RATINGS FOR SELECTED CLASS REPRESENTATIVES AND APPROPRIATE
ACCOMPANIMENTS FOR THE CLASS

Main Item Class Representative	Hedonic Rating	Accompaniments for All Items in Class	Hedonic Rating
Sandwiches		Relishes[1]	
Hamburgers	6.95	Chopped Onion	4.17
Cheeseburgers	6.96	Dill Pickles	5.53
Frankfurters	6.18	Sweet Pickle Relish	4.86
Grilled Cheese	6.72	Mixed Sweet Pickles	4.43
Turkey Club Sandwich	6.42		
Salads		Salad Dressing[2]	
Lettuce and Tomato	6.28	Thousand Island	6.11
Lettuce	6.19	French	6.12
Tossed Green	6.56	Vinegar & Oil	4.70
		Russian	5.16
		Blue Cheese	4.83
Ice Cream		Sauces[3]	
Ice Cream	7.32	Butterscotch	3.77
Ice Cream Sundae	7.05	Hot Fudge	5.58
		Pineapple	4.80
		Miscellaneous[4]	
		Mixed Nuts	5.66
		Carrot Sticks	5.49
		Celery Sticks	5.12
		Green Olives	4.52
		Ripe Black Olives	4.44

[1] The desired serving frequencies for the relishes are much lower than for the sandwiches which reflects the fact that different ones are consumed with different sandwiches.
[2] The desired frequency for the first two salad dressings is approximately the same as the frequency for the salads. The lower values for the other dressings reflect the fact that they are not as popular.
[3] The combined frequency for the three sauces is approximately equal to the desired frequency for sundaes. Therefore, these frequencies are probably accurate predictors of desired frequency of serving.
[4] No main item is listed as these foods can be paired with any combination of alternative items since they do not have strong culturally based associations. These frequencies are probably accurate predictors of desired serving frequency.

solution is carefully selected menu choices from the categories of items that are frequently preferred.

Lunch and dinner eating habits and preferences are more varied. Although some groups demand soup and sandwich combinations at lunch, most prefer a rotation of the various kinds of combination lunches: e.g., soup/sandwich; salad/ sandwich; casserole/vegetable; short order such as hamburgers, hot dogs, etc.; or a regular cafeteria selection. Dinner courses and item categories are relatively invariate and thus determine menu structure in terms of meal components. For example, steaks, roasts, and chops are traditional dinner entrées; some casseroles and other extended meats are acceptable if frequency is rather low. However, the daily selection is random with no rotation among categories expected. Combination preferences[4] and variety are of great importance in planning dinner menus.

Consumption of food depends on its acceptability, if extraneous factors such as illness and satiety are ignored. Preference and flawlessness are necessary to acceptability. A preferred food is acceptable if familiar and properly prepared. Thus, preference is the index to consumption.

NUTRITIONAL NEEDS

An institutional population includes individuals with widely varying physiological requirements for the various nutrients. The exact needs are unknown but commonly represented by an estimate of central tendency, i.e., a population mean. For purposes of evaluation, estimates commonly employed are half (calories excepted) the Recommended Dietary Allowances (RDA) for the appropriate age-sex groups (National Research Council–National Academy of Sciences 1968). These recommendations are devised to meet the needs of most of the group (Sebrell 1969; Miller and Voria 1969). (Fig. 2.5).

Because people vary in their individual requirements for the various nutrients, institutional food service is obliged to provide some acceptable alternatives in terms of the quantity provided. While portion control must be maintained, additional servings of some food items should be routinely available. Of course, the cost of these items must be included in costing the menu. In some situations, caloric value may be one of the important considerations in selection of alternate choice items. For example, the daily calorie total of the alternate items might be the mean minus 1000 calories in order to facilitate weight control.

The nutritional adequacy of the diet or menu set is usually only checked against a food guide such as the Basic 4, except in hospitals and a few other institutions when a computer is available. This is ordinarily satisfactory and sufficient if a variety of natural foods is served.

Unless food consumption can be assumed, nutritional analyses are inappropriate and invalid (both paper and/or chemical analyses are irrelevant and unreliable), and lead to a false sense of security. Individuals differ in their preferences for various food items, and hence in their consumption of them. If a single rich source of a critical nutrient were relied upon to provide the quantity required and if the food were consistently refused, the individual's need for that nutrient would not be met. Therefore, in planning institutional menus it is obligatory that a variety of nutrient sources be provided. Traditionally, liver

---

[4] A food combination has been defined by Eindhoven and Peryam (1959) as: "... several foods, individually prepared, that are served and eaten together or successively. When two foods are combined in this way the individual components partially lose their identity in favor of the combination which has its own preference rating." Examples of combinations are steak and baked potatoes, fish and fries, ham and sweet potatoes, and roast beef and mashed potatoes. Quoted with permission of the Institute of Food Technology.

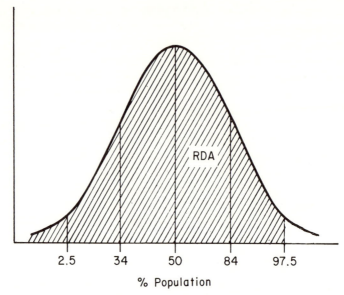

% Population

FIG. 2.5. DISTRIBUTION OF NUTRITIONAL NEEDS FOR ANY
NUTRIENT EXCEPT CALORIES

and some of the less popular, though rich sources of vitamins and minerals, have been used to balance the nutritive content on paper. This practice is misleading and professionally dishonest.

MENTAL SET AND CONSUMER EXPECTATIONS

Acceptability of a meal-as-a-whole and of each of its components depends on the mental set used as a standard of comparison. Normally, people use different sets in evaluating food they prepare at home, food consumed at a friend's home, and in restaurants or institutions. Food from the same batches served in these different situations will receive different ratings due to differences in expectations that are associated with the different frames of reference.

Observation reveals that at home (a) variety may be severely limited due to budget constraints and/or (b) quality may be poor or highly variable due to lack of expertise or indifference of the cook, yet the food is accepted and enjoyed. Why? Two plausible explanations are (a) the consumer accepts what he cannot change and (b) critical comments are repressed in order to keep peace. Thus, the mental set encourages acceptance and enjoyment of the food.

When one visits friends, one also selects an accepting mental set in order to perserve the friendship. However, one is aware of and rates the level of expertise in cookery. Yet, one is customarily polite and compliments the cook.

Four general mental sets apply in judging restaurant food according to the type of restaurant, i.e., fast food, moderate price, elegant, or unusual (ethnic or foreign). Cost plays an important role in determining acceptability; the higher the price, the higher the expectations. Generally, one expects "acceptable" quality and rapid service from a fast food facility; delay is intolerable. Expectations from a moderate priced restaurant are probably elastic and ambiguous reflecting the variations in quality commonly experienced. In a high priced restaurant, slight imperfections in food or service may result in an irate customer. The customer is visibly paying for expertise, and accordingly expects it. Variety is also expected. However, when one selects a restaurant for an unusual eating experience, one expects items to be well prepared and generally typical for the type selected. Some very unusual items are expected to be listed as a "conversation piece."

Institutional food is appraised using still another mental set. Just after World War I, institutional populations considered themselves fortunate if the food were hot and neither burned nor oversalted. But, today good food is expected; it may be plain but not monotonous.

MONOTONY OR VARIETY

Monotony is a psychological construct representing the dissatisfaction which arises from frequent or cyclic repetition of food items or aesthetic factors such as color, texture, shape, etc. As a result of monotony, the usual impulse to repeat the food is reduced. Dissatisfaction, and therefore monotony, is a matter of degree. Long-term success of a cycle menu is largely determined by the consumers perception of its position along the monotony-variety continuum.

Food acceptance and consumption are inversely related to monotony (Zellmer 1969). Various aspects of the relationship have been studied. Siegal and Pilgrim (1958) tested the following hypotheses[5]:

(a) Monotony in eating is some positive function of the number of times an item of food has been consumed totally or in part.
(b) In time, monotony in eating dissipates very slowly or not at all.
(c) A high initial level of acceptance slows the growth of monotony in eating.
(d) The growth of monotony in eating is in large part affected by personality characteristics.
(e) Monotony in eating is overtly expressed in the lowered acceptance of food.

Reported findings supported all hypotheses except "d"; i.e., monotony develops, although at perhaps a different rate, for those with various personality characteristics such as masculinity vs femininity, depression vs contentment, etc. Subsequent studies by these and other investigators indicate numerous complex inter-relationships that require further study (Schutz and Pilgrim 1958).

---

[5] Siegel and Pilgrim (1958). Quoted with permission of the University of Illinois Press.

Adequate variety is difficult to define. For a given population group, generalizations which summarize item toleration may be represented by a specific repetition interval. For example, Group A might tolerate or accept fish once in 7 days; Group B once in 10 days. The FACT scale is a convenient prototype questionnaire for obtaining required data.

Generally, the lower the acceptability rating, the greater the length of repetition interval required. Some items are essentially or absolutely unacceptable to a particular population; in this case the repetition interval is infinity and these items should be omitted from the recipe file. In planning cycle menus, the maximum length of the repetition interval is equal to the length of the cycle; items whose repetition interval exceeds this period are omitted. Items that may only be included once are usually retained in the recipe file for use as substitute items if deterioration and/or storage cost of ingredients is low.

The number of elemental KINDs of food is limited. The number available is more restricted. Beef, pork, lamb, chicken and turkey, either whole or in pieces is the common restriction for meals. Variety meats and game are possibilities but frequency is limited either by lack of acceptability or availability. Because of this limitation, some random plan of rotation is desirable in order to maximize variety. A meat block plan is often used (Fig. 2.6). The concept for distributing item categories can be extended to other meal components too, but tends to introduce rigidities in combining foods.

Other alternative methods may be used to avoid sameness. Use of sauces, garnishes, or interesting combinations and controlled repetition of color, texture, shape, consistency, and preparation method are common procedures for introducing variety.

Meal	Sunday	Monday	Tuesday	Wednesday	Thursday	Friday	Saturday
Lunch		Cheese	Cold Cuts	Bacon	Sliced Ham	Eggs	Diced Pork
Dinner	Sliced Beef	Diced Pork	Ground Beef	Whole Chicken	Diced Beef	Fish	Ground Beef
Lunch		Cold Cuts	Cottage Cheese	Ground Beef	Meat Salad	Sliced Cheese	Diced Beef
Dinner	Sliced Turkey	Cube Steak	Ham or Lamb	Fish	Sliced Pork	Whole Chicken	Variety Meat
Lunch		Ground Beef	Sliced Cheese	Diced Turkey	Cold Cuts	Fish	Sliced Ham
Dinner	Beef Steak	Sliced Turkey	Chops Pork	Ground Beef	Cube Steak	Diced Beef	Whole Chicken

FIG. 2.6. SAMPLE MEAT-BLOCK PLAN; LUNCH AND DINNER 3-WEEK CYCLE

KIND

KIND is defined as: A food group set up on the basis of a common characteristic, e.g., apple is a kind of fruit, zucchini is a kind of vegetable. Controlled repetition of KIND is the most important consideration in planning for menu variety. In planning menus by manual methods, a tally system is used to prevent gross repetition (see Chap. 6, Mechanics of Menu Planning). Using the computer, precise repetition intervals provide a consistent means of control.

Intervals of two types may be specified: overall and meal component. The overall interval precludes repetition of the KIND, in any form, within the specified number of days. For example, if the overall interval for the KIND *Apples* is "3," apples may not be served more often than once in 3 days. The meal component interval precludes repetition of the KIND in the same meal component, within the specified number of days. This interval is usually longer than the overall KIND interval. For example, if the salad component interval for the KIND *Apples* is "5," apple salads may not be served more often than once in 5 days. In combination, these two KIND controls allow Apple Juice at breakfast on Monday and Waldorf Salad on Wednesday but preclude Apple-Celery Salad on Monday and Waldorf Salad on Wednesday. Controls for all other KINDs work similarly.

Color

Color is the second most important factor to be controlled in planning for variety in institutional menus. Interesting but harmonious color combinations are important in merchandizing food in a cafeteria and in stimulating patients' appetites.

In a cafeteria the customer selects foods to meet his needs and satisfy his tastes. All other things being equal, color probably will determine the selection. Colorful foods always sell—because of eye appeal the items are selected on impulse. The arrangement affects overall sales. The colors of food items for the hot food and cold food sections should be visualized separately, in order as arranged on the serving line. Items next to each other should not clash. Nor should there be too much sameness of color, i.e., hot food items should not be all neutral or brown.

In planning menus for those who select from a printed listing, e.g., hospital patients, the importance of visualizing the color combinations is increased. Items should be planned so that a grossly unappetizing combination cannot be selected. Otherwise, when the tray arrives, psychological stimulation may not be sufficient to overcome inertia and the food will remain uneaten. Colors should not clash; there should be harmony on the main plate.

Birren (1963)[6] has made a point that menu planners often overlook:

Colors for foods involve personal and emotional interpretations. No generalizations can be accepted as absolute. Nevertheless, it is good

---

[6]Birren (1963). Quoted with permission of the Institute of Food Technologists.

"business" to avoid personal views for a more objective approach to the way in which *most* persons seem to react.

The psychological effects of the various colors on appetite have been studied. According to Birren (1963), red, red-orange, peach, pink, tan, brown, "butter" yellow, light and clear green are usually good colors for foods. Purple, violet, yellow-green, orange-yellow, gray, olive and "mustardy" yellow are poor food colors.

Other Factors

Texture and shape are two other considerations in planning for menu variety. Their importance remains undefined although they always contribute to the appraisal of the meal. Unlike KIND and color, awareness of these factors typically results from an unexpected stimulus. For example, all soft foods or all round or square foods call attention to texture and shape, respectively. And, defense mechanisms are aroused when a hard substance is encountered in an item such as a hamburger, i.e., one rejects the mouthful because of possible damage to teeth. Variation in both factors is necessary in order to avoid menu monotony.

Szczesniak *et al.* (1963) have developed rating scales for evaluating the textural characteristics of foods: hardness, brittleness, chewiness, gumminess, viscosity, and adhesiveness. Too much of any one of these results in rejection of the food or foods responsible, usually because of muscle fatigue. Therefore, in planning menus excess of any textural characteristic must be avoided. On the other hand, too little texture is boring; consumption declines.

An assortment of shapes makes an important though usually subconscious contribution to menu variety. The current emphasis on portion control has resulted in the monotony of slices, squares, or balls.

Consistency, temperature, and preparation method are usually listed as factors to be considered in planning menus by manual methods. Variety is desirable but is usually achieved without particular emphasis. However, when menus are planned by computer, some controls may be necessary. Consistency is controlled by limiting the number of runny items on the plate. Temperature variation is especially important for the ill or elderly, both hot and cold foods should be included in all meals. Variation in preparation method is primarily a work load factor rather than a consumer consideration. A Boiled Dinner or Fried Chicken and French Fries is commonly accepted.

Use of interesting recipe names or terms relieves menu monotony on paper but reduces effective communication. In restaurants the same base food is often used for many entrées or desserts, etc., or the same sauce is used with different base foods. This practice reduces work load effectively. In this situation it presents no problem as one selects only one entrée, etc. However, this practice is not well accepted by captive groups especially if followed consistently. Selections are more limited so the restriction of choice is more apparent.

Cost as a consumer consideration has two aspects that are relevant to menu planning, (a) absolute cost and (b) relative cost. The absolute cost is the price to be paid for a meal or item and it is compared to the money amount available for purchases. The relative cost is an abstraction based on a subjective evaluation of both food and service. It is evaluated as the marginal utility of spending X dollars or cents for the specific meal or item. That is, the purchase price is evaluated against the desirability of the meal or item. One aspect of desirability is frequency of consumption; a preferred item that has not been consumed recently will have a high marginal utility and impulse buying will result. Another aspect is the consumer's concept of quality; a gap exists between consumer expectations and the quality of food and service that can be provided because labor costs are greater than generally recognized. Hence, the relative cost often appears high to the consumer.

Policies that guide selection of items for the recipe pool are based in part on consideration of these aspects of cost. The absolute price a consumer is willing to pay determines the types of food and service that are appropriate; recipes and menu must be in accord. Thus, the menu planner must know how much money various segments of the prospective consumer group have available. Using this information, one or more entrée and/or meal price classes are selected. The recipe file is then developed by selecting a pool of items for each meal component that includes an adequate number of items from each price class.

The menu planner must also be cognizant of the two aspects of relative cost and the ways in which they influence consumer selections. Use of this information requires that items be selected for the menu that have "magnetic" power, i.e., high marginal utility, such as steaks, roasts, etc. In affluent America, the consumer desires and usually is willing to pay for these items. If he is accustomed to them but the menu emphasizes ground meat and extended entrées, even though the cost is somewhat lower, the relative cost will be too high. But, when relative cost is high, consumer satisfaction is low. Therefore, some expensive items must be included in order to build demand for food, satisfaction, and/or sales. Conversely, items lacking in magnetic power must be eliminated from the recipe pool if they require above average preparation labor time as the consumer will not regard these as "good buys," so demand will be low. Moreover, recipes and menus must be simple, so that purchase price will largely be determined by and reflect food cost. Relative cost evaluations will then distribute selections among items and encourage purchasing.

Institutionally, cost as a consumer consideration is a concept that applies primarily to school children and college students. These are the only two groups that have some option to purchase foods or meals as desired. For example, if a meal contains items that will not be acceptable, the child carries his lunch that day. With cafeteria service a college student may select items as desired, as long as he can pay for them. However, individuals in other institutional groups usually do not have these options. Because they are more captive they are more restricted in terms of possible alternative responses; e.g., they may refuse an item or may select alternate items but the cost is not a decision factor.

BIBLIOGRAPHY

BIRREN, F. 1963. Color and human appetite. Food Technol. *17*, 553–555.

CUSSLER, M., and DEGIVE, M. L. 1952. Twixt the Cup and the Lip: Psychological and Socio-cultural Factors Affecting Food Habits. Twayne Publishers, New York.

DE GARINE, I. 1970. The social and cultural background of food habits in developing countries (traditional societies). Nutr. Newsletter *8*, 9–22.

EINDHOVEN, J., and PERYAM, D. R. 1959. Measurement of preferences for food combinations. Food Technol. *13*, No. 7, 379–382.

EPPRIGHT, E. S. 1947. Factors influencing food acceptance. J. Am. Dietet. Assoc. *23*, 579–587.

GORDON, J. A., and KILGORE, V. 1971. Planning ethnic menus. The food habits of six groups—American Black, Jewish, Puerto Rican, Italian, Irish, and Chinese—are described for consideration in planning ethnic menus. Hospitals *45*, No. 21, 87–91.

KENNEDY, B. M. 1952. Food preferences of pre-army age California boys. Food Technol. *6*, 93–97.

MASLOW, A. H. 1943. A theory of human motivations: the basic needs. Psychol. Rev. *50*, 370–396.

MASLOW, A. H. 1968. A theory of human motivation: the basic needs. *In* Perspectives in Human Behavior. H. H. Kassarjian, and T. S. Robertson (Editors). Scott, Foresman & Co., Glenview, Ill.

MILLER, D. F., and VORIA, L. 1969. Chronologic changes in the recommended dietary allowances. J. Am. Dietet. Assoc. *54*, 109–117.

MOSKOWITZ, H. R. 1972. Personal communication. U.S. Army Natick Laboratories, Mass.

National Research Council—National Academy of Sciences. 1968. Recommended Dietary Allowances, 7th Edition, Food Nutr. Board, Natl. Res. Council—Natl. Acad. Sci., Washington, D.C.

PERYAM, D. R., and PILGRIM, F. J. 1957. Hedonic scale method of measuring food preference. Food Technol. *11*, 9–14.

PILGRIM, F. J. 1957. The components of food acceptance and their measurement. Am. J. Clin. Nutr. *5*, 171–175.

PILGRIM, F. J. 1961. Group attitudes and behavior toward food. What foods do people accept or reject? J. Am. Dietet. Assoc. *38*, 439–443.

SCHUTZ, H. G. 1965. A food action rating scale for measuring food acceptance. J. Food Sci. *30*, 365–374.

SCHUTZ, H. G., and PILGRIM, F. J. 1958. A field study of food monotony. Psychol. Repts. *4*, 559–565.

SEBRELL, W. H., JR. 1969. Recommended dietary allowances—1968 revision. J. Am. Dietet. Assoc. *54*, 103–108.

SIEGEL, P. S., and PILGRIM, F. J. 1958. The effect of monotony on the acceptance of food. Am. J. Psychol. *71*, 756–759.

SZCZESNIAK, A. S., BRANDT, M. A., and FRIEDMAN, H. H. 1963. Development of standard rating scales for mechanical parameters of texture and correlation between the objective and the sensory methods of texture evaluation. J. Food Sci. *28*, 397–403.

TOWNSEND, C. W. 1928. Food prejudices. Sci. Monthly *27*, 703–705.

WAGNER, P. M. 1966. The aesthetics of food. J. Am. Dietet. Assoc. *49*, 30.

ZELLMER, G. 1969. Food acceptance/frequency of serving has a disparate effect on acceptance. Hospitals *44*, 75–77, 80–81.

CHAPTER 3

Worker Considerations

Worker considerations include (a) the needs of the workers (as perceived by the workers and management) and (b) the factors related to efficient utilization of labor time and equipment capacities (discussed in the following chapter). Bigness and complexity of food service organizations have accentuated the need to plan for both aspects.

Food service workers in the aggregate are like any other large group of people. For any trait that might be measured, representatives can be found for each possible point on a rating scale and the overall shape of the distribution is normal or skewed the same as in the population-as-a-whole. Hence, the reference food service worker can be characterized as a cluster of points representing central tendencies on an infinite number of trait scales, each point representing the mean of the normal or skewed distribution of the trait, as the case may be. It follows that food service workers will be highly variable in attitudes, skills, and potential they bring to and contribute to the food service organization. Hence, they cannot be regarded as interchangeable parts for scheduling purposes.

Management is concerned with the workers' needs as they determine attitudes, productivity, and ability to meet variable production demands. A large number of concepts of the workers' needs are possible. The needs of the individual workers combine in the aggregate to shape collective attitudes that may or may not restrict menu planning alternatives. Cohesiveness of the work group will determine the amount and kind of individual differences in attitude that will be accepted, and, hence, that the manager will have to plan for. The needs of the individual workers also determine their individual productivity and in the aggregate, the productivity of the group. If productivity is low, the menu planner must plan menus using simply prepared items. The ability to meet variable production demands depends on responsiveness and cooperation; if the needs of the individual workers emphasize belongingness, achievement, etc., the menu planner has more freedom in selecting items requiring various treatments, skills, and levels of complexity. However, if the need is for security, the recipe pool must be limited to the familiar.

The traditional concept envisions a well-trained, conscientious, highly motivated, highly flexible individual who is capable of performing many jobs well. This may be true of the tradition-directed employee with many years of experience in the same small food service unit where he has performed many functions using relatively simple equipment. This worker's need is for continuity of the relationship. Because the situation is stable, the menu planner is free to select menu items based on consumer needs with minimal restrictions due to worker needs.

In contrast, one can envision a casually trained, indifferent individual with a multitude of outside commitments who can fill only a limited number of jobs. This worker's need is for simple preparation with minimal skills requirement and nontaxing production demand. Although this may result in monotony for the consumer, this employee reality greatly restricts the recipe pool available to the menu planner.

Or, one might envision a partially trained, conscientious, highly motivated, super achievement oriented person who will attempt any task. This worker needs continuous challenge in order to find security in the rewards of accomplishment. The menu planner must compromise by balancing standard items with new or difficult items, because this person tends to become over extended.

The above characterizations of "the worker" are a small sample of those commonly encountered in food service. Ideally, and often in small food service units, the needs of each individual worker are considered in developing the menu. But, in the larger unit the menu planner cannot effectively serve an infinite number of masters. Indeed, it is impossible to consider individual differences when planning the menu. Therefore, one customarily plans for the average level of skill, ability, motivation, speed and requirement for challenge. Standardized recipes, i.e., ones that yield a repeatable quality and quantity independent of the particular cook preparing them, provide a reliable basis for planning time, energy, and equipment allocations. The standardization process generates necessary information for the scheduling aspects of the menu planning process. These aspects will be dealt with in detail in the following chapter.

The current emphasis on self-actualization requires that work be planned for an individual worker so as to facilitate utilization of his skills and abilities to the extent possible, although not in an exploitative way. Thus, some workers will require rewarding challenges and opportunities to be creative. On the other hand, some people prefer to work at less than their capacity in order to free time and energy for alternate activities. Although the menu must be planned for average needs, the manager must recognize these differences among workers and adjust for them in distributing work assignments in order that production will be feasible.

The worker is also concerned with the time, energy, and equipment available to accomplish the tasks created by the menu items. Hence, he studies the menu listing. Items requiring many steps in preparation or several final finishing steps at serving time create time pressures. When extra time is available, as when the census is low or other items require little preparation work, the challenge of the extra steps is acceptable. Otherwise, excessive time pressures develop causing fatigue and intense frustration. While the worker will adjust to the occasional miscalculation of time requirements, a crisis-to-crisis situation results in a degenerative spiral. Thus, to avoid this outcome, the menu planner must know the overall time requirements for each item as well as timing and length of the peak activity period. Then time can be plotted. When more than one item requires attention at the same time, a decision can be made to reschedule preparation, if possible, or to eliminate one of the items.

Energy requirements are also important; wide variation is undesirable. The employee rations energy for the working day as a part of the total day. Frustration and fatigue result if the allocated time is consistently either too little or too great. To alleviate either of these situations, the menu planner must know the pattern of customer census (a) within the day, (b) among days in the week, (c) among weeks in the month, and (d) among months or seasons of the year. Moreover, the relative demand for alternative items must be known. With these pieces of information, overall demand can be predicted and, therefore, time and energy requirements.

Availability of needed equipment when required is also of concern to the food service worker. When available equipment is inadequate to meet production requirements, frustration results, as quality must be compromised or production delayed, both of which have negative consequences. When necessary equipment is unavailable, for whatever reason, even greater frustration results. If the equipment is permanently unavailable, recipes requiring such equipment should be eliminated from the recipe pool to avoid their inadvertant use. If the equipment is temporarily unavailable but shortage or conflict of use occurs frequently, either additional equipment must be purchased or the menu planner must carefully plan to distribute equipment usage. In summary, this group of workers' needs must be met in order to avoid annoying them with pressures and frustrations that create degenerative spirals.

CHAPTER 4

Management Considerations

The menu provides the means for management control over (a) the size of the overall demand for food and its distribution among the various classes of food, (b) utilization of facilities and equipment in food production, (c) utilization of employee time and skills, and (d) costs incurred. Moreover, the menu via the recipe, determines qualitative and quantitative requirements for ingredients, and, hence, the magnitude and complexity of the purchasing and inventory management systems.

DEMAND FOR FOOD

In restaurant service the menu is a merchandizing tool. Consequently, the selection of items, discriptors, order or arrangement, printing, etc., are part of the strategy in attracting a planned number of customers (Dahl 1945). Hence, the sales menu is planned to attract sales. As the entrées are the main attraction most effort is directed to balancing the selection of items in this class (see Chap. 6).

As in restaurant food service, the overall demand for food in institutions is a function of the acceptability of the entrée and perhaps the dessert (Dickins et al. 1945). For example, in residence hall food service, when the entrée is unacceptable, those students who can afford to do so will purchase a meal elsewhere; the others will complain and/or consume extra portions of the other meal components. On the other hand, although the dinner meal census is usually 75% of the residents on a Monday night, if a particularly acceptable menu is served 90% of the residents may appear. Thus, the menu is an important control agent in determining the expected meal census, and, hence, ability to achieve the mission of meeting the nutritive needs of the consumers.

Similarly, the demand for the various other classes of food can be controlled. When two unacceptable vegetables are offered as the only alternatives, total consumption from the vegetable class will be decreased. If the salad is acceptable and quantities are unlimited, the consumers may compensate by taking an extra salad. Unless this behavior is anticipated and production quantities adjusted, vegetables will be overproduced.

UTILIZATION OF FACILITIES AND EQUIPMENT

Facilities and equipment are expensive to obtain and maintain. Therefore, they must be used to good advantage in food production (West et al. 1966). The selection of menu items controls usage. A trade-off is made between under-utilization and creation of production bottlenecks.

Production demand must be planned to conform to production capacity.

Facilities and equipment are regarded as given; they restrict (a) the quantity of an item, or of several items requiring use of the same piece of equipment and (b) the variety of items that can be produced.

For example, if the demand for French fries exceeds the capacity of the fryers, assuming additional equipment cannot be purchased, an equally popular starchy food may be offered as a choice. Or alternatively, an alternate entrée that is customarily served with rice such as Sweet and Sour Pork might be selected to reduce the demand.

A major piece of equipment is often used to produce several items for a meal. To prevent production bottlenecks, feasibility must be verified as the menu is planned. Working backward from the service time the menu planner plots the blocks of time required for preparation and clean-up for each of the items along a time scale (See Fig. 14.11 and 14.12, Chap. 14) (Brown 1969; Ivanicky *et al.* 1969). Given that quality deteriorates with holding time, the blocks of time are planned as close to serving time as possible. When time blocks overlap, the combination is considered unfeasible and alternate items are evaluated.

In an early paper, West and Okey (1929)[1] pointed to a basic problem of production scheduling:

> What seems fundamentally wrong is the tendency to regard large-quantity cookery as an engineering problem, to be solved mathematically from the point of view of labor alone, and without any intelligent appreciation of the effects of prolonged or excessive heating upon flavor and food value.
>
> We believe that it is possible, by working out a time schedule which will avoid the heating of perishable foods in excessively large containers and the unnecessary prolongation of the heating process on steam tables to serve appetizing, nutritious vegetables, even from the largest institutional kitchens.

The variety of items that can be produced has traditionally been restricted by lack of the specific production equipment required or by its use in producing other items. With the advent of acceptable convenience foods at justifiable costs, this problem has been minimized.

Menu variety is also restricted by availability of service equipment. For example, unless one has chafing dishes, buffet service is difficult; a parfait served in a custard cup is lacking in appeal. Ordinarily, this restricts the selection of recipes for the working file.

UTILIZATION OF EMPLOYEE TIME AND SKILLS

Good employees are expensive to attract and retain. Therefore, they must be utilized to good advantage in food production. The selection of menu items controls utilization of their time and skills. A trade-off is made between under-

---

[1]Copyright by the American Home Economics Association, and quoted with permission.

utilization and creation of undue pressure. Production demand must be planned to conform to production capacity.

For purposes of menu planning, in the short-run, available time and skills are regarded as given. Generally, people work at 1 of 4 standard rates according to their level of motivation: (a) leisurely, (b) accommodating or normal, (c) urgent, and (d) frantic. The first results in low productivity and the last in unproductive activity and pressure. The objective in menu planning is to select items that can be produced, given the average level of skills for the particular job, using the man-hours available to the fullest extent possible when the employees work at the normal pace.

Given data on the standard number of man-hours required to produce each item, the menu planner can plot block man-hour requirements against a time scale in determining the feasibility of producing the various items for the meal. When the time blocks overlap, production is considered infeasible and alternate items are evaluated.

Available man-hours and skills may limit menu variety. Ordinarily this restricts selection of items for the working recipe file. Items requiring an excessive number of steps in preparation are simplified or omitted unless convenience items are available at justifiable cost. Items that require a level of skill that is not available are omitted unless convenience items can be substituted.

COSTS INCURRED

One of the classic papers in institutional food service deals with fundamental issues: *The Cost and Nutritional Effect of Making an Institutional Diet Palatable* (West and Okey 1929). Traditionally, the major goal of institutional food service has been to supply the best possible food—which is defined as (a) wholesome, palatable, well-prepared under acceptable standards of sanitary control, and (b) attractively served—at the planned cost. This goal is ambiguous and has been interpreted differently within each institution over time and among institutions. Nonetheless, the concept is consistent with goals of (a) consumer satisfaction as measured by consumption in the long-run and (b) financial success in the long-run, resulting from the cumulative effects of reasonable cost control and stable or increased volume.

The menu determines production requirements and, hence, the variable costs of men, materials, and machines. Fixed costs are not affected by menu selections.

Although it is theoretically possible to ascertain the precise cost of producing a menu, customarily one predicts menu cost from a combination of (a) raw food cost, (b) labor cost, and (c) prorated costs for supplies, equipment, and administration. Recipe costing provides data on raw food cost; however, accuracy is limited by the frequency of costing; computerized recipe costing programs facilitate frequent costing. The average labor cost per meal has been used as a rough estimate; recently methods for determining actual man-hour costs have been reported (Brown 1969; Ivanicky *et al.* 1969).

The menu planner determines the degree of menu control over cost. Theoretically, the menu planner uses costed recipes and keeps a running cost total, adding the cost of each item as it is selected. High- and low-cost items are selected so that the final total cost for each meal, day, or the period as a whole does not exceed the planned allocation. In practice, menu planners rarely have access to a current file of costed recipes; considerable financial risk is involved and cost control is limited.

The tightest possible control over meal or daily costs can be achieved by linear programming methods when sufficient reliable data are available. Using raw food costs and labor costs, "least cost" solutions are obtained (Balintfy 1966). Moderate cost control can also be achieved by a system using a target mean for the menu planning period (Eckstein 1967). Raw food cost, labor cost, etc., can be used in computing cost status.

The reader should note that in the long-run, a least cost solution is probably incompatible with customer satisfaction, and, hence, stability of the operation. Constraints added to improve satisfaction shift the costs upward from the least cost to a moderate but feasible cost range.

PURCHASING AND INVENTORY MANAGEMENT SYSTEMS

The purchasing and inventory management system is designed to supply ingredients of the desired quality, in required quantities, as needed for production. The production menu usually specifies both recipe and number of servings to be prepared. The recipes list ingredients, general specifications and quantities. Knowledge of the necessary qualities of ingredients and expected variation forms the basis for determining ingredient specifications. Thus, the menu basically determines requirements of the supply system. Transactions and problems in logistics are beyond the scope of this book.

BIBLIOGRAPHY

BALINTFY, J. L. 1966. Linear programming models for menu planning. *In* Hospital Industrial Engineering: A Guide to the Improvement of Hospital Management Systems. H. E. Smalley, and J. R. Freeman (Editors). Van Nostrand Reinhold Co., New York.

BROWN, R. M. 1969. Estimating dietary labor by use of work modules. Hospitals *43*, No. 20, 103–104.

DAHL, J. O. 1945. Menu Making for Professionals in Quantity Cookery. Published by the author, Stamford, Conn.

DICKINS, D., FANELLI, A. A., and FERGUSON, V. 1954. Attractive menu items. J. Am. Dietet. Assoc. *30*, 881–885.

ECKSTEIN, E. F. 1967. Menu planning by computer: the random approach. J. Am. Dietet. Assoc. *51*, 529–533.

IVANICKY, M. C., MASON, H. A., and VIEROW, S. C. 1969. Food preparation: labor time versus production quantity. Hospitals *43*, No. 20, 99–102.

WEST, B. B., and OKEY, R. 1929. The cost and nutritional effect of making an institutional diet palatable. J. Home Econ. *21*, 254–260.

WEST, B. B., WOOD, L., and HARGER, V. F. 1966. Food Service in Institutions, 4th Edition. John Wiley & Sons, New York.

CHAPTER 5

Menu Patterns and Meal Patterns

MENU PATTERNS

Two basic types of menu patterns are used in institutional food service, (a) set, i.e., one item per meal component and (b) selective, i.e., two or more choices per meal component. Although restaurants have usually offered a selective menu, until the 1950's the set menu was the customary menu pattern in institutional food service.

The set or nonselective menu is most appropriately used in situations where the consumer is unable to make decisions, e.g., young children, senile adults, critically or mentally ill patients. However, from the managers view, a set menu may be necessary because of cost, time, or facility limitations; simplification usually reduces requirements.

A well-balanced set menu is difficult to plan because (a) validity of nutritional adequacy rests on the assumption that all foods will be consumed in desired quantities; (b) restricting the variety of possible menu items to those universally accepted leads to monotony; (c) utilization of employee skills and time is generally uneven among workers, reflecting wide shifts in requirements according to the particular combination of items to be prepared; and (d) equipment usage is uneven, multiple units of the same type are needed to prepare the maximum quantity but the types of equipment required vary randomly with the menu. Planning for other consumer considerations such as color, texture, shape, and item variety is more easily accomplished because fewer items must be checked. Methods of planning set menus will be discussed in the following chapter.

The selective menu pattern is preferred in institutional food service as it allows more flexibility in dealing with individual differences in food habits and preferences (Santos and Cutler 1964). Also, it results in increased patient contact which meets a fundamental need for attention (Foss and Ohlson 1962). Moreover, effective utilization of employees and facilities is possible if the work load is equally distributed. However, more personnel and equipment may be required (Cabot 1971).

Proponents of selective menu systems emphasize the benefits associated with increased consumer satisfaction resulting from (a) greater ability to meet consumer needs and (b) increased attention. Opponents emphasize the associated problems and costs resulting from (a) increased probability that nutritional needs may not be met (feared but only substantiated by one published study) (Wakefield and Potgieter 1958), (b) more complex problems in planning and managing production, and (c) greater complexity in planning the menu itself. One must acknowledge the validity of both arguments and make a trade-off that is appropriate, given the particular institutional situation.

A well-balanced selective menu is difficult to plan because of the uncertainty in pairing choices; whim, weather, and many other unpredictable factors determine actual choices and, hence, actual production demand (Pilgrim 1957). Thus, nutritional adequacy, expected per capita costs, and work load must be based on assumptions of probable item combinations (Flynn 1963). Absolute variety is easily achieved by selection from various classes of foods. But repetition of KIND, color, texture, flavor, and shape are more difficult to control because of the number of menu items to be checked. Similarly, although increased variety may result in more even utilization of employee facilities, chances of planning several items requiring the same piece of equipment at the same time are increased. Methods of planning selective menus will be developed in the following chapter.

MEAL PATTERNS

Institutional food service units, except for school lunch, provide three or more meals per day to their customers. Until the 1940's the institutional meal pattern was breakfast, dinner, and supper. Two reasons for this pattern were usually cited: (a) patients should only eat a light meal before retiring and (b) the overlap of employee shifts (i.e., 6-2:30 and 10:30-7) provided the additional labor need for preparation of the main meal.

Currently, the customary meal pattern in the United States is breakfast, lunch, and dinner with the main meal in the evening when the majority of family members can assemble. As this meal pattern is most acceptable to the customers, this pattern is usually followed in institutional food service. In addition, there is some evidence that luncheon type entrées such as salad or sandwich plates, caseroles, or short order items require more preparation labor than dinner entrées such as roasts, etc.

Even more recently, 4 and 5 meal plans have been introduced in hospitals and nursing homes. They have been accepted when carefully planned and implemented. These plans are discussed in Chap. 7 and 8.

BIBLIOGRAPHY

CABOT, E. E. 1971. Selective menu raises satisfaction—and costs. Mod. Hosp. *116*, No. 2, 139-140.

ELMAN, K. 1963. Is the selective menu worthwhile?—Yes. Mod. Hosp. *100*, No. 5, 100.

FLYNN, H. W. 1963. Is the selective menu worthwhile?—No. Mod. Hosp. *100*, No. 5, 101-102.

FOSS, J. A., and OHLSON, M. A. 1962. Of what worth is the selective menu? J. Am. Dietet. Assoc. *41*, 29-34.

PILGRIM, F. J. 1957. The components of food acceptance and their measurement. Am. J. Clin. Nutr. *4*, 171-175.

SANTOS, L., and CUTLAR, K. 1964. How hospitals implement selective menu systems. Hospitals *38*, No. 9, 93-96.

WAKEFIELD, L., and POTGIETER, M. 1958. Nutritional value of patient selected versus nonselected menus. Hospitals *32*, No. 21, 72, 74-75.

CHAPTER 6

Mechanics of Menu Planning

The key concept is "Work Smarter, Not Harder." Manual methods of planning menus are designed to simplify the task. Customary means include (a) arrangement of the workplace with idea generators, such as recipe files, cookbooks, current magazines, and old menus; (b) systems for keeping track of repetition; and (c) order of item selection.

Computerization of the routine aspects requires a detailed definition of the task. This chapter provides the basis for determining which aspects can be feasibly computerized and provides a model for design of various segments of a program.

GENERAL CONSIDERATIONS

Ostensibly, selection of individual menu items is based on a series of simple yes–no decisions; a no answer terminates the process thus eliminating the item from further consideration for the particular menu slot. The preceding four chapters have described the complex of factors that must be evaluated and summarized as the criteria used in the accept-reject decision process.

Moreover, when manual methods are employed, the human factor has a distinct, although variable, effect on item selection. It turns out that human beings vary in sensitivity to aesthetic factors, and, hence, menu planners vary in the degree to which they consciously evaluate prospective menu items for suitability in terms of color, texture, etc. Furthermore, when the budget is tight, attention and effort are directed to selection of low-cost items. Since, as a human being, one can only focus on a limited number of objectives at one time, the other factors tend to be neglected. This neglect generates other problems resulting in pressure to increase the priority of the previously neglected factors. The net result is a crisis-to-crisis situation with cyclic repetition of each type of problem. Of course, this puts the menu planner on the defensive, and generates a host of other dysfunctional effects.

Another problem also has been noted. When a person works intensively on a complex problem such as planning a menu, he soon loses objectivity. That is, he identifies with the menu and becomes unable to see production problems, repetition, etc. This is natural; the usual mechanism for restoring partial objectivity is to let the menu "cool off" a day or more before reviewing it.

THE WORKPLACE AND IDEA GENERATORS

Because of the complexity of the task, the menu planner needs a workplace that is well arranged and free from distractions and interruptions such as a ringing telephone.

Planning aids such as previous menus, recipes files, cookbooks, and pictures are useful for generating ideas (Blair and Volume Feeding Management Magazine 1967; Blair 1971; Institutions/VF Magazine 1972; Morris and Outland 1966; Weiss and Weiss 1971; Wilkinson 1971). Production records, preference data, recipe costs, delivery schedules, market statements of availability of seasonal items, and other such data are necessary if informed decisions are to be made. Item search time is reduced if recipes are classified according to season, meal, meal component, color, etc. (Tables 6.1 to 6.3).

Sufficient time must be allotted for the task; however, Parkinson's Law is pertinent, "Work expands to fill the time available for its completion..." (Parkinson 1957). And, a word of caution about menu planning aids. It is easy to become side-tracked. Time spent in this activity, though necessary, may so reduce available time as to prevent adequate evaluation of prospective menu items according to the predetermined criteria.

DELIVERY SCHEDULE CONSTRAINTS

A menu item cannot be produced unless all ingredients are on hand. Hence, the delivery schedule and the probability of an on-time delivery may determine whether an item can be planned for a particular meal. For example, if poultry is delivered between 11 a.m. and 1 p.m. on Tuesdays, roast turkey cannot be

TABLE 6.1

SAMPLE RECIPE CLASSIFICATION BY SEASON

Fall	Winter	Spring	Summer
Entrées	Entrées	Entrées	Entrées
.	.	.	.
.	.	.	.
.	.	.	.
Desserts	Desserts	Desserts	Desserts
Pie	Pie	Pie	Pie
Mince	Mince	Pineapple	Key Lime
Pumpkin	Pumpkin	Chiffon	
Cake	Cake	Cake	Cake
.	.	.	.
.	.	.	.
.	.	.	.
Fruit (fresh)	Fruit (fresh)	Fruit (fresh)	Fruit (fresh)
Apples	Apples	Strawberries	Melons
Oranges	Bananas		Peaches
Pears (Bosc)	Pears (d'Anjou)		Pears (Bartlett)
Grapes (Tokay)			Plums
			Grapes (Green)
Steamed Puddings	Steamed Puddings		Whipped Pudding
Plum	Plum		Spanish Cream
Chocolate	Chocolate		

TABLE 6.2

SAMPLE RECIPE CLASSIFICATIONS

Dinner Entrées	Vegetables
Beef	"A"
Roasts	Broccoli
Steaks	.
Diced	.
Ground, etc.	.
Pork	Zucchini
Green	"B"
Cured	Beets
Veal—steaks, chops	.
Chicken	.
Whole	.
Diced	Squash
Turkey	Salads (side)
Sliced	Fruit
Diced	Vegetable
Rabbit	Cottage Cheese
Variety Meats	Gelatin
Fish	Salads (entrée)
	Meat
Supper or Luncheon Entrées	Cheese
Beef	Fish
Ground	Desserts
Diced	Pie
Pork	Cake
Veal	Pudding
Chicken	Cookies
Turkey	Gelatin
Variety Meats	Fruit (cooked)
Luncheon Meats	Fruit (canned)
Fish	Fruit (fresh)
Egg, Nut	Ice Cream and Sherbet
Cheese	Steamed Puddings
Legume	Breads
	Purchased Breads
Starchy Foods	Purchased Rolls
Potatoes	Biscuits
Pasta	Muffins
Rice	Pastry
Sweet Potatoes	

served for Tuesday dinner unless the lead time is extended, i.e., the turkey is delivered frozen the previous week. For example, in school lunch, entrées must be selected for Monday lunch that do not require meat that must be thawed prior to cooking because it is unsafe to thaw meat on Friday for Monday. Moreover, fruits must be at the proper degree of ripeness; but, despite specification of degree of ripeness they may be green when they arrive. The menu planner should "play safe" by planning an alternate and/or planning an early delivery.

TABLE 6.3

SAMPLE CLASSIFICATION BY COLOR

Salads
  Red
    Jellied Cherry Marshmallow
    Jellied Banana Nut
    Fruited Strawberry Gelatin
    Cranberry Ring Mold
  Orange
    Mandarin Orange & Marshmallow
    Fruited Orange Gelatin
    Jellied Citrus

  Green
    Molded Pear and Lime
    Under-the-Sea
    Lime and Cottage Cheese
    Molded Pineapple Cucumber
  Yellow
    Jellied Cider Fruit
    Jellied Waldorf
    Molded Pineapple & Cottage Cheese

SYSTEMS FOR VARIETY CONTROL

Most systems for controlling variety consist of a classification (mutually exclusive and collectively exhaustive) and a method for controlling frequency. Classification is a means of simplification; all items in a class are treated as though they were equivalent so as to reduce the problem of evaluation. Three methods of controlling frequency have been introduced to replace earlier intuitive methods (a) frequency/unit of time, (b) separation days, and (c) repetition intervals.

Using the first method, data is obtained on desired frequency of consumption using a survey method such as FACT (see Chap. 2). Foods are then classified as standard items (served at every meal), daily, weekly, biweekly, once per period, etc. (McCune 1960). Then a simple tally and check system is used for control.

The term "separation days" implies precise information concerning the minimum (or maximum) number of days that must elapse before an item can be served again (Dougherty *et al.* 1971; Schuh *et al.* 1967). A modified FACT scale is commonly employed to obtain the data. Using manual methods, the menu planner checks back the specified number of days to determine whether the item can be served again; if so, it is repeated.

The third method uses both overall and a meal component repetition intervals arranged in a matrix (Table 6.4) (Eckstein 1969). The overall restriction was designed to prevent serving a given KIND in any form, at any meal within the specified time interval, e.g., apple will not be selected more than once in a three-day period. If apple juice is selected for Monday breakfast, applesauce, baked apple, etc., might be selected for Thursday lunch or any succeeding meal, but not before. In addition, the meal component interval restriction prevents serving a given KIND as the same meal component within another specified time interval. Apple dessert items such as Apple Crisp and Apple Pie could not occur more than once in an eight-day meal period.

In order to simplify the problem of selecting appropriate foods for a meal,

TABLE 6.4

SAMPLE KIND CONTROL MATRIX, REPETITION INTERVALS (DAYS)

Code No.	KIND	Overall	Meal Component Intervals					
			Meat	Starch	Veg	Salad	Dessert	Bread
1	Apple	3	10	14	10	5	8	14
2	Apricot	6	21^1	0^2	21	4	10	10
3	Banana	3	21	0	21	3	10	10
.	—	—	—	—	—	—	—	—
.	—	—	—	—	—	—	—	—
.	—	—	—	—	—	—	—	—
7	Chocolate	4	0	0	0	0	4	10
.	—	—	—	—	—	—	—	—
.	—	—	—	—	—	—	—	—
.	—	—	—	—	—	—	—	—
88	Cabbage	3	18	0	8	4	0	0
.	—	—	—	—	—	—	—	—
.	—	—	—	—	—	—	—	—
.	—	—	—	—	—	—	—	—
95	Peas	3	4	10	3	21	0	0
.	—	—	—	—	—	—	—	—
.	—	—	—	—	—	—	—	—
.	—	—	—	—	—	—	—	—
99	Zucchini	10	0	0	16	0	0	0

[1] Items to be included only once per 21-day cycle.
[2] Zero indicates repetition is unrestricted.

many institutions have arbitrarily classified categories and items as either luncheon or dinner items, usually in conjunction with a predetermined menu structure (Table 6.2). For example: sandwich plates; casseroles containing meat, starchy food, and vegetables (one dish meals); and salad plates are customarily classed as luncheon entrées. Solid meats, poultry, and fish as dinner entrées. Similarly, cookies, gelatin-based desserts, puddings, etc., are luncheon desserts and pies, cakes, ice cream, etc., are dinner desserts. Category repetition intervals are then specified (Eckstein 1969). When a meal component is unnecessary (e.g., no separate starchy food is required when offering Shrimp Creole on Steamed Rice) a 1-in. line is drawn as a placeholder to indicate that the omission was deliberate.

Monotony resulting from repetition of KIND decreases food consumption (as discussed in Chap. 2). When the item name includes the KIND, repetition is easily detected (Table 6.5). In other cases, knowledge of ingredients is required (Table 6.6). Simple tallies for KINDs likely to be repeated are useful; e.g., cheese, tomatoes, chocolate, etc.

Color is also important in providing variety. One executive states (Eliason 1966)[1]:

---

[1] Quoted with permission of Ahrens Publishing Co.

TABLE 6.5

SAMPLE ITEM NAMES THAT SPECIFY KIND

KIND	Item Name
Tomato	Tomato Soup Tomato Beef Stewed Tomatoes, etc.
Cheese	Grilled Cheese Sandwich Macaroni & Cheese Canadian Chedder Cheese Soup, etc.
Apple	Baked Apple Apple Turnover Apple Fritters Apple Pancakes Applesauce, etc.

TABLE 6.6

SAMPLE ITEM NAMES WHERE KIND IS NOT APPARENT

KIND	Item Name
Tomato	Stuffed Peppers Lasagna Spaghetti Ruby Consomme, etc.
Chocolate	Marble Cake Devil's Food Cake Mocha Ice Cream Black Cow

We consider color so important to our vegetable counter that we use a color pattern in planning our menus. One line on our menu calls for a red vegetable, another green, another yellow, and another light green or white. This assures us of a variety of color and in order to be sure of the proper balance of that color we use a diagram. . . .directing the placement of each item on the counter.

Orange	Light green	Red	Other
White	Dark Green	Yellow	

The color of a particular item may not be apparent from the recipe name. For this reason some menu planners keep an index of items (particularly salads and desserts) arranged according to color.

A "meat block" system has been used by the military to distribute varieties and cuts of meat according to preference and cost factors (Navy Subsistence Office 1964). After the frequency of serving each type is decided (beef, pork,

Block "A"   Distribution of meats and meat substitutes

	Meal	Sun	Mon	Tues	Wed	Thurs	Fri	Sat
Week #1	L	—	Cold Cuts	Beef	Cheese	Beef	Eggs	Beef
	D	Beef	Chicken	Ham	Beef	Veal	Beef	Turkey
Week #2	L	—	Beef	Chicken	Ham	Cheese	Fish	Beef
	D	Pork	Variety Meat	Veal	Beef	Rabbit	Beef	Corned Beef
Week #3	L	—	Beef	Cold Cuts	Beef	Cheese or Eggs	Beef	Beef
	D	Chicken	Ham	Beef	Turkey	Pork	Fish	Lamb

Block "B"   Distribution of cuts of meat and meat substitutes

	Meal	Sun	Mon	Tues	Wed	Thurs	Fri	Sat
Week #1	L	—	—	Ground	—	Ground Patty	—	Cubes
	D	Slice	Pieces	Slice	Cubes	Chops	Ribs	Slice
Week #2	L	—	Ground	Diced	Slice	—	Flaked	Ground Patty
	D	Chops	Slice	Cutlet	Ground	Pieces	Slice	Slice
Week #3	L	—	Ground	—	Slice	—	Ground Patty	Ground
	D	Pieces	Slice	Ground	—	Chops	Steak	—

Block "C"   Use of blocks "A" and "B" to select menu items

	Meal	Sun	Mon	Tues	Wed	Thurs	Fri	Sat
Week #1	L	—	—	Pizza	Grilled Cheese Sandwich	Hamburger	Spanish Omlet	Beef Chow Mein
	D	Beef Steak	Chicken Fricassee	Baked Ham	Beef Stew	Veal Chops	Short Ribs	Roast Turkey
Week #2	L	—	Sloppy Joes	Chicken Salad Plate	Ham Sandwich	Macaroni & Cheese	Tuna Sandwich	Hamburger
	D	Pork Chops	Grilled Liver	Veal Cutlet	Meat Balls	Fried Rabbit	Roast Beef	Corned Beef
Week #3	L	—	Spaghetti	—	Roast Beef Sandwich	Cheese Souffle	Hamburger	Tacos
	D	Fried Chicken	Ham Steak	Meat Loaf	Roast Turkey	Pork Chops	Halibut Steak	Roast Lamb

FIG. 6.1. SAMPLE OF STEPWISE PROCEDURE FOR DEVELOPING MEAT
BLOCK PLAN FOR A 3-WEEK CYCLE MENU

fish, etc.; whole, diced, ground, etc.) these are blocked randomly (Fig. 6.1). This is an effective means of control.

MENU STRUCTURE

Meal patterns and custom largely determine menu structure. Historically, the main meal has been served at noon in institutions. This meal pattern is Breakfast, Dinner and Supper (Table 6.7). However, the currently accepted meal pat-

TABLE 6.7

SAMPLE MEAL PATTERN: BREAKFAST, DINNER, SUPPER

Breakfast
  Fruit or juice (rotated)
  Cooked cereal or assorted cold cereals
  Entrée (rotate pattern)
    Meat and eggs
    Hot cakes
    French toast
  Bread Item
  Beverage
Dinner
  Appetizer
  Entrée
  Starchy Food
  Vegetable
  Salad
  Dessert
  Bread item—dinner roll or quick bread
  Beverage
Supper
  Entrée (rotate pattern)
    Soup–sandwich
    Soup–salad plate
    Casserole–vegetable
  Salad (if necessary)
  Dessert
  Bread item (if necessary)
  Beverage

tern is Breakfast, Lunch, and Dinner, with approximately half of the calories provided at the evening meal (Table 6.8). Because a small segment of the American population has recently shifted toward a pattern of consuming 6 small meals, 4-, 5-, and 6-meal patterns have been developed for some institutions (Hagberg 1971; Norton 1967; Reid 1969).

Another variation in structure allows the consumer some choice in selecting a meal. Formerly, institutional menus were set, i.e., offered no choice. Today, most institutions offer two or more alternate items for at least one meal component such as the entrée. Menu planning strategies differ according to whether a set or a selective menu is to be planned.

TABLE 6.8

SAMPLE MEAL PATTERN: BREAKFAST, LUNCH, DINNER

Breakfast
  Fruit or juice (rotated)
  Cooked cereal or assorted cold cereals
  Entrée (rotate pattern)
    Meat and eggs
    Meat and pastry
    Hot cakes
    French toast
  Bread item
  Beverage
Lunch
  Entrée (rotate pattern)
    Soup–sandwich
    Soup–salad plate
    Casserole–vegetable
  Salad (if necessary)
  Dessert–canned or fresh fruit, cookies, gelatin, ice cream, pudding
  Bread item (if necessary)
  Beverage
Dinner
  Appetizer (optional) or relish (optional)
  Entrée
  Starchy food
  Vegetable
  Salad
  Dessert–pie, cake, ice cream, cooked fruit dessert
  Bread item–dinner roll or quick bread
  Beverage

Set Menus

Because the customer has no choice, the menu planner is obligated to limit variety to those items most likely to be consumed. Set menus are usually developed in ten steps as follows:

Step 1. Distribute the dinner and lunch entrées over the cycle, varying the category and preparation method (Fig. 6.2).

Step 2. Select a starchy food, *if required*, to accompany each entrée or draw a 1-in. line as a placeholder to indicate deliberate omission.

Step 3. Select a vegetable to accompany each entrée, planning contrasts in color, texture, shape, etc.

Step 4. Select lunch and dinner salads, varying the category among days.

Step 5. Select lunch and dinner desserts, varying this category among days.

Step 6. Select soups, if any.

Step 7. Select lunch and dinner breads.

Step 8. Select breakfast entrées.

Step 9. Select breakfast cereals and breads.

Step 10. Select fruit or juice.

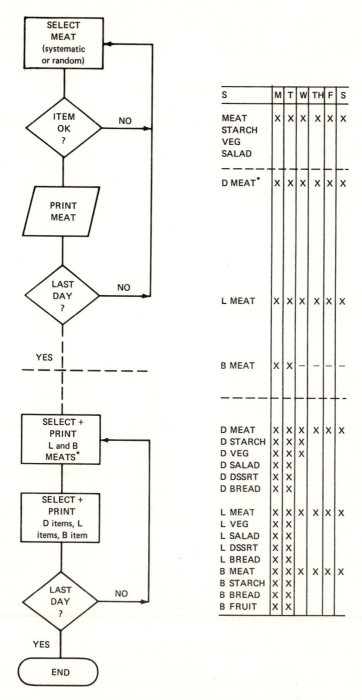

FIG. 6.2. MEAT BLOCK FOR A SET MENU

As part of the selection criteria in evaluating each prospective menu item, the menu planner checks vertically within the day for nutritional adequacy and cost control. Menus are checked horizontally among days for repetition (West *et al.* 1966). For other discussions of the mechanics of menu planning see also Dahl (1939), Hoke (1954), Treat and Richards (1966).

Selective Menus

Because the customer has a choice and will choose what he likes rather than what he should eat (Aykroyd 1961; Wakefield and Potgieter 1958) the menu planner is obligated to provide needed nutrients in the combinations most likely to be consumed. Other items are added to meet the needs of various population subgroups and to provide interest. Consumption data are used as predictors. A balanced selection is achieved by means of structure—assignment of one item from each category and/or color required. The steps in planning a three week selective menu are summarized below:

Step 1. Divide the menu planning task according to work section, i.e., meat and vegetable section, pantry, bakeshop, etc.

Step 2. Begin by planning items for the meat and vegetable sections.

Step 3. Review the classes of entrées to be selected for lunch and dinner each day—if more than three classes are served the classes will be fixed (Table 6.9); otherwise, a meat block pattern is an excellent guide (Fig. 6.1).

Step 4. Select from the most expensive class of entrées first; select other entrées in decreasing order of cost.

Step 5. Check for production feasibility (men and machines).

Step 6. Select starchy foods for lunch and dinner to complement the entrées in terms of color, texture, consistency, and shape.

Step 7. Select vegetables for lunch and dinner to complement the entrées and starches checking distribution of color, texture and consistency, shape, preparation method, KIND, acceptability.

Step 8. Select soups and/or appetizers for lunch and dinner—usually one light and one heavy soup—the heavy soup should be planned to complement the light or sandwich entree since these are most often paired.

Step 9. Select salads to complement the most likely combinations of items (Table 6.9). Select one salad from each class (e.g., fruit, vegetable, protein, gelatin) starting with the gelatin salad since it is a base and repetition of KIND of salad ingredient from the other three types is to be avoided.

Step 10. Check for production feasibility in the pantry.

Step 11. Select desserts to complement the salads from each of the customary classifications for lunch and dinner distributing the workload among pieces of equipment.

TABLE 6.9

SAMPLE MENU PLANNING GUIDE FOR MEAT AND VEGETABLE SECTION

Meal Component	Sunday	Monday	Tuesday
Lunch Entrées			
Beef Casserole	BBQ Beef	Beef Biscuit Roll/Gravy	Beef Chow Mein
Turkey	Turkey Turnover	Turkey Tetrazzini	Turkey Loaf
Meat Substitute	Cheese Omelet	Fish Sticks	Ham & Limas
Sandwich	Bacon-Lettuce-Tomato	Corned Beef	Poor Boy
	Hamburger	Hamburger	Hamburger
Lunch Starch			
	Steamed Rice	Parsley Buttered Potato	Steamed Rice Mashed Potato
Lunch Vegetables			
Green	Buttered Peas	Spinach/Egg	Buttered Green Beans
Yellow	Baked Squash	Parsley Carrots	Creamed Corn
Other	Cauliflower au Gratin	Mixed Vegetables	
Lunch Soups			
Light	Vegetable	Tomato Bouillon	Beef Noodle
Heavy	Cream of Mushroom	Split Pea	Clam Chowder
Dinner Entrées			
Roasts	Beef	Pork	Turkey
"Solids"	Lamb Chop	Beef Pot Roast	Swiss Steak
Poultry[1]	Fried Chicken	Turkey Drums	Liver & Bacon
Casseroles	Beef Stew	Meat Loaf	Sweet & Sour Pork
Meat Substitute	Curried Crab	Halibut Steaks	Baked Salmon
Dinner Starch			
	Mashed Potato	Baked Potato	Sage Dressing
	Scalloped Potato	Buttered Noodles	Steamed Rice
	Dumpling	Julienne Potato	Lyonnaise Potato
Dinner Vegetables			
Green	Buttered Broccoli	Asparagus Spears	Snow Peas
Yellow	Toasted Carrots	Sweet Potatoes	Orange Squash
Other			
Dinner Soups			
Light	Consommé	Turkey Rice	Vegetable Bouillon
Heavy	Gaspacho	Pepper Pot	Potato Soup

[1] When the roast is poultry a variety meat or other item replaces the regular poultry item.

Step 12. Select dinner and lunch breads.
Step 13. Select breakfast entrées (variable ones).
Step 14. Select hot cereal.
Step 15. Select breakfast bread items.
Step 16. Select fruits and juices.
Step 17. Put menu away for a day or so to "cool off"; then recheck for appeal to customers, production feasibility, cost, etc.

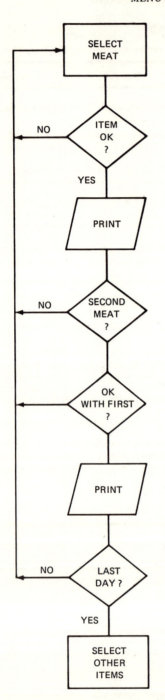

S	M	T	W	TH	F	S
D MEAT 1	X	X	X	X	X	
D MEAT 2	X	X	X	X			
STARCH						
VEG.						

FIG. 6.3. MEAT BLOCK FOR A SELECTIVE MENU

The method of filling in items is depicted in Fig. 6.3. A partial list of alternate lunch and dinner items prepared in the meat and vegetable section as shown in Table 6.9 illustrates selection from representative classes of items.

Cycle Menus

A cycle menu is a series of menus that is repeated at the end of a specified period (Hubbard *et al.* 1961). The purposes of using a cycle are: (A) To reduce the frequency of planning menus, thus saving time. (B) To increase control over production. Reuse of the menu facilitates implementation of feedback information in adjusting production requirements according to previous demand.

The length of a cycle may be 1 to 6 weeks. In a hospital where mean patient stay is 5 days, a short cycle of 7 days may be used. In this case, menu production requirements are largely known—the only variable is quantity. However, such a menu is not very satisfactory to the staff. Where patient stay is long-term, as in a nursing home, cycle length is customarily six weeks.

The cycle has a beginning, a middle, and an end. The beginning and end must fit together with no repetition and the middle must not slump with an abundance of unpopular items (Fig. 6.4). Table 6.10 is a sample three-week cycle menu for breakfast and lunch.

		WEEK #1							WEEK #2							WEEK #3							
DAYS		1	2	3	4	5	6	7	8	9	10	11	12	13	14	15	16	17	18	19	20	21	1
MEAL COMP.																								
BREAK	1	a	X					X	X							X	a						a	a
	2	X	X					X	X									U					X	X
	3	X	X					X	X														X	X
	4	X	X					X	X														X	X
	5	X	X					X	X														X	X
LUNCH	1	Y	Y	U				Y	Y	U		U											Y	Y
	2	Y	Y					Y	Y														Y	Y
	3	Y	Y					Y	Y		U						U						Y	Y
	4	Y	Y					a	Y														b	Y
	5	Y	Y					Y	Y														Y	Y
DINNER	1	Z	Z				U	Z	Z	U	U	U											Z	Z
	2	Z	Z					Z	Z													U	Z	Z
	3	Z	Z					Z	Z	U		U											Z	Z
	4	b	Z					Z	Z														Z	b
	5	a	Z					Z	Z														Z	a
	6	Z	Z					Z	Z		U												Z	Z

FIG. 6.4. UNACCEPTABLE MENU MODEL

Explanation of Symbols:
a, b—Repetition of KINDS U—Unacceptable item
X, Y, Z—Acceptable breakfast, lunch, and dinner items, respectively
KIND "a" is served at (a) breakfast and dinner of Sunday of week No. 1; (b) Sunday breakfast of weeks No. 1 and No. 3; (c) Saturday breakfast of week No. 3 and Sunday breakfast of No. 1 and therefore two days in succession. KIND "b" is served as dinner ingredients on Sunday of week No. 1 and as Saturday lunch dessert ingredients of week No. 3 and therefore two days in succession.

TABLE 6.10

SAMPLE 3-WEEK CYCLE MENU (2 ALTERNATIVES)

Name:
Points:
Search:
Adjustment:
Total Time:

Week 1 Summer

	Monday	Tuesday	Wednesday	Thursday	Friday	Saturday	Sunday
	Orange Juice	Apple Juice	Tomato Juice	Grape Juice	Pineapple-Grapefruit Juice	Orange Juice	Tomato Juice
	Banana	Canteloupe Wedge	Sliced Peaches	Strawberries	Bing Cherries	Canteloupe Wedge	Blueberries/Cream
	Cream of Wheat	Oatmeal	Ralston	Cream of Rice	Farina	Zoom	Steamed Rice
	Corn Flakes	Puffed Rice	Shredded Wheat	Frosted Flakes	Special K	Rice Krispies	Team
	Poached Egg	Hot Cakes/Boysenberry Syrup	Fried Egg	French Toast/Syrup	Scrambled Eggs	Scrapple/Syrup	Cheese Omelet
	Ham Steak	Bacon Strips	Sausage Patty	Bacon Strips	Sausage Links	Hard or Soft Cooked Eggs	Grilled Bacon Strips
	Buttered White Toast	English Muffin	Buttered Whole Wheat-Toast	Buttered Toast	Bran Muffin	Buttered Toast	English Muffin
	Cinnamon Roll	Maple Bar	Pineapple Coffee Cake	Glazed Doughnut	Cinnamon Toast	Bagel	Pecan Rolls
	Assorted Jam & Jelly	Assorted Jam & Jelly	Assorted Jam & Jelly	Assorted Jam & Jelly	Assorted Jam & Jelly	Assorted Jam & Jelly	Assorted Jam & Jelly
	Coffee-Tea-Milk	Coffee-Tea-Milk	Coffee-Tea-Milk	Coffee-Tea-Milk	Coffee-Tea-Milk	Coffee-Tea-Milk	Coffee-Tea-Milk
	Alphabet Soup	Hamburger Creole	Vegetable Soup	Barley Soup	Beef Chow Mein	Beef Noodle Soup	Vegetable Bouillon
	Corn Chowder	Curried Turkey/Rice	Potato Soup	Cream of Celery Soup	Tacos/Enchiladas	Cream of Asparagus Soup	Minestrone Soup
	French Dip Sandwich	Tossed Greens/1000 Island Dressing	Crab Salad Plate	Cheeseburger/Chips	Avocado & Lettuce/Vinegar & Oil Dressing	Fruit & Cold Cut Plate	Roast Beef Sandwich
	Ham & Swiss on Rye	Placed Fruit Salad/Poppy Seed Dressing	Cold Cuts/Hard Roll	Corned Beef on Rye	Marinated Asparagus	Cinnamon Toast Triangles	Ham Turnover
	Orange Sherbet	Sugar Cookies	Lemon Chiffon Tart	Fresh Apricot & Green Grapes	Lemon Sherbet	Turkey Salad Plate	Chocolate Cup Cake/Mocha Frosting
	Green Grapes	Tapioca Cream Pudding	Watermelon Wedge	Chocolate Brownie	Fresh Fruit Cup	Butterscotch Tart	Pineapple
	Coffee-Tea-Milk	Coffee-Tea-Milk	Coffee-Tea-Milk	Coffee-Tea-Milk	Coffee-Tea-Milk	Cranberry Chiffon Square	Coffee-Tea-Milk
						Coffee-Tea-Milk	

Week 2 Summer

Monday	Tuesday	Wednesday	Thursday	Friday	Saturday	Sunday
Prune Juice	Grapefruit Juice	Pineapple Juice	Apple Juice	Grapefruit-Orange Juice	Tomato Juice	Orange Juice
Sliced Peaches	Honeydew Melon	Banana	Canteloupe Wedge	Blackberries	Pineapple Rings	Cranshaw Melon
Oatmeal	Corn Meal Mush	Wheat Hearts	Ralston	Farina	Oatmeal	Zoom
Pep	Puffed Wheat	Cocoa Krispies	Granola	Cheerios	Rice Chex	Raisin Bran
Hawaiian Hotcakes	Soft and Hard Cooked Eggs	Ham Steak	Eggs Over Easy	Orange French Toast	Corned Beef Hash	Buckwheat Cakes/ Maple Syrup
Coconut Syrup	Bacon Strips	Poached Egg	Fried Potatoes	Bacon Strips	Poached Egg	Sausage Links
Country Sausage	Blueberry Buckle	Rye Toast	Bear Claws	Nut Muffins	Whole Wheat Toast	Butterscotch Rolls
Buttered White Toast	Whole Wheat Toast	Cinnamon Rolls	Raisin Toast	Buttered White Toast	English Muffin	Cinnamon Toast
Sweet Rolls (Snails)	Assorted Jam & Jelly	Assorted Jam & Jelly	Assorted Jam & Jelly	Assorted Jam & Jelly	Assorted Jam & Jelly	Assorted Jam & Jelly
Assorted Jam & Jelly	Coffee-Tea-Milk	Coffee-Tea-Milk	Coffee-Tea-Milk	Coffee-Tea-Milk	Coffee-Tea-Milk	Coffee-Tea-Milk
Coffee-Tea-Milk						
Beef Stew	Tomato Soup	Pepper Pot Soup	Creamed Chipped Beef on Toast Points	Manhattan Clam Chowder	Vegetable Chowder	Beef Noodle Soup
Spaghetti/Meat Sauce	Vegetable Soup	Chicken Rice Soup	Ham Biscuit Roll/ Vegetable Gravy	Cream of Mushroom Soup	Ruby Consommé	Cheese Soup
Tossed Greens/ French Dressing	Hot Dog & Potato Salad	Stuffed Tomato Salad Plate	Lettuce, Egg & Asparagus/ Italian Dressing	Tuna Salad Plate	Hamburger Sandwich Plate	Turkey Club Sandwich
Garlic Toast	Grilled Cheese Sandwich	Cold Tongue & Potato Salad	Jellied Pineapple & Celery Salad	Chef's Salad/Hard Roll	Cold Cuts & Swiss Cheese/Poppy Seed Roll	Pastrami
Vanilla Ice Cream	Coconut Cream Pudding	Hard Roll	Rainbow Gelatin Cubes	Gingersnaps	Strawberry Tart	Watermelon Wedge
Chocolate Chip Cookies	Green Grapes	Orange Whip	Lime Sherbet	Peach & Plum Cobbler	Chocolate Rivel Ice Cream	Spice Cupcake/ Burnt Sugar Icing
Coffee-Tea-Milk	Coffee-Tea-Milk	Butterscotch Brownie	Coffee-Tea-Milk	Coffee-Tea-Milk	Coffee-Tea-Milk	Coffee-Tea-Milk
		Coffee-Tea-Milk				

TABLE 6.10 (*Continued*)

Week 3 Summer

Monday	Tuesday	Wednesday	Thursday	Friday	Saturday	Sunday
Pineapple Juice	Apple Juice	Tomato Juice	Orange Juice	Grape Juice	Prune Juice	Grapefruit Juice
Blueberries	Fruit Cocktail	Pear Halves	Honeydew Melon	Banana	Canteloupe Wedge	Pineapple Tidbits
Cream of Wheat	Oatmeal	Ralston	Cream of Rice	Corn Meal Mush	Wheatena	Malt-o-Meal
Sugar Corn Pops	Wheaties	Cheerios	Corn Chex	Raisin Bran	Puffed Rice	Special K
Scrambled Eggs	French Toast/Syrup	Fried Shredded Wheat[1]	Shirred Egg	Buttermilk Hot Cakes/Syrup	Creamed Eggs on Toast	Fried Eggs
Bacon Strips	Canadian Bacon	Sausage Links	Bacon Strips	Bacon Strips	Sausage Patty	Hash Browns
Buttered White Toast	Nut Muffin	Jelly Bismark	Bran Muffin	Chocolate Doughnut	English Muffin	Cinnamon Twist
Bagel	Whole Wheat Toast	Buttered Toast	Cinnamon Toast	Buttered Toast	Raisin Toast	Corn Cake
Assorted Jam & Jelly	Assorted Jam & Jelly	Assorted Jam & Jelly	Assorted Jam & Jelly	Assorted Jam & Jelly	Assorted Jam & Jelly	Assorted Jam & Jelly
Coffee-Tea-Milk	Coffee-Tea-Milk	Coffee-Tea-Milk	Coffee-Tea-Milk	Coffee-Tea-Milk	Coffee-Tea-Milk	Coffee-Tea-Milk

Monday	Tuesday	Wednesday	Thursday	Friday	Saturday	Sunday
Vegetarian Vegetable Soup	Chili Con Carne	French Onion Soup	Corn Chowder	Oyster Stew	Spanish Rice/Cheese & Bacon	Julienne Soup
Tomato Rice Soup	Pork Chop Suey/Rice	Mock Turtle Soup	Vegetable Soup	Cream of Celery Soup	Stuffed Zucchini	Dutch Potato Soup
Corned Beef & Potato Salad	Guacamole Salad	Hot Meat Loaf Sandwich Plate	Balogna & Cheese Sandwich Plate	Crab Louis	Tossed Greens/Italian Dressing	Poor Boy Sandwich
Egg Salad Sandwich Plate	Marinated Cucumbers	Ham Sandwich Plate	Turkey Turnover	Stuffed Egg & Tomato Salad Plate	Lime Tart	Bacon/Lettuce/& Tomato Sandwich
Maple Chiffon Pudding	Refrigerator Cheese Cake	Oatmeal Cookies	Fresh Fruit Cup	Chocolate Chiffon Pudding	Vanilla Ice Cream	Watermelon
Snowball	Lemon Meringue Tart	Peach Ice Cream	Coconut Bar Cookie	Angel Food Cup Cake	Coffee-Tea-Milk	Rasberry Whip
Coffee-Tea-Milk	Coffee-Tea-Milk	Coffee-Tea-Milk	Coffee-Tea-Milk	Coffee-Tea-Milk		Coffee-Tea-Milk

[1] To make: (1) Melt a little butter or margarine in frying pan, (2) dip shredded wheat biscuits in milk, (3) cover and heat through, turning occasionally. Serve with sugar.

Two alternative methods are used in planning for seasonal variation when using a cycle menu. The first method, used with short cycles, e.g., three weeks, repeats about four times per season. A separate cycle is planned for each season: fall—Sept., Oct., Nov.; winter—Dec., Jan., Febr.; spring—Mar., Apr., May; summer—June, July, Aug. Seasonal items are included frequently; basic items are included but with low frequency with this cycle since they are served throughout the year. When a longer cycle is necessary, e.g., a 6-week cycle that is repeated 7 times, the second method is used in which alternatives are planned for some of the items. However, it is more difficult to plan for sufficient seasonal variation and standard items are served throughout the year whether desirable or not.

TABLE 6.11

SAMPLE PRODUCTION MENU, CENSUS 600

Breakfast	Lunch	Dinner
	Monday	
(200)[1]	(400)	(600)
Apple Juice (200)	Pizza (475)	Glazed Ham Steak (675)
Oatmeal (75)	Frozen Cauliflower (100)	Creamed Frozen Peas (300)
Assorted Dry Cereals	Lettuce Wedge, 1000	Baked Fresh Squash (100)
French Toast/Syrup (150)	Island Dressing (300)	Pineapple Ring with Kadota
Buttered Toast, Jam	Potato Roll/Butter (425)	Fig and Cream Cheese (200)
Coffee, Tea, Milk	Peach Betty	Raisin Bread/Butter
		Mystery Pudding (400)
	Tuesday	
(100)	(350)	(550)
Orange Juice (150)	Hamburger on Bun (400)	Roast Round of Beef (300)
Wheat-oata (50)	Mustard, Relish, Catsup,	Spaghetti/Tomato Sauce (300)
Assorted Dry Cereals	Mayonnaise	Buttered Geeen Beans (300)
Soft- Hard-Cooked Eggs (75)	Macaroni Salad on	Lemon Jello with Diced Pears,
Buttered Toast, Jam	Lettuce (75)	Sliced Peaches, Frozen
Coffee, Tea, Milk	Carrot Sticks (400)	Cherries (600)
	Delicious Apple (400)	Homemade Style Wheat Bread/
	Banana Bar (350)	Butter
		Gingerbread/Whipped Cream
		(400)
	Wednesday	
(200)	(400)	(575)
Apricot Nectar (100)	Old Fashioned Bean Soup/	Half Broiled Chicken (575)
Cream of Wheat (60)	Crackers (300)	Mashed Potatoes, Gravy (600)
Assorted Dry Cereals	Chef's Salad Bowl (400)	Buttered Frozen Broccoli (150)
Hot Cakes/Blueberries (175)	Russian Dressing	Spears/Hollandaise Sauce
Buttered Toast, Jam	Hot Garlic/Parmesan (500)	Salad—Pear Half (1), (450)
Coffee, Tea, Milk	Cheese French Bread	Peach Slices (2), Spiced Crab
	Dished Special Ice Cream	Apple
	(500)	Egg Knot Rolls/Butter
		Refrigerator Cheese Cake (525)

[1] Forecast number of servings required.

MENU FORMAT

The menu format is determined by the purpose of the menu, i.e., for production or for sales. The production menu is often written in block style and provides information for the cook such as ingredient state, recipe number, and forecast (Table 6.11).

The institutional sales menu varies from a simple block listing to a formal menu almost as elaborate as many restaurant menus. In the latter case, emphasis is achieved by (a) arrangement of items with appropriate spacing (Fig. 6.5 and

Fried Chicken with Almonds
Steamed Rice
Asparagus Spears with Butter Sauce
Molded Cider Fruit Salad
Poppy Seed Roll   Whipped Butter
Chocolate Cake with Mocha Frosting
Coffee   Tea   Milk

Fried Chicken with Almonds
Steamed Rice   Asparagus Spears in Butter Sauce
Molded Cider Fruit Salad
Poppy Seed Roll   Whipped Butter
Chocolate Cake with Mocha Frosting
Coffee   Tea   Milk

FIG. 6.5. BLOCK FORMAT (ABOVE) AND CENTERED FORMAT (BELOW)
FOR NONSELECTIVE MENUS

6.6); (b) varied use of type—size, style, and boldness (Fig. 6.7, 6.8, 6.9); and (c) use of color and patterns (Fig. 6.10). Note: Standard accompaniments such as sugar, salt and pepper are not listed except on hospital menus.

MENU TERMINOLOGY

The purpose of menu item names is to communicate to the customer a message which calls to mind a concept of the item so that an accept-reject decision can be made. If the customer visualizes 'fruit cup' as being composed of melon balls, banana slices, and diced oranges he does not anticipate or appreciate a dish of canned fruit cocktail. Accurate but interesting descriptors can be used to aid the customer in visualizing the item (Table 6.12). If one lists Chocolate Pudding with Whipped Cream, substitution of whipped topping is illegal under provisions of labeling laws. Similarly, frozen peas may not be listed as Garden Fresh Peas, etc.

When restaurant menus contain foreign or unfamiliar terms, part of the service rendered by the waiter is description of the item. Inasmuch as this service is unavailable in most institutional food service units, unfamiliar terminology

Roast Turkey with Giblet Gravy
Baked Ham
Braised Pot Roast
Grilled Liver with Onions

Mashed Potatoes
Parsley Dumplings
Sage Dressing

Whole Green Beans in Butter Sauce
Julienne Carrots
Cauliflower au Gratin

Sliced Tomatoes on Cress with French Dressing
Tossed Green Salad with Piquant Dressing
Peach and Pineapple Salad

Hot Biscuits   Butter   Honey
French Rolls   Butter
Egg Knot Rolls   Butter

Coconut Cream Pie
Apple Crisp
Rainbow Gelatin Cubes
Ice Cream

Coffee   Sanka   Tea   Milk   Skim Milk

Entrées

Roast Turkey with Giblet Gravy   Baked Ham
Braised Pot Roast

Vegetables

Mashed Potatoes   Parsley Dumplings   Sage Dressing
Whole Green Beans in Butter Sauce
Julienne Carrots   Cauliflowerets au Gratin

Salads

Sliced Tomatoes on Cress with French Dressing
Tossed Green Salad with Piquant Dressing
Peach and Pineapple Salad

Bread Items

Hot Biscuits   French Rolls   Egg Knot Rolls
Butter   Rose Hip Jelly   Honey

Desserts

Coconut Cream Pie   Apple Crisp
Rainbow Gelatin Cubes   Ice Cream

Beverages

Coffee   Sanka   Tea
Milk   Skim Milk

FIG. 6.6. BLOCK FORMAT (ABOVE) AND CENTERED FORMAT (BELOW)
FOR SELECTIVE MENUS

Roast Turkey with Giblet Gravy
Baked Ham
Braised Pot Roast

Mashed Potatoes
Parsley Dumplings
Sage Dressing

Whole Green Beans in Butter Sauce
Julienne Carrots
Cauliflowerets au Gratin

Sliced Tomatoes on Cress with French Dressing
Tossed Green Salad with Piquant Dressing
Peach and Pineapple Salad

Hot Biscuits   Butter   Honey
French Rolls   Butter
Egg Knot Rolls

Coconut Cream Pie
Apple Crisp
Rainbow Gelatin Cubes
Ice Cream

Coffee   Sanka   Tea   Milk   Skim Milk

Entrees

Roast Turkey with Giblet Gravy
Braised Pot Roast   Baked Ham

Vegetables

Mashed Potatoes   Parsley Dumplings   Sage Dressing
Whole Green Beans in Butter Sauce
Julienne Carrots   Cauliflowerets au Gratin

Salads

Sliced Tomatoes on Cress with French Dressing
Tossed Green Salad with Piquant Dressing
Peach and Pineapple Salad

Bread Items

Hot Biscuits   French Rolls   Egg Knot Rolls
Butter   Rose Hip Jelly   Honey

Desserts

Coconut Cream Pie   Apple Crisp
Rainbow Gelatin Cubes   Ice Cream

Beverages

Coffee   Sanka   Tea
Milk   Skim Milk

FIG. 6.7. SAMPLE MENUS SHOWING EFFECTS OF DIFFERENT
SIZES IN TYPE

Roman

Fried Chicken with Almonds
Steamed Rice
Asparagus Spears with Butter Sauce
Molded Cider Fruit Salad
Poppy Seed Roll   Whipped Butter
Chocolate Cake with Mocha Frosting
Coffee   Tea   Milk

Fried Chicken with Almonds
Steamed Rice   Asparagus Spears with Butter Sauce
Molded Cider Fruit Salad
Poppy Seed Roll   Whipped Butter
Chocolate Cake with Mocha Frosting
Coffee   Tea   Milk

Entrees
Roast Turkey with Giblet Gravy
Braised Pot Roast   Baked Ham

Vegetables
Mashed Potatoes   Parsley Dumplings   Sage Dressing
Whole Green Beans with Butter Sauce
Julienne Carrots   Cauliflowerets au Gratin

Salads
Sliced Tomatoes on Cress with French Dressing
Tossed Green Salad with Piquant Dressing
Peach and Pineapple Salad

Bread Items
Hot Biscuits   French Rolls   Egg Knot Rolls
Butter   Rose Hip Jelly   Honey

Desserts
Coconut Cream Pie   Apple Crisp
Rainbow Gelatin Cubes   Ice Cream

Beverages
Coffee   Sanka   Tea
Milk   Skim Milk

Modern

Fried Chicken with Almonds
Steamed Rice
Asparagus Spears with Butter Sauce
Molded Cider Fruit Salad
Poppy Seed Roll   Whipped Butter
Chocolate Cake with Mocha Frosting
Coffee   Tea   Milk

Fried Chicken with Almonds
Steamed Rice   Asparagus Spears with Butter Sauce
Molded Cider Fruit Salad
Poppy Seed Roll   Whipped Butter
Chocolate Cake with Mocha Frosting
Coffee   Tea   Milk

Entrees
Roast Turkey with Giblet Gravy
Braised Pot Roast   Baked Ham

Vegetables
Mashed Potatoes   Parsley Dumplings   Sage Dressing
Whole Green Beans with Butter Sauce
Julienne Carrots   Cauliflowerets au Gratin

Salads
Sliced Tomatoes on Cress with French Dressing
Tossed Green Salad with Piquant Dressing
Peach and Pineapple Salad

Bread Items
Hot Biscuits   French Rolls   Egg Knot Rolls
Butter   Rose Hip Jelly   Honey

Desserts
Coconut Cream Pie   Apple Crisp
Rainbow Gelatin Cubes   Ice Cream

Beverages
Coffee   Sanka   Tea
Milk   Skim Milk

Italics

Fried Chicken with Almonds
Steamed Rice
Asparagus Spears with Butter Sauce
Molded Cider Fruit Salad
Poppy Seed Roll   Whipped Butter
Chocolate Cake with Mocha Frosting
Coffee   Tea   Milk

Fried Chicken with Almonds
Steamed Rice   Asparagus Spears with Butter Sauce
Molded Cider Fruit Salad
Poppy Seed Roll   Whipped Butter
Chocolate Cake with Mocha Frosting
Coffee   Tea   Milk

Entrees
Roast Turkey with Giblet Gravy
Braised Pot Roast   Baked Ham

Vegetables
Mashed Potatoes   Parsley Dumplings   Sage Dressing
Whole Green Beans with Butter Sauce
Julienne Carrots   Cauliflowerets au Gratin

Salads
Sliced Tomatoes on Cress with French Dressing
Tossed Green Salad with Piquant Dressing
Peach and Pineapple Salad

Bread Items
Hot Biscuits   French Rolls   Egg Knot Rolls
Butter   Rose Hip Jelly   Honey

Desserts
Coconut Cream Pie   Apple Crisp
Rainbow Gelatin Cubes   Ice Cream

Beverages
Coffee   Sanka   Tea
Milk   Skim Milk

FIG. 6.8. SAMPLE MENUS SHOWING DIFFERENT EFFECTS PRODUCED BY THE THREE STANDARD TYPE STYLES

Entrees
Roast Turkey with Giblet Gravy
Braised Pot Roast   Baked Ham

Vegetables
Mashed Potatoes   Parsley Dumplings   Sage Dressing
Whole Green Beans with Butter Sauce
Julienne Carrots   Cauliflowerets au Gratin

Salads
Sliced Tomatoes on Cress with French Dressing
Tossed Green Salad with Piquant Dressing
Peach and Pineapple Salad

Bread Items
Hot Biscuits   French Rolls   Egg Knot Rolls
Butter   Rose Hip Jelly   Honey

Desserts
Coconut Cream Pie   Apple Crisp
Rainbow Gelatin Cubes   Ice Cream

Beverages
Coffee   Sanka   Tea
Milk   Skim Milk

ENTREES
Roast Turkey with Giblet Gravy
Braised Pot Roast   Baked Ham

VEGETABLES
Mashed Potatoes   Parsley Dumplings   Sage Dressing
Whole Green Beans with Butter Sauce
Julienne Carrots   Cauliflowerets au Gratin

SALADS
Sliced Tomatoes on Cress with French Dressing
Tossed Green Salad with Piquant Dressing
Peach and Pineapple Salad

BREAD ITEMS
Hot Biscuits   French Rolls   Egg Knot Rolls
Butter   Rose Hip Jelly   Honey

DESSERTS
Coconut Cream Pie   Apple Crisp
Rainbow Gelatin Cubes   Ice Cream

BEVERAGES
Coffee   Sanka   Tea
Milk   Skim Milk

FIG. 6.9. SAMPLE MENUS SHOWING EFFECTS OF VARYING
BOLDNESS OF TYPE AND USE OF CAPITAL LETTERS

Entrees
Roast Turkey with Giblet Gravy
Braised Pot Roast   Baked Ham

Vegetables
Mashed Potatoes   Parsley Dumplings   Sage Dressing
Whole Green Beans in Butter Sauce
Julienne Carrots   Cauliflowerets au Gratin

Salads
Sliced Tomatoes on Cress with French Dressing
Tossed Green Salad with Piquant Dressing
Peach and Pineapple Salad

Bread Items
Hot Biscuits   French Rolls   Egg Knot Rolls
Butter   Rose Hip Jelly   Honey

Desserts
Coconut Cream Pie   Apple Crisp
Rainbow Gelatin Cubes   Ice Cream

Beverages
Coffee   Sanka   Tea
Milk   Skim Milk

(a) Good Example

Entrees
Roast Turkey with Giblet Gravy
Braised Pot Roast   Baked Ham

Vegetables
Mashed Potatoes   Parsley Dumplings   Sage Dressings
Whole Green Beans in Butter Sauce
Julienne Carrots   Cauliflowerets au Gratin

Salads
Sliced Tomatoes on Cress with French Dressing
Tossed Green Salad with Piquant Dressing
Peach and Pineapple Salad

Bread Items
Hot Biscuits   French Rolls   Egg Knot Rolls
Butter   Rose Hip Jelly   Honey

Desserts
Coconut Cream Pie   Apple Crisp
Rainbow Gelatin Cubes   Ice Cream

Beverages
Coffee   Sanka   Tea
Milk   Skim Milk

(b) Poor Example

FIG. 6.10.   SAMPLE MENUS SHOWING EFFECT OF USING PATTERNS

TABLE 6.12

EXAMPLES OF POOR ITEM DESCRIPTORS[1]

Descriptor	Explanation Required for Clarity
Mock Drum Sticks	Veal and pork cubes on skewers, dipped in batter and fried
Chicken a la Maryland	Chicken parts braised in cream
Scrapple	Cornmeal mush with added pork scraps; fried like a potato cake
Perfection Salad	Lemon gelatin containing a tart cabbage-celery-pimiento mixture
Petti-johns	Porridge similar to oatmeal made from rolled wheat
Western Sandwich	Spicy ground beef-tomato mixture served on a bun
Denver Sandwich	Scrambled eggs with ham, green peppers, and onions served on toast
Rissole Potatoes	Oven browned potatoes
Pepper Pot Soup	Cream soup with potatoes and green pepper

[1] A descriptor is poor if it fails to convey the correct image of the food. With a transient group, simple descriptors are necessary. With a long-term or cosmopolitan group, familiarity with terms will enlarge the pool of good descriptors.

should be avoided (Bing 1960). Nonetheless, the menu planner should obtain a standard dictionary of food terms and be familiar with foreign terms that are used frequently (Shannon 1962; Waldo 1967).

Moreover, in selecting recipes for the recipe pool, the menu planner should be careful to select recipes that are authentic, especially if they are adapted from foreign cookery. Several standard references should be consulted to verify authenticity (Given 1959; Waldo 1967). While many acceptable variations are used within a country, imitations using inexpensive substitute ingredients should not be used without adding a descriptor to the item name to indicate to the consumer that the item has been modified. The knowledgeable and discriminating consumer becomes irate when served an item so cheapened. Also, the practice is illegal under provisions of the labeling laws. For example, the name "Grasshopper Sundae" connotes a serving of ice cream topped with equal parts of creme de menthe and creme de cocoa. Substitution of a flavored green sugar syrup is an unacceptable practice. In this case, a more acceptable item name would be "Mock Grasshopper Sundae."

MENU COSTING

Menu costing is the process of computing the expected cost of the meal. A variety of methods are used.

The simplest method, used with a set menu, is the sum of (a) current raw food cost per serving (or purchase price for convenience foods) of the items listed; (b) the mean cost of sugar, salt, pepper, condiments, etc.; (c) the mean labor cost (total man-hour cost divided by census); and (d) prorated supply and administrative costs. When a selective menu is costed, the expected number of servings of each item is used in computing cost as shown in Table 6.11.

A more sophisticated system, using more accurate recipe costing, provides a more reliable estimate of the expected menu cost. Raw food cost is computed in the conventional manner. Labor cost for the item is computed from empirical observations and is summarized as the mode or estimated mean using work modules (standard times for performing elemental tasks such as fetch from refrigerator, open package, place on pan, etc.) (Ivanicky et al. 1969). Supply costs directly attributed to the item, e.g., souffle cups for cranberry sauce, are included; others are prorated. Administrative costs are prorated. The sum of these costs is the menu cost.

Actual costs frequently exceed estimated costs because penalty or salvage costs are incurred. Penalty costs result from forecasting errors in which item demand exceeds supply and other items must be substituted. In addition to the actual cost of the substitute food, supplies, and labor there is a negative effect on total sales if the substitute is less profitable or fewer items are selected. Salvage costs result from forecasting errors in which supply exceeds demand and items must be stored and reheated (additional labor and storage costs), or reworked— e.g., roast beef diced for stew or baked chicken breast ground for chicken salad (additional labor, storage costs, and lower profit).

TABLE 6.13

EXAMPLES OF GOOD ITEM DESCRIPTORS[1]

Baked Ham
Baked Hash
Barbecued Chicken
Beef Stew
Braised Liver and Onions
Broccoli Spears with Lemon Butter
Candied Sweet Potatoes
Chicken Pie
Corned Beef and Cabbage
Cottage Cheese and Peach Salad
Cream of Chicken Soup
Creamed Tuna on Toast
Macaroni and Cheese
Meatballs and Spaghetti
Oven Browned Potatoes
Pork Chops with Dressing
Salmon Loaf
Split Pea Soup

[1] Good item descriptors require no explanation as they are generally familiar.

TABLE 6.14

CRITICAL COST TABLE—IMPUTED VALUES

Meal	Meal Component	Minimum[1] ($)	Maximum[2] ($)
Dinner	Entrée	0.18	0.51
	Starchy Food	0.23	0.54
	Vegetable	0.31	0.59
	Salad	0.39	0.64
	Dessert	0.51	0.70
	Bread Item	0.57	0.75
	Beverage	0.63	0.81
Lunch A	Soup	0.67	0.85
	Salad Plate	0.80	1.07
	Dessert	0.89	1.15
	Bread Item	0.93	1.20
	Beverage	1.03	1.25
Breakfast	Fruit or Juice	1.11	1.31
	Entrée	1.29	1.43
	Bread Item	1.35	1.48
	Beverage	1.38	1.58
. . . . . .	. . . .	. . . .	. . . .
Lunch B	Casserole	0.81	1.03
	Vegetable	0.85	1.10
	.		
	.		
	.		

[1] Total daily minimum raw food cost allowed is $1.38.
[2] Total daily maximum raw food cost allowed is $1.58.

In order to control the overall menu cost, the menu planner must know the relative cost position after selecting each meal component in order to ensure feasibility of including all meal components. The simplest method is to construct a Critical Cost Table (Table 6.14) and compare the sum of (a) the cumulative cost of previously selected items and (b) the prospective menu item. If the total exceeds the range, the item is rejected and other items are selected and tested.

MENU REVIEW

Menu review by a committee is the part of the menu planning process in which adjustments and refinements are made. Experience has shown that these committees have variable success depending on the political climate established. If the menu planner is relatively secure and sincere in wanting a good critique, many problems can be avoided. On the other hand, if the menu planner is so threatened that review degenerates into trivial comments, committee members play safe and give tacit consent; nothing is accomplished as the problems remain.

One must also recognize that once a menu is complete, it is difficult to select a substitute item that will meet all criteria without requiring other item changes;

therefore, compromises must be reached. To minimize the number of changes required after the basic menu is complete, one must have explicit menu planning policies, adequate data, judgment, artistic flair, and the ability to consider numerous factors simultaneously.

In reviewing the initial menu set, one thoroughly rechecks it for horizontal and vertical balance of the following factors—nutritional adequacy, cost, acceptability, variety, production feasibility. Thereafter, the menu is rechecked each time the cycle is repeated. In this case, production records are examined; seasonal adjustments for cost or availability are also added. Additions and corrections to the menu are made as necessary.

Another function of a menu review committee is to review the menu planning policies and selection criteria to provide guidance in planning the menus. The ten mistakes in menu writing (Table 6.15) cited by Sandler (1968) are areas for discussion that each review committee needs to consider intermittently in order to make continuous improvement in the menu.

TABLE 6.15

TEN MISTAKES IN MENU WRITING[1]

Mistake No.	Mistake
1	You don't know your customers
2	You copy your competitor's menu
3	You don't know what you're selling
4	You hang on to slow volume items
5	Your food costing is inaccurate
6	You build in high labor cost
7	You don't know how to buy
8	Your menu only works part time
9	You list when you should sell
10	You settle for sameness

[1] Adapted from Sandler (1968). With permission of Fast Food.

MENU PLANNING EXERCISES

For Nonselective (Set) Menus

Menu Pattern in Planning Set Menus

Breakfast
Juice or fruit
Entrée: (2 of these) eggs, meat, hot cakes, hot bread
Cooked cereal
Bread item (if necessary)
Beverage (print routinely)

Lunch (3 plate options, rotate type; bread as necessary; beverage)
1. Soup, sandwich, dessert
2. Casserole, salad, dessert
3. Soup, salad plate, dessert
4. Beverage (print routinely)

Dinner
Meat or meat substitute
Starchy food: potato, rice, etc.
Vegetable
Salad
Dessert
Bread item
Beverage (print routinely)

Exercise No. 1.–Plan 5 lunch menus suitable for school children aged 9-12 yr. Use the type "A" meal plan to meet nutritional requirements. It is hazardous to thaw meat on Friday for Monday lunch; select your entrée accordingly. Ballance the menus for color, texture, and flavor.

Note time requirements: (a) total time, (b) recipe search, (c) evaluation of prospective items, and (d) adjustments.

Exercise No. 2.–Plan a one-week menu (breakfast, lunch, dinner) for a co-ed dormitory with a heterogeneous population. Follow menu pattern for set menu. Assume:

(A) Meat is delivered Tuesday and Thursday between 11 a.m. and 1 p.m.
(B) Frozen food is delivered on Thursday between 8 and 10 a.m.
(C) Staples are delivered on Thursday between 8 a.m. and 2 p.m.
(D) Produce is delivered on Tuesday, Thursday, and Saturday between 7 and 9 a.m.
(E) Bread and dairy delivered daily in time for breakfast.
(F) Oven space is limited.
(G) Major cleaning is done on Saturday afternoon.
(H) Sunday dinner is served at noon and the evening meal is omitted.

Note time requirements: (a) total time, (b) recipe search, (c) evaluation of prospective items, and (d) adjustments.

For Selective Menus

Dinner Menu Pattern
Soups (2)
Entrées (4)
Mashed potatoes
Starchy food
Vegetables (3)
Salads (3)

Tossed salad
Cake
Cream pie
Fruit pie
Other dessert
Ice cream
Bread item (3)
Beverages

Exercise No. 1.–Plan a one-week menu for a hospital staff cafeteria. Include the indicated number of items for each meal component. Plan for attractive hot and cold food displays. Customers will select items that seem to be complementary; plan for this in selecting the alternative items. Mark items for expected ethnic acceptability as follows: (a) Northern Blacks, (b) Oriental, (c) Chicano, and (d) German.

Note time requirements: (a) total time, (b) recipe search, (c) evaluation of prospective items, and (d) adjustments.

Exercise No. 2.–Plan a 3-week cycle menu for a retirement home using any one of the four seasonal groups below. Assume population composed of WASPs (White Anglo-Saxon Protestants) and Reform Jews. Plan two alternatives for each meal component listed for the menu pattern in planning set menus. Distribute KINDs to avoid monotony.

Season	Months
Fall	September, October, November
Winter	December, January, February
Spring	March, April, May
Summer	June, July, August

Note time requirements (a) total time, (b) recipe search, (c) evaluation of prospective items, and (d) adjustments.

SAMPLE QUESIONS FOR DINNER MENU PLANNING MODELS

For Manual Set Menus

Meat
- Was this category served in the last X days?
- Was this item served in the last Y days?
- Was this gravy or sauce served in the last Z days?
- Was this item served the same day last week?
- Is this item too expensive, given the average?

Starchy Food
- Was this category served in the last X days?
- Was this item served in the last Y days?
- If this item is not a potato, is a potato needed?

Vegetable
- Was this vegetable served in the last X days?
- Is this vegetable unpopular? If answer is yes, has anything else unpopular been selected?
- Is the color OK?
- Is the texture OK?
- Is the shape OK?
- Are there too many runny items?
- Are there too many fried items?
- Is there a production problem of work load or timing?

Salad
- Was this category served in the last X days?
- Was this item served in the last Y days?
- Is there a preparation or production problem?
- Does this salad contain the same vegetable that is served as a vegetable?
- Does this salad also contain a member of the cabbage family?

Dessert
- Was this category served in the last X days?
- Was this item served in the last Y days?
- Is KIND OK?
- Do both salad and dessert contain fruit?
- Is color OK?
- Are texture and shape OK?

Bread Item
- Was this bread item served in the last X days?
- Is there a production problem?

Are cost and nutrition OK? —

For Manual Selective Menus (3 Items + Constants)

Meats (categories are predetermined)
- Was this item served in the last X days?
- Is the preparation method varied?
- Are handwork and timing OK?
- Is color varied?
- Are price levels represented?

Starchy Food
- Is potato needed?
- Was this type of potato served in the last Q days?
- Does this starchy food complement a meat?
- Is rice needed?
- Has dressing been served too frequently?

Vegetables (hospital—A and B vegetable?)
- Does this vegetable complement a meat?
- Is color varied?
- Are texture and consistency varied?
- Is shape varied?
- Is there a production problem of handwork or timing?
- Is there an acceptable choice of vegetables?

Salads (constants = tossed and cottage cheese)—select fruit, gelatin, and other salads
- Is the color of the salad bar OK?
- Are the salads OK with the entrées?
- Are there contrasts in texture?
- Are the salads acceptable? Good choices?
- Is there a production problem of handwork or timing?

Desserts (category control; constant = ice cream)
- Is the color of the dessert bar OK?
- Are the choices acceptable?
- Is there a production problem of handwork or timing?

Breads (category control—yeast and quick)
- Is the assortment varied enough?

Beverage
- Print routinely.

BIBLIOGRAPHY

AYKROYD, W. R. 1961. Reflections on human food patterns. Nutrition *15*, No. 2, 65–70.

BING, J. H. 1960. Write the menu for the readers. Mod. Hosp. *95*, No. 1, 108–110.

BLAIR, E. C., and VFM Magazine. 1967. Professional's Recipe Master. Ahrens Publishing Co., New York.

BLAIR, E. C. 1971. Volume Feeding Menu Selector. Institutions/VF Magazine, Chicago.

DAHL, J. O. 1939. Menu Making for Professionals in Quantity Cookery. Published by the author, Stamford, Conn.

DOUGHERTY, D. A., TUTHILL, B. H., and MOORE, A. N. 1971. Menu planning by computer at the medical center, UMC. *In* Computer Assisted Food Management Systems. A. N. Moore, and B. H. Tuthill (Editors). Technical Education Services, University of Missouri-Columbia, Columbia.

ECKSTEIN, E. F. 1969. Menu planning by computer: the random approach to planning for consumer acceptability and nutritional needs. Ph.D. Dissertation. Kansas State Univ.

ELIASON, W. W. 1966. Cafeteria menu planning. *In* Profitable Cafeteria Operation. E. Miller (Editor). Ahrens Publishing Co., New York.

GIVEN, M. 1959. Meta Given's Modern Encyclopedia of Cooking, Vol. 1 and 2 (Revised Ed.). J. G. Ferguson Publishing Co., Chicago.

HAGBERG, E. W. 1971. Patients eat better on five meals a day. Hospitals *45*, No. 24, 104–105.

HOKE, A. 1954. Restaurant Menu Planning, Revised Edition. Hotel Monthly Press, Evanston, Ill.

HUBBARD, R. M. I., SHARP, J. L., and L. M. GRANT. 1961. Pros and cons of cycle menus. J. Am. Dietet. Assoc. *39*, No. 4, 339–340.

Institutions/VF Magazine. 1972. Food Industry Census. Institutions/VF Magazine, Chicago.

IVANICKY, M. C., MASON, H. A., and VIEROW, S. C. 1969. Food preparation time versus production quantity. Hospitals *43*, No. 20, 99–102.

MCCUNE, E. 1960. Food preference survey: Guide to better menus. Hospitals *34*, No. 10, 70–74.

MORRIS, M., and OUTLAND, J. G. 1966. Rotating Seasonal Menus. Ahrens Publishing Co., New York.

Navy Subsistence Offices, Bur. Supplies and Accounts. 1964. Food Operations Reference Manual. NAVSANDA Publ. *421*, Oct. 30.

NORTON, M. 1967. Zip-age hospital nutrition; frequent feedings can help patient and hospital. Hospitals *41*, No. 14, 89–92.

PARKINSON, C. N. 1957. Parkinson's Law. Vallentine Books, New York.

REID, W. R. 1969. New hospital uses four-meal plan with success. Hospitals *43*, No. 4, 77–81.

SANDLER, B. 1968. Ten mistakes in menu writing. Fast Food *67*, No. 3, 114–115, 117–120.

SCHUH, D. D., MOORE, A. N., and TUTHILL, B. H. 1967. Measuring food acceptability by frequency ratings. J. Am. Dietet. Assoc. *51*, 340–343.

SHANNON, E. 1962. American Dictionary of Culinary Terms: a Comprehensive Guide to the Vocabulary of the Kitchen. A. S. Barnes & Co., New York.

TREAT, N., and RICHARDS, L. 1966. Quantity Cookery. Little, Brown & Co., Boston.

WAKEFIELD, L., and POTGIETER, M. 1958. Nutritional value of patient selected versus nonselected menus. Hospitals *32*, No. 21, 72, 74–75.

WALDO, M. 1967. Dictionary of International Food and Cooking Terms. Macmillan Co., New York.

WEISS, E., and WEISS, H. 1971. Catering Handbook. Ahrens Publishing Co., New York.

WEST, B. B., WOOD, L., and HARGER, V. F. 1966. Planning, food standards, and service. *In* Food Service in Institutions. John Wiley & Sons, New York.

WILKINSON, J. (Editor). 1971. The Professional Chef's Catering Recipes. Institutions/VF Magazine, Chicago.

MENU PLANNING FOR SUBGROUPS

CHAPTER 7

Menu Planning for Hospital Patients, Staff and Guests

The task of planning a good hospital menu is complicated and difficult because of the need to plan for requirements of three very different consumer groups, namely patients, staff, and visitors. Some hospitals attempt to use one master menu for all three groups; others prefer separate menus with some common items. Still others plan only a patient menu and provide short order and/or vending machines to meet the needs of staff and guests. Diverse philosophical issues and situational factors must be weighed in determining appropriateness in any given hospital.

Also at issue is whether the master menu should be planned as a general diet to meet normal nutritional requirements (adaptable for staff) or whether requirements of therapeutic diets should determine menu choices. According to Reed (1960), if a general menu is planned to reduce processing requirements in food preparation, it is difficult to assure that diet requirements will be met satisfactorily and some additional items will be necessary to meet individual or special diet needs. Whereas, if therapeutic diet requirements determine menu choices a large number of alternatives will be selected to provide for expected contingencies; this simplifies the task of writing therapeutic diets. Unfortunately, unless carefully planned, work load and/or cost may be excessive. Resolution of this problem depends on the ratio of therapeutic to general diets.

PLANNING FOR THE NEEDS OF PATIENTS

The hospital patient is a captive consumer who generally requires room service. Obviously, time and distance create some problems that somewhat restrict the types of items that can be served. For example, in transit a rennet custard disintegrates to curds and whey; a 3-min egg becomes hard cooked; a souffle falls; fragile cookies crumble. However, operational problems of this nature are not critical in planning menus.

Considerations in planning patient menus, aside from operational constraints, can be categorized as (a) psychological, (b) physiological, and (c) public relations. These *should* guide menu policy.

Psychological Needs

Hospitalization is generally a traumatic experience for the patient. Aside from physical stress, the emotional stress is immense. Stresses include the fears, anxieties, insecurities, etc., of an unfamiliar environment and treatment (Vigeurs 1959). Mealtime may provide the only familiar aspect the patient can relate to; hence, it may be critical to morale and recovery. Therefore, mealtime trauma is to be minimized.

How does the patient view hospital food? According to a study by the National Opinion Research Center (Sheatsley, 1965)[1]

> The person who has an unhappy stay in the hospital for reasons quite apart from the food served to him is in no mood to enjoy his meals, however attractively they may be served, and he may feel compelled to add these to his list of complaints. Conversely, the patient who has an easy and painless stay, who receives unexpectedly good medical news, or who enjoys the attention of hospital personnel, is not likely to complain about his food even though the fare is but average.

Feldman (1962) reviewed the results of opinionaires designed to determine patients' response to hospital food after discharge. In summarizing numerous surveys, he stated that most patients are satisfied with both the food and service. On the other hand, the common wisdom asserts that hospital food is likely to be inedible or insipid at best. While the average patient is satisfied, those from higher socioeconomic groups who are accustomed to top quality food elaborately prepared, are not. These people are exceedingly verbal and society accords their opinion greater than normal weight. Hence, the stereotype of hospital food.

Physicians generally report that patients dislike hospital food. Feldman attributes this to the high visibility of a vocal minority who exert pressure on the physician to either try to improve the food or assure them that the next time he will place them in another hospital.

For a combination of physical and psychological reasons, patients are often apathetic about marking a menu; decisions may be poor. Consequently, mealtime may be frustrating when the tray arrives with an array of food items that is unrelated to current needs. Usually the menu is distributed the previous day in order to allow necessary lead time for preparation planning. During the interval, patient status may be entirely changed and previous choices are unacceptable (Robinson 1971). Thus, patient response to the menu is highly variable; it must be monitored continuously.

At home one arranges one's dietary pattern for convenience in accordance with one's life style. The general diet in a hospital is planned to meet the aggregate needs of patients in a general way. Limited means of accommodation to individual needs of patients are planned for, be it between meal feedings, reduced portion size, or whatever.

---

[1] Reprinted with permission from American Hospital Association.

The hospital therapeutic dietary regimen is arranged for dietary control in order that (a) physical discomfort of the patient be minimized or at least not increased, or (b) that observations by the physician-dietitian team be facilitated in order to allow effective planning of a diet therapy program of variable duration. In this case, although considerable effort is made to accommodate individual desires, diet restrictions may generate a traumatic situation.

Given the expected emotional-psychological status of the usual patient, a primary objective in planning the master menu is to specify familiar items that are acceptable to the majority and can be combined into attractive customary combinations. Familiar items provide security; if they are acceptable, the probability of consumption is increased. Most people "eat with their eyes" so color, texture, and shape harmony must be planned if the meal is to be attractive. An attractive meal motivates an otherwise apathetic consumer. If the meal is flavorful, more is likely to be eaten. Thus, all four considerations are necessary if consumption is to be optimized.

Physiological Needs

Menu planning considerations related to physiological needs of patients include (a) nutritional requirements, and (b) modified preparation necessary to cope with physiological impairment. In the aggregate patients' basic nutritional needs are normally distributed. The objective in planning the master menu is to ensure that expected combinations of foods will provide a nutritionally adequate diet except for calories. One assumes some provision is made for portion size adjustment and/or optional items to allow for wide variation in caloric need.

Modified diets comprise 15–85% of the patient meals in hospitals. Typical modifications include diets of the following types: liquid, soft, bland, low sodium, low fat, low residue, diabetic, calorie restricted, and mechanical soft (Kapfer 1968). Aside from the liquid diets, the modified diets are generally expected to be nutritionally adequate. Alternate choices on the master menu must include suitable, or easily modified, items for all of these diets (Table 7.1).

Modified diets are usually derived from the Soft Diet (Table 7.1). Hence, in selecting alternatives for each meal component, at least one choice is planned for the Soft Diet. Another common practice is to routinely list an "A" vegetable (e.g., spinach, green beans, etc.) and a "B" vegetable (e.g., peas, carrots, beets, etc.) at both lunch and dinner since diabetic diets will require one or both.

Another routine consideration in constructing the master menu is to restrict the number of common "gas formers" such as legumes, onions, and members of the cabbage family (broccoli, cauliflower, Brussels sprouts, etc.). Portion size is also commonly restricted.

Pediatric Menus

Menus for infants of various ages are routinely prepared as standard modifications from the master menu. These serve as guides for planning menus for

TABLE 7.1

SAMPLE MASTER MENU WITH MODIFICATIONS FOR SOME STANDARD THERAPEUTIC DIETS

Tuesday—12/5/72—5th Week

Juices/Fruits
S1. Orange Juice[1]

S2. Apricot Nectar
S3. Stewed Prunes
    Apple Juice
    Grape Juice
    Prune Juice
    Cranberry Juice
    Half Grapefruit
    Canned Apricot
    Pureed Apricot

Cereals
S1. Oatmeal*

S2. Cream of Wheat/SF
S4. Puffed Rice
 3. SF Oatmeal
    Rice Krispies (Peds)

Entrées
S1. Scrambled Eggs*

S2. Bacon
    Scrambled Whites
    Soft Cooked Egg
    Hard Cooked Egg
    Osterized Hard Cooked Egg

Breads
S6. Strawberry Snail Sweet Roll
S7. Sugared Raised Donut
    Plus Standard Items

Beverages: Standard Items

Soups
S1. Ham Bone Soup

S2. Broth/SF
    Crackers/SF

Entrées
S1. Turkey Dumpling Casserole/

    2 Jubilee Grapes

S2. Veal Scallopini/2 Jubilee Grapes
S9. Main Plate Cottage Cheese & Marinated
    Vegetable Salad/French Dressing
 5. Roast Turkey/Giblet Gravy/Cranberry
    Jelly*
 6. SF Ground Turkey
 7. SF Gravy
    Chopped Turkey
    Baby Chicken

Starches
S1. Buttered Noodles
S2. Mashed Potatoes*
 4. SF Noodles
    SF Mashed Potatoes

Vegetables
S1. Buttered Summer Squash*

S2. Buttered Spinach/Lemon Wedge
 3. SF Puréed Summer Squash
 4. SF Summer Squash

Salads/Dressings
S1. Tossed Green Salad/Shoestring Beets/

    Green Goddess Dressing

S2. Scarlet Peach Molded Salad
 3. Tossed Green Salad/French Dressing
 6. SF French Dressing
 7. Zero Dressing/SF
    Plus Standard Dressings

Desserts
S1. Apricot Pie

S2. Canned Plum
S8. Sherbet* (Plain)
S11. Fresh Fruit in Season (½ banana)
 4. SF Apricot Pie
 5. Dietetic Royal Anne Cherries
    Puréed Peach
    Canned Peach
    Plus Standard Items

Breads: Standard Items

Beverages: Standard Items

TABLE 7.1 (Continued)

Soups	Vegetables
S1. Cream of Tomato Soup	S1. Baby Lima Beans
S2. Broth/SF	S2. Buttered Carrots*
4. Bland Strained Cream of Tomato Soup*	3. SF Puréed Carrots
Crackers/SF	4. SF Carrots

Soups
S1. Cream of Tomato Soup

S2. Broth/SF
4. Bland Strained Cream of Tomato
   Soup*
   Crackers/SF

Entrées
S1. Grilled Cube Steak/Brown Gravy/
    Radish Rose

S2. Tamale Pie/Parsley
4. SF Cube Steak/SF Gravy/Parsley
5. SFND Cube Steak/Brown Gravy*
6. SF Ground Beef
   Chopped SFND Cube Steak
   Baby Lamb

Starches
S1. Au Gratin Potatoes

S2. Steamed Potato*
4. SF Mashed Potatoes
   SF Rice
   Mashed Potatoes

Vegetables
S1. Baby Lima Beans

S2. Buttered Carrots*
3. SF Puréed Carrots
4. SF Carrots

Salads/Dressings
Tossed Green Salad
Fresh Spring Vegetable Salad #1
Plus Standard Dressings

Desserts
S1. Pineapple Upside Down Cake

S2. Applesauce
S11. Fresh Fruit in Season (Pineapple)
3. Loaf Cake*
5. Dietetic Apricot
Plus Standard Items

Breads: Standard Items

Beverages: Standard Items

Source: Courtesy of the Department of Nutrition and Dietetics, University of California Hospitals, San Francisco.
[1] Legend for symbols: S—Item goes on select menu. Underlining—The regular item. *—A soft menu item. SF—Salt free. ND—Low calorie/low fat. Numbers before items—Coding system for tray line.

individual children. Infants are highly variable in the age at which they are able to tolerate and have been introduced to each class of new foods. Therefore, the mother should be consulted before preparing a custom-made menu (Synar 1963).

The hospital is an unfamiliar environment that adds to the insecurity and anxiety of illness. Often under such stress a preschool child shows regressive behavior such as refusing foods customarily eaten, asking for a bottle, etc. Under such conditions, it is inappropriate to attempt to introduce new foods; it simply makes mealtime traumatic. Moreover, points emphasized in Chap. 10 in relation to general food habits and preferences of children are pertinent.

In planning a general pediatric menu it is not sufficient to reduce portions and print the regular adult patient selections on colorful paper with pictures of animals, etc. While a family member usually will select items for a young child or the nurse will ask a child which of several choices is preferred, youngsters 8 yr old and up generally mark their own menus. Therefore, menu terminology is important in communicating an image of the alternate items. According to Bachrach (1970)[2]

[2] Reprinted with permission from American Hospital Association.

Pediatric patients, many of whom have never read a restaurant menu, often have difficulty in reading hospital menus. . . . One can imagine . . . the confusion these children encounter when they meet such sophisticated menu items as hot vichysoisse, chateau potatoes . . . etc. . . . Because dietetic terminology is so much a part of the dietitian's world, it may be difficult for her to understand that many persons are unfamiliar with what she considers basic vocabulary.

As the writer was helping a hospitalized 12-yr-old boy select his menu items, the boy grumbled innocently, "Why don't they write it in English?"

Another young patient, disappointed with his luncheon, saw the boy in the next bed enjoying a hot dog on a bun. When asked why he hadn't ordered a hot dog, the boy said it wasn't on the menu. When the item, listed as "frankfurter on a bun," was pointed out to him, he asked, "Oh, is that what a frankfurter is?"

At the same hospital, a look of horror appeared on one child's face as he hurriedly removed a plump black olive from his mouth and exclaimed, "Gosh, what a terrible grape!"

Another challenge is to select items that pediatric patients can eat with ease. For example, preschool-aged children do not have enough muscular coordination to use a spoon to cut up an elusive, slippery peach half in syrup into bite-size portions. According to Bachrach (1972), "The acrobatics performed by these youngsters in attacking the peach would make amusing episodes on 'Candid Camera'." The obvious alternative solutions are to serve salad cut peaches, sliced peaches, or to cut the peach half into bite-size pieces before serving. The alert dietitian will observe similar problems and plan appropriate menu modifications for the specific age group.

Although the general pediatric menu presents interesting challenges, modified diets for children are even more challenging, primarily because of restrictions and necessary changes in eating habits. Insofar as possible items used for the same modification for adults are planned, however, a number of unique items must be anticipated in planning the production load (Synar 1963).

Public Relations

A physician is usually a staff member in several hospitals; he generally suggests a preferred hospital to a patient. The physician routinely monitors patient response to hospital care; feedback determines patient load. Accordingly, in the past decade some hospitals instituted "vini-care" (Anon. 1968; Funk and Prescott 1967), buffet service for ambulatory patients on a general diet, gourmet dinners (Anon. 1963), and the like in order to create a favorable image. Each of these adds unique menu planning challenges that are similar to those faced in planning restaurant menus. Chapter 14, Planning Menus for Restaurant Customers, provides an extended discussion of these topics.

PLANNING FOR STAFF NEEDS

The hospital staff represents a large pool of potential customers since patient care requires 3 shifts, 7 days per week. However, unlike the patients, this group is not captive since each individual has the alternative of a brown-bag meal.

As a group, behavior is similar to that observed in an industrial in-plant cafeteria. When prices are low, as when subsidized, participation is good, all other things being equal. When prices are raised a fraction, participation drops off rapidly and brown-bag meals appear. Also, the food service is the scapegoat for other pressures and problems; griping is chronic. Great efforts in merchandizing, e.g., special meals with appropriate decor and music, are required to raise participation but the effect is transient.

Moreover, sales to staff are often related to patient acceptance of particular items (transmitted via the grapevine). For example, Chicken and Parsley Dumplings was served on Sunday and was popular with patients and staff. When the cycle was repeated and the weekend staff was again favored with this entrée, a delegation of weekday employees demanded that this item be served on a weekday to avoid discrimination! On the other hand, when less acceptable items are served to both patients and staff the manager is accused of serving left-overs to the staff. Staff generally expect an array of food items comparable to offerings in commercial cafeterias; often just to look at, not to purchase. Apparently, the array registers as management concern for staff needs.

Moreover, there is some evidence that the level of service in the staff cafeteria influences the mental set which determines staff attitude toward patient food service. Cabot (1972) has indicated[3]

> Bad food or bad service in the cafeteria results in discontented employees who won't provide the desired level of patient care. If employees are treated with discourtesy in the cafeteria, if the plates are merely thrown together, are not garnished or handled properly, this cannot help but affect nursing personnel's standard for patient food service trays and entrées. However, if the employees receive courteous attention, if their plates are well assembled and the food is garnished and placed neatly on plates, this higher standard becomes the level of service that nursing would expect the patients to receive.

Thus, the cafeteria service is important in setting up a situation in which the nursing personnel conveys a positive or negative attitude to the patient by association.

A short cycle menu with a period of 2 or 3 weeks is adequate for patient service since the average patient stay is approximately 5 days. On the other hand, a six week cycle is more satisfactory with staff since turnover is hopefully low. This dilemma is usually resolved by providing short order service and/or extra choices for the staff.

Since staff members usually purchase only one meal per shift, responsibility for nutritional adequacy of the diet rests with the individual. However, in order to encourage consumption, a wide variety of fruits and vegetables should be provided.

---

[3] Quoted with permission of McGraw-Hill, Inc.

PLANNING FOR THE NEEDS OF VISITORS

The hospital visitor who requires a meal is usually visiting a patient who is critically ill. The visitor is often in an agitated state. He either desires to minimize eating time so as to return to the bedside or to extend it to fill waiting time. In the first case food-to-go or vending machines best meet the visitor's needs. In the second, regular cafeteria service suffices.

WORKER CONSIDERATIONS

The general worker considerations discussed in Chap. 3 apply in hospital food service. However, quality control and scheduling problems are especially difficult due to the necessity of preparing numerous special diet items in small quantities, i.e., six servings or less. Items tend to dehydrate or become overcooked and preparation is time-consuming. The number and kinds of special diet items must be anticipated and allowances made when planning the master menu.

MANAGEMENT CONSIDERATIONS

The general considerations are discussed in Chap. 4; all apply to hospital food service. Furthermore, three additional sets of considerations affect design of the master menu: (a) meal pattern, (b) catering requirements, and (c) holiday menu requirements. And, the menu must be written for remote readers.

According to Hartman (1960)[4]

> In most parts of the United States, family meals follow a 'breakfast, lunch, dinner' scheme. Unfortunately, too many hospitals seem to offer the 'breakfast, dinner, supper' plan. The usual rationalization is that the larger meal at midday is more practicable from a staffing standpoint. Seldom is the heavy noon-day meal justified for its benefit to the patient.

Three meals are commonly served in hospitals. However, during the 1960's 4 and 5 feeding plans were developed as an attempt to better meet the needs of patients (Reid 1969). The three major factors that caused this shift were (a) the general change in American eating habits toward several snack meals plus one heavy meal (Norton 1967), (b) increased use of technology resulting in a large increase in the proportion of "hold" trays where service must be delayed until completion of X-rays or laboratory tests, and (c) the number of patients requiring between-meal feeding. Acceptance of the 4- and 5-meal plans has been related to the effectiveness of planning prior to implementation.

Two types of menu planning considerations result from the 4- and 5-meal plans. First, the light meals must be planned to utilize available preportioned or ready foods. Second, production planning problems resulting from the 9-to-5 schedule of employees may overly restrict the variety of items that can be prepared for the 2 major meals unless convenience foods are utilized.

---

[4] Quoted with permission of McGraw-Hill, Inc.

The catering load in many hospitals is quite heavy; regularly scheduled dinners and luncheons for various medical staff groups are served almost daily. These meals are generally prepared by the regular dietary staff in addition to the regular patient meals. In order to cope with the load the master menu must be carefully planned. Patient and staff menus will necessarily be simplified to free sufficient time for preparation of the additional items.

Since the late 1960's, a number of hospitals have used an a la carte menu as a simplification to reduce the requirements in purchasing, inventory management, and food preparation. As in a restaurant, the same menu is used every day. A number of alternatives are planned for each meal component. For example, for breakfast 5 juices and 4 fruits, 2 hot cereals, 5 cold cereals, 4 kinds of eggs, pancakes, and French Toast. For lunch and dinner, nine or more entrées are listed. Steak, prime rib, chicken, etc., are offered as well as lighter entrées such as sandwiches. Selections are limited to the most popular items. For a discussion of considerations in planning an a la carte menu see Chap. 14.

The problem of planning a menu to meet the needs of the special group is simplified if a regular banquet file is maintained for each group. Information to be compiled includes (a) name and size of the group, (b) contact person and telephone number, (c) type of meal desired, (d) price range, and (e) previous menus. In addition, costed prototype menus should be prepared so as to provide the contact person several alternative menus to select from (Table 7.2).

Hospitals customarily serve the traditional holiday meals on each of the major holidays. These meals are generally blocked in before planning surrounding meals in order to minimize repetition of items or KINDS. As some of the items are prepared infrequently or require more complex preparation than usual items, extra preparation time should be allotted.

MENU READABILITY

The hospital menu should be written for the readers who are not at their peak of alertness or decisiveness and who vary in familiarity with menu terminology. According to Bing (1960)[5]

> The menu is a powerful medium of communication. No other routinely issued hospital order has a larger or more interested readership, or a greater influence on hospital costs, on the utilization of employees, the satisfaction and well-being of the patients, the morale of staff members or on the general reputation of the hospital and its administrators. Because of this, the menu should meet the basic requirements of all published writing: It should be written for the readers.
>
> A well written hospital menu (this includes the menu for house diets, therapeutic diets, and the cafeteria) can be understood by everyone who reads it. It is clear, concise and unequivocal. It is consistent in format and

---

[5] Quoted with permission of McGraw-Hill, Inc.

TABLE 7.2

SAMPLE OF COSTED PROTOTYPE MENUS FOR BANQUETS FOR IN-HOSPITAL GROUPS

Entrée	1.25	1.50	1.75	2.00	2.25	2.50	2.75	3.00	3.25	3.50 … 4.50
Baked Ham/Pineapple Sauce						A	B	C		
Beef Cubes in Sour Cream					A	B				
Breaded Pork Chops									A	B
Breaded Veal Cutlets							A	B	C	
Chicken Fricassée							A	B	C	
Cube Steak/Brown Gravy							A	B	C	
Fried Rabbit							A	B	C	
Halibut Steak au Gratin							A	B	C	
Ham Steak							A	B	C	
Meat Loaf/Brown Gravy		A	B	C						
Oven Fried Chicken								A	B	
Polish Sausage		A	B							
Roast Beef au Jus										C
Roast Turkey/Giblet Gravy						A	B	C		
Salisbury Steak			A	B	C					
Salmon Steak & Lemon Butter								A	B	
Swiss Steak								A	B	
Veal Scallopini										A

Price Range (Dollars)

Base A

Tomato Juice Cocktail	Cranberry Juice Cocktail
Mashed Potatoes	Buttered Noodles
Buttered Green Beans	Buttered Peas
Mixed Greens	Relish Plate
Ice Cream Slice	Sherbet
Rolls & Butter	
Coffee Tea	Milk

Base B

Tomato Juice Cocktail			Cranberry Juice Cocktail
Fruit Cup			Relish Plate
Mashed Potatoes	Baked Potatoes	Buttered Noodles	Steamed Rice
Buttered Green Beans			Buttered Peas
Mixed Greens			Cole Slaw
Ice Cream Slice		Sherbet	Short Cake
Pudding with Whipped Topping			
Rolls & Butter			
Coffee Tea			Milk

Base C

Tomato Juice Cocktail		Ruby Consomme
Fruit Cup		Relish Plate
Mashed Potatoes	Baked Potatoes	Scalloped Potatoes
	Parsley Dumplings	
Buttered Mixed Vegetables		Julienne Carrots
Sautéed Asparagus Spears		Corn in Butter Sauce
Mixed Greens with Avocado Slices		Cole Slaw with Creamy Dressing
Fruit and Cottage Cheese Salad		Cucumbers in Sour Cream
Chocolate Ice Cream Sundae		Apple Pie with Lemon Sauce
Coconut Cream Cake		Chocolate Eclairs
Coffee Tea	Sherbet	Milk

terminology. It holds out no false promises to the consumer, and it gives basic but definite instructions to the employees whose work it directs.

After the menu has been planned it should be edited so as to convey to the reader precisely the items intended. Editing considerations include (a) correctness of terminology, (b) use of foreign names and/or phrases and other adjectives, (c) freedom from ambiguity, (d) consistency of format, and (e) accuracy and completeness of listing.

Menu terms should not be deliberately misleading, i.e., whipped cream should not be listed if whipped topping is used or Breaded Pork Chops when only one chop is served per person. And, correct technical terms should not be used when they have no meaning to the reader. For example, Roast Top Clod might better be called Pot Roast of Beef. Moreover, as Bing (1960) also reminds us[6]

> Imagination, which plays such an important part in the planning of menus, should be forgotten when writing them. The tough, outer stalks of celery are not magically tenderized by being described as "celery hearts." The popularity of a good, honest beef stew depends almost entirely on its ingredients and its preparation; listing it as "braised beef cubes with fresh vegetables" does not necessarily contribute to its acceptance. Speaking of vegetables, the factual "mixed vegetables" is to be preferred to the more romantic "medley of vegetables" or to the exotic "macedoine of vegetables," particularly if the consumers are already aware that the cooks use the same recipe for all three.

Foreign names and phrases should be avoided except when they are the common descriptor for the item. Thus, au gratin potatoes, pizza, tacos, etc., are acceptable whereas Carbonnade Planande and Blanquette de Veau are not. A waiter is not available to interpret the names; if they are meaningless to the patient, they do not enhance the appeal of menu listing and therefore should be avoided.

Use of descriptors, i.e., adjectives or phrases, should be limited to those that indicate preparation state or mode or that distinguish among somewhat similar items. Thus, Hot Toast is redundant; it should be served hot, otherwise it is misleading. On the other hand, Cinnamon Toast, Garlic Toast, Raisin Toast are different items that must be differentiated from regular toast.

Ambiguous terms such as "assorted breads" are inappropriate since only one type is served to each patient, although an assortment may be distributed among the patients. Similarly, "assorted cake," "assorted fresh fruit," etc., should not be used. However, if an employee brings a cart around and offers the patient a choice, such a term may be used.

Consistency of format is important in assisting the patient in selecting all desired meal components. By listing them in expected order of consumption he is more likely to choose combinations he will enjoy. Moreover, the menu planner and production personnel are less likely to omit items.

---

[6]Quoted with permission of McGraw-Hill, Inc.

Accuracy and completeness of the listing is important. The menu listing should be checked to see that (a) all items were transferred from the rough draft, (b) all words are spelled correctly, and (c) all items such as salt, pepper, butter, etc., are included. Since the patient is remote from the kitchen, failure to include all items results in unnecessary trips to the patient's room to supply needed items.

BIBLIOGRAPHY

ANON. 1963. Gourmet gift meals served to patients. Hospitals *37*, No. 22, 47, 50.

ANON. 1968. Vinicare for special diets. Hosp. Nursing Home Food Mgmt. *4*, No. 6, 35–36.

BACHRACH, B. 1970. Pediatric menu terminology. Hospitals *44*, No. 9, 84–85.

BACHRACH, B. 1972. Personal communication. Chicago, Ill.

BING, J. H. 1960. Write the menu for the readers. Mod. Hosp. *95*, No. 1, 106, 108–110.

CABOT, E. 1972. Poorly managed cafeterias damage employee morale, hospital image. Mod. Hosp. *118*, No. 3, 132.

FELDMAN, J. J. 1962. Patient's opinions of hospital food. J. Am. Dietet. Assoc. *40*, 325–329.

FUNK, L. D., and PRESCOTT, J. H. 1967. Study shows wine aids patient attitudes. Mod. Hosp. *108*, No. 3, 182–184.

HAGBERG, E. W. 1971. Patients eat better on five meals per day. Hospitals *45*, No. 24, 104–105.

HARTMAN, J. 1960. Right size meals at the right time will cut down patient complaints. Mod. Hosp. *95*, No. 3, 148, 150.

JERNIGAN, A. K. 1970. Suggestions for feeding of hospitalized children. Hospitals *44*, No. 9, 88–89.

KAPFER, E. 1968. Considerations for menu planning in hospitals. Hospitals *48*, No. 1, 80.

LYNCH, H. D. 1958. Your Child is What He Eats. Henry Regney Co., Chicago.

MCWILLIAMS, M. 1967. Nutrition for the Growing Years. John Wiley & Sons, New York.

NORTON, M. 1967. Zip-age hospital nutrition: Frequent feedings can help patient and hospital. Hospitals *41*, No. 14, 89–92.

REED, R. JR. 1960. Menu processing takes to methods of engineering. Mod. Hosp. *94*, No. 4, 150–156.

REID, W. R. 1969. New hospital uses four-meal plan with success. Hospitals *43*, No. 4, 77–81.

ROBINSON, N. E. 1971. The unit menu system. Hospitals *45*, No. 16, 84–86.

SHEATSLEY, P. B. 1965. How total hospital shapes patient's opinion of food. Hospitals *39*, No. 2, 105–111.

SYNAR, E. J. 1963. A modified diet calls for a modified approach to the child patient. Hospitals *37*, No. 23, 86, 93.

VIGEURS, R. T. 1959. Be kind to "impossible" patients: they're scared. Mod. Hosp. *92*, No. 1, 70–71.

CHAPTER 8

Menu Planning for Nursing Home Patients

Planning nursing home menus is a challenging task due to unique patient needs, a restricted budget, and use of unskilled labor. The most difficult problem is to get the patient to eat.

PLANNING FOR PATIENT NEEDS

With the advent of Medicare legislation, planning for the needs of the patient became a reality in nursing home food service. According to Cashman (1967) dietetic or nutritional service is a requirement for certification of a nursing home or extended care facility under Medicare. This service can be provided in three alternate ways (a) a full-time, (b) part-time, or (c) consulting basis.

Nursing home patients can be categorized as (a) bedridden critically ill adults or (b) ambulatory custodial care patients, i.e., senile, retarded, or mild mental cases of variable age and activity. Although age ranges of 35-95 have been reported, most patients are over 65.

In general, food consumption by both groups of patients is highly variable so nutritional needs may not be met by dietary intake. Nonetheless, a nutritionally adequate diet should be presented (Table 8.1).

The first problem is to get the patient to eat. A master menu can and should be planned but substitutions will be necessary because of differences in needs and preferences among the patients. The dietitian must visit the patients and develop a profile of food habits and preferences for each. Unlike the hospital situation, the nursing home patient is a long-term captive customer, therefore his individual needs must be met or he may withdraw and refuse to eat.

According to Sebrell (1966)[1]

> Every aspect of the patient's life should be investigated. In addition to the history of indigestion, constipation, flatulence, specific food intolerance and other evidence of digestion malfunction, the other factors should be noted. Does the patient enjoy his food? What sort of diet did he have when he was a youngster?

A set menu is prepared for the general diet patients since the majority are not capable of selecting a meal. The general diet is often mechanically soft to some degree, i.e., meats are chopped, fruit diced, vegetables chopped or shredded to compensate for the physical handicaps associated with age such as poor fitting

---

[1] Quoted with permission from Enloe, Stalvey and Associates.

TABLE 8.1

NUTRITIONAL REQUIREMENTS (RDA)[1] OF ADULTS IN NURSING HOMES

Age (Yr) From Up To	Weight (Kg)	Weight (Lb)	Height (Cm)	Height (In.)	Kcal	Protein (Gm)	Fat-Soluble Vitamins					Water-Soluble Vitamins					Minerals				
							Vitamin A Activity (IU)	Vitamin D Activity (IU)	Vitamin E Activity (IU)	Ascorbic Acid (Mg)	Folacin[2] (Mg)	Niacin (Mg Equiv)[3]	Ribo-flavin (Mg)	Thia-min (Mg)	Vita-min B6 (Mg)	Vita-min B12 (µg)	Calcium (Gm)	Phos-phorus (Gm)	Iodine (µg)	Iron (Mg)	Mag-nesium (Mg)
Males 55–75+	70	154	171	67	2,400	65	5,000	—	30	60	0.4	14	1.7	1.2	2.0	6	0.8	0.8	110	10	350
Females 55–75+	58	128	157	62	1,700	55	5,000	—	25	55	0.4	13	1.5	1.0	2.0	6	0.8	0.8	80	10	300

Source: Adapted from *Recommended Daily Dietary Allowances*, Food and Nutrition Board, National Academy of Sciences—National Research Council.

[1] The allowance levels are intended to cover individual variations among most normal persons as they live in the United States under usual environmental stresses. The recommended allowances can be attained with a variety of common foods, providing other nutrients for which human requirements have been less well defined.

[2] The folacin allowances refer to dietary sources as determined by *Lactobacillus casei* assay. Pure forms of folacin may be effective in doses less than ⅓ of the RDA.

[3] Niacin equivalents include dietary sources of the vitamin itself plus 1 mg equivalent for each 60 mg of dietary tryptophan.

dentures, palsy, etc. (Anderson 1971). Modified diets are planned from the master menu; these are similar to those used in hospitals but are often not as rigorous since the patients are chronic rather than acute cases and are expected to continue on them for an extended period of time.

In constructing the master menu all of the basic considerations outlined in Chap. 2 are pertinent. Color interest must be provided by the meal components themselves since garnishing is often limited to an occasional shake of paprika, given the budgetary restrictions. Flavor interest must also be planned; bland and strong flavored foods should be balanced and preparation methods varied.

Of the consumer considerations, variety is the most difficult factor to manage. Patients tend to accept and expect foods they are accustomed to and reject new items. Or, menu acceptability may be evaluated in terms of the variety of ethnic or religious dietary staples that are included. If the group is relatively homogeneous, planning for acceptability is not difficult and individual differences can be accommodated. However, if the group is divided into several major ethnic or religious groups, planning is very difficult since all are served approximately the same menu. By late life, food habits and preferences are largely unchangeable; the Chinese want their rice; the Germans, their kraut, etc. (Hankin and Antonmattei 1960). These must be provided.

On the other hand, since the patients are long-term captive consumers adequate variety is necessary. Variation in the number and types of meal components adds interest, e.g., random distribution of soup-sandwich combinations, salad plate, and casserole-vegetable combinations. As much variety of KIND as can be afforded should be planned, subject to group preferences. Many casseroles have a tomato sauce base; frequency of including tomatoes should be carefully controlled.

Although most nursing home food service units operate with a severely restricted budget, some are experimenting with wine service (Lane 1972B). Because wine is a mild tranquilizer, some physicians advocate its use. Hence, selection of wines is added to the menu planning task in some nursing homes.

OTHER CONSIDERATIONS

Budgetary restrictions are usually severe, a mean raw food cost of $1.25 per day has been reported recently (Kroll 1971). However, many food allowances are considered below the "irreducible minimum" (West et al. 1966). Consequently, item variety is reduced. And, a light entrée such as creamed tuna, scrambled eggs, macaroni and cheese, etc., is often served as the major protein source of the day.

Unskilled kitchen help is usually employed (Lane 1972A). The cook is usually experienced though untrained. Item variety is usually further reduced by her lack of skill. Preparation must be simplified as convenience foods are generally too expensive to provide a justifiable alternative.

In recent years a number of nursing homes have experimented with 4 or 5 meal plans.   According to a bulletin of the California State Department of Public Health (1966) some advantages are[2]

(A) The patients eat better when food is offered frequently. Less food is wasted.

(B) Most patients anticipate meal time and the extra scheduled meals provide an activity that helps fill the day.

(C) Patients seem more content throughout the day and night. In some patients, medications for sleeping have been eliminated or reduced.

(D) Dehydration, a frequent problem with nursing home patients, is reduced because fluids are given with each meal.

(E) Patients don't need to be awakened and prepared for breakfast as early as with the three meal plan. The continental breakfast served in bed satisfies early morning hunger and leaves the patients more relaxed while waiting for morning care.

(F) The plan conforms more closely to the eating pattern of the elderly. Observation of eating habits shows that most older people eat many small meals rather than three big meals.

Moreover, work load may be reduced when only two major meals are to be prepared. The head cook usually prepares these meals and less skilled and less costly personnel prepare the continental breakfast and late supper (Table 8.2). See also Chap. 7 for discussion of this meal plan in hospitals.

TABLE 8.2

SAMPLE THREE-TWO MEAL PATTERN FOR NURSING HOMES

Time	Meal Components
7:00 a.m.	Beverage (coffee, tea, milk, cocoa) Bread item (toast, doughnut, roll, or quick coffee cake) Juice (optional)
10:00 a.m.	Fruit or juice Cereal with milk (hot or cold) 2 eggs or 1 egg plus ham or sausage Toast with spread Beverage (coffee, tea, milk)
12:00–1:00 p.m.	Juice or soup Cookies or crackers
3:30–4:00 p.m.	Meat or meat substitute Starchy food (potatoes, rice, noodles, etc.) Cooked vegetable Salad Fruit or dessert Beverage (coffee or tea)
8:00–9:00 p.m.	Protein source (sandwich, cottage cheese, custard, milk, milkshake, or eggnog) Juice or hot beverage

Source: Adapted from State of California (1966).

----

[2] Quoted with permission, California State Dept. of Public Health.

BIBLIOGRAPHY

ANDERSON, E. L.   1971.   Eating patterns before and after dentures.   J. Am. Dietet. Assoc. *58*, 421–426.

CASHMAN, J. W.   1967.   An overview of Medicare.   J. Am. Dietet. Assoc. *50*, 17–18.

HANKIN, J. H., and ANTONMATTEI, J. C.   1960.   Survey of food service practices in nursing homes. Am. J. Public Health *50*, 1137–1144.

KROLL, A. P.   1971.   Menu planning for the geriatric patient.   Hospitals *45*, No. 1, 64–66.

LANE, M. M.   1972A.   Food service in nursing homes need not be "substandard."   Nursing Homes *21*, No. 1, 34–35.

LANE, M. M.   1972B.   Some pros and cons on wine in the nursing home. Nursing Homes *20*, No. 12, 27–28.

MAGGIORE, J., and ZACCARELLI, BR. H.   1971.   Nursing Home Menu Planning, Food Purchasing and Management. Institutions Magazine, Chicago.

SEBRELL, W. H.   1966.   It's not age that interferes with nutrition in the elderly. Nutr. Today *1*, No. 2, 15–19.

State of California.   1966.   The three-two plan for food service.   Bureau of Licensing and Certification, Dept. Public Health, State of California, Berkeley.

U.S. Public Health Service.   (Not Dated) Nursing homes and homes for the aged: a guide to nutrition and food service. U.S. Dept. Health, Education, Welfare, Washington, D.C.

WEST, B. B., WOOD, L., and HARGER, V.   1966.   Food Service in Institutions.   John Wiley & Sons, New York.

CHAPTER 9

Menu Planning for Retirement Home Residents

The majority of retirement home residents are relatively healthy senior citizens. A dispensary is usually maintained for a small number of convalescent patients, though acute cases are hospitalized.

The budgeted food allowance varies widely among retirement homes—from a subsistence minimum to a copious allowance. Accordingly, menu offerings and levels of service vary. The critical factor is the degree of correspondence between the expectations and charges to the residents for the service provided.

PUBLIC RELATIONS AND PSYCHOLOGICAL NEEDS

Retired people usually have empty time to be filled; mealtime provides a major social diversion (Weinberg 1972). The menu is often a major topic of conversation. Residents are long-term consumers but they may not be captive if kitchen facilities are provided in the apartments or if commercial restaurants are convenient and not overly expensive. When acceptable meals are offered residents will congregate in the dining room and planned consumption of food is more likely.

In order to meet the physical and psychological needs of retirement home residents, acceptable menus must be planned so that the probability of consumption is high. As with other population groups, knowledge of the food habits and preferences of the group is necessary in order to plan acceptable menus.

Some generalizations concerning the food habits of senior citizens are part of our folklore but as Beeuwkes (1960) has pointed out, the reliability of available information concerning food habits of the elderly is questionable. Responses of a small number of willing and able participants are aggregated and summarized. The obtained information is valid, *if* and only if, the participants are truly representative of elderly people as a whole. Without information on the food habits of nonparticipants, this assumption cannot be verified.

The population of senior citizens is composed of the same economic, social, cultural and religious subgroups as the general American population. However, for economic, social or cultural reasons the group at a retirement home will be relatively homogeneous. If the food habits and preferences of the particular group are known, acceptable menus can be planned. But menus planned for one group are not expected to be transferable among retirement homes unless the groups are very similar.

The major consideration in planning menus is to make the food attractive in order to encourage consumption. Hence, color, texture, and flavor contrasts and garnishing are important.

Moreover, monotony must be avoided. This is challenging since older people generally prefer familiar food (Beeuwkes 1960) and preparation methods. However, KIND and item variety must be planned. Monotony-breakers also create interest, e.g., foreign meals with appropriate music and decor, parties, etc. Wine service has been recommended since wine is a mild tranquilizer (Pelcovits 1971).

Additional interest is created by varying the style of meal service. Breakfast and lunch are often served cafeteria style with waitresses to assist as necessary. Dinner is usually more formal; when a selective menu is provided waitresses take the guests' orders. Elaborate buffet service for Sunday supper has been successful in some retirement homes.

NUTRITIONAL AND PHYSIOLOGICAL NEEDS

Nutritional requirements of senior citizens are based on metabolic demand and activity levels, both of which generally decrease with age (Pelcovits 1972). Caloric requirements are approximately 22% below those for sex and build at age 25. However, eating habits (items and quantities) are established when young and are not easily changed. Hence, acceptable foods with low calorie density and high satiety value are desired—seemingly mutually exclusive goals. Moreover, since absorption is often impaired, increased quantities of minerals and vitamins must be provided. Because individual needs differ, provision for portion size adjustments and low-calorie substitutes is desirable.

A number of minor physical impairments associated with age also require minor modification of food items (a) poor fitting dentures—soft or chopped meats and cooked fruits or vegetables, (b) intestinal inefficiency—low residue diet, (c) palsy—thickened liquids, etc. Because activity level is usually low, gas formers such as legumes, onions, and members of the cabbage family should be served in reduced portions or with reduced frequency.

Breakfast, lunch, and dinner are usually served in retirement homes since this meal pattern is customary for most of the residents. However, Pelcovits (1972) has indicated many eat fewer meals for various reasons. The concept of five meals has been advocated because (a) the extra meals help fill empty time and (b) frequent hot feedings comfort those suffering from chills due to poor circulation. Success has been variable. There is some evidence that suggests that people become accustomed to consuming a fixed number of meal components of specific size. Consequently, they are likely to feel that they are not getting enough to eat when five smaller meals are served.

All of these consumer considerations combine to make menu planning a challenging task. A number of management considerations also impose additional constraints.

MANAGEMENT CONSIDERATIONS

Aside from budgetary restrictions which vary widely as noted above, menu selections are limited by (a) the number of kitchen employees and their general level of skill and (b) the catering load.

Generally, the cook is experienced but untrained; helpers are few and untrained. This limits the complexity of foods that can be prepared unless the budget is sufficient to allow use of gourmet convenience foods.

The catering load varies widely according to administrative policies. Often, small dinner parties can be arranged when scheduled in advance. Holidays also require special meals. Birthdays are often celebrated with a community party. Special menus are required in each case. A preplanned list of alternate menus for special dinners simplifies the task for both the manager and the resident.

BIBLIOGRAPHY

ANON. 1971. Nutrition and eating problems of the elderly. J. Am. Dietet. Assoc. *58*, 43–48.
BEEUWKES, A. M. 1960. Studying the food habits of the elderly. J. Am. Dietet. Assoc. *37*, 215–218.
PELCOVITS, J. 1971. Nutrition for older Americans. J. Am. Dietet. Assoc. *58*, 17–18.
PELCOVITS, J. 1972. Nutrition to meet the human needs of older Americans. J. Am. Dietet. Assoc. *60*, 297–300.
WEINBERG, J. 1972. Psychologic implications of the nutritional needs of the elderly. J. Am. Dietet. Assoc. *60*, 293–296.

CHAPTER 10

Menu Planning for Adolescents and Children

Menu planning considerations differ according to (a) the number of meals to be provided, (b) sex and age range of the group, and (c) whether normal or handicapped. On the other hand, the institutional framework is a major determinant of the type and level of food service provided. Therefore, discussion is organized into sections as follows (a) secondary schools, (b) elementary schools, (c) nursery schools, and (d) other institutions.

GENERAL CONSIDERATIONS

In planning menus for school lunches, a common assumption is that one master menu is appropriate for all schools in an entire district. Proponents of the one menu system emphasize the advantage that all students are offered the same food. This is important in answering charges of discrimination. At the same time, if the various school populations *have* different food preferences, then participation and satisfaction may be low in all schools. In this case, menus planned according to the preferences of the individual school population would better meet the needs of the students. The major advantage in using a master menu for all schools, which is rarely admitted publically, is that it reduces costs of purchasing, supply, inventory, supervision, and surveillance. A policy decision determines whether one master menu or individual school menus are planned.

The need for and planned extent of variety in menu items is also a function of policy. A number of positions are taken as revealed by study of a sampling of menus. On one end of the continuum one sees menus that are limited to about three dozen items per month, for all components. These items are redistributed among the school days each month but new items are rarely introduced. In some cases, an entrée item such as a hamburger is served every Thursday. On the other end of the continuum are menus containing many unfamiliar and/or foreign foods. While such menus sound interesting to sophisticated professional menu planners and gourmets, children and parents reading them are put off.

Ostensibly, the invariate menus contain only the most accepted foods and therefore should meet the needs of the majority. Hence, maximum participation and satisfaction should result. This is probably true for the primary students. However, monotony and failure to participate are the characteristic reactions of older students who have consumed the same items and combinations year after year. Think back and remind yourself of what you know.

A large number of items are well-accepted by most children and young people, although the composition of the recipe pool will vary somewhat with

the regional and/or ethnic background of each particular group. Common ingredients and menu items can be combined and distributed throughout the
month to achieve any desired degree of variety. Wide variety is welcomed when
the items are familiar.

When a central kitchen is used as a large food processing plant to supply
satellite schools, the pool of items that can be produced and still meet delivery
schedules is reduced. Some items simply require more time or labor than can be
made available, e.g., lasagna. Moreover, the larger the quantities involved, the
more critical scheduling becomes. The extent of menu item restriction resulting
from production constraints varies with the individual district depending on (a)
the number of meals to be produced, (b) the distance from the central kitchen
to the schools and thus the transport and delivery time required, (c) the kind,
size, and quantity of production equipment available, and (d) the number and
level of skill of production personnel available.

SECONDARY SCHOOLS

General Considerations

It is well known that the general diet of teenagers is frequently inadequate to
meet nutritional needs (Table 10.1) (Hampton *et al.* 1961; Huenemann *et al.*
1966, 1967, 1968; Shapiro 1963). Recent studies have also shown that, con-
trary to popular opinion, the average level of physical activity is low although
teenagers are constantly busy. And, customary schedules make regular meals
difficult to obtain—teenagers awaken late and rush off to school, snack during
noon meetings, after school go directly to scheduled activities and return home
late at night after dinner (Shapiro 1963). The hungry teenager obtains whatever
is available in refrigerator or cupboard. Many meals are skipped and snacking is
prevalent.

A study by Huenemann et al. (1967) showed that boys preferred the dinner
meal to others but that breakfast is almost as popular. On the other hand, girls
prefer lunch. Moreover, dinner tended to be more popular with upper middle
class Caucasians than with other social or racial groups.

Those who preferred breakfast gave as a reason its effect in assuaging hunger.
The appeal of the lunch meal was related to social factors whereas dinner was
preferred because of the food itself, i.e , the type, quantity, method of preparation and wide variety of items customarily offered. These findings have important implications in menu planning.

Moreover, teenagers devote considerable attention to establishing independence while simultaneously conforming to group norms and practices. Hence,
the selective menu coupled with cafeteria service has fundamental appeal. If a
nutritionally adequate diet is to be obtained, the most likely combinations of
items should provide needed nutrients.

The cost of meals provided in school lunchrooms is often subsidized by state

TABLE 10.1

NUTRITIONAL REQUIREMENTS (RDA)[1] OF ADOLESCENTS

Age (Yr) From Up To	Weight (Kg)	Weight (Lb)	Height (Cm)	Height (In.)	Kcal	Protein (Gm)	Fat-Soluble Vitamins			Water-Soluble Vitamins							Minerals				
							Vitamin A Activity (IU)	Vitamin D (IU)	Vitamin E Activity (IU)	Ascorbic Acid (Mg)	Folacin[2] (Mg)	Niacin (Mg Equiv)[3]	Riboflavin (Mg)	Thiamin (Mg)	Vitamin B6 (Mg)	Vitamin B12 (µg)	Calcium (Gm)	Phosphorus (Gm)	Iodine (µg)	Iron (Mg)	Magnesium (Mg)
Males																					
12–14	43	95	151	59	2,700	50	5,000	400	20	45	0.4	18	1.4	1.4	1.6	5	1.4	1.4	135	18	350
14–18	59	130	170	67	3,000	60	5,000	400	25	55	0.4	20	1.5	1.5	1.8	5	1.4	1.4	150	18	400
18–22	67	147	175	69	2,800	60	5,000	400	30	60	0.4	18	1.6	1.4	2.0	5	0.8	0.8	140	10	400
Females																					
12–14	44	97	154	61	2,300	50	5,000	400	20	45	0.4	15	1.4	1.2	1.6	5	1.3	1.3	115	18	350
14–16	52	114	157	62	2,400	55	5,000	400	25	50	0.4	16	1.4	1.2	1.8	5	1.3	1.3	120	18	350
16–18	54	119	160	63	2,300	55	5,000	400	25	50	0.4	15	1.5	1.2	2.0	5	1.3	1.3	115	18	350
18–22	58	128	163	64	2,000	55	5,000	400	25	55	0.4	13	1.5	1.0	2.0	5	0.8	0.8	100	18	350

Source: Adapted from *Recommended Daily Dietary Allowances*, Food and Nutrition Board, National Academy of Sciences—National Research Council.

[1] The allowance levels are intended to cover individual variations among most normal persons as they live in the United States under usual environmental stresses. The recommended allowances can be attained with a variety of common foods, providing other nutrients for which human requirements have been less well defined.

[2] The folacin allowances refer to dietary sources as determined by *Lactobacillus casei* assay. Pure forms of folacin may be effective in doses less than ¼ of the RDA.

[3] Niacin equivalents include dietary sources of the vitamin itself plus 1 mg equivalent for each 60 mg of dietary tryptophan.

and/or federal monies. Hence, the cost to the student is relatively low. Nonetheless, many teenagers cannot afford to purchase meals. The demand for meals is elastic; if the price is very low essentially all will purchase the meals if the foods are acceptable and properly prepared but if the price is raised as little as a nickel, the demand drops off rapidly (Bard 1968).

Two of the traditional goals of school food service are to provide an opportunity for (a) nutrition education and (b) increased exposure to a variety of unusual, ethnic, regional, or cultural foods. Nutrition education is initiated through a planned series of units in grades 1 to 6; lecture, reading, demonstration and menu writing and other methods are used (Cronan 1962). Follow-up programs for high school students are taught in health, physical education, and Home Economics classes. Ulibari (1972) reports development of a program in cafeteria management that attracts some students; this program has a nutrition education component. There is some evidence that tasting parties are somewhat successful in introducing new vegetables; however, large numbers of students do not accept unfamiliar items. No matter how rich the nutrient content of the food, it cannot be relied on in meeting nutritional needs unless it is consumed.

Type "A" Lunch Program—Philosophy and Participation

This program which is administered by the USDA provides for cash reimbursement when requirements are met (Table 10.2). In addition, donated commodities are made available in variable quantities according to supply.

Student participation varies widely among schools committed to the program. A number of factors are probably involved: (a) number and location of competitive snack bars and relative speed of service, (b) acceptability of the food, i.e., items, combinations, and preparation, (c) number of choices, (d) speed of service, and (e) dining room atmosphere. Student involvement in menu planning has been shown to improve participation (Parker 1968).

When set menus are served under the type "A" plan, if the entrée or two other meal components are unacceptable the student usually purchases lunch at the snack bar or brings a brown-bag lunch. When the student population is relatively homogeneous, set menus can be planned that are acceptable to all. But when the population is heterogeneous, the set menu is likely to contain items that are unacceptable to one or more subgroups; overall participation is reduced. The selective menu, when alternatives are carefully planned, is more likely to be acceptable to a population with diverse food habits and preferences.

The basic type "A" lunch is composed of the following meal components (a) main dish, (b) vegetable, (c) salad, (d) bread item, (e) dessert, and (f) milk (State of California 1967A).For those students desiring a low-calorie meal, an approved (State of California 1967B) salad-plate meal has been developed that consists of (a) protein-rich salad, (b) fruit or vegetable relish or salad, (c) bread item or sandwich, (d) fruit dessert, and (e) milk. Another variation designed to meet the

TABLE 10.2

THE TYPE A LUNCH[1]

Milk	Required: 1/2 pt of fluid, whole, unflavored milk served as a beverage. In addition, it is desirable to use a nonfat dry milk in the preparation of dishes in the menus.
Protein-rich food	Required: 2 oz cooked lean meat, or equivalent. The edible portion of the meat is counted.
	Equivalents are: 2 oz poultry; 2 oz fish; 2 oz cheese; 1 egg; 1/2 c dry beans or peas (cooked); 4 T peanut butter; or combination of these.
	To be counted in meeting this requirement, the foods must be served in a main dish or in a main dish plus only one other dish (a protein-rich salad *or* sandwich *or* dessert). In other words, two dishes in a menu are the maximum number which may be counted toward supplying the protein requirement. More than one protein food may be used in a protein dish. Some possible combinations are as follows:
	1 oz cooked meat + 1 oz cheese = 1 serving
	1 oz cooked poultry + 1/2 egg = 1 serving
	1–1/2 oz cheese + 1 T peanut butter = 1 serving
Fruit/vegetable combination	Required: 3/4 c, served in at least 2 dishes.
	The menu should include:
	1 raw item each day
	1 serving of an ascorbic acid-rich (vitamin C) food each day. (These are oranges, grapefruit, broccoli, cabbage, tomatoes, green peppers, and others.)
	1 serving of a carotene-rich (vitamin A-value) food at least twice a week. (These are dark-green leafy vegetables and deep-yellow fruits and vegetables.)
	Full-strength vegetable or fruit juice may be counted to meet not more than 1/4 c of this requirement. Some possible fruit/vegetable combinations are as follows:
	3/8 c vegetable + 3/8 c fruit = 6/8 or 3/4 c serving
	1/4 c vegetable + 1/4 c fruit/vegetable + 1/4 c fruit = 3/4 c serving
	3/8 c vegetable + 2/8 c vegetable + 1/8 c fruit = 6/8 c or 3/4 c serving
	1/4 c fruit juice (full strength) + 3/8 c vegetable + 1/8 c fruit = 3/4 c serving
	2/8 c vegetable + 2/8 c fruit/vegetable + 3 oz 75% frozen orange juice bar = 3/4 c serving
	2/8 c vegetable + 2/8 c fruit/vegetable + 2 oz 100% frozen orange juice bar = 3/4 c serving
Bread	Required: 1 slice whole grain or enriched bread; or a serving of cornbread, biscuits, rolls, muffins, and so forth made of whole grain or enriched flour.
Table fat	Required: 2 tsp butter or fortified margarine. Part may be used on the bread and part in another food, such as a vegetable, cream sauce, or dessert.

[1] Lunches served to high school students should follow the basic Type A pattern, but the amounts should be increased by 1/3 to 1/2 those given.

needs of students desiring a quick lunch to free time for noontime activities consists of (a) protein-rich sandwich, (b) salad or raw vegetable, (c) fruit or cookie, and (d) milk.

Another problem related to the structure of the type "A" meal is that nutritional requirements are based on the needs of children, aged 9 to 12 yr. Portion size is supposed to be increased to meet the needs of older students; in practice, since the cash reimbursement is the same, inadequate portions are frequently served. Moreover, when two choices are listed they must be nutritional equivalents, i.e., if one entrée contains half the protein requirement so must the other. Although necessary, this constraint complicates the problem of planning good alternates.

Optional Meals—Breakfast and Dinner

Breakfast programs have been developed to meet the needs of children and teenagers who are unable to learn because they are too hungry (Foods Research and Action Center 1972). By law the minimum breakfast is to include (a) ½ pt of whole milk, (b) ½ cup fruit or fruit or vegetable juice, and (c) 1 slice of bread or equivalent grain product. In addition, programs are directed to provide a protein-rich food "as often as is practicable" which, since reimbursement is 15¢ per meal, is never in most cases. Moreover, the minimum requirement is somewhat inadequate to meet the needs of a child in the 9 to 12 yr age group; it is grossly inadequate to meet the needs of teenagers (Foods Research and Action Center 1972). Menu planning requirements would depend on policy decisions regarding the number and type of additional meal components to be added, if any. In any case, variety is restricted by the low budget, which results in lower participation than expected.

With the advent of double or triple sessions in high schools serious consideration should be given to the need for providing a dinner meal. No federally-funded programs have been proposed to date, but if multisession useage continues to expand, development of a dinner program can be expected. Menu planning requirements would be considerably different because of the difference in student expectations in regard to the types of items appropriate for dinner (Shapiro 1963). Since the same student population would not be expected to consume breakfast, lunch, and dinner meals at the school, vertical checking for repetition among meals would be unnecessary.

Management Considerations

In addition to nutritional, budgetary, and participation problems the menu planner must be concerned with (a) aesthetics, (b) man-hours and level of skills available for preparation, (c) scheduling problems, and (d) catering requirements.

Aesthetic factors such as harmony or interest in color, texture, and shape are important in motivating students to eat various meal components. If the item looks good, the teenager may try an unfamiliar food. The mechanics of planning for aesthetic acceptability were discussed in Chap. 6.

Employee considerations have a sizeable impact on menu item selections. Generally the cook is experienced but training is often limited to attendance at local workshops. And cook's helpers are usually willing but unskilled. Consequently, expected skill and efficiency are low. Convenience foods would provide a logical solution but usually cost and/or legal restrictions prevent their use.

Because secondary school feeding programs operate on a 5-day-on, 2-day-off schedule, production requirements restrict feasibility of preparing some items on specific days of the week. For example, since it is inadvisable to thaw meat on Friday for Monday, entrées such as Roast Turkey cannot be planned for Monday. Moreover, the long vacations in summer, and at Christmas and Easter also create scheduling problems that must be considered in selecting menu items. Because prepreparation is necessary for some items such as gelatin salads, these cannot be planned for the first meal following a vacation. On the other hand, since many items are perishable, just prior to vacations, menus must be planned to use up the quantities on hand.

Generally, the number, kind, and approximate date of banquets to be served can be forecast in advance since the majority of these are annual affairs such as awards banquets. The mechanics of providing menu options to regular groups is discussed in Chap. 6. On days when a banquet is to be served, and usually on the preceding day, the regular student lunch menu must be simplified since the regular employees must produce both meals.

ELEMENTARY SCHOOLS

General Considerations

Many children come to school hungry (Bard 1968; Foods Research and Action Center 1972); the school lunch reduces physical need so that attention can be focused on learning objectives. Unless the food is consumed, it does not meet this need; therefore, menu planning objectives should be designed to plan acceptable meals that will be consumed. Their nutritional requirements are defined in Table 10.3.

Younger children should be served small portions with additional portions available. When large portions are served the child tends to eat the entire portion of preferred items, and therefore is unable to eat other items needed for their nutrient contribution.

Food habits and preferences vary widely among students from various social, cultural, religious, and economic backgrounds. And the food related behavior of children is often a function of need for attention or security, expectation of rewards, etc. Also some children have had limited exposure to foods other than those served in the home. Hence, many are reluctant to try new foods. All of these factors increase the challenge of planning acceptable menus.

If the student population is relatively homogeneous in socioeconomic background, a set menu is more practical for children in the primary grades since

TABLE 10.3

NUTRITIONAL REQUIREMENTS (RDA)[1] OF CHILDREN

	Age (Yr)		Weight		Height				Fat-Soluble Vitamins			Water-Soluble Vitamins							Minerals				
	From Up To		(Kg)	(Lb)	(Cm)	(In.)	Kcal	Protein (Gm)	Vitamin A Activity (IU)	Vitamin D (IU)	Vitamin E Activity (IU)	Ascorbic Acid (Mg)	Folacin[2] (Mg)	Niacin (Mg Equiv)[3]	Ribo-flavin (Mg)	Thia-min (Mg)	Vita-min B_6 (Mg)	Vita-min B_{12} (μg)	Calcium (Gm)	Phos-phorus (Gm)	Iodine (μg)	Iron (Mg)	Mag-nesium (Mg)
Children	6-8		23	51	121	48	2,000	35	3,500	400	15	40	0.2	13	1.1	1.0	1.0	4	0.9	0.9	100	10	250
	8-10		28	62	131	52	2,200	40	3,500	400	15	40	0.3	15	1.2	1.1	1.2	5	1.0	1.0	110	10	250
Males	10-12		35	77	140	55	2,500	45	4,500	400	20	40	0.4	17	1.3	1.3	1.4	5	1.2	1.2	125	10	300
Females	10-12		35	77	142	56	2,250	50	4,500	400	20	40	0.4	15	1.3	1.1	1.4	5	1.2	1.2	110	18	300

Source: Adapted from *Recommended Daily Dietary Allowances*, Food and Nutrition Board, National Academy of Sciences–National Research Council.

[1] The allowance levels are intended to cover individual variations among most normal persons as they live in the United States under usual environmental stresses. The recommended allowances can be attained with a variety of common foods, providing other nutrients for which human requirements have been less well defined.

[2] The folacin allowances refer to dietary sources as determined by *Lactobacillus casei* assay. Pure forms of folacin may be effective in doses less than ¼ of the RDA.

[3] Niacin equivalents include dietary sources of the vitamin itself plus 1 mg equivalent for each 60 mg of dietary tryptophan.

many are confused by the problem of selecting a meal. When the group is heterogeneous, several alternate plate-lunch combinations might provide a feasible solution. Generally, a selective menu will best meet the needs of older groups.

Whether the elementary school child will purchase a lunch on a specific day is frequently determined by the "sound" of the menu when the mother reads it in the newspaper or hears it announced on the radio at breakfast. Therefore, familiar descriptive names for items are desirable.

The cost of the meal is also a major determinant. When the program is subsidized with federal or state monies, cost to the student is low and demand is relatively large. When the price is raised as little as a nickel demand drops off, especially if there are several children to be provided with lunch money.

Type "A" Lunch—Philosophy and Participation (Also See Above)

Participation varies widely within and among school districts, states, and regions of the United States. A number of factors are involved such as (a) acceptability of the food, i.e., appropriateness of items offered given the socioeconomic background of the group, quality of food preparation, variety offered compared to variety accepted, etc., (b) cost to the student, and (c) speed of service.

From the standpoint of menu planning, the problems of food acceptability are most pertinent. Generally, acceptable combinations of foods can be planned for White Anglo-Saxon Protestant groups. However, rigidities designed to simplify the task of nutritional accounting create problems in planning for other population subgroups. For example, a sizeable number of Blacks, Orientals, and Jews are lactose-intolerant (Bayless and Huang 1969; Bayless and Rosensweig 1966; Huang and Bayless 1968); and the requirement of "½ pt whole pasteurized milk, to be used as a beverage" presents a problem. Either the meal will be purchased and the milk traded or discarded or the students will not participate. An adjustment that would allow an increased meat portion would improve acceptability of the meals. Another requirement that adds to the acceptability problem is that of including one high vitamin C food per day. Although numerous sources are available (Table 10.4), cabbage and tomatoes tend to predominate since they are relatively inexpensive. Since cabbage is not a preferred vegetable, great waste occurs and the nutritive need is not met.

Another problem relates to the use of donated commodities. According to the Food Service Office, California State Department of Education (State of California 1967A), donated food commodities made available to the schools by the USDA are of two types: (a) foods purchased with funds appropriated by Congress for school lunch purposes that are for use only in type "A" lunches (designated Section 6 Commodities); and (b) foods purchased under the government price support and surplus removal program (designated Section 36 Commodities) which may be used in any nonprofit school lunch program. It is

TABLE 10.4

VEGETABLES AND FRUITS CONTAINING ASCORBIC ACID
(TO BE SERVED EVERY DAY)

	Good Sources		Fair Sources
Fruits	Grapefruit Grapefruit juice Grapefruit-orange juice Guavas Kumquats Mangoes[1]	Oranges Orange juice Papayas[1] Strawberries Tangerines Tangerine juice	Cantaloupe[1] Honeydew melon Raspberries, red Tangelos Tangelo juice
Vegetables	Broccoli[1] Brussels sprouts Cauliflower Collards[1] Cress, garden[1]	Kale[1] Kohlrabi Mustard greens[1] Peppers, sweet, red[1] Peppers, green	Asparagus[1] Cabbage Dandelion greens[1] Okra Potatoes (cooked in skins) Rutabagas Sauerkraut Spinach[1] Sweet potatoes[1] Tomatoes[1] Tomato juice, paste, or purée[1] Turnips Turnip greens[1]

[1] Also a good source of vitamin A. Adapted from the most recent listing of fruits and vegetables which nationwide are good sources of vitamin C value. List developed by USDA.

financially advantageous for a district to utilize commodities to the extent possible. When force issue tactics (i.e., requirement to serve more frequently than warranted by acceptability in order to avoid discarding) are required, monotonous repetition leads to dislike. Moreover, when some commodities are added to extend standard products, acceptability declines.

A problem that directly affects acceptability of menu items is the level of product quality and consistency in quality control. Because most cooks are experienced but untrained, quality control is a problem. Greasy entrées, raw or overcooked vegetables, tacky puddings, etc., result in negative responses by children; the cumulative and aggregate effects are the same, namely brown-bag lunches. Unless quality can be controlled, items such as these should not be placed on the menu.

The commitment to increase student exposure to new foods has dysfunctional effects when such items are planned as sources of nutrients. The student may remain hungry and nutritive needs are not met! New items should be introduced in addition to or as choices, thus giving the child the option of selecting or rejecting the item.

TABLE 10.5

SAMPLE SCHOOL BREAKFAST MENUS
(ADEQUATE NUTRITIONALLY)

9–12 Year Olds	High School
Orange juice (½ c)	Orange juice (1 c)
Egg (1)	Egg (1)
Ham (½ oz)	Ham (1 oz)
Whole wheat bread (1 slice)	Whole wheat bread (2 slices)
Butter (1 pat)	Butter (2 pats)
Milk (½ pt)	Milk (½ pt)
Tomato juice (½ c)	Tomato juice (½ c)
Oatmeal (½ c) with raisins (¼ c)	Oatmeal (1 c) with raisins (½ c)
Corn muffin	Corn muffin
Butter (1 pat)	Butter (2 pats)
Milk (½ pt)	Milk (½ pt)

Source: Food Research and Action Center (1972). Reproduced with permission of the Gazette Press and the author.

Optional Meals—Breakfast and Dinner

Breakfast programs have been introduced in some school districts in order to meet the needs of a large number of students who come to school hungry (Foods Research and Action Center 1972). Menu planning requirements are minimal since the number of meal components is small and items are acceptable and not particularly monotonous (Table 10.5). However, some variety does increase participation.

With the advent of double and triple sessions provision of dinner meals becomes important. Although no federal programs have been developed to date, if multisession useage continues to expand, initiation to dinner programs can be expected. Menu planning problems are expected to be similar to those encountered in planning lunch.

NURSERY SCHOOLS

The preschool child, aged 2 to 5, brings to the nursery school or daycare center food habits that reflect the personality and practices of the mother (Mayer 1970). These determine the initial responses of the child to the food served. In some cases the mother establishes arbitrary rules governing mealtime behavior and requires the child to comply. The result may be a contest of wills with the child becoming nervous, suspicious, and petulent. Other mothers allow their children to eat whenever and whatever they desire. Nursery school personnel usually strive to make mealtime pleasant and to help the children develop healthy, relaxed food habits while improving table manners and social behavior.

Children of this age group are often erratic in their food habits and preferences. Moreover, physical activity varies widely from day to day; appetite varies accordingly. Temporary physical disturbance such as colds, fatigue, etc., may result in regressive eating behavior. Although the individual may vary, generalizations for the group can be used in meeting the menu planning challenge:

(A) A child will eat what he is accustomed to eating at home.
(B) When most of the peer group consumes a food with enjoyment, a child is more likely to try it; he may eat it at the nursery school and reject it at home.
(C) Simple foods are preferred by WASP children; minority children prefer foods common to their ethnic or religious group.
(D) Finger foods are enjoyed by many children; however, a fastidious child may reject them.
(E) A child can be trained to accept and enjoy foods served at the nursery school that are not served in the home.

However, in regard to the last point, Sweeny (1927) made a point that is still pertinent:[1]

> There are factors other than food requirements which must be definitely considered in planning the children's midday meal. The cost of the food and labor involved in its preparation are equally important. It is obviously unfair to train a child to like and enjoy foods which his family cannot afford, and to cultivate standards that the average mother, doing all her own housework, has neither the time nor the energy to meet.

Nutrition

The nutrient needs for children of this age group are well defined (Table 10.3) (Food & Nutrition Board, NAS-NRC 1968). These are easily met when a well-balanced variety of acceptable items and combinations are planned.

Introducing New Foods

Because a child's exposure to foods is usually limited to foods served in the home, a number of standard WASP foods may be new to the child. When new foods are introduced as a learning experience and the child is not pressured into tasting, acceptance may be good. However, new foods should not be relied on as a source of nutrients until they are well accepted.

OTHER INSTITUTIONS

Hospitals

Pediatric menus are customarily prepared as modified diets from the master menu for infants and children up to age eight. Older children, unless otherwise

---

[1] Quoted by permission from the American Home Economics Association, Washington, D.C.

restricted, select their meals from the general menu. Special considerations in planning pediatric menus are discussed in Chap. 7.

Handicapped Children

The general principles of menu planning for children of each age group apply to handicapped children as well. However, there are some additional challenges to be met.

Institutions whose major function is rehabilitative rather than custodial care must cope with secondary psychological problems. Mealtime provides a unique opportunity to work with the children.

In planning menus for blind children, texture and flavor contrasts are particularly important in providing interest in the meals. A set menu is customarily provided since selections are difficult unless menus are marked in advance.

Deaf children enjoy cafeteria service. Color, texture, flavor, and shape harmonies are particularly important in creating and maintaining interest in food.

Mentally defective children also have special needs that determine menu offerings. Walker (1955) has made some provocative points. Master menus are difficult to plan for the following reasons:

(A) Cost restrictions and the aggregate effect of individual difficulties reduce the pool of items that should be considered; items should be selected that the majority can or will consume.

(B) The nutritional needs of the various age groups differ; alternatives must be selected to meet several levels of need.

(C) New foods are difficult to introduce; the mentally defective child is reluctant to try new foods.

(D) Variety in preparation method alternatives is restricted; foods must be selected or prepared so that they have a texture and/or consistency that can be adapted for variable levels of motor control, e.g., many meats must be ground for those who have difficulty in swallowing and liquids must be thickened for ease in handling.

(E) Color interest is more important; color appeal on the main plate and among accompanying components is an important means of stimulating interest in the meal and in increasing the probability of consumption.

Unfortunately, menus for mentally handicapped children have often been limited to gruels, soups, and stews. The recent finding that some mental retardation was due to metabolic disorders created interest in providing better diets for mentally defective children. Much work needs to be done.

Correctional Institutions

The considerations in planning menus for youths in correctional institutions are basically the same as for other groups of youths. The major difference lies in the paranoidal fear of being served unwholesome or poisonous food. This emotional state is attributed to a long history of insecurity, fear, and distrust. Therefore, new items are not readily accepted nor are casseroles since the youths cannot satisfactorily identify the individual ingredients in a mixed dish. Quality control of flavor and texture, and absence of defects is also critical since one experience may prejudice the group against ever eating the item again. For example, if a fly or a hair is discovered in a roll, bread products may be totally rejected.

BIBLIOGRAPHY

BARD, B. 1968. The School Lunchroom: Time of Trial. John Wiley & Sons, New York.
BAYLESS, T. M., and HUANG, S. S. 1969. Inadequate intestinal digestion of lactose. Am. J. Clin. Nutr. 22, 250.
BAYLESS, T. M., and ROSENWEIG, N. S. 1966. A racial difference in incidence of lactose intolerance. J. Am. Med. Assoc. 197, 968.
CRONAN, M. L. 1962. The School Lunch. Chas. A. Bennet Co., Peoria, Ill.
Foods Research and Action Center. 1972. If We Had Ham, We Could Have Ham and Eggs . . . If We Had Eggs. A Study of the National School Breakfast Program. Gazette Press, Yonkers, NY.
HAMPTON, M. C., SHAPIRO, L. R., and HUENEMANN, R. L. 1961. Helping teen-age girls improve their diets: report of a pilot study. J. Home Econ. 53, 835–838.
HUANG, S. S., and BAYLESS, T. M. 1968. Milk and lactose intolerance in healthy Orientals. Science 160, 83.
HUENEMANN, R. L., SHAPIRO, L. R., HAMPTON, M. C., and MITCHELL, B. W. 1966. A longitudinal study of gross body composition and body conformation and their association with food and activity in a teenage population. Am. J. Clin. Nutr. 18, 325–338.
HUENEMANN, R. L., SHAPIRO, L. R., HAMPTON, M. C., and MITCHELL, B. W. 1967. Teen-agers' activities and attitudes toward activity. J. Am. Dietet. Assoc. 51, 433–440.
HUENEMANN, R. L., SHAPIRO, L. R., HAMPTON, M. C., and MITCHELL, B. W. 1968. Food and eating practices of teen-agers. J. Am. Dietet. Assoc. 53, 17–24.
KOONCE, T. M. 1972. Does breakfast help? School Foodservice J. 26, 51–54.
LAW, H. M., LEWIS, H. F., GRANT, V. C., and BACHEMIN, D. S. 1972. Sophomore high school students' attitudes toward school lunch. J. Am. Dietet. Assoc. 60, 38–41.
MAYER, J. 1970. Feeding the preschool child. Postgrad. Med. 47, 267–270.
National Academy of Sciences–National Research Council. 1968. Recommended Dietary Allowances, 7th Edition, Revised 1968. Food Nutr. Board, Natl. Acad. Sci.–Natl. Res. Council Publ. 1694.
PARKER, D. 1968. Increased participation . . . the key to holding down prices. School Lunch J. 22, 70–72.
PAYNE, E. C. 1963. Cycle menu terminology. Hospitals 44, No. 1, 84–85.
SHAPIRO, L. R. 1963. Food habits of California children. California's Health 21, No. 2, 9–13.
State of California. 1967A. Beginning Menu Planning: A Course for School Food Service Personnel. Food Serv. Office, Div. Public School Admin., Dept. Educ., State of California, Sacramento.
State of California. 1967B. Advanced Menu Planning: A Course for School Food Service Personnel. Food Serv. Office, Div. Public School Admin., Dept. Educ., State of California, Sacramento.
SWEENY, M. 1927. Some observations on the feeding of young children. J. Home Econ. 19, 307–312.
ULIBARI, R. 1972. One person's view of the school lunch program. School Foodservice J. 26, 19–20.
WALKER, G. H. 1955. Nutrition in mentally deficient children. J. Am. Dietet. Assoc. 31, 494–497.

CHAPTER 11

Menu Planning for College Student Consumers

RESPONSIBILITY FOR MEETING THE NEEDS OF STUDENTS

College and university food service is big business, according to recent figures. It is the largest segment of the institutional food service industry. More than $1/3$ of the food consumed institutionally is consumed on campuses (Anon. 1972B).

Traditionally, the term "college feeding" has been practically synonymous with residence halls feeding despite the large volume of business done by restaurants in Student Unions. As a simplification, it sufficed when the typical campus was isolated in a country setting. However, many 2- and 4-yr colleges are commuter campuses with somewhat different problems and needs (Anderson 1971). Since these are similar to those faced by commercial restaurants, the reader should see Chap. 14 for a discussion of alternate menu planning strategies.

General Considerations

Residence halls commonly serve 20 meals per week: breakfast, lunch, and dinner on Monday through Saturday, and brunch and dinner on Sunday. Styles of service vary from family style to cafeteria. Philosophical bases for menu policy also vary widely (Goodfriend 1970).

For many years a major objective of some institutions has been to minimize cost to the student so that no student would be denied an education because of the cost of dormitory living. In other cases, the food service was expected to make a profit to be used in supporting other programs. Here again, low cost food was served. However, in affluent America either policy has dysfunctional effects. For example, when extended meats and meat substitutes predominate as dinner entrées, the students who are accustomed to roasts, steaks, and chops will not accept the meals. They will eat in restaurants or, if possible, move to apartments (Hazeltine 1970).

Moreover, students often come to college with preconceived negative ideas about food service in dormitories or other campus food service facilities (Nugent 1965). If food is monotonous, unfamiliar, ill-prepared, or service is slow, these ideas are reinforced. As a result, the student is less likely to consume the variety and quantity of food necessary to meet physiological requirements.

Another objective has been to increase students' food experience. In former times, and today in relatively isolated areas, this may be a desirable policy. However, the student in an urban campus area usually has opportunity for as much food exposure as he desires. If foods are to be served for this purpose, they should be offered in addition to, not in lieu of, acceptable items.

Food habits of college students are an outgrowth of childhood and adolescent patterns. General habits and time commitments often interfere with eating regular complete meals. Findings of studies of food habits and preferences from the past 20 yr can be summarized as follows:

(A) Meal attendance in dormitories located in a small college town: breakfast, 80%; lunch, 90%; dinner, 80%. Weekend breakfast much lower and dinner on Friday and Saturday night reduced.

(B) When a standard breakfast was consumed, nutritional adequacy of the diet as compared to the appropriate RDA, was more likely (Odland *et al.* 1955).

(C) When freely available, milk consumption varies among campuses although men are more likely to consume adequate amounts than women (Odland *et al.* 1955; Myers *et al.* 1963; Mirone and Whitehead 1957).

(D) Men and women rate most foods similarly (Kennedy 1958; Knickrehm *et al.* 1969).

The traditional breakfast-lunch-dinner meal pattern often does not meet the needs of large student subgroups. Student schedules are highly variable and it is inconvenient for many students to return to the residence halls for some meals. In other cases, hours and life-style do not fit with scheduled mealtimes. Various alternatives are being explored in an effort to meet student needs (Anon. 1972A). To help meet student needs, at some universities a continental breakfast may be obtained in lieu of the regular breakfast (Anon. 1967C). This self-service meal is commonly served between 8:30 and 11:00 a.m. At least one university is experimenting with continuous feeding (Friese 1971). Vending machines, when adequate in number and variety—and when properly serviced—also provide a feasible alternative to the student.

Another consideration relates to the continuing student need to establish independence. In some cases, students who have been accustomed to eating items of marginal acceptability will regularly select the alternate. In this respect one infers that their zone of acceptance or indifference has been reduced. On the other hand, some students will become more venturesome and will try new items just to show that they are cosmopolitan. If a selective menu is used, one cannot predict whether the item-mix consumed will be nutritionally adequate, unless one has preference and frequency data for a representative sample of individuals for most of the foods.

Subgroup Needs

College and university students commonly are a heterogeneous population representing various racial, religious, social, and cultural groups. Because of this diversity, menu planning considerations are numerous and "acceptability-to-all" is difficult to achieve.

Generally, a selective menu is desirable because alternates can be specified that appeal to the various subgroups. This increases the probability of consumption; nutrient intake can be predicted and evaluated for adequacy. The RDA for men and women, aged 18–22 yr (Table 2.1 in Chap. 2) is the standard for measuring nutritional adequacy of the diet.

In a recent pilot study of racial differences, preference ratings for 416 standard foods were obtained by Eckstein (1972) (Table 11.1). Ratings were ob-

TABLE 11.1

PILOT STUDY RESULTS: ITEMS LIKED[1] AND DISLIKED[2]

Liked	Disliked
Items normally liked and flatly disliked by all three races	
Apple Pie	Cervelat
Apples	Knickerbocker Soup
Barbecued Spareribs	Mulligatawny Soup
Beef Stew	Parsnips
Cantaloupe	Peanut Butter Cake
Cheeseburger	Pepper Pot Soup
Corn on the Cob	Pickled Green Beans
French Bread	Pineapple Cheese Salad
French Fried Potatoes	
Hamburger Sandwich	
Hashed Brown Potatoes	
Hot Roast Beef Sandwich	
Hot Turkey Sandwich	
Ice Cream Sundae	
Orange Juice	
Oranges	
Roast Beef	
Spaghetti	
Turkey	
Turkey/Gravy	
Caucasians	
Applesauce	Black Eyed Peas
Bacon, Lettuce and Tomato Sandwich	Butterscotch Cream Pie
Baked Potatoes	Canned Apples
Banana Split	Cabbage and Pepper Salad
Blueberry Muffins	Cheese Soup
Brownies	Chocolate Chip Bread Pudding
Danish Pastry	Cucumber/Onion/Pepper Salad
Devils Food Cake	Figs (canned)
English Muffins	Fried Oysters
Fruit Salad	Garden Cottage Cheese Salad
Grapes	Iced Coffee
Grilled Cheese Sandwich	Meatball Submarine
Ham	Mustard Greens
Hot Rolls	Okra
Lemonade	Rutabagas
Mashed Potatoes	Succotash
Meat Loaf	Turnip Greens
Milk	Vegetable Slaw
Milkshake	
Mixed Fruit Salad	
Pot Roast	

Table II.1 (*Continued*)

Liked	Disliked
Pumpkin Pie	
Steak	
Strawberry Shortcake	
Sweet Rolls	
Tangerines	
Tossed Green Salad	
Blacks	
American Cheese	Banana Salad
Bacon	Bean Soup
Baked Potatoes	Butterscotch Cream Pie
Biscuits	Butterscotch Sauce
Brownies	Carrot and Raisin Salad
Chicken	Cheese Soup
Chicken Noodle Soup	Cherry Cake Pudding
Chocolate Milk	Corn Chowder
Devils Food Cake	Cucumber and Onion Salad
Dill Pickles	Eggplant
Doughnuts	Farina
Frankfurters	Fish Chowder
Fried Chicken	Fried Oysters
Gingerbread	Frijole Salad
Grape Juice	Kidney Beans
Grapes	Lemon Pudding Sauce
Grape Soda	Lobster Newberg
Grilled Cheese Sandwich	Manhattan Clam Chowder
Ham	Meatball Submarine
Hot Rolls	Mince Pie
Ice Cream	Pineapple Pie
Instant Orange Juice	Raisin Pie
Mashed Potatoes	Rice Pilaff
Peaches (fresh)	Sauerbraten
Peaches (canned)	Scalloped Tuna and Peas
Peanut Butter Cookies	Spareribs with Sauerkraut
Pineapple	Waldorf Salad
Pizza	Wax Beans
Plums	Western Sandwich
Potato Salad	
Raisin Bread	
Sherbet	
Sweet Potatoes	
Sweet Rolls	
Tangerines	
Tuna Salad	
Turkey	
Turkey Noodle Soup	
Vanilla Wafers	
Watermelon	
Orientals	
Asparagus	Apple Stuffing
Bacon	Banana Salad
Banana Split	Beer
Beef Pot Pie	Bread Pudding
Beef/Barbecue Sauce	Cabbage Pepper Salad

Liked	Disliked
Chicken	Cherry Cake Pudding
Chocolate Milk	Chocolate Chip Bread Pudding
Chow Mein	Creole Soup
Cola	Cucumber and Onion Salad
Danish Pastry	Frijole Salad
Eggs to Order	Garden Cottage Cheese Salad
Farina	Grits
French Fried Onion Rings	Mustard Greens
French Toast	Raisin Pie
Fried Chicken	Raisin Stuffing
Fried Rice	Rutabagas
Grapefruit	Sauerbraten
Grilled Cheese and Ham Sandwich	Succotash
Lobster	Turnip Greens
Milk	
Milkshake	
Mixed Nuts	
Peaches	
Pears	
Pizza	
Pork Roast	
Pot Roast	
Rice	
Roast Pork/Gravy	
Sausage Links	
Scrambled Eggs	
Sloppy Joe	
Steak	
Strawberry Shortcake	
Submarine	
Sweet and Sour Pork	
Tacos	
Tea	
Thousand Island Dressing	
Veal Roast	
Watermelon	

Source: Eckstein (1972).
[1] Liked items are those with a mean rating greater than 7.0 on a 9-point Hedonic Scale.
[2] Disliked items are those with a mean rating less than 3.0 on a 9-point Hedonic Scale.

tained from a random sampling of men and women college students at the University of California, Berkeley from three races, i.e., Caucasian, Black, and Oriental. Although findings are tentative because of small sample size, a number of differences did emerge. Findings can be summarized as follows:

(A) Caucasians—A rather small number of foods (27) were "liked" by the group as a whole. Ratings for individual foods were distributed over the scale. "Disliked" foods were primarily southern vegetables and less familiar items, e.g., Cheese Soup.

(B) Blacks—A somewhat larger number of foods (40) were "liked" by the group as a whole. Ratings for foods tended to be concentrated at both ends of the scale. While a number of traditional southern favorites were well liked, southern vegetables were not. Thirty-one foods were "disliked." These were primarily foods that are served infrequently so "unfamiliar" might be a more appropriate term. A "never" column was provided to allow the respondent to indicate that he/she had never eaten the item but this column was seldom used.

(C) Orientals—A similar number of foods (41) were "liked" by the group as a whole. Ratings tended to be distributed over the upper end of the scale. A larger number of breakfast foods were rated "liked." "Disliked" foods included beer, southern vegetables, and items that are uncommon in the west. The "never" column was used frequently by this group. Although traditional favorites are evident, clearly this group enjoys the standard American diet.

Vegetarians constitute another subgroup whose dietary needs require menu modifications. A number of campuses have reported alternate methods of meeting needs of vegetarian students (Anon. 1972C; Cappadonna 1972). For information on vegetarian food habits see Chap. 28.

Special Diet Needs

Freedom from disease is not a requirement for attending college. Hence, the college student population is expected to include individuals with most of the chronic diseases of the general American population, i.e., diabetes, ulcers, allergies, etc. Moreover, students are equally susceptible to common contagious illnesses of a temporary nature such as flu.

Ordinarily, only a limited number of special diet items or menus are available to the students. Usually, the student is hospitalized if the condition is acute and requires special dietary treatment. If it is controlled, the student may easily select appropriate foods from the regular menu. In other cases, unless special items can be obtained from the food service unit the student will be obliged to live in an apartment.

However, colleges·and universities are increasingly involved with programs for special groups of diabetics, obese persons, etc. In these cases special therapeutic diets may be required for the entire group or various subsets of it. See Chap. 7, Planning Menus for Hospital Patients, for suggestions on methods of planning the master menu.

PACK LUNCHES

When the student population is small and class scheduling permits all students a lunch period between 11:30 and 1:30, all students can be expected to return to the residence hall for lunch. However, on many campuses this is impossible for a significant number of students. Therefore, pack lunches must be provided.

Pack lunches can be just as monotonous as regular lunches so items must be planned unless an array of items is provided and the student chooses and makes his own lunch. Although food poisoning is a potential hazard, if sandwich makings as well as the bread are refrigerator cold, chances of food poisoning are low since bread is an excellent insulator. Therefore, customary meat sandwiches can be provided.

PUBLIC RELATIONS AND MENU PLANNING

Menu Committee

Student complaints about dormitory food are universal and chronic whether the food is good or not. A menu committee composed of student and food service representatives listens to complaints, determines their validity, and recommends appropriate actions. Student demands for additional services are also evaluated. At some institutions, the student members of the committee may prepare a suggested menu. In any case, recommendations must be implemented in menu design unless very good reasons can be given that show why implementation is not feasible. Otherwise, negative student reaction will create other problems.

Special Meals and Catering

A number of regularly scheduled special banquets are served to student groups during the academic year. In addition monotony-breakers are served at random intervals. Moreover, the residence hall usually provides meals for groups attending institutes or conventions if these are housed in the residence hall (Anon. 1968). Each of these poses special menu planning problems.

Student groups usually schedule similar banquets annually. Therefore a banquet file, as described in Chap. 6, and a set of predetermined alternate menus simplify the task. A file of special menus of Polynesian, Mexican, German, Indian, and other nationality groups is useful in meeting unexpected requirements.

Monotony-breakers can be effective in breaking up the students' mental set that condemns or rejects residence halls food because of boredom. Universities vary in the approach used. Common monotony-breakers include (a) ice cream socials, (b) watermelon feeds, (c) luaus, (d) outdoor barbecues, and (e) nationality meals with appropriate music and decor (Anon. 1967AB, 1969). The latter three require considerable planning but type menus are readily available in cookbooks. During exam times snacks are often served at 10 p.m. to provide a study break since students will be up late.

Groups attending institutes or conventions are served a different quality of food from student fare because food cost allowance is more generous and greater efforts in pleasing the customer are customary. Better cuts of meat and more expensive salads, desserts, etc., are selected. Thus, the menu planner must have an alternate set of recipes in order to plan acceptable meals. The basic menu planning considerations regarding harmony and contrast of color, texture, flavor, and variety requirements are the same. Worker and management considerations also must be taken into account.

MANAGEMENT CONSIDERATIONS (SEE ALSO CHAP. 4)

Residence halls food service, on most campuses today, is big business (Goodfriend 1970). Therefore, management considerations differ from those of independent units commonly encountered in retirement or nursing homes. Observed differences include (a) consequences of consumer dissatisfaction, (b) levels of employee skills, (c) importance of production scheduling, and (d) problems in disposal of leftovers.

Whereas the dissatisfied hospital or nursing home patient or retirement home guest may refuse to eat and/or complain, the student may demonstrate or destroy. Hence, menu acceptability is a more critical factor.

College and university food service employees in all classifications are likely to be more skilled than those in similar positions in other institutions. This can be attributed to (a) college and university policy to employ only civil service or union employees that meet basic job requirements, (b) effectiveness of uniform interviewing and screening procedures, (c) extensive use of orientation and training programs, and (d) professional supervision. Thus, in spite of the lack of a chef, most college and university food service units should be able to consistently produce good quality food.

The production scheduling problems associated with producing 20, 200, or 2000 meals differ tremendously. In large dormitories, production scheduling is probably the most critical management consideration because of the problems in logistics of supplying raw materials and in coordinating use of men and machines. When a long line of students forms behind each of eight serving lines, any delay in resupplying the lines creates a major crisis. Therefore, production must be carefully planned.

Overproduction is not a critical problem in a facility serving 50 people; 5% extra is only 2.5 more servings and these easily can be absorbed. On the other hand, 5% of 2000 is 100 portions, too large a number of portions to dump. While most dormitories feeding this number of students have adequate freezer space to accommodate this many portions of a freezable entrée, clearly 100 portions of each meal component cannot be frozen routinely. Moreover, some items do not freeze well.

Therefore, it is customary, although inadvisable, to serve salad and/or dessert items at succeeding meals until the excess is used, reducing the production quantity of the planned items accordingly. When limits of one salad or dessert are enforced, the leftover remains untouched unless the planned item is less popular. However, the planned item may run out before the end of the serving period leaving no choice to later customers. When the number of salads or desserts is unlimited, the astute students take extra portions of the leftover items as well as the new ones. They then return the uneaten portions to the scrapping line for disposal since they know that once served the item must be disposed of. Of course, difficulties in forecasting are increased unless one monitors the scrap line and watches to see if this pattern develops.

ATHLETIC DORMITORIES

Food service in athletic dormitories may be managed independently or as a unit of the general campus residence halls food service system. Problems peculiar to feeding athletes as a group are the same.   Management considerations generally differ in type and magnitude.

Athletes are commonly housed in separate dormitories because their training schedules require somewhat different hours from the regular student schedules, e.g., 6 a.m.–10 p.m. vs. 7:30 a.m.–2 a.m.   Moreover, light meals are usually required at least 3 hr prior to a competitive event in order that digestion be completed.   Consequently, fat, protein, and fiber content should be reduced. Gas formers should also be omitted.   To reduce the possibility of dehydration, several cups of liquid should be planned; soups, juices, etc., but not coffee or tea since the caffeine may stimulate the already nervous athletes.   Subsequently, late but heavy meals may be required (Am. Assoc. for Health, Physical Education and Recreation 1971). Thus, athletes' schedules partly determine the type and timing of meals.

Nutritional requirements, except for calories are the same as for other college men (Sharman 1972).   Caloric requirements for some groups of athletes are greater than for other college men because of greatly increased physical activity (Bogert *et al.* 1972). Caloric requirements vary from 4000–5000 in preseason training in long-distance swimming, track, and football. At the beginning of the training period, protein requirements are also increased but in meeting the increased caloric need, protein intake is usually adequate. A daily sweat loss of several liters of fluid is not uncommon; salt loss averages several grams. Increased fluid and salt intake is also necessary. Perhaps 3–4 gm of sodium per day may be required; since normal intake varies between 5 and 15 gm, supplementation is probably unnecessary.   However, carbonated beverages, fruit ades, salted nuts, pretzels, potato chips, etc., can be consumed ad libitum without nutritional hazard, if the diet is otherwise adequate, since the caloric requirement is so high.

The basic problems in planning menus for athletes are (a) meeting unusually high caloric requirements on a long-term basis, (b) catering to mythical needs of the athletes for specific items, and (c) catering to individual preferences. Taken together, these create a menu planning challenge!

Of the three, meeting caloric requirements is probably the easiest to meet. Once basic nutrient needs are met, calorie-rich foods can be added according to group preferences. The athletes are usually obsessed with the need to maintain superior health. They will eat quantities of the foods they associate with health.

On the other hand, many of their notions of requirements have little factual basis. Usually, concepts of need are related to some outstanding eccentricity of a famous coach, who is unlikely to have had any training in nutrition. According to the American Association for Health, Physical Education, and Recreation (1971), some of the common myths are:[1]

  (A) No candy, sweets, pastries, or cakes should be eaten during training; bread and potatoes should be restricted. (Except for the pastries these are largely carbohydrate sources to be added after other requirements are met in making up needed calories.).
  (B) No fats, no fried foods, no oily dressing should be eaten. (No basis except for precompetition meals, if diet is otherwise adequate.)
  (C) Steak is the best source of protein for athletes. (Most expensive and best liked but otherwise no better than other solid meats.)
  (D) Next to meat, eggs are the most important source of protein; two to four a day should be eaten—raw or poached, never fried or hard-cooked. (Good source of protein but cholesterol is a problem.)

Needless to say, the menu planner has to make adjustments in resolving these conflicts.

The general worker and management considerations discussed in Chap. 3 and 4 apply in planning menus for athletic dormitories. However, there are some differences that relate to whether it is independent or a unit in the residence halls food service system.

When food service in the athletic dormitory is independent of the residence halls food service system, problems in supplying foods are simplified by the elimination of system middlemen between the dietitian and the purveyor. On the other hand, residence halls food service usually employs a purchasing agent who writes specifications for foods; and the size of purchases results in both a price break and purveyor eagerness to please. Availability of foods may be more of a problem to the manager of an independent dormitory.

Another problem encountered when athletic dormitories are part of a larger system results from the difference in nutritional needs of the athletes compared to those of the general student population. A higher proportion of calorie-rich foods is served so a different set of recipes is needed. This may create a unique problem in supply of ingredients and/or items when the latter are prepared at a commissary. This supply problem may affect production scheduling.

BIBLIOGRAPHY

AM. ASSOC. FOR HEALTH, PHYSICAL EDUCATION, AND RECREATION.   1971.
    Nutrition for athletes: a handbook for coaches.   Am. Assoc. Health, Phys. Educ.,
    Recreation, Washington, D.C.

---

[1] Quoted by permission of American Association for Health, Physical Education, and Recreation.

ANDERSON, B. R. 1971. Food must sell itself to commuters. Coll. Management 6, No. 7, 38–39.

ANON. 1967A. Steak-out starts campus tradition. Coll. Univ. Business 42, No. 1, 63.

ANON. 1967B. A "trip" every Thursday boosts dining hall sales. Coll. Univ. Business 43, No. 1, 38.

ANON. 1967C. Serve late breakfast continental style. Coll. Univ. Business 42, No. 4, 88–89.

ANON. 1968. Catering with a flair is good public relations. Coll. Univ. Business 44, No. 4, 94–95.

ANON. 1969. Convenience foods, cosmopolitan atmosphere broaden dining experience. Coll. Univ. Business 47, No. 6, 61.

ANON. 1972A. College and university food services. Coll. Management 7, No. 2, 5.

ANON. 1972B. Colleges and universities are biggest eaters. Coll. Management 7, No. 2, 14.

ANON. 1972C. Into organic foods. Coll. Management 7, No. 2, 14.

BOGERT, J., BRIGGS, G. M., and CALLOWAY, D. H. 1972. Nutrition and physical work performance. In Nutrition and Physical Fitness. W. B. Saunders Co., Philadelphia.

CAPPADONNA, M. V. 1972. Student vegetarianism takes root at UM. Coll. Univ. Business 52, No. 3, 52–53.

ECKSTEIN, E. F. 1972. Food preferences of minority students at UC Berkeley. (Unpublished.)

FRIESE, J. C. 1971. Continuous feeding closes hunger gap while opening up employee efficiency. Coll. Univ. Business 50, No. 6, 62–63.

GOODFRIEND, H. 1970. "Hot lunch" syndrome may be a cold comfort if students won't eat the food. Coll. Univ. Business 49, No. 4, 66, 70, 72, 74, 77, 81.

HAZELTINE, K. 1970. Urban food service must meet students halfway—before they take their appetites elsewhere. Coll. Univ. Business 48, No. 5, 94, 96, 98.

KENNEDY, B. M. 1958. Food preferences of college women. J. Am. Dietet. Assoc. 34, 501–506.

KNICKREHM, M. E., COTNER, C. G., and KENDRICK, J. G. 1969. Acceptance of menu items by college students. J. Am. Dietet. Assoc. 55, 117–120.

LAMB, M. W., ADAMS, V. J., and GODFREY, J. 1954. Food preferences of college women. J. Am. Dietet. Assoc. 30, 1120–1125.

MIRONE, L., and WHITEHEAD, E. L. 1957. Milk drinking by college students. J. Am. Dietet. Assoc. 33, 1266–1269.

MYERS, M. L., SULLIVAN, E. M., and STARE, F. J. 1963. Food consumed by university students. J. Am. Dietet. Assoc. 43, 336–343.

NUGENT, M. 1965. Help students expand food preferences. Coll. Univ. Business 38, No. 2, 59.

ODLAND, L. M., PAGE, L., and GUILD, L. P. 1955. Nutrient intakes and food habits of Montana students. J. Am. Dietet. Assoc. 31, 1134–1142.

SHARMAN, I. M. 1972. Food to run. Nutr. Food Sci. 29, 2–4.

CHAPTER 12

Menu Planning for Industrial Cafeteria Customers

The needs of workers purchasing meals at in-plant cafeterias vary according to (a) the amount and type of physical activity required by the job, (b) the amount of money available for purchasing the meal, when not provided as a part of wages, (c) the meal to be purchased, and (d) variety, since they are long-term consumers. Other considerations in planning menus include (a) length of service period, (b) length of the employees' lunch period compared to the amount of time required to obtain and consume the meal, (c) policies regarding pairing of items as alternate menu choices, expected run-out time for entrées, and (d) catering load.

RESPONSIBILITY IN MEETING EMPLOYEES' NEEDS

During World War II a number of studies indicated that industrial work performance was below the expected standard due to chronic failure to meet nutritional needs (Simonson et al. 1948). In-plant cafeterias were instituted in major plants to fill this need. The nutritive needs of a specific group depend on (a) age distribution, (b) sex, (c) amount and type of job-related activity. Moreover, employees' concept of the type and quantity of food necessary to meet physiological needs varies widely.

Factory workers engaged in heavy physical labor require and expect heavy meals—meat and potatoes, casseroles, heavy soups, etc. On the other hand, clerical workers (usually women), light assembly workers, and executives who are largely sedentary, require and expect a light lunch—soup-sandwich combination, salad plate, etc. When both groups must be served from a common cafeteria counter menu selections must contain several alternatives for each group.

Over the years, nutritionists have proposed various standards for evaluating the nutritional adequacy of in-plant cafeteria meals. Recently, Lease et al. (1963) stated that from the standpoint of public health, the lunch should contain a fair share of protein, vitamins, and minerals in proportion to caloric content. Accordingly, if the meal is planned to provide $\frac{1}{2}$ of the calories it should provide $\frac{1}{2}$ of the recommended quantities of other nutrients as well.

Originally, in order to encourage consumption of meals in the cafeteria, food was served at no out-of-pocket cost to the workers; however, meals were included as part of the wages for tax purposes. For various reasons, workers today (except food service workers in some institutions) are paid higher wages and purchase their own meals. Since there may be many personal demands on a scarce financial resource to which individuals assign different priorities, a variable amount of money is available for purchasing lunch. The mean amount available determines the mean check average. This, in turn, determines the range and selection of items to be offered.

Variety within the meal and among days is a major consideration since industrial workers are a long-term consumer group that eat at the cafeteria day in and day out. The mechanics of KIND control are discussed in Chap. 6. Monotony-breakers are also important in creating interest in the food service. Common monotony-breakers include (a) foreign meals with appropriate music and decor, (b) loss-leader feature items, in which a popular item is sold at or below cost in order to attract customers, and (c) seasonal specials.

OTHER CONSIDERATIONS

In some industrial plants that operate on a 24-hr basis with 3 shifts, the cafeteria may be expected to remain open for 12 hr or more. In this case, soup, sandwiches, and short order items are usually available continuously. However, since the greatest volume of business is usually at lunch time and demand is quite light at other meals, hours of service usually have been reduced. Instead, a variety of vending machines have been installed to meet the needs of workers on other shifts.

The next factor to be considered is the length of the workers' lunch hour and the amount of time required to obtain and consume the meal. Although the length of the lunch period is fixed, the amount of time required to obtain lunch is a function of (a) distance of workplace from the cafeteria; long distance means travel time reduces eating time; (b) whether meal periods are staggered so that only a part of the work force lines up for meals at any one time; (c) percentage participation—the higher the participation, the longer the lines, all other things being equal; (d) average seat turnover time—depends on whether all workers have the same amount of time for lunch; and (e) the actual length of the line and its speed. When time is relatively short, the number of item choices must be reduced in order to maximize speed in selecting a lunch. However, if seat turnover is too slow some workers will be standing holding their lunch. If total time to obtain the lunch is too great the employees will bring brown-bag lunches to be consumed at their desks. A common means of accommodating workers in this case is to send a mobile truck to each building to provide hot foods.

Policies regarding the pairing of alternate choices can be important in determining customer satisfaction and production control. When a highly acceptable and a highly unacceptable item are paired, the acceptable item runs out first. Consequently, later customers have no choice. What is management's responsibility? Is the same amount of choice obligatory for customers whose lunch period is at the beginning of the service period and those whose scheduled period is toward the end? What does this mean in terms of distributing the work load?

Commonly, pairing of items is random and intuitively constrained; customer acceptability is highly variable, and production forecasting unreliable. Clearly, a better strategy can be devised. Another strategy that has been employed is to rank entrées, etc. Pairs of items of approximately equal rank are then used as alternate items. This strategy has the advantage that for popular items, production requirements are about evenly divided which distributes the production load. Also, the probability of running out of either alternative is somewhat lower. Unfortunately, from the consumer standpoint, this strategy also occasionally results in a forced choice between two unacceptable alternatives as when lamb and liver are paired. Moreover, it is probable that the total number of servings sold is reduced by a significant number of people who do not select either item.

A more reasonable strategy is to pair items for acceptability, deleting pairs whose items are marginally acceptable, i.e., unacceptable to $1/3$ of the group. Such items should occasionally be offered as a third choice, if the total quantity that can be sold is great enough to be economically feasible.

Most in-plant food service units cater some company functions. The frequency and types are dependent on the facilities available. If a plush executive dining room and a skilled chef are available, executive dinner parties may be frequent, especially if the plant is not located near an excellent restaurant. Typical club menus are customarily served.

Small office parties usually require coffee and doughnuts, cake, or cookies. Occasionally tea sandwiches, etc., are required. Menu planning is minimal but in planning the overall production work load an allowance for this production requirement must be made.

Annual events such as the Christmas Party and the Summer Picnic are sometimes catered by the food service unit. These present some special problems in production, scheduling, and transport that must be considered in planning the menu.

When production must be planned around the normal work load, items should be selected that can be (a) preprepared ahead and frozen or (b) served with minimal preparation. Otherwise, tension increases and quality decreases.

Scheduling of men, materials, and machines requires careful coordination. Extra personnel are usually required in order that the regular food service personnel not become so fatigued that they are unable to attend the event. A material problem, such as ingredient or subassembly, should be anticipated and minimized. The abnormally large quantities of produce, meat, etc., may exceed walk-in capacity unless delivery and storage are carefully planned. Extra lead time for prepreparation is also necessary because of the extra quantities. Moreover, extra racks of already completed subassemblies may require storage space in the walk-in; the volume requirements can be estimated. Furthermore, most entrées selected for catered events require cooking or reheating in the oven, e.g., roast beef, baked ham, roast chicken or turkey. Therefore, cafeteria meals should be planned with entrées that can be prepared in the steam-jacketed kettles, e.g., spaghetti, chili, curried lamb, etc., in order to free scarce oven space.

Transport of the prepared foods to the service facility also presents some unfamiliar problems. Meats are commonly transported in hotel pans; if no oven is available for holding and/or reheating, time is critical unless the meat can be served cold. Salads are usually packed into covered plastic tubs and present no special problems; serving utensils must be included. Cooked vegetables can be cooked about half done and placed in insulated beverage servers; they will finish cooking by retained heat during transit. Desserts and breads are usually no problem, except to prevent staling. Items such as cupcakes, cookies, and doughnuts are easy to handle because there is no cut edge to dry out.

VENDED FOOD

In many industrial plants the traditional cafeteria has been replaced by vending machines that largely provide calories and stimulants since these are very profitable. In other cases, the cafeteria prepares and supplies the company-owned vending machines. This makes a greater variety of foods possible; a menu is often prepared from the master menu. Items are selected to (a) utilize leftovers, (b) duplicate cafeteria foods, or (c) supplement cafeteria items. The alternative policy set is determined by the specific situational requirements.

BIBLIOGRAPHY

LEASE, E. J., ANDERSON, H. S., MALPHRUS, R. K., and LEASE, J. G. 1963. Industrial lunches and public health. J. Am. Dietet. Assoc. *43*, 34–38.
SIMONSON, E., BROZEK, J., and KEYS, A. 1948. Effect of meals on visual performance and fatigue. J. Appl. Physiol. *1*, 270.

CHAPTER 13

Menu Planning for Adults in State Institutions

Inmates of state institutions are generally long-term consumers—either prisoners or mental patients. While public sentiment favors a least-cost diet, nutritive needs of the inmates should be met. In some states, a standard ration allowance is used as a basis for determining the distinct types and quantities of food to be used in planning menus in all institutions.

RESPONSIBILITY IN PLANNING FOR THE NEEDS OF INMATES

Inmates in state institutions are a long-term totally captive consumer group. Therefore, menus must be planned to provide all nutrients in necessary quantities (Table 13.1). Unless the food is consumed in quantities planned, it does not meet the nutritional needs of the inmates and nutritional calculations reduce to a paper exercise. Therefore, acceptability of the food items and combinations is fundamental in meeting nutritional needs.

Although in general, prisoners and mental patients come from all religious and ethnic groups, the populations mix at a particular institution will reflect the distribution in the local population. Thus, religious and ethnic concentration will vary among institutions. However, there is some evidence that minority groups are more than proportionally represented. Menu offerings should reflect the food habits and preferences of the predominant groups.

Prisoners and mental patients are subject to the same chronic diseases which require modified diets as the general American population. When the number of modified diets to be prepared is large, the major modifications should be planned in preparing the master menu (see Chap. 7). Otherwise, item substitution to accommodate individual needs should suffice.

PLANNING PRISON MEALS

Rector (1929) stated, "It is the consensus of opinion among prison officials that more serious disciplinary problems arise over dissatisfaction with the menu than from any other cause." Nevertheless, until recently the needs of prisoners were largely ignored; the attitude seemed to be, "If they don't eat it, it's their problem." But in recent years the rash of sit-ins, hunger strikes, and other demonstrations in the dining room has forced management to plan more acceptable meals. The report by Rector (1929) also pointed out a number of ideas which are still relevant and should guide menu planning:[1]

The feeding of prisoners is a matter of first importance. It involves not

---

[1] Quoted with permission of Osborne Associates, Inc.

TABLE 13.1

NUTRITIONAL REQUIREMENTS (RDA)[1] OF ADULTS

	Age[2] (Yr) From Up To	Weight (Kg)	Weight (Lb)	Height (Cm)	Height (In.)	Kcal	Protein (Gm)	Fat-Soluble Vitamins Vitamin A Activity (IU)	Vitamin D (IU)	Vitamin E Activity (IU)	Water-Soluble Vitamins Ascorbic Acid (Mg)	Folacin[3] (Mg)	Niacin (Mg Equiv)[4]	Ribo-flavin (Mg)	Thiamine (Mg)	Vitamin B6 (Mg)	Vitamin B12 (µg)	Minerals Calcium (Gm)	Phosphorus (Gm)	Iodine (µg)	Iron (Mg)	Magnesium (Mg)
Males	18–22	67	147	175	69	2,800	60	5,000	400	30	60	0.4	18	1.6	1.4	2.0	5	0.8	0.8	140	10	400
	22–35	70	154	175	69	2,800	65	5,000	—	30	60	0.4	18	1.7	1.4	2.0	5	0.8	0.8	140	10	350
	35–55	70	154	173	68	2,600	65	5,000	—	30	60	0.4	17	1.7	1.3	2.0	5	0.8	0.8	125	10	350
	55–75+	70	154	171	67	2,400	65	5,000	400	30	60	0.4	14	1.7	1.2	2.0	6	0.8	0.8	110	10	350
Females	18–22	58	128	163	64	2,000	55	5,000	—	25	55	0.4	13	1.5	1.0	2.0	5	0.8	0.8	100	18	350
	22–35	58	128	163	64	2,000	55	5,000	—	25	55	0.4	13	1.5	1.0	2.0	5	0.8	0.8	100	18	300
	35–55	58	128	160	63	1,850	55	5,000	—	25	55	0.4	13	1.5	1.0	2.0	5	0.8	0.8	90	18	300
	55–75+	58	128	157	62	1,700	55	5,000	—	25	55	0.4	13	1.5	1.0	2.0	6	0.8	0.8	80	10	300

Source: Food and Nutrition Board, National Academy of Sciences–National Research Council.

[1] The allowance levels are intended to cover individual variations among most normal persons as they live in the United States under usual environmental stresses. The recommended allowances can be attained with a variety of common foods, providing other nutrients for which human requirements have been less well defined.

[2] Entries on lines for age range 22–35 yr represent the reference man and woman at age 22. All other entries represent allowances for the midpoint of the specified age range.

[3] The folacin allowances refer to dietary sources as determined by *Lactobacillus casei* assay. Pure forms of folacin may be effective in doses less than ¼ of the RDA.

[4] Niacin equivalents include dietary sources of the vitamin itself plus 1 mg equivalent for each 60 mg of dietary tryptophan.

only the health but efficiency and morale of the prison population. . . .
Exigencies of the situation make it impossible to give any consideration
to individual likes and dislikes for food. . . . If monotony of diet is to be
avoided—and it is highly important that it should be—there must be careful planning of the menus. . . . Finally the preparation of food must be
such as to present a balanced diet sufficient for the physiological needs
of the inmates under the changed environment in which they are placed.

Many inmates are subjected to radical change in their dietary habits
upon beginning prison life. Some who have been accustomed to finer
foods and dietary luxuries find the plain food and manner of serving unappetizing. It is hard to adjust themselves to the changed conditions. For
another group comprised of the floaters and nomadic type of individuals
who have never had a settled habitation or method of living, the prison
may offer the opportunity for better fare and in greater abundance than
that to which they have been accustomed. Between these two extremes
lie other groups whose reaction to the prison dietary regime is less pro-
nounced, but of sufficient emphasis to make it necessary to plan carefully
for the best service possible with the facilities and equipment at hand.

Generally, prison food is plain and monotonous, reflecting very tight budgetary restrictions. The prison farm often supplies many of the basic ingredients
at no cost, which helps somewhat. A nonselective menu is served almost universally in order to reduce cost and work, although prisoners usually supply
the preparation labor. Moreover, a basic pattern menu has been developed in
some states (Table 13.2) in order to facilitate ingredient supply, control costs,
and meet nutritive and acceptability requirements of inmates.

In selecting menu items the menu planner has some unique considerations to
deal with. The prisoners often regard the food as inedible and refuse to eat.
Poor food is regarded as evidence of a conspiracy against them. This response is
prompted by a mental set that regards everything with suspicion and distrust.
Furthermore, off-color or off-flavor food is regarded as unwholesome, probably
poisonous. And, if the dietary staples, e.g., bread, rice, potatoes, or tortillas,
etc., are not selected with the particular group in mind, the prisoners may feel
that they are being starved to death. Thus, in order to plan acceptable meals,
the menu planner needs to be mindful of the unique frame of reference of the
prisoners.

Caloric needs of the prisoners vary widely, from about 2200 for the sedentary
prisoner confined to his cell to 4000 or more for the one sentenced to hard
labor. Menus must be planned to accommodate these differences in needs.

PLANNING MENTAL HOSPITAL MEALS

Until the 1950's, each state maintained large mental hospitals with populations in the thousands. A combination of more effective drug therapy and a
philosophy of releasing patients for home and community out-patient care
have resulted in a drastic reduction in the number of institutionalized mental
patients.

TABLE 13.2

FS-VI-01—BASIC PATTERN MENU FOR ADULT GENERAL INMATE, STATE OF CALIFORNIA, DEPARTMENT OF CORRECTIONS

Breakfast

1. One fruit—variety during the week:
    3 meals with citrus fruit
    4 meals with dried fruit
    (A maximum of two meals of prunes shall be served.)
2. Cereal—variety during the week:
    1 meal of ready-to-eat prepared cereal, 3–6 meals of cooked cereal
    (Oatmeal to be used a maximum of two meals a week.)
3. Entrée—variety during the week:
    2 meals with eggs
    3 meals with hot cakes, french toast, or bakery products
    1 meal of potatoes or meat hash—(6-oz portion)
4. Bread
5. Margarine
6. Coffee
7. Milk—4-oz for cooked cereal, 6-oz for dry cereal
8. Sugar for cereal and coffee
9. Syrup, honey, jelly, or jam as entrée indicates

Dinner or Supper[1]

1. Meat, fish, or poultry—once a day—variety during the week:[2]

	Lb
1 meal frankfurters	1/4
1 meal stew—boneless meat or short ribs	1/5
1 meal roast	0.40 boned weight
1 meal fish	0.33 fillet
1 meal hamburger or sausage	1/4 boneless
1 meal meatloaf	1/4 boneless
1 meal steak, roast or chops	0.40 boneless

2. Potato or substitute
3. Vegetable, cooked
4. Salad or raw vegetable relish
5. Dessert or fruit[3]
6. Bread
7. Milk or tea

Supper or Lunch[1]

1. Main dish—variety during the week:
    3 meals of beans
    3 meals of rice
    2 meals of macaroni pastes
    1 meal meat and potato
2. Salad
3. Hot vegetables
4. Bread
5. Margarine
6. Dessert or fruit[3]
7. Coffee

Source: Adapted from Chap. 6 of *Food Ration Analysis*, State of California, Dept. of Corrections with permission of Charles E. Dubois, R.D., Departmental Food Administrator.
[1] Soup shall be served once a day, either noon or night. A maximum of 10 meals a week of potatoes shall be served. Hot bread or hot rolls shall be served once a day or a minimum of 4 days a week.
[2] Poultry once a month.
[3] Bakery and Dessert Schedule—Variety during the week: 1 meal with pie, 2 meals with cookies, 2 meals with cake, 2 meals with pudding, 2 meals with flavored gelatin, 5 meals with canned or fresh fruit.

Mental patients are not emotionally inert. Like other people they respond to food items and manner of service according to cultural, religious, and personal cues, even if they repress the response because of mental agony. Because food symbolizes love and acceptance and it is consumed in a social setting, mealtime takes on added importance for the mental patient. Food may provide the means of reaching some patients; in any case, it is important in the total treatment of the mental patient (Ross 1962).

Modern mental institutions often provide cafeteria service for the majority of inmates, since drug therapy enables them to function reasonably well. One mental hospital reported instituting selective menus in anticipation of benefits to the patient in relearning to make decisions about what he wished to eat that would be similar to those required in normal living (Ralli 1957).

After instituting the selective menu the dietary staff noted the following: (a) many psychiatric patients needed training in making choices, otherwise they unthinkingly selected the same items as the person ahead of them in line, (b) supervision is needed in controlling the number of items and portion size, and (c) some patients need assistance in selecting items if the line is to move at an acceptable pace. Patient response was gratifying; patients were more content and responsible.

On the other hand, Armstrong (1972) reported a study implying benefits from serving family-style meals rather than cafeteria-style meals. She concluded that family-style meals provide opportunity for increased rapport and understanding between patients and staff as a result of the informal interaction at mealtime. It is known that certain types of patients show typical eating habits, e.g., paranoid patients may be suspicious of the wholesomeness of the food, schizoid patients prefer to eat alone, regressed patients are often untidy so spill much food, depressed patients may refuse food, and immature patients may grossly overeat. Staff observations of eating habits may provide increased understanding of patients' problems thus enhancing therapeutic efforts.

Both cafeteria-style service and family-style service can be used to therapeutic advantage with mental patients. Perhaps both should be used; family service with new or difficult patients and cafeteria-style service with those needing to build self-confidence in ability to make decisions prior to release.

In planning menus for mental patients both the general consumer and general management considerations discussed in Chap. 2 and 4 are applicable. Color, texture, shape, and flavor contrasts are important in creating interest in the food and in increasing its general acceptability. Common preparation methods, items, and combinations should be used for the security provided. Totally new items may be upsetting; some patients may react with anger and fear.

Although a selective menu may be planned for the majority, a set menu and ward or room service is still necessary for some patients. Modified diets of all types may be required. These should all be planned from the master menu.

As in prison systems, a food plan based on a standard ration requirement that will meet nutritive needs, is often used to simplify procurement of ingredients and to reduce costs. One such plan has been reported by Flack (1955).

BIBLIOGRAPHY

ARMSTRONG, R. G.   1972.   Staff-shared, family-style luncheon in a mental hospital—therapeutic advantages. J. Am. Dietet. Assoc. *60*, 323–325.

FLACK, K. E.   1955.   Administrative problems in a large hospital system. J. Am. Dietet. Assoc. *31*, 497–500.

RALLI, F. M.   1957.   Selective menus in a psychiatric hospital. J. Am. Dietet. Assoc. *33*, 1172, 1174.

RECTOR, L.   1929.   Health and Medical Service in American Prisons and Reformatories. National Society of Penal Information, New York.

ROSS, M.   1962.   Food in the mental hospital. J. Am. Dietet. Assoc. *40*, 318–320.

CHAPTER 14

Menu Planning for Restaurant Customers[1]

Restaurant customers differ from institutional consumers in that they are not captive; therefore, the restaurant must build a reputation that ensures repeat sales and sufficient volume. Restaurants are business organizations whose major purposes are to (a) make a profit and (b) to ensure continuance of the business by means of sustained sales. These basic factors change the priorities assigned to the various basic principles discussed in Chap. 1 to 6; nonetheless, they are still applicable. Additional differences will be noted below according to the type of restaurant operation, i.e., table service, cafeteria or buffet, and short-order takeout.

Generally, the complexity of the menu planning problem is determined by the category of restaurant, the expected check average, and the image to be projected (Fig. 14.1). Although there is some overlap in check average and service pace, the menu planning problems are quite distinct as are the production problems. Menu planning is both an art and a science. The descriptive information below reviews the scientific aspects; the menu planner must supply artistic food senses.

TABLE SERVICE RESTAURANT

Restaurants offering table service usually have more complex menus than do other types of restaurants. Complexity, in general, follows the expected check average which is adjusted to cover the added costs of waiter service and atmosphere. As a group, restaurants in this category range from those with minimal service, that expect moderate turnover and volume of business during the meal hours, to those with maximum service and expecting little or no turnover and a small volume of business. In the latter case, the mean check average must be large in order for a sufficient profit to be realized.

Each restaurant or chain selects a theme and creates an image such as French, Italian, Mexican, Polynesian, organic foods, etc. Decor, advertising, menu content, and menu format are designed to provide harmonious reinforcement of the image. This is important. The customer will be more likely to respond positively to the atmosphere of the dining experience if the menu selections reinforce the image of the restaurant, assuming of course, that the image is attractive. Thus, specific classes of food are excluded from consideration in menu planning and other classes are emphasized. Within these limits, the basic principles relating to aesthetics apply.

---

[1] A list of pertinent trade journals and Americanized ethnic cookbooks is given in the Appendix.

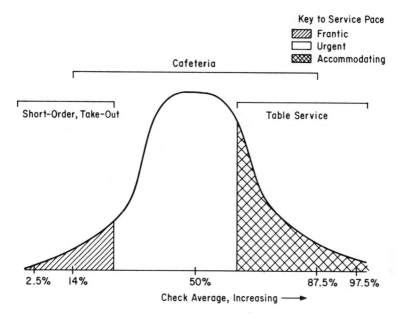

FIG. 14.1. MODEL FOR RESTAURANT SERVICE AS RELATED TO CHECK AVERAGE

Production problems are a limiting factor in planning menus for table service restaurants. The astute waiter senses when the customer will be ready for the next course and times the production order so that preparation will be completed at the desired time. Well-developed judgment is required to plan the trade-off between (a) ordering items too soon and risking loss of quality and (b) ordering items too late and risking the ire of customers kept waiting between courses. To ease this problem alternate items should be selected that require approximately equal cooking or finishing time, if partial preparation is feasible.

In planning menus for restaurants with table service, three basic types of menu pattern are possible (a) a la carte, (b) table d'hote, and (c) a combination of the two. Each presents different problems in menu planning.

A la carte menus are lists of various alternatives for each meal component or course. The customer selects the number of courses he desires and specific items according to impulse, preferences, and funds available. The entrées are selected first; items for other courses are selected for compatibility with the entrées. Items are selected for each course according to (a) preferences of the expected target customer group, (b) price—a range is commonly provided, and (c) specialty items to attract impulse selection. In general, the list of entrées is prominently displayed with larger and/or bolder type and additional description. An extensive descriptive treatment of menu formats to enhance marketing potential is contained in a book by Seaberg (1971).

Table d'hote menus are set menus; the customer has no choice of items. In some cases only one menu is served each day; in this case it is usually posted. As soon as the customer is seated, the first course is served and succeeding courses follow in planned order. In other cases, the restaurant offers several alternate 'package' meals each of which is a set menu with stated items for each meal component. Usually, the alternate menus represent different price ranges as well as types of entrées and number of courses (other items may be essentially the same). The customer thus selects his meal according to his preference for the entrée, price range, and quantity of food.

The combination menus offer a limited number of table d'hote menus plus an assortment of a la carte items. Usually there is some overlap as some of the a la carte items are included in the table d'hote meals. Portions served a la carte are generally larger. This type of menu provides the diner with the greatest number of alternatives and is often used in restaurants serving foreign foods. This enables the unfamiliar diner to select a menu of complementary foods and the experienced diner to select favorites and/or try new items.

Another factor that determines menu offerings is the pattern of patronage. If the customers are transient, the same menu can be used every day, with minor changes for seasonal variation. Whereas, if the same customers frequent the restaurant daily or on specific days of the week, greater variety will be required. Three strategies are commonly employed in such cases: (a) a different menu is provided for each day of the week—a cycle menu may be used, (b) a longer list of real alternatives is provided, or (c) a moderately long list of alternatives is provided with daily specialty items as clip-ons.

With this descriptive framework for the variations of the menu planning task defined, the mechanics of menu item selection will be considered next. General principles are outlined in Chap. 6.

Selection of Table d'Hote Items (See Fig. 14.2, 14.3)

The first task is to determine the number of items that will be adequate to satisfy consumer preferences and allow a sufficient price range. The second task is to select the entrée base for the menu—the item or items expected to provide the greatest profit. The decision is a trade-off between high volume of low-profit items and low volume of high-profit items. Next, additional entrées are selected to appeal to various segments of the customer group, whether ethnic, economic, or health need. The successful selection takes into account competitors' offerings as well.

Having selected the entrées, complementary items for other courses are selected for each of the entrées. Alternatively, one may list essentially the same items for the other courses for each of the menus. For example, Baked Potato with Sour Cream Dressing, Buttered Peas, Tossed Salad, and Vanilla Ice Cream may accompany all of the entrées. The high general acceptance of these items has resulted in overusage among restaurants. Other simple but appropriate

Symbol   Interpretation

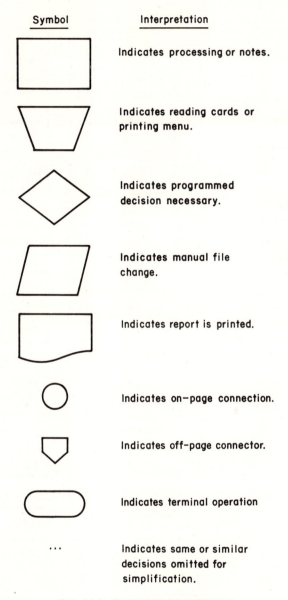

Indicates processing or notes.

Indicates reading cards or
printing menu.

Indicates programmed
decision necessary.

Indicates manual file
change.

Indicates report is printed.

Indicates on–page connection.

Indicates off-page connector.

Indicates terminal operation

Indicates same or similar
decisions omitted for
simplification.

FIG. 14.2. FLOW CHART SYMBOLS

items should be used to attract patronage. These items should be selected to
reinforce the image of the restaurant, thus increasing the positive responses to
dining.

In electing to use a table d'hote menu one immediately simplifies purchasing

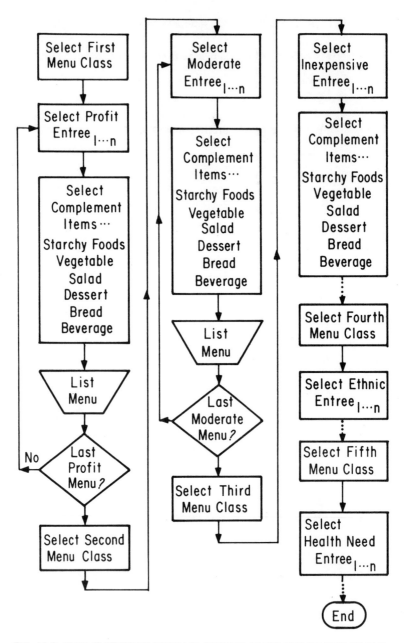

FIG. 14.3. TABLE SERVICE MENU PLANNING FLOW CHART FOR TABLE
d' HOTE MENUS

and inventory tasks. The limited number of offerings require only a limited number of ingredients. Moreover, production requirements are reduced as some items can be prepared in large batches thus reducing the per unit production time.

Selection of a la Carte Menu Items

A la carte menus are selective menus. The a la carte menu is more difficult to plan than the table d'hote menu because it is usually more extensive and emphasis must be given to selected items in each section. The first task is to determine the number of entrées and variety of preparation methods to be employed, such as charcoal broiling, French frying, roasting, etc. Next, one must determine the price range. Then, in keeping with the image of the restaurant, one must determine the kinds of meat, if any, to be served such as beef, pork, fish, etc., or specialty items such as rabbit, squid, abalone, etc. Specific items are then selected so as to obtain a distribution among preparation methods, price categories, and kinds of meat, etc. Ideas for entrées may be obtained from many sources: Atkinson (1971), Culinary Institute of America (1971), Fowler *et al.* (1970), Gancel (1969), and Saulnier (not dated), School of Hotel Administration (1967), Simon and Howe (1970), and Wenzel (1966).

The next section to be planned is usually the appetizers and/or soups. The first decision is what categories to include, that is soups, fruit and/or vegetable juice cocktails, seafood cocktails, assorted relishes, or specialty items.

The selection of soups is usually less than five. When more than three are listed, a separate section featuring the soups is usually established. Types are determined by the image of the restaurant, e.g., bisques and chowders predominate at seafood restaurants, specialty soups such as Minestrone are found at Italian restaurants and Sizzling Rice Soup is one of the distinguishing features of Northern Chinese cuisine, etc. High status restaurants often feature chilled soups such as Jellied Consomme, or Vichysoisse. When Soup de Jour (soup of the day) is the only soup listed, it is included with the appetizers. Ald (1969) is a good source for soup recipes.

Standard fruit, vegetable juice, and seafood cocktails are commonly listed. These include fruit cups, tomato or V-8 juice, crab or shrimp cocktails. However, specialty items may be featured in nationality restaurants, e.g., Sashimi (raw fish) in Japanese restaurants, antipasto in Italian restaurants, assorted pastries in Chinese restaurants, etc. Ideas for appetizers are available from many sources (Atkinson 1971; Culinary Institute of America 1971; Fowler *et al.* 1970; Gancel 1969; Saulnier (not dated); School of Hotel Administration 1967; Simon and Howe 1970; and Wenzel 1966).

The third section to be planned is usually the starchy foods and/or vegetables if these are not a part of the entrée. These items may be grouped together or separately depending on the number of items in each category.

Here again, the image of the restaurant determines the types and extent of offerings. A steak and roast beef or seafood restaurant usually only offers baked potatoes or French fries. Few vegetables, if any, are offered. On the other hand, a Northern Chinese restaurant often lists several types each of noodles and dumplings plus fried and steamed rice. The listings for vegetables are usually extensive.

The fourth section to be planned is the salad section. The first decision is whether the selection shall be limited to side salads or shall include salad plates as entrées. When the offerings are limited to side salads, often tossed salad with assorted dressings, cole slaw, potato salad, or fruit and cottage cheese salad are the only alternatives. However, when salad plates are featured, the range is increased. It often includes meat, fish, exotic fruit, and/or other ingredients in massive artistic arrangements. Ideas for side salads and salad plate combinations are available from many sources such as Atkinson (1971), Culinary Institute of America (1971), Fowler et al. (1970), Gancel (1969), Saulnier (not dated), School of Hotel Administration (1967) Simon and Howe (1970), and Wenzel (1966).

The fifth section to be planned is the dessert section. The first decision concerns the type and extent of offerings; this depends on the price the target customer group is expected to pay for a meal and the image of the restaurant. The meagre and unimaginative listing of chocolate, strawberry, and vanilla ice cream supplemented with orange sherbet is customary in moderate-price restaurants. Others in this price class add pie or cake for variety. These restaurants, as a whole, would be more successful if they were more imaginative, establishing a "better" moderate price restaurant than competitors. On the other hand, high status restaurants commonly serve elaborate, rich, and often flaming desserts. Listings of dessert ideas can be obtained from Atkinson (1971), Crane (1964), Culinary Institute of America (1971), Fowler et al. (1970), Gancel (1969), Kaufman (1968), Saulnier (not dated), School of Hotel Administration (1967), Simon and Howe (1970), and Wenzel (1966).

The sixth meal component to be planned is the bread item. In some cases the bread item is served routinely; two assortments are commonly served (a) crackers, bread sticks, and hard rolls or (b) hot soft rolls and/or quick breads. In other restaurants, breads are featured as part of the restaurant's image. Commercially-prepared variety breads, homemade quick breads, or individual loaves of bread may be selected. Local availability of quality products or production capability limit the variety that can be featured. Ideas for bread items can be obtained from a variety of sources such as Amendola (1960), Atkinson (1971), Culinary Institute of America (1971), Fowler et al. (1970), Gancel (1969), Saulnier (not dated), School of Hotel Administration (1967), Simon and Howe (1970), and Wenzel (1966).

The last section to be planned is the list of beverages, both nonalcoholic and alcoholic. These are listed separately on the menu. Customarily, the nonalcoholic beverages are listed at the bottom of the menu. Coffee, tea, milk, and a decafeinated coffee are minimal offerings. However, a variety of teas such as Jasmine, Earl Grey, Russian Caravan, etc., are featured in some restaurants. Similarly, a variety of coffees such as Columbian, Kona, Espresso, Turkish Coffee, etc., may be served. Ideas for increasing the variety of coffees may be obtained from the Coffee Brewing Center, 120 Wall St., New York 10005.

The selection of alcoholic beverages requires many decisions. Standard cocktails may be offered. Or, wines and beers may be selected to complement menu offerings or local tastes. A separate Wine List may be provided or suggested wines may be listed opposite the entrées (Seaberg 1971). Dessert wines and cordials may be included in the dessert listing (Seaberg 1971). Information about wine service can be obtained from the Wine Institute and a number of other sources (Brodner *et al*. 1962; Grossman 1959; Haszonics and Barratt 1963; Schoonmaker 1964; Trader Vic 1948; Voegele and Woolley 1961).

The major difficulty in planning a la carte menus is to provide adequate variety for each course without creating expensive or difficult production problems. One means of reducing the production problem is to limit the cuts of meat and/ or the basic types of sauces used; treatment and seasonings are used to produce variety. Similar means are employed for other courses. While the gourmet appreciates fine differences among items, the average customer does not distinguish such differences and may feel tricked if the price differential is significant. Figure 14.4 depicts the process of item selection.

Selection of Items for Combination Menus

The problem of selecting complete table d'hote menus plus an array of a la carte items is complex and challenging. The first task is to select the table d'hote menus; 3 or 4 generally suffice. As these are the focal point of the menu they must be appealing, varied, easily produced, as well as profitable given the expected volume of sales. The basic considerations discussed above apply. However, it is also necessary that the entrées be selected so that the customer does *not* infer that they are reworked or disguised leftovers. For this reason, meatloaves, one-dish casseroles and the like are usually avoided. Figure 14.5 is a flowchart depicting the process of item selection.

The second task is to select the a la carte items for each course. The a la carte items must be competitive, not just names listed to fill menu space. Also, they must increase variety by appealing to specific customer groups and be amenable to batch preparation or production with minimal loss of quality and/or shortorder finish preparation. Selection of such items is discussed at length above.

The table d'hote portion of the menu may be directed to special segments of the customer group. One such group is weight-watchers and in order to avoid charges of false labeling, the menu planner should list the calories contributed by each menu item as well as the total for the meal. Many fashionable menus for weight-watchers are not actually low in calories, except that portion sizes are reduced. The most reliable caloric values for American foods can be obtained from (Church and Church 1970; Watt and Merrill 1963). Vegetarian, low salt, and low cholesterol menus might attract significant patronage.

Children's menus are often table d'hote; usually 2 or 3 alternate menus are

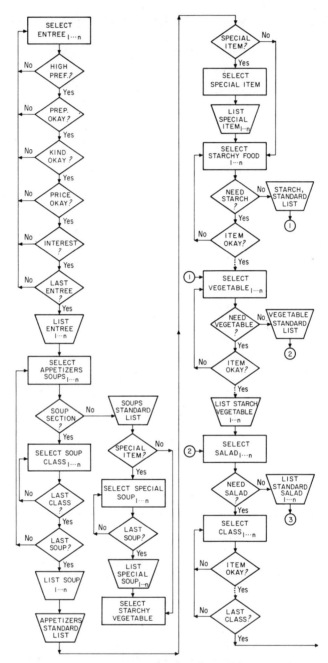

FIG. 14.4. TABLE SERVICE MENU PLANNING FLOW CHART FOR A LA CARTE
MENUS

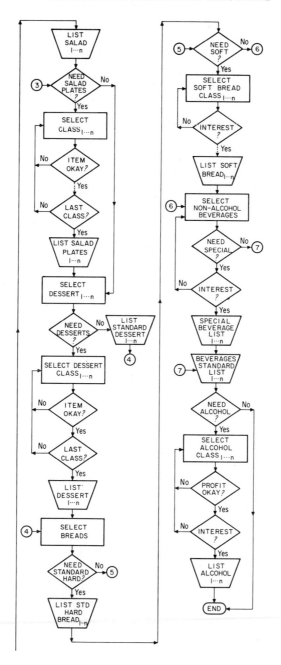

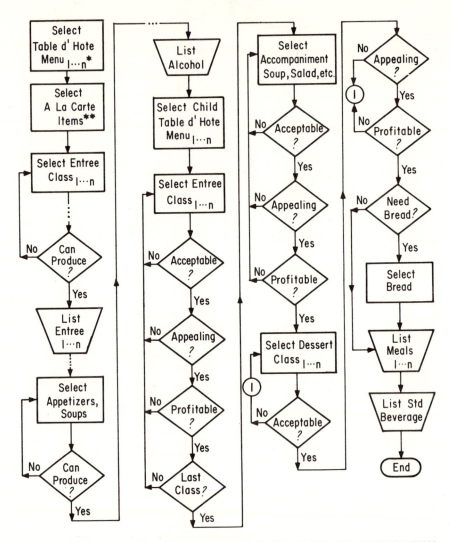

FIG. 14.5. TABLE SERVICE MENU PLANNING FLOW CHART FOR COMBINATION
MENU

*See Fig. 14.3 for details.
**See Fig. 14.4 for details.

listed. Hamburgers, French fries, etc., are usually offered on the menu regardless of the price class of the restaurant. When the a la carte items are well-accepted by children, addition of a price column for a child's portion may eliminate the need for a special menu. Generalizations concerning children's foodways are discussed in Chap. 10.

CAFETERIA OR BUFFET SERVICE

Selective menus offering numerous choices to the consumer in terms of both meal components and alternative items are characteristic of these types of service. Restaurants with both types of service range from moderately priced with expectations for moderate turnover to those with relatively inexpensive fare expecting a high turnover to provide a fairly large volume of business; a high volume of low-profit items produces a moderate overall profit.

In addition to restaurants offering only cafeteria or buffet service, some table service restaurants may utilize a Salad Bar or Dessert Buffet as a conversation piece. The principles guiding selection of the various categories of items for a buffet are the same whether part or all of the service is buffet style.

Selection of Cafeteria Items

In selecting items for this style of service (Fig. 14.6), particular attention is paid to (a) selection of complementary items among the meal components so that customers are encouraged to purchase entire meals, (b) aesthetic qualities of the alternate items so that attractive displays can be arranged, and (c) selection of alternates from the various price ranges in order to attract several market segments. Other factors to be considered include (a) production feasibility in large quantity, (b) ability to retain quality for an indeterminate period of time, and (c) ease of portioning. Each of these restricts the size of the pool of items that are available as menu choices (Fig. 14.7).

One of the difficulties of cafeteria service is that the diner may go through the line and purchase bread, butter and a beverage (often with refills available in the dining room), and then occupy a seat for as long as he desires. This presents a management problem since check average is low and a valuable seat is occupied.

One means of reducing the incidence of this problem through menu planning is to stimulate impulse buying by presenting an attractive array of items that are customarily served together. For example, when Roast Turkey is the entrée, dressing or sweet potatoes, some variety of cranberry salad, and pumpkin pie are usually offered. These will be selected more frequently than when the entrée is Breaded Pork Chops or Baked Chicken. Other accepted combinations are listed in Table 14.1.

TABLE 14.1

SAMPLE COMPATIBLE COMBINATIONS

Roast Turkey, Cranberries, Squash or Pumpkin, Mince Pie or Plum Pudding
Roast Beef, Mashed Potatoes, Apple Pie
Baked Ham, Sweet Potatoes
Corned Beef, Boiled Potatoes or Rye Bread, Cabbage or Sauerkraut
Steak, French Fries, Tossed Salad
Spaghetti, Tossed Salad, French Bread

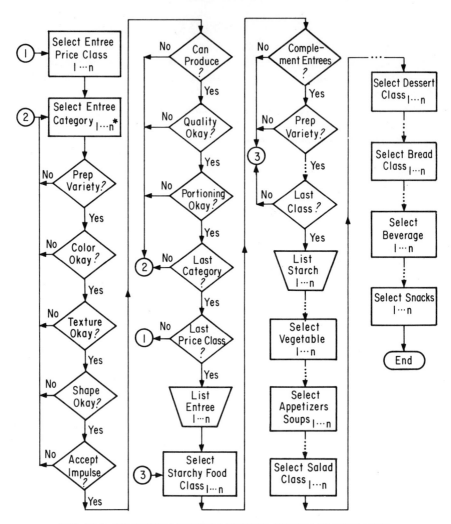

FIG. 14.6. CAFETERIA SERVICE MENU PLANNING FLOW CHART

*Category refers to beef, pork, poultry, fish, etc.

The bases for this strategy are the facts that we are psychologically conditioned to select items associated with good times and are culturally conditioned to accept certain combinations of items as a result of frequent exposure to the combinations. Moreover, we are subconsciously stimulated to select all components of an accepted combination so as to achieve a feeling of completeness. This strategy is effective with customers who can afford to purchase a meal but who are apathetic and/or indecisive. Moreover, other customers with partial meals are encouraged to purchase additional items to complete the meal.

MENU

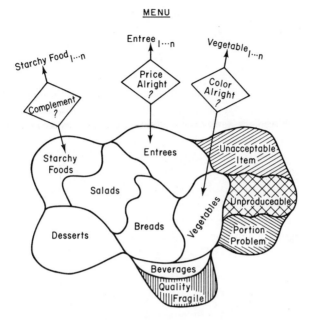

FIG. 14.7. POOL OF AVAILABLE ITEMS SHOWING EFFECTS OF LIMITING FACTORS AND EFFECTS OF SELECTION FACTORS

An important factor in stimulating impulse buying is the aesthetic appeal of the array of food items. While arrangement and garniture are important to the sales of individual items, the challenge from the standpoint of menu planning is to select complementary and contrasting colors and textures to create an enticing and harmonious effect within each section of the cafeteria line. This requires that the menu planner have a mental image of the visual characteristics of each item. A good selection of items will facilitate their arrangement in an attractive pattern. In order to assure color variety, menu writing policy at one restaurant (Eliason 1966) requires that vegetables be selected according to color as follows:

Orange	Light Green	Red	Other
White	Dark Green	Yellow	

Other restaurants have similar policies governing color variety in the salad and dessert sections.

Another factor in menu item selection is directed to sales volume. In the aggregate, customers vary in the amount of money they will spend for a meal according to their values and/or economic status. Definite market segments can usually be identified. Unless the pool of customers willing to pay a specific sum for a meal is large or the frequency of eating out is high a cafeteria must offer a selection of items in various price ranges to attract customers from several market segments in order to maintain a satisfactory volume of sales.

To plan menus for several price categories, the menu planner selects items from the pool of items in each cost/price range for each meal component and then evaluates each item for suitability according to other criteria such as acceptability, color, etc. For this purpose, it is necessary to have separate rank-order listings, by total cost per serving with sales price, for each meal component (Table 14.2). Given the rank-order listing, cutlines are established to determine which items currently fall into each price range pool. Cutlines may be set arbitrarily or according to logical cost groupings within the pool of items for each meal component.

Another factor that must be considered when selecting menu items for cafeteria service is production feasibility. Production feasibility is somewhat a function of aggregate demand for all items and the specific demand for the individual item. The aggregate demand for all items is determined by the volume of sales

TABLE 14.2

SAMPLE RANK-ORDER LISTING OF ENTRÉES BY TOTAL COST PER SERVING WITH SALES PRICE; ARBITRARY AND LOGICAL COST GROUPINGS ARE INDICATED

Logical Group	Item Name	Total Cost per Serving[1] ($)	Actual Sales Price ($)
	Roast Veal/Dressing/Gravy	0.757	0.80
	Lasagne	0.712	0.70
	Veal Scallopini	0.707	0.80
	Oven Fried Chicken/Country Gravy/ Cranberry Sauce	0.667	0.60
	Chop Suey on Rice	0.581	0.60
	Lamb Stew	0.577	0.60
	Baked Ham/Pineapple Sauce	0.575	0.70
	Beef Burgundy on Noodles	0.483	0.75
	Chicken Fried Cubed Steak/Brown Gravy	0.463	0.60
	Roast Beef au Jus	0.447	0.70
	Salisbury Steak	0.352	0.60
	Meat Loaf/Brown Gravy	0.344	0.55
	Tamale Pie	0.324	0.55
	Cheese Souffle/Mushroom Sauce	0.311	0.55
	Beef Croquettes/Brown Gravy	0.297	0.55
	Halibut au Gratin	0.236	0.70
	Ravioli (Italian) Half Order	0.171	0.35
	Baked Beans & Franks	0.147	0.50

70¢ cutline after Oven Fried Chicken group; 30¢ cutline after Cheese Souffle/Mushroom Sauce.

[1] Values are assigned rather than actual.

and is highly correlated with check average. One selects a target volume of sales and plans items and strategies to achieve it. A relatively high check average indicates sales success; sales generate production demand. When the overall production demand is heavy, only simple items can be produced. When the overall demand is low, complicated items can be produced that would be infeasible when volume is heavy. Since demand is unknown, complicated items usually are eliminated from consideration in order to reduce the probability of production problems.

If one studies the general pattern of the aggregate demand for food in a cafeteria, one notes that 1 of 3 patterns usually emerges (Fig. 14.8 to 14.10). In Fig. 14.8, the customers arrive all at once or close together; a line forms and de-

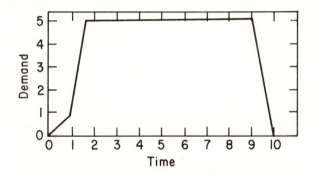

FIG. 14.8. AGGREGATE DEMAND PATTERN WHEN A CUS-
TOMER QUEUE DEVELOPS AND IS MAINTAINED THROUGH-
OUT THE SERVING PERIOD

mand is continuous until the end of the serving period when it falls off rapidly. This pattern of activity requires that many batches or essentially continuous production be prepared. In this case, simple preparation is advantageous as production pressure is great.

In Fig. 14.9, the customers arrive in groups at intervals; thus, there are alternate variable-length periods of activity and slack throughout the serving period which are usually longer than in the first case. Here, items requiring finish preparation are feasible if slack periods are sufficiently long.

In Fig. 14.10, customer arrival rate and timing are random and unpredictable. For this reason, simple items and those with two-stage preparation are preferred so that they can be prepared rapidly when needed, or finish-preparation delayed until the item is demanded.

From the foregoing, it is clear that aggregate demand patterns function primarily to limit the size of the pool of alternate items that may be selected for each meal component. Aggregate demand itself sets the outer limits or boundary for production requirements and also influences feasibility of producing specific items, given the other items to be produced.

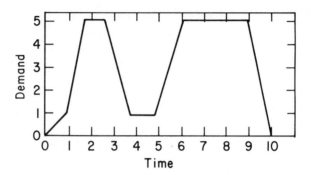

FIG. 14.9. AGGREGATE DEMAND PATTERN WHEN CUSTOM-
ERS ARRIVE INTERMITTENTLY IN GROUPS DURING THE
SERVING PERIOD

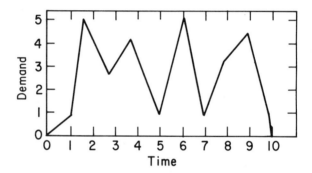

FIG. 14.10. AGGREGATE DEMAND PATTERN WHEN CUSTOM-
ERS ARRIVE AT RANDOM RATES AND TIMES DURING THE
SERVING PERIOD

The specific demand for each item is important in the selection of all items.
If, for example, demand for an individual item, given the alternatives, is low
then quality control may be impossible and it may not be feasible to produce
the item for this reason. In some cases the batch size required in order to maintain quality is small and labor cost so disproportionately large that production is
infeasible. On the other hand, if one item is very much more popular than the alternate items, it may be infeasible to produce it in the required quantities due to
equipment and/or labor limitations. In this case, the solution is to pair it with an
equally attractive item so as to divide the sales between the items and thus spread
the equipment useage or reduce the labor requirement, whichever is necessary.
Or, a complicated item that sells moderately well can be produced when the
other alternatives are high volume items requiring little preparation.

Production feasibility is ascertained by plotting the cumulative and aggregate
equipment and labor requirements for each time period. Items are accepted as
long as preparation equipment and labor time are available (Table 14.3, Fig.
14.11, 14.12).

TABLE 14.3

SIMPLIFIED SAMPLE MENU FOR RESTAURANT X FOR USE IN
COMPUTING EQUIPMENT AND MAN-HOUR REQUIREMENTS

No.	Menu Item	No. of Servings
	BREAKFAST (6:30 to 11:00 a.m.)	
1	Assorted Fruits and Juices	70
2	Hot Cereal–Regular	30
3	Fried Eggs	100
4	Scrambled Eggs	50
5	Hot Cakes	35
6	French Toast	15
7	Sausage Links	50
8	Bacon Strips	75
9	English Muffins	100
10	Pastries or Donuts	50
11	Coffee Tea Milk	250
	LUNCH (11:00 a.m. to 2:00 p.m.)	
12	Old Fashioned Bean Soup–Homemade	100
13	Vegetable Soup–Canned	50
14	Cheeseburgers and Hamburgers	150
15	Beef Stew–Frozen	100
16	Chili con Carne–Canned	50
17	Macaroni and Cheese–Frozen	25
18	Fishwiches	50
19	Cold Sandwiches	100
20	Cole Slaw	50
21	Potato Salad	40
22	Gelatin Salad	25
23	French Fries	200
24	Milkshakes	100
25	Carbonated Beverages	100
11	Coffee Tea Milk	
	DINNER (5:30 to 9:00 p.m.)	
26	Juice Appetizers	50
27	Roast Beef with Gravy	200
28	Half Fried Chicken	100
29	Glazed Ham	100
30	Meat Loaf with Gravy	75
31	Mashed Potatoes–Instant	275
32	Baked Potatoes	100
33	French Fries	100
34	Mixed Vegetables–Frozen	200
35	Buttered Peas–Frozen	250
36	Tossed Salad	300
37	Cottage Cheese Salad	50
38	Gelatin Salad	50
39	Assorted Pies–Purchased	200
40	Assorted Cakes–Purchased	75
41	Assorted Rolls–Purchased	550
11	Coffee Tea Milk	

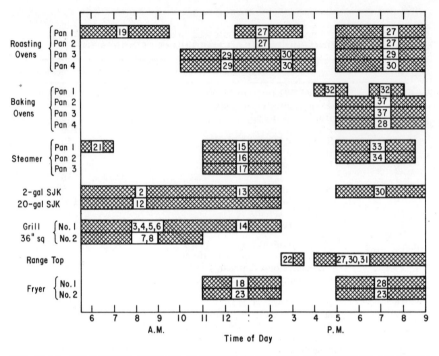

FIG. 14.11. EQUIPMENT USEAGE REQUIREMENTS FOR PRODUCTION OF MENU
IN TABLE 14.3

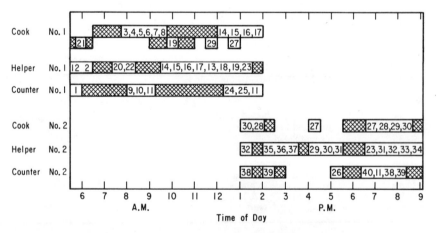

FIG. 14.12. MAN-HOUR USEAGE REQUIREMENTS FOR PRODUCTION OF MENU
IN TABLE 14.3

The ability to retain acceptable serving quality for an indeterminate length of time is another factor to consider in selection of items for cafeteria menus. Here again, the aggregate demand pattern will be the determining factor. When demand is continuous, preparation is essentially continuous, i.e., preparation of vegetables at 3–5 min intervals throughout the serving period, so this quality is less important. When demand alternates between high and low, timing must be strictly controlled and items must be less fragile. When demand is erratic, this quality is essential.

In general, items whose appeal depends on a fragile textural quality such as crispness are not suitable for cafeteria service as control is exceedingly difficult; sogginess reduces acceptability of the item. Green vegetables also present a problem as irreversible color changes make them increasingly less acceptable. Unless item turnover is rapid these factors limit the pool of available items, making variety difficult to achieve.

Ease of portioning is also a factor to be considered. Some items are so difficult to portion uniformly that they must be eliminated from the pool of alternate items. Others require so much time to portion that they would reduce line speed. These must be paired with easy-serve items or eliminated from the pool of alternate items.

Another constraint that usually further delimits the subset of items that can be considered for a given meal component results from the policy to select items from each category. For example, the salad alternatives usually include a fruit salad, a cooked vegetable salad, a gelatin-based salad, a cottage cheese and fruit salad, a variation of tossed salad, and some other type which may be a relish plate, a starchy salad, etc. Or in the case of desserts, alternatives include canned fruit, gelatin, cake, pie, pudding, ice cream, etc.

These are the major considerations that underlie decisions to select one item rather than another for a particular cafeteria menu. Because of similarities in planning cafeteria and buffet menus, the step-by-step process for selection of meal components for buffet menus is described below.

Selection of Buffet Items

The appeal of a buffet is in the artistic arrangement of a large variety of items, perhaps as many as 15 or 20 for each meal component. An ice carving may be used as the focal point and conversation piece. Repeat business depends not only on the number of items and their arrangement but also upon the selection itself. The opportunity of trying new items adds to the eating adventure. Thus, novelty items are included with standard items in each section.

When a buffet is featured daily, some portion of the items must change each day in order to retain appeal. Since the pool of possible items is exceedingly large, variety is easily attained. Generally, the Sunday buffet features more elegant and elaborate items. A fish buffet may be featured on Fridays or during Lent. Another means of creating interest is to emphasize the cuisines of various nations at regular or irregular intervals. Good sources for information on buffet service are Finance (1958), Waldner and Mitterhauser (1968). A book on gueridon and lamp cookery (Fuller 1964) provides additional ideas.

Although the pool of items that may be used in planning buffet menus is exceedingly large and restrictions are fewer, those that are imposed are crucial to success. These include: (a) total cost per portion, (b) production feasibility, (c) the relative popularity of alternate items, (d) ability to retain quality for an indeterminate length of time, and (e) ease of portioning. These are discussed below in regard to selection of items for each section of the buffet. Figure 14.13 depicts the decision process.

The first task is to select the entrées. The number and their types are determined by the price class of the restaurant. Standard items such as roast beef, fried chicken, baked ham, and the like, are commonly served. Portions of these are limited in the less expensive restaurants. Various types of meatballs, cold cuts, and cheeses round out the offerings in the less expensive buffets. On the other hand, expensive buffets feature Beef Stroganoff; Beef Burgundy; crab, shrimp, or lobster dishes; rabbit; squab; etc. Some may also feature a variant of the fondue pot for cooking selected morsels at the table; in this case, a round table is used to facilitate customer reach for self-cooking and -service.

The relative popularity of alternate items is important and must be known in order to predict the cost for the total quantity consumed. This is necessary in order to determine the economic feasibility of serving each item. Given a budgeted allowance for entrées, one allocates a portion to each. Feasibility is determined by multiplying the demand (expected number of servings required) by the per unit cost; e.g., 200 servings of entrée X at 50¢ per serving = $100; 400 servings of entrée Y at 25¢ per serving = $100. The number of servings and costs are summed. They are adjusted until desired quantities and costs are obtained.

Production feasibility must also be determined before final selection of entrées is made. Given the relative demand for each item, one must determine whether the required quantities can be produced given limitations on facilities, personnel, and time. Theoretically, one plots quantity vs time; actually, in most instances lack of reliable data forces the menu planner to make an intuitive guess which must suffice.

The ability to retain quality for an indeterminate length of time is also crucial. Although total demand for an individual item can be predicted with some certainty, demand throughout the 3–4 hr serving period will be uneven and cannot be predicted. For this reason, some pans of fully prepared food may have to be held. Thus, it is essential that items be selected that will mellow on holding rather than deteriorate. Of course, some items requiring only a few minutes of preparation time can be used, especially convenience foods.

Another consideration is the ease with which the item can be portioned. For aesthetic reasons entrées that tend to crumble leaving a messy serving platter, should be avoided. The alternative is to serve them on small platters. However, a supply problem is likely to develop since small platters must be continually replaced. Furthermore, as the customer is balancing a plate in one hand, he has only one hand with which to serve himself. Therefore, portions should be precut so as to be easily lifted with tongs or a spatula.

Other hot foods including starchy items and vegetables are selected next. Items such as rice and pasta are served in limited quantities. Vegetables are selected to harmonize and/or add contrasting color. The number and types of these items are usually a function of popularity and demand. Cost is controlled by selecting alternate items with similar per serving costs. Production feasibility, ability to retain quality for an indeterminate period, and ease of portioning are also considerations that pertain to this group of items.

Salads are selected next. Here color, texture, and variety are key considerations. Customarily, several items are selected from each of the classes of salads: (a) vegetables—fresh and marinated, (b) fruit—fresh and canned, (c) gelatin-based, (d) cottage cheese and . . ., (e) starch-based, such as Club Salad, and (f) relishes—fresh and pickled. The cost of salad ingredients varies widely among seasons. Ideally, recipes are costed monthly; in practice, recipes are often marked to indicate the seasons in which they can be served profitably. Using prepared fruits and vegetables allows the menu planner increased flexibility in selecting these salads since the production problem is reduced. If covered and refrigerated prior to placing on the buffet, most salads can retain their fresh appetizing appearance for a reasonable period of time; thus, perishability is not a limiting factor. Ease of portioning is characteristic of most salad materials; however, gelatin salads should be precut.

The dessert section is planned next. It is relatively easy to plan since production feasibility, stability of product quality and portioning present only minor problems so are not ordinarily limiting factors in selection. Moreover, the cost per serving of small portions of desserts is relatively low and invariate; costing is done at infrequent intervals and is used primarily to limit the pool of item choices. When the diner reaches this section his appetite is satisfied, therefore light and decorative desserts or small portions of rich ones suffice. The major challenge is to select a colorful and interesting assortment of cakes, pies and tarts, puddings, gelatin desserts, and cookies.

The bread section is planned last. Variety breads make customers feel special. Conventional sliced bread may be available in fancy baskets—it satisfies those wanting regular style while presentation is more in harmony with other items. Commercial availability of a wide assortment of bread items simplifies the planning task. Many kinds of crackers, bread sticks, hard and soft rolls, and variety breads such as Swedish Limpe, Shepherd's bread, and Sour Dough Bread are generally available. Coffee cakes and quick breads such as biscuits, muffins, and fruit breads are easily produced from mixes when not commercially available; thus, production feasibility is not usually a limiting factor. Here again, cost per

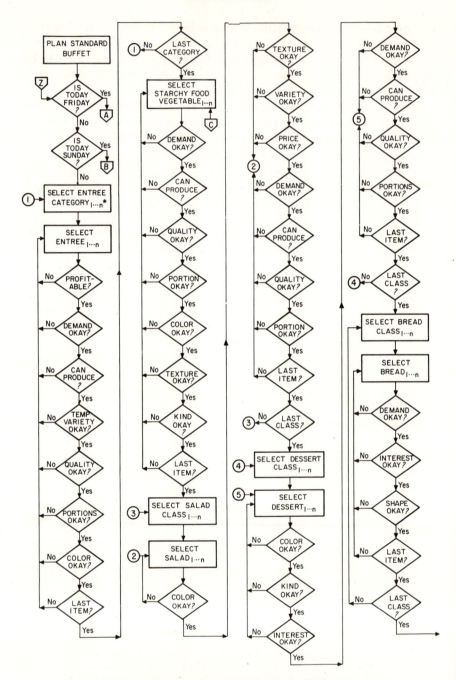

FIG. 14.13. BUFFET SERVICE MENU PLANNING FLOW CHART

*Category refers to beef, pork, poultry, fish, etc.

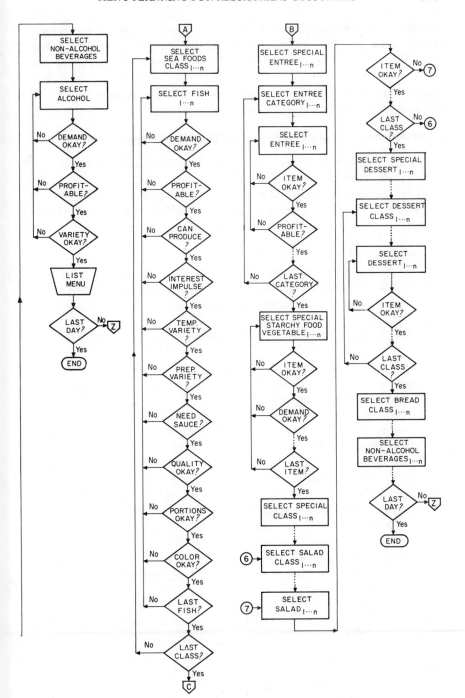

serving is relatively low and serves primarily to limit the pool of items available to the menu planner. If quantities per tray are adjusted to demand, staling is minimal. From a planning standpoint, the portioning problem is unimportant.

Beverages, both alcoholic and nonalcoholic may be served from the buffet although usually these are served by waitresses. The standard beverages are generally ad libitum; cocktails are purchased separately.

SHORT-ORDER AND TAKEOUT SERVICE

Two general classes of restaurants utilize one or both of these types of service: (a) short-order, sit down and (b) short-order, takeout. Usually, restaurants in these classes offer limited menus of low-to-moderate cost items. An extra large volume of sales coupled with lower facilities and service labor costs combine to provide a satisfactory profit in the well-managed operation.

Short-Order, Sit Down

A number of kinds of restaurants are included in this class: (a) coffee shops, (b) lunch counters, and (c) fast-food, short-order operations. In these restaurants customers are seated at counters, booths, or tables or some combination of these.

Coffee Shops.—One of the distinguishing features of a coffee shop is that it is open long hours and usually caters to a transient clientele. Unlike other short-order restaurants, breakfast, lunch, and dinner meals are provided. Breakfast is often available around the clock. Lunch may be available from 11 until 3 o'clock and dinner from 4 until midnight.

Breakfast menus usually provide the standard fare, a combination of table d'hote meals and a la carte items. Table d'hote menus are designed to appeal to a range of sizes of appetites and prices. Typical patterns include: (a) juice, bread item, and beverage; (b) fruit or juice, cold cereal, and beverage; (c) juice, one egg any style, toast, and beverage; (d) juice, one egg any style, meat, toast, and beverage; (e) fruit or juice, pancakes or waffle, and beverage; and (f) fruit or juice, pancakes or waffle, one egg any style or meat, and beverage. Variants of these patterns include (a) increasing the number of eggs, (b) substitution of one meat for another, and (c) addition or substitution of fried potatoes. A la carte items usually include (a) additional fruits and juices, (b) more elaborate preparation of eggs such as omlets, and (c) more expensive kinds of meat. All of these items are prepared to order.

Lunch menus also are a combination of table d'hote meals and a la carte selections. Typical table d'hote meal patterns include: (a) soup, cold sandwich, and beverage, (b) grilled sandwich, fries or chips, and fountain beverage, and (c) grilled sandwich, salad, dessert, and beverage. A la carte selections include: (a) soups, (b) cold sandwiches, (c) grilled sandwiches and other hot sandwiches, (d) salad plates, (e) fountain items, (f) desserts, and (g) beverages. A limited number of standard items are usually offered in each section. Daily and/or seasonal specials are added as clip-ons.

Since the clientele is largely transient, the same menu can be used every day. Hence, the menu planning problem is minimal. The flowchart (Fig. 14.5) provides a general model for item selection. Once the basic menu is planned, few changes in the selection of items are made. The principles guiding selection of items are (a) popularity and profitability and (b) short-order production feasibility. Relative popularity of various items can be obtained from Gallup Polls printed in Food Service Magazine; however, local differences must be ascertained. Profitability, being a function of volume, efficiency in production, procurement, and other factors, must be computed for the individual unit. Short-order production feasibility is a function of demand vs labor and equipment available. Lunch production usually peaks between 11:30 a.m. and 2 p.m. often following the curve shown in Fig. 14.14.

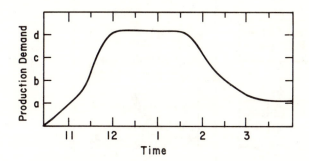

FIG. 14.14. THE LUNCH PRODUCTION DEMAND

The dinner menu resembles the lunch menu but usually is more extensive and expensive. Here again, a combination of table d'hote and a la carte selections are offered. Typical table d'hote meals include (a) soup de jour, cold meat sandwich, salad, dessert, and beverage; (b) grilled sandwich including steak sandwiches, fries or chips, and beverage; (c) hot sandwich such as roast beef or roast turkey, mashed potatoes, vegetable de jour, or salad, dessert, and beverage. A la carte dinner sections and selections are often identical with lunch.

Lunch Counters.—Unlike coffee shops, the lunch counter clientele is usually composed of two segments: (a) regular customers from nearby offices, and (b) shoppers. Office workers desire quick midmorning or midafternoon coffee-break combinations plus an inexpensive and satisfying lunch (filling or low-calorie). Shoppers usually pause for a snack but may be enticed into impulse buying of a meal. The menu is designed to meet the needs of both groups.

For this reason, the menu often provides (a) a very simple breakfast such as bread item and beverage or cold cereal and beverage between 7:30 a.m. and 11:00 a.m.; (b) a limited short-order lunch menu between 11:00 a.m. and 2:00 p.m.; and (c) a bread item or dessert and beverage until 4:30 p.m. All items are usually a la carte. The flow chart in Fig. 14.15 provides a general model for item selection.

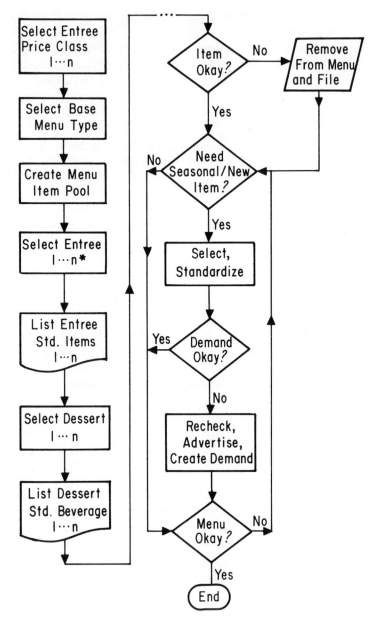

FIG. 14.15. FAST-FOOD, SHORT-ORDER MENU AND ANALYSIS
FLOW CHART

*See Fig. 14.4 for sample considerations that may apply.

Typical breakfast breads include commercially available donuts, pastries, English muffins, and toast. The short-order lunch menu is the same as that provided by most coffee shops. However, the quality is often lower and the portion size smaller. Some lunch counters also serve canned entrées such as chili, baked beans, or macaroni and cheese, heated to order. Typical afternoon coffee-break fare usually includes pastries, cake, pie, and fountain items. Daily and/or seasonal specials are added as menu clip-ons.

The menu for a lunch counter operation is relatively easy to plan since the majority of items are served daily. The most challenging aspect is to select the special items, including the low-calorie plate lunches. Some regular customers will eat the same lunch for 20 yr; the cook will know their expected arrival time and plan to prepare the meal so it is ready when they arrive. Others seem to require variety. If the menu is too limited, these customers will become dissatisfied and will increase their variety by lunching at a competitor's establishment. To reduce the probability of this outcome, a limited variety of items is introduced. But, facilities, time, and skill in food preparation are often lacking. Therefore, convenience foods can be used to advantage.

Low-calorie plate lunches present a problem. Limiting portion size and substituting fresh fruit and vegetables for fries and chips reduce calories somewhat. But, as this diet must be followed for long periods, additional variety is necessary. Ideas for low-calorie plate lunches can be obtained from many sources such as the American Heart Association and the National Dairy Council; however, calories of individual items and totals should be marked.

Fast-Food, Short-Order.—Restaurants of this type provide little service so 1 of 2 systems of order timing are often employed. In the first, the customer reads the menu, gives his order to an order clerk and receives a number. When his order is called he obtains the meal and pays the cashier. In the second, the customer reads the menu, gives his order to an order clerk via a call box, and receives his meal from a waitress who also presents the check, which he pays at the door.

The menu in this type of service ranges from a very limited one to a quite extensive array. However, all entrées are either convenience foods or are grilled, broiled, or fried to order. French fries and a tossed salad are commonly served with all items; vegetables and soups are seldom available. Desserts are commonly commercially prepared pies and cakes or ice cream. Standard beverages are also provided.

The challenge in planning this type of menu is to provide sufficient variety without increasing the production load (Fig. 14.15). This is achieved by planning a base menu using one of several strategies:

(A) Use of equivalent preparation time items when the base is the same, e.g., pizza where the topping and garnish provide variety, or salad plates where the base and bed are the same, the body and garnish provide variety.

(B) Use of equivalent preparation time items where the base and/or garnish differ, e.g., pancakes made from buckwheat, buttermilk, and regular batter with nuts, fruits, etc.; or hot and cold sandwiches where the breads, fillings, and garnishes differ.

(C) Use of similar preparation time items, e.g., fried chicken wings, drumsticks, thighs and breasts, etc.

(D) Use of different cuts of meat, prepared in the same way, and requiring similar preparation times, e.g., various steaks, chops, burgers, etc.

Once the basic strategy is selected, the task is to develop a pool of alternate items. Next, one selects and tests items for relative popularity, removing the less popular items until a menu is obtained that provides the maximum volume for the long-run. Then the menu planning task reduces to monitoring sales for need to change items. Seasonal features are added to the pool to increase variety. Also, it is obligatory to find new items and create a demand for them as a means of oneupmanship to attract customers away from competitors. Figure 14.16 illustrates this process.

Short-Order, Takeout.—Restaurants of this type provide no service except packaging of food. The challenge in planning the menu is to select an array of items that will maximize sales volume. Volume is a function of customer through-put and the number of items selected per customer, measured by check average. Each restaurant usually specializes in a particular type of food such as hamburgers, pizzas, fish and chips, tacos and enchiladas, ice cream, etc.

Most restaurants of this type are chain franchise operations. Menu, control systems, layout, etc., are given to the unit in order to protect the image. The following discussion does not pertain to chain operations.

Success of these fast-food restaurants depends on meeting the consumers' needs in terms of food and service, commonly defined as speed. To some degree, those units located on major highways to serve a large volume transient clientele can erode standards and still maintain a satisfactory sales volume. However, most units rely on repeat business which is a function of novelty, speed, and quality.

In regard to novelty, the customer is looking for a type of food that he does not usually prepare at home, hence the popularity of takeout fried foods, Chinese foods, etc. Therefore, an image determining food-related concept forms the basis for volume sales. A popular type of novelty entrée such as pizza, fish and chips, tacos and enchiladas, etc., serves as the basis for menu planning. A limited number of additional items are promoted that complement the entrée, complete the meal, and increase the check average. However, addition of canned soup or a commonly available convenience entrée does not increase sales or variety from the consumers' standpoint since these items are available at home. Initially or if there is no competition among units offering the same type of food, novelty will attract customers. Later, service and quality determine which operation is patronized.

Service speed or through-put of customers is partially determined by the

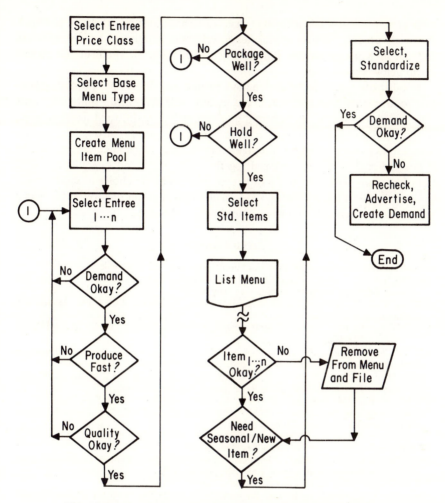

FIG. 14.16. SHORT-ORDER MENU PLANNING AND ANALYSIS

ordering and delivery system. A number of gimmicks have been used such as meal numbers or color codes which reduce the consumers' decision-making problem and increase the speed and accuracy of order taking. Similarly, the meals are prepackaged by number or color for delivery to the customers. If limited choice of beverage is desired, beverages are prepackaged and the customer selects these as he pays the cashier.

In planning a menu for a fast-food operation one must recognize that the items are not really prepared to order. Rather, the most popular ones are produced continuously and others are produced at discrete intervals to maintain a predetermined supply level. Therefore, the menu is limited to those items that can retain acceptable quality when packaged in closed containers for variable time periods. Hot sandwiches that need to retain moisture are easily managed. However, products whose appeal lies in crispness deteriorate rapidly; breather foil and moisture permeable films have helped alleviate this problem, but quality is still below standard.

Food quality is basically determined by item suitability and speed of service; raw food quality and preparation are usually well controlled. Suitability rests on a complex of factors: (a) inherent qualities such as texture and flavor interest, (b) popularity of the items as it determines item turnover, (c) serving temperature acceptability—items must be acceptable over a range of temperatures, especially if hot and cold items are packaged together since they tend to equilibrate with both becoming tepid. In this regard, cole slaw is a better choice of salad since it presents less of a hazard than potato salad and will retain quality better than a gelatin salad which will melt when placed next to hot foods.

BIBLIOGRAPHY

ALD, R. 1969. The Complete Soup Cookbook. Prentice-Hall, Englewood Cliffs, N.J.

AMENDOLA, J. 1960. Bakers Manual for Quantity Baking and Pastry Making, 2nd Revised Edition. Ahrens Publishing Co., New York.

AMENDOLA, J. 1970. Ice Carving Made Easy. National Restaurant Association, Chicago.

ATKINSON, A. B. 1971. Volume Feeding Menu Selector. E. C. Blair (Editor). Institutions/VF Magazine, Chicago.

BRODNER, J., CARLSON, H. M., and MASCHAL, H. T. 1962. Profitable Food and Beverage Operation, 4th Edition, Revised. Ahrens Publishing Co., New York.

CHURCH, C. F., and CHURCH, H. N. 1970. Bowes & Church Food Values of Portions Commonly Used, 11th Edition. J. B. Lippincott Co., Philadelphia.

CRANE, W. E. 1964. Delectable Desserts. Ahrens Publishing Co., New York.

Culinary Institute of America 1971. The Professional Chef, 3rd Revised Edition. Institutions/VF Magazine, Chicago.

ELIASON, W. W. 1966. Cafeteria menu planning. In Profitable Cafeteria Operation. E. Miller (Editor). Ahrens Publishing Co., New York.

ERICSON, M. H. 1971. Quantity Recipes. Cornell Hotel and Restaurant Quarterly, School of Hotel Administration, Cornell University, Ithaca, N.Y.

FINANCE, C. 1958. Buffet Catering. Ahrens Publishing Co., New York.

FOWLER, S. F., WEST, B. B., and SHUGART, G. S. 1970. Food for 50, 5th Edition. John Wiley & Sons, New York.

FULLER, J. 1964. Gueridon and Lamp Cookery. Ahrens Publishing Co., New York.

GANCEL, J. E. 1969. Gancel's Culinary Encyclopedia of Modern Cooking. National Restaurant Association, Chicago.

GROSSMAN, H. 1959. Practical Bar Management. Ahrens Publishing Co., New York.

HASZONICS, J., and BARRATT, S. 1963. Wine Merchandising. Radio City Book Store, New York.

KAUFMAN, W. E. 1968. Appetizers and Canapes. Doubleday & Co., Garden City, N.Y.

SAULNIER, L. (Not Dated) A Repertoire of the Cuisine. National Restaurant Association (Importer), Chicago. (French)

School of Hotel Administration. 1967. Tested Quantity Recipes. Cornell University, Ithaca, N.Y.

SCHOONMAKER, F. 1964. Encyclopedia of Wine. Hastings Books, Philadelphia.

SEABERG, A. G. 1971. Menu Design—Merchandising and Marketing. Institutions/VF Magazine, Chicago.

SIMON, A. L., and HOWE, R. 1970. Dictionary of Gastronomy. McGraw-Hill Book Co., New York.

TRADER VIC. 1948. Bartender's Guide. Doubleday & Co., Garden City, N.Y.
VOEGELE, M. C., and WOOLLEY, G. H. 1961. Drink Dictionary. Ahrens Publishing Co.,
New York.
WALDNER, G. K., and MITTERHAUSER, K. 1968. The Professional Chef's Book of Buf-
fets. Institutions/VF Magazine, Chicago.
WATT, B. K., and MERRILL, L. 1963. Composition of Foods: Raw, Processed, Prepared.
USDA Agr. Handbook 8.
WENZEL, G. L. 1966. Wenzel's Menu Maker. Radio City Book Store, New York.

Basic Computer Concepts[1]

For most food service units, application of computer technology in menu planning requires tremendous adjustment in concepts, procedures, and organization. Most applications in other fields develop from manual methods to automated data processing (ADP) methods using tabulator cards and then to electronic data processing (EDP). In part, transitional problems can be attributed to the common practice of skipping the ADP stage in developing menu planning applications, where some basic problems would be solved.

This chapter describes some basic computer concepts. Subsequent chapters will discuss the history of menu planning by computer and operational problems in developing a menu planning program.

THE COMPUTER

The computer is a group of five different types of modular units that are coupled in series or in parallel depending on the power of the control unit and/ or job requirements. The types of units are (a) input, i.e., card, tape, disc, terminal typewriter, etc; (b) control, i.e., operating system to accept, time, and terminate jobs or run off-line equipment; (c) central processing unit (CPU) to perform arithmetic, i.e., addition, subtraction, multiplication, and division, or logical comparisons; (d) memory, i.e., storage of data and instructions for processing; and (e) output, i.e., print reports, punch cards, write tapes or discs, type messages on terminal typewriter.

As used here the adjective modular refers to the fact that the various input-output devices, i.e., card reader, card punch, tape, disc, terminal typewriter, etc., are compatible with or can be used with a variety of computer systems. For example, when the five units are used in series or sequentially, first, the program and data are read, stored in memory; next, processing is initiated and completed; then, some output such as a printed report is generated. When the units operate

---

[1]The reader who intends to work as a member of a computer applications team will need a course in programming and general computer applications in addition to the introduction provided in this chapter.

in parallel, while the CPU is making various mathematical computations, the card reader may be reading the next job into memory and the printer may be printing the reports generated by the previous job and the card punch may be punching a new data deck. Thus, a number of tasks can be performed by the various units simultaneously.

The general steps in preparing and submitting a job for computer processing are as follows:

(A) Define the problem in minute detail, listing all objectives; and document decisions, assumptions, and hypotheses.

(B) Plan a set of instructions or program to direct computer processing of the data.

(C) Develop a sample set of data that contains all expected data errors in order to test the program.

(D) Keypunch cards, both instructions and data; desk check for accuracy.

(E) Submit to a dispatcher to be run.

(F) Check preliminary output; debug, i.e., correct errors and/or revise instructions and/or data as necessary and resubmit.

Figure 15.1 depicts the relationships among the basic steps. Figure 15.2 shows intradepartmental considerations local to the dietary department and interdepartmental considerations global to the institution in regard to computer use that must mesh in order to plan for computer use.

Problem definition is a primary responsibility of the dietitian. It is perhaps the most difficult step as one must conceptualize processes which are largely performed intuitively according to the experience of the person. For example, in planning menus the evaluation of prospective menu items is largely subconscious. The amount and kinds of experience of the menu planner determine the quality of judgment exercised, i.e., the comprehensiveness and reliability of evaluation the individual can make. In order for the computer to select alternate menu choices, other than mechanically, the complete subconscious process must be known and simulated in order for the resultant menus to be of comparable quality.

In addition to the problem definition provided by the dietitian, usually a management scientist also will study a particular process using a separate set of tools in the analysis. The additional view is generally beneficial in obtaining a broad, systematic, and generalizeable definition of the problem. According to Gille (1968), "Problem definition consists of finding out everything that is now known about the problem and how it is presently processed, plus everything that should be known, so that a practicable solution can be found for processing the problem. . . ."[2] The overall approach of operations research is the scientific method of inquiry, namely:

---

[2] Quoted with permission of American Data Processing, Detroit.

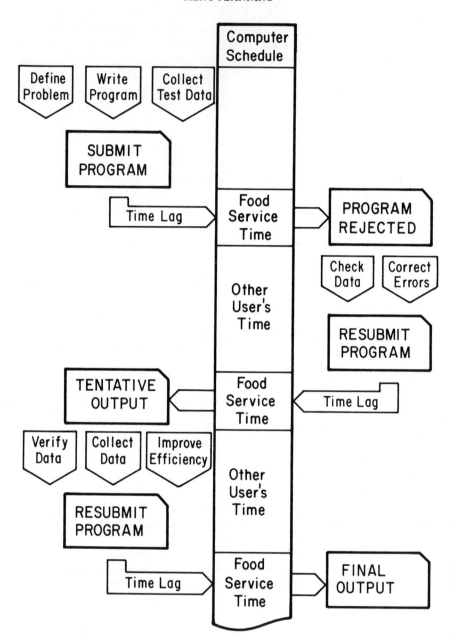

FIG. 15.1. STEPS IN PROGRAM DEVELOPMENT AND DELAY POINTS

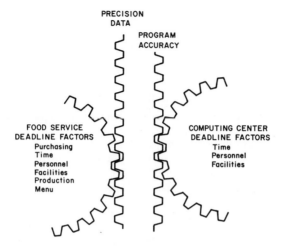

FIG. 15.2. INTERDEPARTMENTAL TIME FACTORS

(A) Definition and fact finding.
(B) Development of alternative methods of solution.
(C) Evaluation of alternatives in terms of short-term and long-term effectiveness.
(D) Implementation and testing.

Conceptual and mathematical models, which are simplified abstractions of reality, are developed to clarify relationships and provide a common means of communication among members of the research team. Sippl (1966)[3] has described model building as follows:

> A problem is encountered in a "real world" setting, i.e., an environment, and it must be translated into quantitative terms; it must be abstracted from its environment by simplifying it—stripping it of its complexities. Superficialities are deleted; cold, clear logic is substituted for the ambiguities of language; relationships of variables are formalized by using the rigorous discipline of mathematics. The problem must be the abstracted representation of the true situation being analyzed. Skill, experience, and judgment are required to handle the modern, complex, sophisticated relationships. The model requires specific representations of relationships—variables, constraints, parameters, reduced to symbols, clearly defined. Functional relationships which link the variables and parameters are established to find the values of the decision variables according to a criterion by which the decision must be judged.
>
> Because a model is essentially a hypothesis based on postulates and assumptions, it develops the preconceived expectation through logic and deduction with empirical evidence for objectivity, intersubjectivity, and optimality.

---

[3] Quoted with the permission of Howard W. Sams & Co., Indianapolis.

However, as Morse (1967)[4] has pointed out, "Like any other model, the computer model will not predict correct results unless it corresponds to the actual operation in all important respects. . . . Unless realism is built into the details of the program and the whole simulation is checked for normal behavior, the computer model is only a complicated and impressive way of making an unverified guess." At the present time, the menu planning process in only partially defined and only simplistic models are available. Much work remains to be done.

The second step, that of preparing the specific instructions for the computer requires technical skill in programming. Usually, a programmer is employed for this purpose. The programmer may have a mathematical background or only technical training in programming. Consequently, when the problem definition is incomplete or incorrect, unanticipated difficulties may arise since the programmer can only write the instructions mechanically. An astute programmer may sense difficulties and be able to ask questions for clarification, but usually problems may only be discovered by intense scrutiny of the output.

The programmer communicates with the computer by means of a programming language which according to Sammet (1967)[5] is ". . . some set of characters and rules for combining them by which the user can communicate with the computer to cause useful work to be done; this communication takes place through another program which is normally called a compiler, and whose purpose is to translate the user's program (called the source program) into machine code (called the object program) which can then be executed by the compiler." Another author (Shaw 1967) defines a programming language as ". . . a language that permits the specification of a variety of different computations, thereby giving the user significant control, either immediate or delayed, over the computer's operation. . ." The dietitian should be familiar with the language used by the particular company computer and should have minimal skill in programming in order to effectively communicate with the programmer.

Flow charts are customarily prepared at several stages in the programming process (MacKinnon 1968). Figure 15.3 is a simple illustration. The preliminary flow chart is designed to aid in problem definition and clarification of relationships among parts of the problem. The final flow chart should accurately represent the program and serves as documentation of contents. It is of tremendous value in adapting a program to new information or situational changes that require new constraints.

A test deck containing expected keypunch errors, missing data, extreme values, etc., is usually constructed for use in checking the completeness and functionality of program statements. A small test deck can inexpensively check program reliability, whereas to run the program with a large data set is costly. The process of developing a menu planning program is shown in Table 15.1.

---

[4] Quoted with permission of MIT Press, Cambridge, Mass.
[5] Quoted with permission of *Computers and Automation*.

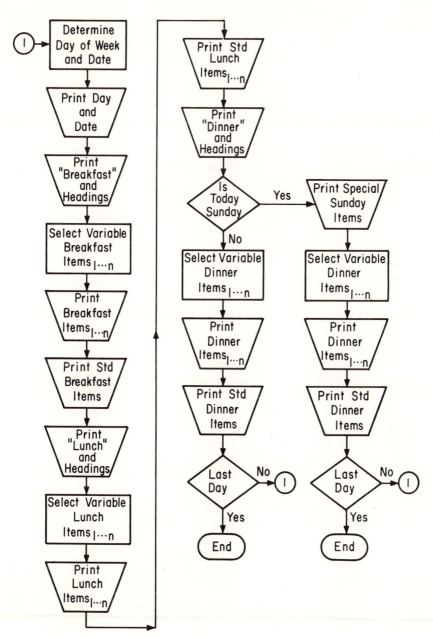

FIG. 15.3. FLOW CHART FOR MENU PRINTING BY COMPUTER

TABLE 15.1

STEPS TO FOLLOW IN A MENU PLANNING PROGRAM

1. Define problem
    Philosophy—assumptions
    Policies
    Operational constraints
2. Collect data—mean and range
    Recipe costs—time and area
    Preferences—subgroup
    Food characteristics
    Production—time and timing
3. Programming and testing
    Aesthetics—color, texture, shape
    Variety—flavor
    Acceptability—item, combination
    Cost—profit
    Nutrients—contribution, totals and mean
    Production
4. Evaluation—refinement
5. Updating—expansion

Computers are usually leased at high dollar rates per hour; the rate depending on the size, capacity, and features of the specific configuration of components. Because the cost is high, the computer must be utilized to the extent possible, i.e., every second. Consequently, jobs are ordered, insofar as possible, in a continuous queue and are processed in order or by priority. Hence, the dispatcher. In some situations, specific time periods are allocated to each department and jobs can *only* be processed during these times regardless of when submitted (Fig. 15.1). In any case, although actual processing time may be a few seconds, turnaround time, i.e., elapsed time between submission and completion, may be several days. Average turnaround time can be planned for by planning multiple job runs spaced to return output at reasonable intervals.

Very few jobs run correctly the first time. Hence, some adjustments are necessary. When changes are made, the program is rerun. This step may be repeated many times before satisfactory output is obtained.

COMPUTER CAPABILITIES

Throughout most of the 1960's discussions of computer capabilities were still favorably biased in order to generate interest in developing applications (Anon. 1968; Hartman 1967; Kotschevar 1967; Casbergue 1966). According to Samet (1969)[6]:

The period when we were delighted that computers worked at all is over. We are only just beginning to realize how challenging is the task of

---

[6] Quoted with permission of *Computer Digest*.

making them work properly for us, just how difficult it is to pose the right problems and just how important it is to specify the correct solutions in full. If only someone would invent a computer that would 'do what I mean, not what I say.'

And by 1968 it became evident that the computer could not solve all problems efficiently and it became fashionable to emphasize limitations (Kovac 1969). Both positions should be evaluated.

The computer has four major attributes that explain its usefulness in food service applications (Table 15.2). These are:

(A) The computer has essentially an infinite memory that is infallible—this means that it can handle the tremendous amounts of data we often deal with.

(B) It performs arithmetic calculations rapidly and accurately—this is especially helpful in computing and analyzing cost and nutritional values.

(C) The computer is consistent regardless of interruptions; under program control it follows the same sequence of steps each time it performs an identical function. Thus, it will consider all factors each time.

(D) It is responsive—a change in instructions or data causes an immediate and permanent change in results.

TABLE 15.2

COMPUTER CHARACTERISTICS

1. Unlimited memory
2. Rapid processing
3. Consistent
4. Flexible—responsive
5. Only follows instructions
6. Complete definition
7. Errors undetected—absurd
8. Decide by comparison
9. Deadlines—time discipline
10. Accuracy—procedure

But the computer also has four limitations that need to be considered. These limitations increase the cost and difficulty of developing applications (Table 15.2). These are:

(A) The computer can *only* follow instructions; it has no experience, judgment, or insight for use in evaluation.

(B) It can only solve problems that can be defined completely and that use quantitative data. With programmed feedback loops it can change data or values of constraints and thus modify subsequent output; in this sense it learns.

(C) The computer cannot detect errors in data unless specific instructions are given. If the data are incorrect, out-of-date, or missing, erroneous results will be obtained. This is more critical than when calculations are performed manually since the error will be consistent and thus effects will be magnified.

(D) The computer can only decide between two alternatives at one time and only by comparison. Therefore, decision-making is based on a series of comparisons progressing systematically along branches of a decision tree.

Obviously, advantages outweigh limitations or computer applications would atrophy. However, these considerations greatly affect design of computer programs.

Until now, discussion has been based on the premise that input and output were widely separated in time. While this is frequently true, time sharing systems make instant feedback possible. Time sharing means that a large number of users, e.g., 30, located in various locations can concurrently use the computer in solution of different problems (Bell 1968A, B; Fano and Corbato 1966; Westerhouse 1969). Large computers perform arithmetic operations in nanoseconds (billionths of a second). There are short periods of time between calculations when reading, printing, etc., are being done which do not require use of the CPU. When many users' programs are stored in memory, instead of waiting for these off-line operations to be completed before resuming calculations, the CPU performs calculations on different programs in rotation. As described by Bell (1968B)[7]

> The round robin algorithm runs each user, in turn, for a fixed quanta of time, and when all users have been served, the process is repeated. If any user cannot run because his is waiting for input or output, or halted, he misses a turn. On completion of input or output the user is put at the head of the queue and run (subject to his allotted time).

Thus, processing of users' data is performed rapidly and systematically using the computer to best advantage. The user is unaware that the computer is working on any other programs. The terminal typewriter enables the programmer to establish a "running dialog" of instructions when using this system in "conversational mode." This instant feedback speeds up programming tremendously.

The major limitation here is that this system works most effectively on problems requiring initial and terminal attention with infrequent attention in intermediate stages. Otherwise, the programmer is placed in the position of making frequent decisions, which builds pressure, which leads to snap judgments. In the case of menu planning, this may lead to the original subconscious intuitive evaluation of prospective menu items with no guarantee of improvement over manual methods.

---

[7] Quoted with permission of *Computer Design*.

SYSTEMS APPROACH

The systems approach was designed to encourage specialists to approach problems in terms of the objectives of the whole, its component parts, and relationships among the parts. It turns out that specialists have usually been optimizing the goals of their specialities in hopes that the cumulative and aggregate effects would be optimal for the whole. Unfortunately, some goals are mutually exclusive, so that the strategy of optimizing parts has been rejected as unsound. Hence, the systems approach has been embraced for its corrective effects.

A fundamental concept of the systems approach is that every system is a subsystem in a higher level system. The ultimate system is divided into subsystems according to purpose. Thus, all systems can be assigned hierarchical positions. This concept is fundamental in assigning priorities in funding continuous analysis and improvement projects for the system and its parts.

According to Brightman *et al.* (1968), "Systems analysis is the process of evaluating all aspects of a particular system and the situation in which it operates."[8] Thus, in analyzing food service systems in a particular institution, it is necessary to evaluate relations between the dietary department and each of the other departments, and policies global to the institution. It is necessary but not sufficient. Food service operations in similar institutions should also be studied to uncover both similarities and differences. A food service system may be defined as a coordinated program in which the food-related components of procurement, storage, preparation, and service are integrated with equipment utilization and methods of management so as to optimize labor utilization, consumer satisfaction, quality control, and cost effectiveness. Moreover, the systems analysts have contributed the following perspective (Freshwater 1969):[9]

> . . . the degree of success . . . of a food service operation cannot be measured only in terms of sales volume, profit and loss figures, and the rate of return on capital investment. Such intangible factors as employee morale, menu acceptance, and the psychological impact of the dining atmosphere upon the consumer have a dynamic impact on . . . consumer decisions. . . . An increasing number of operators, mainly the larger ones, recognize these intangible factors and are attempting to evaluate their impact upon financial progress. There is also a growing realization that survival in an expanding competitive market is dependent upon the determination of profit margins and production costs for specific menu items.

The systems analyst uses the scientific method as a fundamental strategy in developing a well-defined statement about the system and its interactions with its environment. Five standard parts of the analysis include:

---

[8] By permission of MacMillan Co., New York.
[9] Quoted with permission of J. F. Freshwater.

(A) Objectives—these provide a frame of reference for subsequent evaluation and decisions.
(B) Constraints—time, money, quality, skills, etc.—thoroughly documented so that as conditions change, justifications for modifications can be developed.
(C) Relationships among the parts—expected, actual, formal, informal and an evaluation of which are critical to success.
(D) Alternate courses of action or various systems configurations.
(E) Time limits as they affect intrasystem dynamics, intersystem harmony.

With all of the data in hand, one can propose and develop an appropriate food service system. The system should be appraised for effectiveness in providing necessary information. Ten tests that might be applied include (Jones 1968):[10]

1. The system will be vigorously opposed by those whose empires within the organization will suffer because of its implementation. A system which disrupts no one's operating habits in the organization is probably irrelevant.

2. The system will be expensive. It is a mistake to justify an automated system by the savings it will incur because there probably will be no great reduction in the costs of the information produced by the system. The information will become more timely and otherwise more useful, however, and the study that went behind the system might well discover other cost-saving but non-hardware-oriented modifications.

3. A good electronic computer system can do work that cannot be done any other way. If a way can be found to do the job another way, say with a punched card system, even though it may involve more time, then the computer is not being utilized to its highest potential.

4. The reports produced by the systems are real reports, not just listings of data. Recall that the difference between data and information is that information is data presented in the most useful form. A report is a device which transmits information, not data.

5. Information produced by the system and delivered to a station in the organization is *used*. If individuals receive reports from the system that are not used, then they should not get the reports—the system needs further modification.

6. The same report will not go to different levels of decision-makers in the organization. The president of a sales organization is more interested in branch sales totals than in detailed listings of all transactions. The information system should take into account the different needs for information at the different organizational levels and produce and deliver reports accordingly.

7. The automated system is not part of the conventional accounting system and control of the data processing department does not lie with the accounting department. . . . conventional accounting systems have failed to provide modern large businesses with the information they need.

---

[10] Quoted with permission of United Business Publishers.

Putting a resource as potentially valuable as data processing as a bookkeeping tool of the conventional system is a serious mistake.

8. Top executives are familiar with data processing and appreciate what good an information system can do for the organization.

9. The system is viewed by the organization's decision-makers as a decision-making tool rather than as a means to reduce accounting costs.

10. Experts were called in *before* the system was designed and implemented, and they were called in for advice in designing the new system, not reassurance that the new system already designed is good.

The menu planning subsystem is embedded at the center of the food service system. It utilizes information generated by other food service subsystems, e.g., availability and prices of foods or processing time and capacities of equipment. It also generates data for use by other food service subsystems, e.g., quantity and quality of ingredients and/or food items to be purchased, number of employees and level and distribution of production skills required. Consequently, a systems review of the entire food service system is necessary prior to development of a computerized menu planning subsystem. Considerations related to consumers, workers, and management were discussed in detail in Chap. 2, 3, and 4, respectively.

BIBLIOGRAPHY

ANON. 1968. Computers today: a new realism. Institutions *62*, No. 3, 91–102.

BELL, C. G. 1968A. Fundamentals of time shared computers. Part I. Computer Design *7*, No. 2, 44–59.

BELL, C. G. 1968B. Fundamentals of time shared computers. Part II. Computer Design *7*, No. 3, 28–44.

BRIGHTMAN, R. W., LUSKIN, B. J., and TILTON, T. 1968. Data Processing for Decision making. An Introduction to Third-generation Information Systems. Macmillan Co., New York.

CASBERGUE, J. P. 1966. Computers are changing methods of management in food service. Food Exec. *29*, No. 1, 12–14.

FANO, R. M., and CORBATO, F. J. 1966. Time sharing on computers. Sci. Am. *215*, No. 3, 129–140.

FRESHWATER, J. F. 1969. Selected Research Abstracts of Published and Unpublished Reports Pertaining to the Food Service Industry, including Recommendations for Research Needs. USDA Agr. Res. Serv. *ARS 52-46*.

GILLE, F. H. 1968. Computer Yearbook and Directory, 2nd Edition. American Data Processing, Detroit.

HARTMAN, J. 1967. It's time to get acquainted with your new dietary assistant: the computer. Mod. Hosp. *109*, No. 6, 130.

JONES, C. 1968. Ten Tests. *In* Data Processing for Decision Making. An Introduction to Third-generation Information Systems. R. W. Brightman, B. J. Luskin, and T. Tilton (Editors). Macmillan Co., New York.

KOTSCHEVAR, L. H. 1967. Computer: Fiend or friend? Part I and II. Food Management *3*, No. 3, 10, 53–55.

KOVAC, G. M. 1969. A way out of the maze of the computer myth. Food Technol. *23*, 1131–1138.

MACKINNON, A. 1968. Flow charts methods. Computer Design *7*, No. 2, 72–75.

MORSE, P. M. 1967. Operations Research for Public Systems. MIT Press, Cambridge, Mass.

SAMET, P. A. 1969. Computer quotes. Computer Dig. *4*, No. 1, 2.

SAMMET, J. E.   1967.   Fundamental concepts of programming languages. Computers Automation, Febr., 30–37.

SHAW, C. J. 1967. What a non-programmer should know about programming languages. Computer Group News *1*, No. 4, 1–9.

SIPPL, C. J. 1966. Computer Dictionary and Handbook. Howard W. Sams & Co., Indianapolis.

WESTERHOUSE, R. A. 1969. Time sharing and its applications. Computer Group News *2*, No. 7, 3–7.

CHAPTER 16

History of Menu Planning by Computer

Until the 1950's automated data processing referred to rearrangement and tabulation of data using sorters, collators, and accounting machines. Then computers were introduced to further automate these routine clerical functions. Toward the end of the decade investigations of the usefulness of the computer in decision-making began (McCormick 1968; Myers 1967). Heuristic, i.e., trial and error, programming methods were developed which permit the computer to solve problems using strategies, criteria, etc., which are similar to ones human beings use in solving the same problems. However, progress in developing applications has been hindered by the lack of structure of most decision-making.

Decision-making in institutional food service is no exception. However, a systems study of the dietary department at Sara Mayo Hospital in New Orleans by Balintfy and Balintfy (1964) indicated that if the menu planning subsystem were computerized all information necessary for computerization of other routine functions would be available. At about the same time applications in nutrient analysis, inventory and cost control, etc., were announced (Balintfy 1964 A, B; Brisbane 1964; Johnson and Moore 1966; Tullis *et al.* 1965).

ANTECEDENTS OF MENU PLANNING BY COMPUTER

The problem of finding a nutritionally adequate diet at least cost, i.e., the diet problem, is a classic example of application of linear programming methods. The first formulation of the diet problem was made in 1941 and was originally solved using a calculator (Dantzig 1963). A simplified example is customarily included in discussions of linear programming in textbooks on methods of operations research (Smith 1961). Linear programming solutions to the diet problem have been used to great advantage in formulating various feed blends for animals.

G. J. Stigler developed a model for obtaining a nutritionally adequate subsistance diet at least cost in 1945 based on the 1943 RDA and selected premises regarding nutritional requirements and the nutrient contributions of a small variety of foods (Smith 1961; Stigler 1945). In developing his model, Stigler used a list of 77 food commodities for which the Bureau of Labor Statistics Index of Retail Prices was available, such as flour, cornmeal, margarine, cheese, lard, liver, etc. He specified that the levels of nutrients could exceed RDA rather than meet them exactly. This simplification greatly enhanced the probability of a solution and it turned out that less costly diets could be obtained.

Furthermore, it enabled him to reduce the list of foods by omitting foods that were relatively more expensive sources of nutrients; this was important in reducing the computational load. His final list of prospective foods was wheat flour, evaporated milk, cheddar cheese, beef liver, cabbage, spinach, sweet potatoes, dried lima beans, and dried navy beans. His model produced a least-cost diet at 10.9¢ per day (1939 prices) or $40 per year. The diet solution consisted of 370 lb wheat flour, 57 cans of evaporated milk, 111 lb cabbage, 23 lb spinach, and 285 lb dried navy beans. Unfortunately, such a restricted diet was unpalatable and thus unacceptable.

Another minimum cost subsistance model was developed in 1959 by Beckmann using the 1958 RDA and 25 foods (Smith 1963). The solution contained four foods: lard, frozen orange juice, beef liver, and soy bean meal. Probability of consumption was low since the last two foods were not very acceptable.

At about the same time, the Vajda model was developed in Britain. A model was also developed for a Yugoslavian diet.

In 1959, V. E. Smith (1959) first reported development of the midget model which was designed to provide nutritionally adequate diets at least cost.

In 1961, P. E. Smith (1961) took another approach to the diet problem setting his objective as one of minimizing calories but meeting vitamin and mineral requirements. His optimal diet consisted of 14.08 oz haddock, 40.3 lettuce leaves, 1.4 cup cooked turnip tops, and approximately 1/4 oz wheat germ. This diet provides 349 calories. Like other previous solutions, this one is only a curiosity. The reader should note that computational accuracy exceeds reasonable measurement accuracy.

V. E. Smith (1963) reviewed previous models and solutions to the diet problem in terms of efficiency of meeting cost, and nutritional and palatability requirements. Using several models developed during the 1950's, Smith showed that the linear programming method provides a means of (a) determining the absolute cost of subsistance, based on physiological need—usually defined by the RDA, and (b) the cost of assuring consumption, based on culturally acquired needs—such as variety, item acceptability, etc., which can be obtained from available statistics or by survey.

In developing nutritional constraints, Smith recognized some fundamental sources of difficulty in building nutritional constraints, which are simplified statements designed to assure nutritional adequacy of the diet. Adequacy can be assured if, and only if, (a) nutritional requirements are completely known and are accurate, (b) the nutritional contributions of food items are accurately assessed, and (c) the sum of the nutrients provided is a valid reflection of intake (unless consumption can be assumed it is not). In developing his models, Smith used the best information available concerning (a) nutritional requirements, namely the RDA, and (b) nutritive composition of food items, based on *Bowes and Church Food Values of Portions Commonly Used* (Church and Church 1970). He initially assumed that if items were commonly consumed, they could be considered palatable, and therefore, consumption could be assumed. However, in later models, he abandoned this assumption and attempted to increase palatability with a variety of special constraints.

The Smith midget model was designed to meet nutritional requirements at least-cost with no consideration of palatability of the diet. Nutritional constraints were based on the 1953 RDA and the list of prospective foods and their associated costs were obtained from a 1955 consumer survey in East Lansing, Michigan. The solution contained fresh milk, margarine, carrots, potatoes, picnic ham, and white flour. Smith (1963) made this comment on the most expensive of his least-cost diets:[1]

> With only 6 ingredients, it is dull, and runs heavily to potatoes and flour (over 5 lb a day of the two together, for a family of 3). The 139 lb of milk correspond to 65 qt, or 2.3 qt per day. I suppose the menu will have to consist largely of potato soup, creamed potatoes, creamed carrots, and milk. Nothing can be salted, for no salt is provided in the diet. About twice a month there will be a great day when the picnic ham is bought, and for some time afterward our friends can have scalloped potatoes baked with bits of ham... The most difficult problem is disposing of the 66 lb of flour. There is neither yeast nor baking powder in the diet, so the family may have to eat flour paste.

With this observation in mind, Smith then developed palatability constraints. He noted that while the dietitian normally considers preference in planning meals, she does so in an intuitive or implicit fashion. Whereas, when palatability constraints are included in a programming model they become explicit and thus can be evaluated for validity. Furthermore, explicit inclusion allows computation of the effects on cost.

As a means of improving palatability, Smith (1963) initially added cooking aids to his midget model, i.e., baking powder, baking soda, flavoring extracts, vinegar, and prepared mustard. With this improvement he then observed, "It is interesting to note how rapidly flour loses its superiority as an economical food when one requires the purchase of complementary goods needed in order to use the flour in palatable ways."

Next, Smith developed the small model in which the cooking aids included: baking powder, baking soda, baking chocolate, flavoring extracts, meat sauces, spices, pepper, vinegar, yeast, and prepared mustard. Coffee was also added since a beverage is commonly served. Moreover, maximum quantity limits were established for some of the food commodities at 2 to 3 times mean consumption, as determined by survey. This model resulted in inclusion of a larger number of foods.

Smith then developed the large model using 572 foods and 98 restraints; the computer was necessary in solving such a large problem. The solution contains 62 commodities but was still not acceptable. Whereupon Smith examined the relationship between item acceptability and combination acceptability. He determined that data on the marginal utility of consuming added quantities of a

---

[1] Quoted with permission of the author.

food, given the quantity of that food and others in the diet, was necessary before accurate constraints could be constructed.

Using this model Smith also evaluated the effects of the various nutritional constraints, the economic cost of a nutrient, the cost of habits and preferences, and the effects of substituting preferred foods on the overall cost. He found that (a) some nutrients are more difficult to obtain in the diet since they are more expensive, while others have no effect since they are provided in supplying the scarce nutrients; (b) the relative costs of the various nutrients can be determined by measuring the cost of adding one unit of each nutrient to a given diet, given specific nutrient requirements; (c) the cost of preference is equal to the added cost of the food minus the cost of the quantities of other foods that can be reduced when this food is added; and (d) although there are equivalent sets of nutritional substitutes, when one item is substituted, the quantities of other items must be adjusted and traditional sources of nutrients may not be the ones selected in the least-cost diets. He also found that seasonal variation in composition of the least-cost diet is minimal since this diet consists of staples whose prices are practically invariate.

Smith's contributions have been considerable. After 10 yr of research in developing solutions to the diet problem Smith concluded:[2]

> The principal problem to be solved in putting programming into operational use in institutional feeding or elsewhere is controlling the palatability of the diet. That limitations imposed by consideration of palatability play a powerful role in determining the composition of diets prepared by traditional methods is evident when one compares the cost and composition of the purely nutritional diets . . . with the cost and composition of the low-cost diets ordinarily set forth by students of nutrition.

Peryam (1959) reviewed Stigler's and Smith's work and concluded,[3]

> The diets provided by Stigler's solution or by Smith's simpler models are merely curios; no one would use them, at least not in this country. Habit, custom, preference for flavor, traditional ideas of what is fitting in the way of a meal—in a word, acceptability—demand consideration.

He suggested that one of the difficulties with linear programming solutions was related to the lack of menu structure. That is, people do not eat like animals, rather they consume meals of a culturally determined structure. For example, dinner consists of the following meal components: entrée, starchy food, vegetable, salad, dessert, bread, and beverage. He further noted the need to consider item suitability for each meal, e.g., dry cereal is not suitable for dinner. Moreover, menu combinations are not additive in acceptability since some items such as sweet potatoes have a low acceptability rating except when paired in a culturally accepted combination with ham. Furthermore, he noted that some combinations of foods are acceptable and others are not. However, he did not

---

[2]Quoted with permission of the Journal of Farm Economics.
[3]Quoted with permission of the Journal of Farm Economics.

develop a model using this information. It remained for Balintfy to develop a program to plan hospital menus by computer.

MENU PLANNING BY COMPUTER: LINEAR PROGRAMMING APPLICATIONS

Balintfy and Vetter (1964) reported development of algorithms for planning nonselective menus by computer. According to Balintfy (1964A):[4]

> ... the objectives of palatability in menu planning are carried through by imposing formal requirements on the structure of menu components and also on the variety of menu items within the components. Inasmuch as these requirements are combined with nutritional and economic objectives, a new version of the classical diet problem, the "menu problem" emerges. The menu problem is concerned with finding the optimum combination of menu items which satisfies specified nutritional, structural, and variety requirements for a sequence of days. The optimality condition can be minimization of cost or maximization of consumer's satisfaction, or both. The structural requirements are the customary array of the components in menus. These can be, for instance, appetizer, entrée, cereal, bread, and beverage for breakfast; appetizer, entrée, starch, vegetable, salad, dessert, bread, and beverage for dinner; and similarly for supper. More or less of these components make up the structure of menus depending upon the habits and standard of households and institutions. Finally, the variety requirements are satisfied either through selectivity, i.e., offering more than one menu item per component or by restricting the repetition of items for a number of days or by the combination of both procedures (cafeteria system).

V. E. Smith and P. E. Smith developed models obtaining standard linear programming solutions. On the other hand, Balintfy recognized the problem as an integer programming problem. In his models, portion size is specified since a solution specifying inclusion of two carrot coins would be absurd. Thus, his solutions are stated in terms of whole portions of items.

Balintfy developed multistage linear programming models since menus are customarily planned for an entire cycle at one time. Each day is considered a stage with stated objectives to be optimized. Using branch and bound techniques allows the objectives to be optimized each day but with carryover of nutrients such as calories, vitamin A, etc. This allows solutions in which some nutrient constraints such as ascorbic acid are met daily while others are met on the average over the cycle. Commonly, cost is to be minimized subject to nutritional, variety, color, texture, etc., constraints. The RDA serve as nutritional requirements in the model. Variety, i.e., repetition of item and major ingredients, is controlled by means of "separation days" which specify the number of days or meals that must elapse before repetition can occur. An advantage of the multistage model is that each item can be re-evaluated for each stage and, thus, items previously rejected because of repetition can re-enter the solution set

---

[4]Quoted with permission of the Association for Computing Machinery, Inc.

after individually varying intervals. Color constraints are simply defined (Balintfy and Nebel 1966); for example $1x_2 + 1x_4 + 1x_5 \leqslant 1$, which means that only one meal component (entrée, salad, or dessert) can be red. Texture is controlled similarly.

Furthermore, Balintfy (1970) perceived that the menu planning process combines two separate activities, namely planning or selecting the items to be included in the solution and scheduling their occurrence within and among days, according to frequency criteria. The single stage model was used to plan the list of least cost items. Initially, dietitians scheduled the items in menus but later menus were prepared by computer.

However, a difficulty was encountered in distributing items over the menu cycle. If items were assigned from the beginning of the cycle, the last days were loaded with low preference items. When distributions began at both ends, a middle problem developed. Obviously, low preference items have to be randomly distributed over the cycle so that no day has too many unacceptable items.

Another problem has been encountered with linear programming solutions that has been difficult to solve. Menus planned by this method are arranged in a sequence from least expensive to most expensive with a 6–7 day period of increasing costs as more expensive meal components are selected to replace items proscribed because of variety restrictions. Then a "steady state" develops as items are allowed to re-enter the solution set (Balintfy and Nebel 1966). Menus are planned for an entire cycle at one time, which may be 6 weeks, and patient stay averages 5 days. Since acceptability is highly correlated with cost, patients served meals at the beginning of the cycle are unhappy. According to one user, to avoid this problem, menus are scrambled among days. Unless the entire day's menus are transposed, daily nutritional adequacy cannot be assumed, since items are rarely nutritional equivalents. However, long-run adequacy is not affected. Moreover, the distribution of items over the cycle is destroyed.

Model refinements have continued over the years (Balintfy 1967, 1970; Balintfy et al., 1967A; Balintfy and Blackburn 1968). However, each refinement has raised the minimum cost over the least-cost solutions. The term "optimal cost" might be used to describe these expanded model solutions, but it is ambiguous and unhandy since extensive documentation listing all premises and assumptions would be necessary in order to judge optimality. The term "feasible cost" might be used, but, here again, it is relevant only.

Another problem has also been identified (Eckstein 1971). When the nutrient levels are allowed to exceed requirements by an unspecified amount below an arbitrarily selected upper bound, the quantities of most nutrients are random. Scarce nutrients are provided in minimal quantities as Smith pointed out. Other nutrients are provided according to their distribution in foods supplying the scarce nutrients. Optimally, *the RDA should probably be regarded as target means* to be met in the long-run, i.e., over a week or so, rather than daily.

Another contribution of Balintfy and Prekopa (1966) has been an analysis of the types of random variation that account for variability in the nutrient composition of meals. They have demonstrated that the nutritive composition of meals is related to variability in (a) inherent nutrient composition of the ingredients, (b) portion size and plate waste, and (c) the nutrient contribution of items combined as meals. However, they state that the lack of adequate data on nutrient composition (i.e., range, mean, standard deviation, variance, and covariance) creates problems in forecasting the nutritional adequacy of menus planned manually or by computer. Much research is required to develop data of this nature.

According to Balintfy and Nebel (1966), computerized menu planning probably will always be a joint man-machine decision-making activity because there are a number of aspects of the menu planning process that may never be sufficiently defined to allow incorporation in the model. The computer optimum may not be optimal as judged by dietitians. Therefore, dietitians will need a means of modifying menus as they are generated by computer to assure that all requirements are met.

Balintfy's models were developed to plan nonselective menus. Liggett and others observed that selective menus are commonly used in hospital food service. They developed models for planning selective menus by computer using stochastic linear programming methods.

A major problem in using linear programming methods to obtain a solution to an applied problem such as planning menus is the difficulty of obtaining proper values for the parameters. As indicated above, the true values for nutrient parameters can only be approximated due to inherent variation in ingredient composition, etc. The true value for quantity consumed can only be approximated. It can only be known after the food is consumed; thus, this information is unavailable to the planning process. Preference is the best predictor available. Values for other parameters are also variable. Since the values of most, if not all, of the parameters appear to be random variables, strategies for linear programming under risk (i.e., when the probability distribution is known) and uncertainty (i.e., when the probability distribution is unknown) are appropriate.

Stochastic programming techniques are used when the constraints must be met. Linear programming methods use an objective function that must be maximized or minimized, e.g., cost. However, it is meaningless to minimize this function if its value is a random variable. So, one uses the expected value in place of random variables in computation. Constraints are also restated as expected values.

In planning a menu, at the outset, all values are unknown, being dependent on the values associated with the items selected, since combinations are effectively infinite. However, when the first item is selected, some values become knowns and will affect decisions influencing selection of all successive items for that menu. Thus, as additional items are added and the cumulative values of the parameters approach those of the constraint, the number of items that can satisfy constraints is reduced. In the case of the last meal component, the values are completely known.

The number of constraints and variables, i.e., recipes, in a linear programming problem is large which results in a heavy computational load and high costs for computing. A number of programming tricks have been employed to reduce the computational load and thus obtain the solution more efficiently. For example, the chance-constrained programming technique is used when it is highly desirable that all constraints be met but some can be relaxed if necessary to obtain a solution. For discussion of this technique, see Hillier and Lieberman (1967). Undoubtedly, increasingly sophisticated techniques will be developed to increase program efficiency.

Liggett (1965) discussed some of the statistical and operational problems associated with planning selective menus using linear programming models. Some points of interest are:

(A) Prediction of item choices by a patient or a model of a patient is difficult; a patient's choice among alternate items for a given meal component may be influenced by previous choices from the particular menu or previous menus.

(B) In testing linear programming models, one must be cognizant of and assess the effects of erroneous limits in restricting the selection of menu items. For example, in regard to nutrition constraints, setting excessive limits might cause the Type I error which is the chance of rejecting menu item groups as candidates for the menu plan, when in fact, the groups would satisfy nutrient constraints. On the other hand setting too low a limit might cause the Type II error which is the chance of accepting menu item groups as candidates for the menu plan, when in fact, the groups would not satisfy nutrient constraints.

(C) Since a patient selects only one item from a group of alternate items for a given meal component, the statistical probability of a patient not picking a balanced diet equals the probability of a patient selecting the minimum nutrients from each group of foods on the menu, if choices of meal components are independent. However, as noted in (A) above, they are not. This presents difficulties in using linear programming models.

(D) It is easier to select items at the beginning of the menu cycle than at the end; frequently restrictions reduce the set of prospective menu items available making solutions more difficult.

(E) While individual meals or days may be optimal the entire cycle may not be optimal; short-run and long-run objectives are not identical nor are they met in the same way.

Gue and Liggett (1966) developed a linear programming method in which pairs or triplets of items, e.g., Beef Stew or Meat Loaf, Roast Beef or Broiled Chicken, etc., are constructed for each meal component in which choice is planned. Using this system, the pair or triplet is treated as a single entity for programming purposes. Associated probabilities for each member of the combination are used to compute the cost and nutrient contribution. In theory, the number of possible pairs or triplets is infinite; in practice the number is reduced to a select group for which probability data are available. Combinations are scheduled randomly; additional items are selected to meet structural, nutritional, and palatability requirements at least cost. In subsequent papers (Gue 1969A, B; Gue and Liggett 1966, 1967) have been reported further developments and refinements in their strategy for planning selective menus.

Baust (1967) reviewed previous linear programming applications and their shortcomings, particularly Balintfy's Computer-Assisted Menu Planning (CAMP) system. He noted the following limitations: (a) inadequate control of color and texture, major ingredient repetition, etc., (b) menu item incompatibility resulting from use of absolute rather than cross-correlated preference ratings, and (c) failure to consider kitchen and service facilities and available manpower for production. He concluded, "Until procedures can be developed for quantifying data, an alternative approach to CAMP is necessary." He suggested development of a man-machine system in which feedback on the dietitian's corrections could be used by the computer in "learning" which items are incompatible. At present, problems have been reduced but not resolved.

Langier (1969) reviewed linear programming applications and developed solutions for use in Guatemala and other less developed countries. A large proportion of the people are living on a subsistance diet with a high motivation to meet physiological needs. Furthermore, they do not have great expectations in terms of variety. Hence, use of a linear programming model to determine which common, acceptable food should be added or increased to improve nutritional status at least cost seems feasible. Patrick and Simoes (1971) have developed a linear programming model that creates a list of least cost foods, with associated quantities, for Brazil. This model uses caloric, nutrient, and quantity restrictions as programming constraints.

In 1970, Balintfy reviewed Gue's work and outlined several shortcomings. Among them: (a) since new combinations cannot be generated, as only accepted triplets, etc., are used, an artificial nonrational element affects modeling; (b) nontransferable historical data are used in predicting choice probabilities for standard triplets but imputed values are used for new triplets; (c) nutritional constraints designed to assure levels exceed requirements, but no provision is made to control quantities within limits; and (d) nutritional control is difficult to obtain and menus are more costly. Balintfy then offered three models he developed as a part of his own research project, starting in 1966.

The "balanced meal choice" model is designed to plan 2 separate menus designed for 2 population subgroups with differing nutritional requirements. A choice is always offered for at least one meal component, usually selected arbitrarily for all stages, but wherever possible other items are the same in order to minimize cost. The first meal is selected; then alternate choices for the second meal are selected. Furthermore, genuine choices are possible when the alternate meal items are selected to be compatible with items in the first meal.

The second model is based on the premise that requirements set for the majority subgroup in the population plus structural requirements will be sufficient to ensure acceptable nutrient control. A balanced menu is planned for the majority and alternate items are added without regard for their nutrient contribution.

The third model is designed to plan a set menu first and then alternate items that are nutritional equivalents in terms of content of critical nutrients. This allows consumer freedom of choice while minimizing loss of nutritional control.

These three models represent common methods of planning for the nutritional content of selective menus. Two advantages over other investigators' models are (a) item pairs are not predetermined and (b) selection probability data for the pairs are unnecessary. This enhances menu variety and reduces the work of computerization while allowing control.

Pinto (1971) explained the theoretical basis for planning protein-rich food mixtures that would contain an optimal pattern of the essential amino acids at least cost. Equations and inequalities used in obtaining the solutions were also discussed.

Gelpi *et al.* (1972) reported results of a study designed to compare sets of regular and 11 types of modified diet menus planned with computer assistance to those planned by conventional methods. Mathematical programming techniques developed by Balintfy, as described above, were used in the programs for computer assisted menu planning. Exchange lists and other common simplifying methods were used to control the nutritive content of menus planned by conventional methods.

Selective regular menus planned by both methods were compared on the basis of raw food cost, palatability, and nutritive content in the first segment of this study. The authors concluded that (a) the raw food costs of menus planned by conventional methods were 10% higher than those planned with computer assistance, (b) there was no significant difference in palatability of the menus planned by the two methods, and (c) the computer planned menus provided stipulated levels of selected nutrients more precisely than did conventionally planned menus.

Eleven types of modified diet menus, e.g., diabetic, bland, sodium restricted, etc., planned by conventional and computer assisted methods were compared in the second segment of this study. They were compared on the basis of nutritive content and raw food cost. The authors concluded that (a) the computer planned menus provided stipulated levels of selected nutrients precisely whereas conventionally planned menus violated tolerances for calories, fat, and carbohydrate and (b) conventionally planned menus were unjustifiably more expensive since a mean savings of 40¢ per patient day could be realized by using the computer assisted menu planning system.

In concluding remarks, the authors reminded the reader that these results were obtained using systems designed for research purposes. Such systems are not readily applicable for general use. Moreover, in determining the economic feasibility of using the computer to plan menus, the costs of development and operation of the computer assisted systems must be included in the analysis. However, other than the statement that this research project was the outcome of 7 yr of research and processing time to plan a 2-to-4 week cycle is 4 hr per quarter, no information on time and costs was given.

MENU PLANNING BY COMPUTER: RANDOM SELECTION METHODS

Brown (1966) developed primitive techniques for controlling the palatability of individual nonselective lunch and dinner menus using random selection techniques. Factors included in the model were texture, flavor, color, shape, and method of preparation. Nutritional adequacy was not of primary importance so menu structure requirements were assumed adequate in assuring adequacy comparable to that attained by using Food Guides. Daily menu cost was tallied but not controlled. An item classification system was used to control selection of items from appropriate classes for each specified meal component.

Working independently, at about the same time, Eckstein (1967) developed a somewhat more sophisticated method of planning up to 99 selective dinner menus using the random selection method. Selection criteria included meat cost, color, texture, shape, flavor, calories, and variety, i.e., controlled repetition of items and categories of items. Standard menu structure was used in selecting meal components.

The random approach was designed to simulate the dietitian's methods of selecting menu items. Three random numbers are drawn and are manipulated to generate an item code. The code is then used to retrieve information about the item in order to evaluate its suitability for the meal component under consideration. In essence, the program functions as follows:

(A) For the meal component being selected, e.g., the meat item, an item is selected at random.

(B) The computer evaluates the item on the basis of test criteria built into the program (constraints) and stored in a memory unit of the computer.

(C) An item that fails a test is rejected for that menu. The computer then selects another item at random in the same group and proceeds as above. If, after 50 attempts to find a meal component and no item can be found that will pass all of the tests, the computer goes on to select other meal components using "dummy characteristics" which have been predetermined for the missing meal component. An asterisk is printed on the menu listing where the name of the blank item would appear.

(D) An item that passes all tests is accepted for the menu by the computer; its characteristics are stored for checking purposes. The next meal component, e.g., starchy food, is then chosen at random by the computer and is tested by separate but similar criteria. This process continues until all meal components have been selected. The complete dinner menu is then printed by computer. Thereafter, additional menus are prepared by the same process until the desired number are completed.

Selection criteria normally used by the dietitian formed the basis for program constraints. The cost of the meat item is greater than that of other meal components and it is more variable; therefore, control is important. A 3-day moving average is used to control selection so that costs average 21–30¢, or any other predetermined cost range, except on Sunday when the average is adjusted to allow selection of a more expensive item. If a low cost meat is selected for Sunday dinner, in order to maintain an acceptable average a more expensive meat will be selected for Monday or Tuesday dinner.

Color constraints were primarily designed to prevent repetition on the dinner plate, i.e., no two items among the meat, starchy food and vegetable may have the same color. Generally, two reds or red, red purple, and orange are proscribed.

Texture constraints were devised to prevent monotony. The maximum number of times soft, chewy, and crisp textures can be included is two. And, no more than 1 chewy and 1 crisp item can be selected.

Shape constraints are also designed to increase variety. Three "slices" and two each of "rounds" and "squares" may be selected but other shapes cannot be repeated.

KIND constraints were designed to control repetition of kinds of fruits, vegetables, flavors, etc. Control limits are based on acceptability ratings. Categorical limits, stated as a proportion of the population, include: acceptable-to-some, $\frac{1}{4}$ to $\frac{1}{2}$; acceptable-to-most, $\frac{1}{2}$ to $\frac{3}{4}$; and acceptable-to-all, greater than $\frac{3}{4}$. Constraints for selection of Sunday dinner require that all items selected be acceptable-to-all.

Miscellaneous code numbers and constraints function conjointly with historical data to control selection in three areas. One constraint limits the number of items in a meal that contain fruit. A second controls selection frequency of items whose major ingredient is a member of the cabbage family. A third precludes pairing of a semifluid vegetable, such as cream-style corn, with a meat that is served with a sauce or gravy.

In addition to the general constraints that apply to all meal components, specific ones were designed to control aspects unique to the individual meal components. Three types of constraints for the meat component include (a) automatic selection of an alternate item if a less well-accepted item such as fish or liver is selected, (b) a limit of one tomato-based sauce, i.e., Spanish, BBQ, etc., in 7 days, and (c) a limit of category, i.e., beef, pork, lamb, etc., selection to once in 3 days.

Specific constraints applying to the starchy food component include (a) selection of a potato at least every third day, (b) control of frequency of potato substitutes according to type and acceptability, e.g., rice can be served once in

TABLE 16.1

CRITICAL NUTRIENT VALUES

	Calories Min Max		Protein Min Max (Gm)		Fat Min Max (Gm)		Carbohydrate Min Max (Gm)		Calcium Min Max (Mg)		Iron Min Max (Mg)		Vitamin A Min Max (IU)		Vitamin B$_1$ Min Max (Mg)		Vitamin C Min Max (Mg)	
Daily																			
	1690	2475	38	85	43	123	175	315	0	0	0	0	0	0	0	0	0	115
	1925	2635	43	89	52	129	205	340	0	0	0	0	0	10000	0	0	0	129
	1970	2672	43	90	55	132	210	345	0	0	0	0	1810	12500	0	0	26	136
	2100	2742	44	90	65	133	225	355	0	0	0	0	2210	14000	0	0	33	144
	2440	2965	53	93	80	138	275	385	0	0	0	0	0	15000	0	0	0	150
	2600	3100	55	95	90	145	295	405	0	0	0	0	0	15000	0	0	0	150
Weekly																			
	2700	3000	55	95	90	138	310	360	775	1000	10	18	5000	6500	1	2	50	105

7 days, noodles once in 10 days, and dumplings once in 18 days, and (c) creamed starchy food cannot be paired with a meat that is served with a sauce or gravy. The time limits for the first two constraints were selected arbitrarily based on experience.

The vegetable component normally provides color, texture, and shape interest in a meal. Constraints were designed accordingly using "reasonable" limits. Selection frequency for individual vegetables was based on acceptability, e.g., any vegetable rated acceptable-to-some could only be selected once in 14 days whereas those rated acceptable-to-all could be selected once in 4 days.

Specific constraints were also designed to provide a variety of salads. There were mainly categorical limitations, (a) fruit salads could not be selected for three successive meals, (b) vegetable salads could be selected daily, although not from the same group such as a succession of variation of cole slaw, and (c) the salad cannot repeat the vegetable component, e.g., carrot and raisin salad cannot be paired with buttered carrots.

Two types of specific constraints were designed to control dessert selection. These include (a) limiting selection of a category of dessert, i.e., pie, cake, pudding, etc., to every other day and (b) preventing pairing of a fruit salad with a fruit dessert.

A "history" of items served in the preceding 21-day period is stored in memory. After the entire day's menus have been planned the entire history is shifted back one day and the code numbers for newly selected items are entered in history. This allows the computer to check back in time in checking for repetition of items, etc.

Eckstein (1969) refined the program constraints and expanded the program by adding (a) nutritional constraints, (b) a tally system for evaluating effectiveness of constraints and (c) a breakfast and luncheon cycle menu of 21 days.

Nine nutrients were included: calories, protein, fat, carbohydrate, calcium, iron, vitamin A, thiamin, and ascorbic acid. The RDA were treated as target means; upper and lower bounds were established arbitrarily. To assure that nutrient requirements would be met and all meal components could be selected, upper and lower bounds were assigned for the nutrients at each selection point (Table 16.1).

Although the models developed by Eckstein are probably not as efficient nor as sophisticated from the standpoint of theory in operations research, they are more sophisticated in terms of the concepts in menu planning that are employed. However, a great deal of additional work remains to be done.

BIBLIOGRAPHY

BALINTFY, J. L. 1964A. Menu planning by computer. Assoc. Computing Machinery Commun. 7, 255–259.
BALINTFY, J. L. 1964B. On a basic class of multi-item inventory problems. Management Sci. 10, 287–297.

BALINTFY, J. L. 1966. Linear programming models for menu planning. *In* Hospital Industrial Engineering: A Guide to Improvement of Hospital Management Systems. H. E. Smalley and J. R. Freeman (Editors). Reinhold Publishing Corp., New York.

BALINTFY, J. L. 1967. Computerized Dietary Information System, Vol. I, Data Organization and Collection Procedures. Graduate School Business Admin., Tulane Univ. Res. Paper *14*.

BLAINTFY, J. L. 1970. Computer Assisted Menu Planning and Food Service Management. Graduate School Business Admin., Tulane Univ. Working Paper *41*.

BALINTFY, J. L. and BALINTFY, S. K. 1964. Dietary information processing by computer. Graduate School Business Admin., Tulane Univ. Paper *1*.

BALINTFY, J. L. *et al.* 1967A. Computerized Dietary Information System, Vol. II, Data Processing Systems. Graduate School Business Admin., Tulane Univ. Res. Paper *21*.

BALINTFY, J. L., BLACKBURN, C. R. II, and MORRIS, K. V. 1967B. Computerized Dietary Information Systems, Vol. III, On-line Terminal Systems. Graduate School Business Admin., Tulane Univ. Res. Paper *22*.

BALINTFY, J. L., and BLACKBURN, C. R. II. 1968. Computerized Dietary Information Systems, Vol. IV, Planning and Scheduling Optimum Menus in Multi-stage. Graduate School Business Admin., Tulane Univ.

BALINTFY, J. L., and NEBEL, E. C. 1966. Experiments with computer-assisted menu planning. Hospitals *40*, No. 12, 88–96.

BALINTFY, J. L., and PREKOPA, A. 1966. Nature of random variation in the nutrient composition of meals. Health Serv. Res. *1*, 148–149.

BALINTFY, J. L., and VETTER, E. W. 1964. Computer writes menus. Hospitals *42*, No. 6, 49–52.

BAUST, R. T. 1967. Computer assisted menu planning. Data Processing Mag. *9*, No. 12, 22–24.

BRISBANE, H. M. 1964. Computing menu nutrients by data processing. J. Am. Dietet. Assoc. *44*, 453–455.

BROWN, R. M. 1966. Automated menu planning. M.S. Thesis, Kansas State Univ.

CHURCH, C. F., and CHURCH, H. H. 1970. Bowes & Church Food Values of Portions Commonly Used, 11th Edition. J. B. Lippincott Co., Philadelphia.

DANTZIG, G. B. 1963. Stigler's nutrition model: an example of formulation and solution. *In* Linear Programming and Extensions. Princeton Univ. Press, Princeton, N.J.

ECKSTEIN, E. F. 1967. Menu planning by computer: the random approach. J. Am. Dietet. Assoc. *51*, 529–533.

ECKSTEIN, E. F. 1969. Menu planning by computer: the random approach to planning for consumer acceptability and nutritional needs. Ph.D. Dissertation, Kansas State Univ.

ECKSTEIN, E. F. 1971. Models for control of the nutritive content of menus planned by computer. Food Technol. *25*, 600–602.

ECKSTEIN, E. F., and WAKEFIELD, L. M. 1972. Using the computer for menu planning. Hospitals *46*, No. 6, 92–95.

GELPI, M. J., BALINTFY, J. L., DENNIS, L. C. II, and FINDORFF, I. K. 1972. Integrated nutrition and food cost control by computer. J. Am. Dietet. Assoc. *61*, 637–646.

GUE, R. L. 1969A. Mathematical basis for computer-planned nonselective menus. Hospitals *43*, No. 21, 102–104.

GUE, R. L. 1969B. A reformulation of the menu planning problem. Am. Inst. Ind. Engrs. Trans. *1*, 146–149.

GUE, R. L., and LIGGETT, J. C. 1966. Mathematical programming models for hospital menu planning. J. Ind. Eng. *17*, 395–400.

GUE, R. L., and LIGGETT, J. C. 1967. Selective menu planning by computer. Computer Sci. Center, Inst. Technology, Southern Methodist Univ. Tech. Rept. *CP-67101*.

HILLIER, F. S., and LIEBERMAN, G. J. 1967. Introduction to Operations Research. Holden-Day, San Francisco.

JOHNSON, R. A., and MOORE, A. N. 1966. Inventory and cost control by computer. J. Am. Dietet. Assoc. *49*, 413–417.

LANGIER, J. D. 1969. Economical and Nutritional Diets Using Scarce Resources. Michigan State Univ. Press, East Lansing.

LIGGETT, J. C. 1965. Mathematical programming and hospital menu planning: applications and limitations. M.S. Thesis, Univ. Florida.

MCCORMICK, E. M. 1968. Computers for management decision making: a critical inquiry. *In* Computer Yearbook and Directory, 2nd Edition. American Data Processing, Detroit.

MYERS, C. A. 1967. The Impact of Computers on Management. MIT Press, Cambridge, Mass.

PATRICK, G. F., and SIMOES, M. H. R. 1971. Least-cost diets in Cristalina, Goias, Brazil. Arch. Latinoamericanos Nutr. *21*, 371–380. (Portuguese with English summary)

PERYAM, D. R. 1959. Discussion: linear programming models for the determination of palatable human diets. J. Farm Econ. *41*, 302–305.

PINTO, G. F. 1971. Optimization of protein-rich mixtures. Arch. Latinoamericanos Nutr. *21*, 169–183.

SMITH, P. E. 1961. The diet problem revisited: a linear programming model for convex economists. J. Farm Econ. *43*, 706–712.

SMITH, V. E. 1959. Linear programming models for the determination of palatable human diets. J. Farm Econ. *41*, 272–283.

SMITH, V. E. 1963. Electronic Computation of Human Diets. Bur. Business Econ. Res., Michigan State Univ.

STIGLER, G. J. 1945. The cost of subsistence. J. Farm Econ. *27*, 303–314.

TULLIS, I. F., LAWSON, W., and WILLIAMS, R. 1965. The digital computer in calculating dietary data. J. Am. Dietet. Assoc. *46*, 384–386.

CHAPTER 17

Model Selection and Development

Development of a computer program to plan institutional menus is a complex process. A model is used to specify the relationship among key factors; it guides program development. Mathematical models, which are a series of equations, are the most common type. Three types of equations are common in models for decision-making (Brightman *et al.* 1968). *Definitional equations* define relationships among variables. *Technological equations* express results of physical processes. *Behavioral equations* simulate or predict behavior of customers. A verbal model, though less precise, is often used initially to express these relationships. A flow chart is a combination visual and verbal model that is used for documentation as well as communication.

The computer offers great promise in menu planning because of its speed, accuracy, and consistency in appraising each prospective menu item. However, as Morse (1967) has pointed out:[1]

> Like any other model, the computer model will not predict correct results unless it corresponds to the actual operation in all important respects .... Unless realism is built into the details of the program and unless the whole simulation is checked for normal behavior, the computer model is only a complicated and impressive way of making an unverified guess.

Premature enthusiasm resulting from apparent success with a simplification of the menu planning problem has been widespread in management circles. In an attempt to maintain previous food/labor cost ratios, programs have been designed to plan menus at the lowest cost, given selected criteria. When low cost is emphasized and other values are subordinated, the menu-planning problem is greatly simplified and model development is facilitated. However, the danger is that both the model builder and management may confuse the real world with the model which simulates the situation. Poor menus and poor decisions regarding use of the menus may result. In this case insidious erosion contributes to consumer and worker dissatisfaction.

Another difficulty has also been noted. Once a model is constructed or selected, the decision-maker is reluctant to discard it even if it is not good (Brightman *et al.* 1968). The investment of time, energy, and money results in commitment to the project. For this reason selection or development of a model should not be attempted without a comprehensive situation analysis and thorough investigation of alternative prospective models.

---

[1] Quoted with permission of MIT Press.

MODEL SELECTION

Comprehensive information concerning the premises and assumptions used in model development should be provided in the descriptive materials that accompany the flow chart and sample output. If it does not, an adequate appraisal of model suitability is impossible. And, one may infer incompetence, neglect, and/or deceit; in any case use of the system should be tabled pending receipt of adequate descriptive materials.

Ideally, one should consider several alternative models for menu planning before making a decision. Currently, one has only the choice between accepting a linear programming model or local development of a custom-made model.

In selecting a model for a specific situation one should carefully evaluate the underlying philosophies that guided model development. Universal, global, and local considerations should be systematically reviewed for effects. One expects that universal considerations, for example those that control aesthetic acceptability such as color, texture, shape, and consistency, will be included in the model. As indicated in previous chapters global considerations, i.e., those applying within each segment of the institutional food service industry, are not expected to be relevant to other types of food service units. For these reasons, a model designed to represent hospital feeding requirements is unlikely to fit the realities of school food service situations. Moreover, while universals and globals define what should be done, local considerations determine what can be done. Therefore, a model that is sufficiently generalizeable for wide appeal will probably require extensive modification if it is to be responsive to local needs. Some aspects are independent of the data, others are not.

In addition to these basic considerations a number of others also affect the quality of the menu produced. One should determine the effects of search and selection procedure on menu quality and whether an accurate or an approximate solution will suffice. Next, the level of program and data sophistication should be evaluated. Then a problem definition must be devised that will assure inclusion of all elements necessary in order to obtain the menu quality desired. Finally, one should determine whether the menus should be planned wholly or in part by machine.

Search Procedure

Mechanical repetition of menu items at periodic intervals was an early fear that generated resistance to computerization of the menu planning process. Together, the search procedure and constraints actually determine whether mechanical repetition is likely. Two strategies for selecting prospective menu items for evaluation have been used, namely, systematic and heuristic procedures.

Using a systematic search procedure, which is customary with linear programming methods, all items coded for a specific meal component are evaluated sequentially and the best item or items are selected. Unless constrained, the computer will attempt to utilize the same best item or items every day, hence the necessity of introducing a time-frequency constraint. Even so, unless other constraints cause realignment in the ranking of what is best, mechanical repetition will occur with items repeating at individually different but constant intervals.

Using the heuristic search procedure, an item is selected at random from those coded for the specific meal component and is tested to determine whether it meets criteria. The first item that passes all tests is selected. The particular combination of characteristics required to satisfy constraints is dependent on the aggregate characteristics of previously selected items. Therefore, it is unlikely that mechanical repetition will occur.

Sophisticated Models and Primitive Data

Formulation and refinement of menu planning models is challenging and it provides many subproblems suitable for graduate student research. Hence, increasingly sophisticated models will become available.

By definition, a model represents a simplified version of reality. All aspects of the problem have not been defined, tested for effects, or included in model formulation. The model builder selects the aspects he considers most important. A well-formulated model will produce solutions that are precise, i.e., reproducible given stated conditions. However, precision does not increase the comprehensiveness or accuracy of the problem definition; hence, the relevance of the solution. Therefore, spurious solutions may be obtained. As current models contain only selected aspects, the minimax principel seems to apply. Because all effects cannot be evaluated, selected factors should not be optimized. In all probability, the best strategy is a moderate solution that provides assurance of avoiding defects that might generate greater problems than those solved by the model.

Many different classes of data are required in order to systematically evaluate the suitability of prospective menu items. But, the data base for the institutional food service industry is inadequate, i.e., both spotty and inaccurate. Commonly, required classes of data include mean nutritive requirements of the target consumer group and the following data for each prospective menu item: (a) mean nutritive contribution, (b) mean total portion cost, (c) mean hedonic and desired frequency ratings, and (d) mean man-machine processing time. Other classes of data may also be required depending on the level of sophistication desired.

The quality of computer planned menus reflects the quality of input data as much as the power of the program. Currently, available data in most cases should be regarded as estimates because sampling procedures are not rigorously controlled. Therefore, we are *not* privileged to regard the data as being sufficiently accurate to warrant elegant statistical treatment. Given expected limitations of the data, a model should be selected whose level of sophistication does not imply unjustified accuracy in the solution.

Problem Definition

The appropriate problem definition for a particular food service operation depends on the reason for automating the process, the type of institution, and situational factors. Two major reasons for automating are (a) to reduce the cost of providing nutritionally adequate menus and (b) to improve the quality of the menu by consistent consideration of all factors.

In the first case, the business objective of reducing costs in order to maximize profit or minimize loss is the primary goal. Nutritional requirements are regarded as constraints limiting the degree to which costs may be reduced. Aesthetics and preferences of the target population are low priority factors considered only when they reduce effectiveness in meeting costs and/or nutritional objectives. Work load and equipment usage may also be considered in order to implement cost reduction. Given a monopoly situation or in the short-run, this problem definition may suffice. However, when consumer purchasing power is strong enough to reduce volume of sales, a realignment of priorities is necessary. There is some evidence that the tendency to balance priorities is a natural phenomenon that occurs in the long-run.

The number of combinations of menu items that will meet nutritional requirements is very large; systematically evaluating them to determine the least expensive combinations is computationally infeasible without using the computer. Hence, if this problem definition is accepted, a computer application is necessary.

In the second case, the objective is to use the computer capabilities of speed and consistency in the evaluation of all the characteristics of each prospective menu item so as to optimize selection according to all accepted criteria. This assumes massive quantities of data and a large set of decision rules. The accept-reject decision for the individual item is therefore more objective, i.e., based on complete data and not subject to random application of the criteria. This definition is directed toward a compromise solution that facilitates progress toward long-run goals, i.e., achieves cost and nutritional goals which minimize dysfunctional side effects.

If the menu planning problem is defined—to provide optimal nutrition at minimal cost—then one must show that the food is likely to be consumed and that reductions in food cost have not been negated by increases in other costs. Clearly, if this objective is to be reached the problem definition is similar to the one: *to improve the menu quality by consistent consideration of all factors.* To meet these objectives, the quality of the menu must be defined in detail.

Two other reasons for automating the menu planning process are often cited although they have little effect on formulation of the menu planning model per se. They are (a) to integrate the menu planning process with automated systems of purchasing, inventory management, etc., and (b) to free professional time from a routine repetitive decision-making task. The four reasons for computerizing the menu planning process are neither mutually exclusive nor collectively exhaustive, but they are typical.

Once the reasons for automating the menu planning process are clearly defined and documented an operational definition must be developed. In general, the operational definition used in model development differs for each type of institutional population because the characteristics of the group and the budgeted cost allowance differ. Specific considerations were enumerated in the chapters dealing with the various types. Local situational factors also modify the operational definition. A detailed description of premises and assumptions must be developed as a part of the documentation. Next, a set of decision rules must be developed. These must define actions to be taken at each decision point. Alternative actions must be planned for each expected type of status condition. These are used by the programmer in writing the instructions for the computer to follow in selecting menu items.

Next, criteria for evaluating effectiveness of the computer menu planning program must be stated. According to the particular problem definition developed, expected types and levels of quality will differ. Conceptually, the quality rating of a menu obtained from a professional evaluation is a weighted aggregate average determined by a subjective comparison of the actual with the ideal. Unfortunately, the ideal is often irrelevant because of situational requirements and constraints. For purposes of research, it is acceptable to judge and report the quality of a menu in terms of the selected factors investigated. For practical situations, all factors must be evaluated using the same criteria used by the consumer group as well as management. These criteria must be explicitly defined if effective rather than token or hypercritical evaluation is to be avoided.

Numerous interrelated factors contribute to the quality of a menu. These include all of the consumer, worker, and management considerations discussed in Chap. 2, 3, and 4—preference, nutrition, variety, work load, and cost. Minimum and maximum variation allowable for each aspect of each factor must be specified. In order for a quality menu to be planned, a minimax strategy is required. This requires that problem definition include factor priorities represented by numerical weights.

Machine or Man-machine Menu Planning?

A computer program can be written to plan menus in any way that is desired. Efficiency and costs will vary with the approach and program requirements. Two approaches have been reported:

(A) The machine plans the total menu set which is then reviewed by professional staff; changes are introduced to correct for factors not included in the program (Eckstein 1967).

(B) A man-machine combination plans the menus. The interaction begins with the machine suggesting a menu which is then modified by the dietitian as necessary. The machine then re-evaluates the menu and makes additional changes as necessary. This process is repeated until both man and machine are satisfied (Balintfy et al. 1967).

Each of these approaches is based on a different philosophy. The first acknowledges that the computational load and number of characteristics to be evaluated according to a large number of criteria exceeds human ability. It assumes that given adequate data and selection criteria and using the computer advantages of speed and consistency in evaluation, the computer can produce superior menus. Only minor changes are expected to result from professional review.

In theory, this approach achieves an optimal result—high quality menus are produced and professional time is released for less routine tasks. Difficulties are encountered when program design is inadequate resulting in need for frequent item substitution.

The second approach is predicated on the belief that a man-machine interaction can produce a better menu than either alone. It acknowledges that the computational load is heavy and that using the speed and systematic functioning of constraints, a good menu can be obtained. But, because not all relevant criteria are included in the program, continuous professional review is required to detect and correct menu problems.

This approach has two built-in hazards: (a) the dietitian is pressured into making snap decisions regarding need for menu changes and feasible substitutions and (b) the dietitian is trained to select substitute items that are almost equivalent to those replaced since this minimizes the number of menu changes to be reviewed and, hence, computer time. While professional review is ostensibly designed to compensate for program inadequacies, the man-machine interaction system tends to undermine commitment to this goal-directed activity. Hence, menu quality tends to be progressively eroded as the dietitian is trained in the man-machine interaction.

The first stages of model selection can and should be objective; the final selection is usually subjective. When the local menu planning problem has been defined in detail and the features of alternate menu planning models have been enumerated and evaluated, elimination of unacceptable alternatives can begin. Finally, a small number of good alternatives remain. At this point, after a final review of the advantages and limitations of each, one model is selected intuitively.

MODEL DEVELOPMENT

The number of alternative models for planning menus by computer is limited, as noted above. In order to plan a satisfactory menu for a specific situation, a new model may be required.

The process of model development involves a series of small research projects. A basic framework is developed first. Then each aspect is developed and tested systematically and is integrated with previous parts. The whole is then tested to detect undesirable effects, if any. Adjustments are made as necessary. Additional parts are developed and tested stepwise.

The steps in model development will vary somewhat although in general they will include the following: (a) problem definition, (b) development of a tentative concept of modeling methods, (c) model formulation, and (d) model testing.

Two types of problem definition and pertinent categories of data to be included in descriptive documentation were discussed in the section above. When developing a menu planning model, the depth of detail included in the problem definition is much more important. Insufficient detail is likely to result in inadequate model formulation.

A tentative concept of modeling methods is commonly obtained from a review of the literature. Most research reports contain some descriptive information about the mini-problem and some unique method of dealing with it. In the aggregate these solutions are very helpful. It remains for the model builder to incorporate applicable concepts and develop others as necessary. Logical analysis provides the basis for insightful integrations of the various parts of the model. Model formulation itself is a technical task that requires ability to identify and state relationships unambiguously. If problem definition is accurate and complete, formulation is facilitated.

Once a model is constructed, it must be validated under a variety of real conditions. Usually, several independent sets of historical data are used and the solution obtained using the model is compared with the actual events. A high degree of correspondence should be obtained. Otherwise, the model must be refined to improve the quality of solution obtained.

After a satisfactory model has been obtained, computerization of the menu planning process can begin. Usually data collection and programming proceed concurrently.

BIBLIOGRAPHY

BALINTFY, J. L. *et al.* 1967. Computerized Dietary Information System, Vol. II, Data Processing Programs. Computer Res. Systems, Graduate School Business Admin., Tulane Univ. Res. Paper *21*.

BRIGHTMAN, R. W., LUSKIN, B. J., and TILTON, T. 1968. Data Processing for Decision-Making. An Introduction to Third-generation Information Systems. Macmillan Co., New York.

ECKSTEIN, E. F. 1967. Menu planning by computer: the random approach. J. Am. Dietet. Assoc. *51*, 529–533.

MORSE, P. M. 1967. Operations Research for Public Systems. MIT Press, Cambridge, Mass.

CHAPTER 18

Data Collection and Validation

There is a hazard in using the computer to generate reports. The halo effect of a well-arranged report with figures to X decimal places may mislead the reader to infer unwarranted accuracy. One must carefully monitor the quality of input data and check the quality of the output reports for reasonableness.

The quality of output reports generated by the computer is determined by (a) the validity of input data and (b) the quality of the instructions that determine the processing steps and generation of reports. Format statements can be designed to generate neatly arranged, properly labeled reports. Mathematical accuracy to X places is determined by features of the machine. This does not necessarily improve the accuracy of the output. The number of significant digits in the input data determines the number justified in the output reports.

Data processing requirements for menu planning exceed human capacity when manual methods are employed. But to compensate for lack of experience and professional judgement the computer is programmed to analyze large quantities of data. When computerized systems are used the problem is reversed and inadequacy of the data becomes a limiting factor. Hence, the decision to computerize is usually the signal to conduct a literature search or a series of small research projects to obtain the required classes of data.

Data requirements usually include the following types: (a) expected nutrient contribution of various menu items, (b) food habits and preferences of the consumer group, (c) production data, i.e., man-machine processing times, (d) cost data, and (e) menu item characteristics. Each type is discussed briefly below.

EXPECTED NUTRIENT CONTRIBUTION

The estimated nutrient content of a day's menus is customarily obtained by summing the nutritive contributions of the various items listed on the menu. Validity of this nutrient analysis rests on the validity of the assumptions that (a) all of the items are consumed in the quantities indicated (to be discussed in the following section) and (b) the data used in computations are both relevant and reliable.

Data on the nutritive contribution of the various menu items can be obtained in two ways, namely by chemical and/or biological assay of representative samples of the foods actually served or from standard tables of food composition. As the former method is both time-consuming and costly, one generally resorts to the latter method, although it is less accurate.

Tables of food composition for selected American foods have been available since 1896 (Atwater and Woods 1896). At first, protein, fat, crude fiber, ash, and moisture were listed. As knowledge of nutritional requirements became known additional nutrients were added to the tables (McMasters 1963). Because the nutritional status of the American population became important to national defense during World War II, the tables of food composition were revised and greatly expanded. However, they have not been systematically revised since.

Conceptually, the table values are supposed to represent typical year-round, country-wide values. Therefore, they should be generally applicable.

However, table values, originally obtained by analysis in USDA *Agriculture Handbook 8* were obtained largely by a search of the research literature (Watt and Murphy 1970). However, the number of samples used in computing the mean was not standardized among foods or nutrients. Nor were levels of control standardized by nutrient for the same food; interfering substances confound results to a variable and unknown degree. Therefore, one has reservations about the typicality of the mean value (Harris 1962, 1963; Mayer 1960).

Moreover, since World War II our foods have changed greatly. Many new items are commonly consumed but no composition values are available. Formerly, knowing the name of a menu item enabled one to predict its composition fairly accurately since type and quantity of ingredients were fairly standardized in order to assure product success. However, by using stabilizers, gums, and other nonnutritive texture and bodying agents, traditional eating qualities can be obtained without using the traditional ingredients. Table values for class representatives of each of the alternate ingredient-mixes are not available; use of traditional composition values is meaningless and leads to spurious nutritional analysis of diets.

Food processing methods also have changed. The direction and magnitude of changes in nutrient composition are largely unknown. For example, the standard loaf of bread changed from the homemade type to an airy sponge when the bakery industry changed from batch to continuous processing methods. The loaf is baked at higher temperatures which presumably reduces the thiamin content since it is heat labile. The ratios of ingredients have changed and the number of slices per pound has greatly increased with the expansion in volume. Consequently, one expects the per slice nutrient composition to be reduced. The quantitative effect is at this point undefined.

According to Watt and Murphy (1970) other technological changes that have affected the nutrient composition of our foods and for which limited or no data are available include:

(A) Development of new varieties of fruits and vegetables that can withstand the rigors of mechanical harvesting.
(B) Development of new breeds of poultry, pigs, and steers resulting in meat with a higher protein and lower fat content.
(C) Development of raw and cooked turkey rolls.
(D) Development of cake, cookie, pie crust and muffin mixes and other convenient forms of these items.

(E) Development of nondairy substitutes for milk, cream, whipped cream, etc.

Another difficulty with table values is that the data were largely obtained by chemical analysis of constituents. However, due to the presence of interfering factors the biologically available quantity differs; for the majority of foods the quantitative effect of interfering agents is unknown.

With these data limitations in mind, one must be exceedingly careful in interpreting nutritional analyses. The computer will assure computational accuracy. The user must be careful to avoid drawing unjustified inferences if the quality of data won't support them regardless of the level of computational accuracy used in summarizing the data.

FOOD HABITS AND PREFERENCES

Prior to World War II information on food habits and preferences was intuitive or unorganized. During World War II information concerning the food habits and preferences of the soldier-consumer became critical in planning food to meet his nutritional needs. As a result, the Quartermaster Corps of the Food and Container Institute for the Armed Forces developed systematic methods of data collection and analysis (Jones and Thurstone 1955: Kamen 1962B; Peryam and Pilgrim 1957; Pilgrim 1957). These have served as models for civilian studies. Numerous studies were conducted and the data were published to aid civilian menu planners (Bell *et al*. 1965; Kamen 1962A; Moskowitz *et al*. 1972; Peryam *et al*. 1960; Pilgrim 1961; Vawter and Konishi 1958; Wood and Peryam 1953). In the ensuing decades, studies of the food habits and preferences of various institutional populations have been reported at sporadic intervals. However, these studies are not usually generalizeable because of situational and regional biases. Such data can be used for comparison but some local surveys will be required to provide baseline data. Then assumptions and premises can be checked for validity.

The assumption that all items listed on the menu will be consumed in the quantities indicated is based on another subset of assumptions, namely, (a) an appropriate number and distribution of items are offered, (b) all of the items are acceptable individually (preferred and properly prepared), (c) the combination of items is acceptable, and (d) the quantity of each item is appropriate. Each of these assumptions must be verified.

In the first case, an empirical study of plate waste is called for. A plate waste study consists of the following steps:

(A) A systematic sampling of the weight of specific items and/or the total quantity of food as served to the consumer. Usually an average tare weight, i.e., weight of the plate plus the food minus the average weight of a representative sample of plates, is computed.

(B) A systematic sampling of the weight of the specific item and/or the total quantity of food remaining on the plate when returned to the scrap line. Here again, the average tare weight is usually computed.

(C) The difference between the values for the two samplings equals the quantity consumed. The sample mean plate waste value is then computed.

If the quantity of plate waste is small, it is attributed to individual differences. If it is large, investigation of the cause is indicated. Alternate explanations might include (a) too large a quantity of food, i.e., either too many items or too generous portions or (b) inappropriate distribution of items, e.g., too many starchy foods. If one of these is the cause of nonconsumption, corrective action is simple and validity can easily be restored.

In the case where acceptability of individual items must be verified, at least two types of survey are necessary. First, a preference survey is used to determine the relative proportion of the consumer group that (a) is familiar with the item, (b) totally rejects the item, and (c) rates the item on each scale point. Second, since preference ratings and the desired consumption frequency are imperfectly correlated, it is necessary to determine the number of days that must elapse between serving the same item and its major ingredient(s).

The first consideration is to select the subjects to be surveyed. According to Pilgrim (1957), a number of characteristics determine food preferences. These include age, cultural and socioeconomic background, region of residence in early years, size of town of birth, level of education. To control for these factors, a stratified random sampling plan is usually employed. For example, in surveying a male college popualtion, with a sample size of 800, college class is the basis for stratification. That is, 200 subjects are selected randomly from the freshman, sophomore, junior, and senior classes. When additional factors are used in partitioning the sample, care must be taken that each subgroup remains sufficiently large that valid data can be obtained. As the number of strata increases so must the total sample size. Moreover, one usually expects only a 50% return of the questionnaire and some will be unuseable.

The second consideration is the selection of the classes of foods to be surveyed. Initially, data on the preference ratings for items in all classes are necessary but it is impractical to sample all classes at one time. The questionnaire would be so long that subject cooperation would be difficult to obtain. Therefore, one customarily starts with the limited objective of obtaining data about the preference ratings for the most important and/or critical classes of foods, e.g., entrées, vegetables.

The third consideration is the number of food items that should be surveyed within each food class. The objective is to obtain a large enough sample to be representative. Therefore, if the items are very similar, a small number of items will suffice. However, a class such as entrées contains several subclasses such as breakfast, lunch, and dinner entrées. Each subclass is further divided into categories. For example, breakfast entrée categories include eggs, meats, etc; dinner entrée categories include beef, pork, lamb, variety meats, poultry, fish, etc. Furthermore, the expected range of ratings must be represented in order to determine the dispersion of ratings. Therefore, the number of items to be surveyed in each class must be large enough to include a sufficient number of items for each category and expected scale point, otherwise one cannot obtain reliable ratings.

The fourth group of considerations concerns construction of the questionnaire itself to minimize common rating errors that might distort interpretation of the findings. The three expected types of rating errors are (a) error of leniency, (b) error of central tendency, and (c) error of contrast. Error of leniency means that the subject rates items he prefers according to the best sample he can recall. Directions to the subject should remind him to rate an item according to his average response insofar as possible. Error of central tendency refers to the fact that most poeple tend to avoid rating items using either the highest or lowest rating. Directions to the subject should encourage him to use the full range of scale points. Contrast error refers to the tendency to rate an item higher than normal when it follows a disliked item; it seems more acceptable by contrast. The sequence of items should be arranged to minimize this effect.

Another consideration in questionnaire design is the placement of directions on a page so as to attract the reader's attention. Moreover, the schedule of items and rating points should be arranged to aid the reader in marking the form, e.g., light and dark bands carry the eye across the page, thus increasing the likelihood that ratings refer to the intended items.

Another consideration is the problem of identifying the menu items so as to enable the subject to respond accurately. If the wrong item name is used, the subject may (a) mark the item as though it were unknown or (b) confuse it with another item, giving it an incorrect rating. In both cases the obtained data would be invalid, but the investigator would have no means of determining the extent of this type of error.

To minimize this bias, the common name, obtained from cookbooks and/or restaurant menus, is used. Short descriptive phrases are often added for clarity, e.g., Veal Parmesan (veal cutlet cooked in tomato sauce and topped with grated Italian cheese).

During the pilot testing of the questionnaire, problems associated with the item names can be identified. A test-retest procedure can be used in which the questionnaire is administered and scored, then alternate names can be substituted and the questionnaire readministered to the same group of subjects.

Ratings for the two test samples should be evaluated item by item. If the same items are marked "unknown" in both cases, one concludes that the item is unknown. When the item changes from an unknown to a rated item, then one concludes that the substitute name is more familiar and retains this name for use in the final questionnaire. When an item rating remains essentially the same, both names are retained for use on equivalent forms. Where the rating changes markedly, confusion is indicated and one must carefully evaluate both names to determine which is ambiguous.

The fifth consideration concerns the number of scale points needed. Scale points are intended to represent the midpoints of psychologically equal intervals (Jones 1954; Jones and Thurstone 1955). The number of scale points necessary is determined by mean subject ability to discriminate and report differences in preferences. Several rules of thumb can be obtained from the literature but this should be established by pilot testing a prototype questionnaire. Table 18.1 shows a sample of common scales and associated terminology. Figure 18.1 shows a scale used by children in indicating preferences.

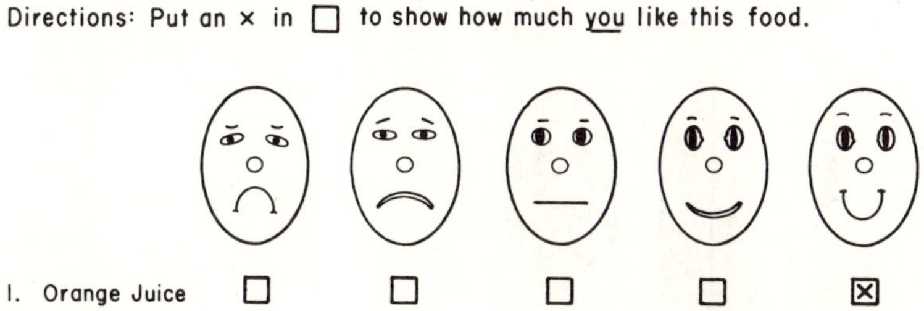

Directions: Put an × in ☐ to show how much you like this food.

I. Orange Juice ☐ ☐ ☐ ☐ ☒

FIG. 18.1. FACIAL HEDONIC SCALE

Experts generally agree that an odd number of scale points is more effective as it allows for a midpoint representing indifference. The original hedonic scale (Peryam and Pilgrim 1957) was constructed as a 9-point scale varying from "like extremely" through "neither like nor dislike" to "dislike extremely." Other investigators have found a 5- or 7-point scale to be equally effective.

The sixth consideration is the length of the questionnaire. Generally, it should not require more than 30 min to complete. It is known that if it is too long, some subjects may express annoyance by deliberately sabotaging the results. Common methods are (a) completely random marking (b) pattern marking, e.g., all items are marked "6" and (c) failure to complete the questionnaire. Prior to data analysis, each questionnare should be screened and defective ones rejected. If many items must be surveyed in order to obtain a representative sampling of food items, then the list of items should be divided among two or more forms. Usually a number of items will be common to both forms for validation purposes. The forms must be tested for equivalence; standard statistical tests can be employed.

A seventh consideration concerns the administration of the questionnaire to a mixed ethnic group. In order to determine the differences in ethnic preferences for a standard sample of menu items, the author administered the same questionnaire to a sample of four different ethnic groups, namely black, ori-

TABLE 18.1

SAMPLE SUCCESSIVE-INTERVAL CATEGORY RATING SCALES

Type Scale	Sample Item	Scale								
		Like Most +4	+3	+2	+1	Neither Like Nor Dislike 0	−1	−2	−3	Dislike −4
Rating	Roast Beef	Like Most				Neither Like Nor Dislike				Dislike
Hedonic[1]	Tomato Soup	Dislike Extremely 1	Dislike Very Much 2	Dislike Moderately 3	Dislike Slightly 4	Neither Like Nor Dislike 5	Like Slightly 6	Like Moderately 7	Like Very Much 8	Like Extremely 9
Modified Hedonic No. 1	Buttered Carrots			Never Tried	Refuse		Accept		Like	
Modified Hedonic No. 2	Baked Halibut		Refuse to Eat It	Don't Care For It		It's OK Might Eat It		Like Fairly Well	One of My Favorites	
FACT	Consomme	Weeks per Month 1 2 3 4		Dinner	Days per Week 1 2 3 4 5 6 7			Lunch / Weeks per Month 1 2 3 4		Days per Week 1 2 3 4 5 6 7

[1] Also see Fig. 18.1.

ental, chicano and caucasian. Because many of the items were unknown to the minority subjects, answering the questionnaire became traumatic and a large proportion failed to complete the questionnaire. Therefore, it became necessary to convince the subjects before starting the questionnaire that information on which items were unknown was exactly the information we were seeking. We explained that for the purposes of assessing menu choice, unknown equals unacceptable. Therefore, if they aided us by providing information about which items were unknown we could avoid loading menus with these items, thus providing more acceptable menus.

These are the major considerations in developing a preference questionnaire. Most also apply to design of a questionnaire to determine the desired frequency of serving each item.

Ostensibly, the desired consumption frequency can be obtained by asking subjects to mark a form listing meal, day, week, and month (see Fig. 2.3, Chap. 2). However, this is an oversimplification, since the desired frequency is reduced if similar items are served in other meals or within a few days. Therefore, a second set of data on the desired frequency of serving the major ingredient must be obtained to be used in conjunction with the first set. The objective of the questionnaire would be to show that, for example, while Waldorf Salad might be served once in 10 days, apple salads might be served once in 5 days and apples might be included in some meal once in 3 days. More frequent inclusion would result in monotony. Schuh *et al.* (1967) have discussed the problem of frequency in a recent paper.

Another consideration is the selection of items to be included. For some items such as condiments (catsup or mustard), sauces (butterscotch or chocolate), toppings (nuts or coconut), etc., the general frequency ratings are meaningless. The objective is to determine for these classes of items whether the item is never consumed or, if it is consumed with which item(s) it is customarily consumed. The optimal form of the questionnaire (Schutz 1972) is therefore a series of matrices by food class with associated condiment, sauce, etc., arranged so the subject can indicate paired items (see Fig. 18.2).

The preference and frequency data for the population as a whole are then plotted in a 3 by 3 matrix (Meiselman *et al.* 1972). One is primarily interested in identifying the items that (a) are highly preferred and can be served with high frequency, and (b) items that are disliked and should be served infrequently (Table 18.2). It turns out that one will find that some items are overserved and some underserved (Table 18.3); appropriate adjustments are easily implemented.

Next, the preference and frequency data should be plotted by ethnic group as described above to obtain the break-out of data. It turns out that a number of items that are rated low-low for the population as a whole will rate high-high for one or more ethnic groups. Obviously, these items must be served with high frequency in order to meet the needs of the ethnic group. Otherwise, one is *not* privileged to assume that food is consumed.

FOOD-USE QUESTIONNAIRE

This survey has been designed to help us determine how you, the consumer, feel about the appropriateness of the various condiments with the foods listed on the left of the grid below. Use the scale given here to fill in the grid, selecting the number that best represents how you feel about the appropriateness of the entrée when paired with each condiment.

Scale:

appropriate ┤─┼─┼─┼─├ inappropriate
          1 2 3 4 5

Sample:

	Salt	Jelly	Sugar
Scrambled Eggs	1		
Toast	5		
Grapefruit Half	5		

Interpretation: The "1" indicates that salt is appropriate on Scrambled Eggs and the "5" indicates that it is inappropriate with Toast and Grapefruit Half.

Directions: Fill in the grid below, working down the columns. If some combination is unfamiliar to you, guess how you would feel about its appropriateness and then circle the number from the scale that you insert in the grid.

Entrées	Catsup	Mustard	Dill Pickles	Horseradish	Tabasco	Soy Sauce	Mayonnaise	Sweet Pickles	Lettuce	Tartar Sauce
Grilled Meat Sandwiches										
Hot Meat Sandwiches										
Roast Meats										
Ham										
Cold Beef Sandwiches										
Scrambled Eggs										
Meat Patties or Meat Logs										
Fishwich										
Grilled Cheese Sandwich										
Cold Turkey Sandwich										
Corned Beef										

FIG. 18.2. SAMPLE FOOD-USE QUESTIONNAIRE WITH MATRIX BY FOOD CLASS WITH ASSOCIATED CONDIMENTS, ETC.

TABLE 18.2

RELATIONSHIP BETWEEN PREFERENCE SCALES FOR EVENING MAIN DISHES (HEDONIC SCALE)

	Low	Moderate	High
Low	A. Sardines; D. Liverwurst	D. Cervelat (cold cuts)	
Moderate	A. Fried Oysters; C. Beef Liver	A. Fish, Shrimp Creole, Breaded Shrimp, Tuna Salad, Seafood Platter, Baked Tuna and Noodles, Lobster Newburg, Salmon; B. Baked Macaroni and Cheese, Lasagna; C. Lamb Roast, Polish Sausage, Lamb Chops, Veal Roast, Spare Ribs and Sauerkraut, Corned Beef, BBQ Beef Cubes, Veal Parmesan	C. Veal Burger, Breaded Veal Steaks, Baked Stuffed Pork, Swedish Meat Balls, Pepper Steak, Italian Sausage, Chile Con Carne, Chile Con Carne/Beans; D. Bologna (cold cuts), Frankfurter, Salami (cold cuts), Sloppy Joe, Turkey Club Sandwich, Submarine Sandwich, Luncheon Meat (cold cuts), Ham (cold cuts), Chicken Club Sandwich, Turkey (cold cuts), Meatball Submarine; D. Tacos, Western Sandwich, Shredded Beef with BBQ Sauce, Hot Tamales; B. Pizza, Spaghetti, Ravioli, Chili Macaroni; C. Ham (canned), Sliced Roast Pork with Gravy, Roast Pork, Ham, Pot Roast, BBQ Spare Ribs, Meat Loaf, Cheeseburger, Grilled Cheese/Ham Sandwich, Hot Roast Beef Sandwich, Bacon-Lettuce-Tomato Sandwich, Hot Turkey Sandwich/Gravy, Grilled Cheese Sandwich, Turkey
High	A. Lobster		C. Roast Beef, Swiss Steak, Grilled Steak, Salisbury Steak, Fried Chicken, Chicken, Turkey Slice with Gravy; D. Hamburger, Pizza

TABLE 18.3

UNDERSERVING/OVERSERVING: EVENING MAIN DISHES (HEDONIC SCALE)

	Low	Moderate	High
Underserved		Veal roast Beef stew Salmon Chili con carne Chop suey Submarine sandwich	Grilled steak Roast beef Pot roast Pork roast Cheeseburger Swiss steak Chicken Salisbury steak
Overserved	Beef liver	Corned beef Baked tuna and noodles El rancho stew Turkey pot pie Barbecued beef cubes Luncheon meat (cold cuts) Frankfurter (with sauerkraut)	Ham Hot turkey sandwich with gravy Spaghetti

Once preference ratings for individual items are established, one can focus attention on the need for data on combination preferences. It is immediately apparent that one cannot hope to determine the exact preference rating for all possible combinations of items. Therefore, one attempts to select class-representative combinations from which to predict ratings for similar combinations. A number of types of combinations can be studied that will yield useful data. These include (a) meal component pairs, e.g., pairs of entrées or salads, etc.; (b) entrée-starchy food pairs; (c) entrée-starchy food-vegetable triplets; (d) soup-sandwich plate; (e) soup-salad plate, etc. However, such ratings are based on historical data which may not be generalizeable to other combinations (Davis 1958).

Combination preference data can be obtained in a variety of ways. The percentage of the population selecting each member of the meal component pairs can be obtained from production records. Data on the other types of combinations can be obtained by preference and frequency surveys constructed in the manner described above for individual items. A recent application of the magnitude estimation technique reported by Moskowitz and Sidel (1971) appears promising. This technique is used to plot the distance between members of pairs, triplets, etc., in psychological space (see Fig. 2.1 in Chap. 2). By judicious selection of a sampling of pairs, etc., one should be able to set anchor points to allow prediction of real combination preferences.

If portion size is grossly inappropriate it will be obvious and corrective action can be taken. Otherwise, until an appropriate number and distribution of individually acceptable items and/or preferred combinations are served, one is *not* in a position to validly assess appropriateness of portion size. When acceptability is controlled, if preparation is acceptable, then a simple plate waste study as described above will indicate need for change in portion size.

When all the food habits and preference data have been used in selecting acceptable menu items and combinations *and* portion sizes are appropriate, one can assume that the food items will be consumed in the quantities indicated. Then nutritional analysis using table values is valid. However, given limitations on table values these must not be interpreted too strictly.

Even the captive consumer usually has some access to foods other than those listed on the menu and included in its nutritional analysis. Some estimate of the quantity and probable nutrient contribution of these items must be made. For this purpose, questions to determine (a) the frequency and (b) the usual quantity of consumption of common snacks are customarily included in the food preference survey. Table values are used to compute their approximate nutrient contribution. This information should be listed with the nutritional analysis of the menu. Also, it should be discussed in any accompanying documentation, so that valid interpretations can be made.

Moreover, some meals are customarily omitted by some customers. The expected meal count and observed meal count are compared to determine the overall population percentage that omits the various meals. In theory, the daily nutrient intake should be divided among all three meals. But, if one of the meals is not regularly consumed by a significant segment of the population and nutrition education efforts directed to changing life style are ineffective, the alternative of dividing the nutrients among the meals that are consumed, should be thoroughly evaluated for desirability.

Food preference surveys are difficult to control as well as being costly to conduct. Nonetheless, a comprehensive data base should be established. At random intervals, a small segment of the population should be sampled as a means of monitoring changes in food preferences. With this quality of data, the computer should be able to plan acceptable menus.

PRODUCTION DATA—MAN-MACHINE PROCESSING TIME

All other things being equal, food will be consumed if it is properly prepared. Assuming use of reliable recipes by motivated competent cooks, product quality is determined by availability of optimal man-machine processing time. If machine processing time is unavailable, a less satisfactory preparation method may be substituted. If machine-processing time, e.g., oven time, is insufficient a speed-up may be effected by increasing the temperature which may damage product quality. If man-processing time is insufficient at any step, short-cuts are taken and/or control is lost; quality inevitably suffers. Thus, in order to assure consumption, data on man-machine processing times must be obtained and used in planning menus.

Standard time study techniques (Kazarian 1969; Brown 1969) are employed to collect data on the length of time required for man to perform each of the basic tasks required in food preparation. The objective is to create a standard performance time for each task. This is defined as the length of time required by the average worker to complete the task using standard techniques and working at the standard pace.

In order for the standard performance index to be reliable, it must be based on a large number of observations. Either a large number of workers must be timed or a smaller number must be timed repeatedly. Because menu variety is necessary to satisfy customer needs, it is difficult to obtain a sufficiently large sampling of observations within a reasonable time period.

In order for the standard performance times to be generalizeable, i.e., applicable to recipes not studied, it is necessary to systematically time requirements for each task in a representative sample of recipes for the expected range of quantities to be produced. This is a lengthy procedure.

Overall processing time does not increase linearly with quantity. Nonetheless, Ivanicky *et al.* (1969) devised a means of predicting labor time on the basis of production quantity. A sample of recipes was selected and steps were divided into elements. Average production times were derived from empirical investigation for each element at five different production quantities. The data were then plotted. Approximate production times for intermediate quantities can be read directly; the trend line can be extended for an estimate to time requirements for somewhat larger quantities.

Machine-processing time varies differently according to the type of task. For example, oven time is not appreciably increased with increasing quantity up to equipment capacity. If capacity is exceeded and additional ovens are not available, the quantity to be produced must be divided into batches; total production time is then a multiple of batch time. The time line is therefore a discontinuous series of steps.

On the other hand, shaping or portioning time increases with quantity. For small quantities the relationship is approximately linear; for larger quantities fatigue would cause time requirements to increase at a faster rate.

The standard time required for task performance forms the basis for blocking preparation time. If recipe preparation requires continuous man-processing time, the standard times for the tasks are summed and the total time is blocked. The same is true for continuous machine-processing time. If, recipe preparation requires man-processing time at discrete intervals interspersed with machine-processing time, each segment is blocked separately within the total time block.

COST DATA

The estimated cost of a recipe is usually based on (a) the direct or variable costs of preparation, i.e., food, labor, and supplies and (b) indirect or fixed costs, i.e., supervision, plant, equipment, etc., which are prorated. The raw food cost is commonly used as an index to total recipe cost in computing the cost of a menu. However, as Stokes (1967) has pointed out the term "raw food cost" is both ambiguous and inaccurate.

Most foods are no longer purchased in the natural state so the ingredient cost is increased by an indeterminate amount by labor and processing costs. Therefore, one should compute the prime cost which is the cost of food, labor, and supplies.

Food cost is usually taken to be the cost of the ingredients used in preparation of a recipe. However, ingredients are purchased in multiples of standard container sizes, irrespective of the quantities required in preparation. If the remainder is likely to spoil and/or be discarded, its cost should be added to the ingredient cost for the recipe.

Labor cost for original preparation of the item is estimated, if at all, from gross data on processing times. However, when standard time data are available, the actual costs of labor in producing each item can be determined. However, when overproduction results from inaccuracies in forecasting additional labor is required to store and reheat or rework an item for service. A correction factor to adjust for this added labor cost should be devised.

The cost of supplies is usually small and is commonly a gross estimate that is prorated. The exception is when special paper supplies costing over 1¢ each portion are used. These are computed separately.

The cost of a meal is not *just* the simple sum of the costs of its major components. The costs of napkins, condiments, etc., are individually trivial; the cumulative and aggregate cost is significant and should be prorated by meal.

MENU ITEM CHARACTERISTICS

Menu item characteristics include (a) color, (b) texture, (c) shape, (d) flavor, (e) KIND, and (f) miscellaneous attributes. For the purposes of menu planning, fairly gross description will suffice. Since item characteristics can be determined by inspection, validity is assured.

DATA MANAGEMENT

Massive quantities of data are accumulated from a variety of research projects and are manipulated in planning menus by computer. In order to manage the data efficiently, the investigator must conceptualize the form of the data from each project and arrange it for convenience in processing, i.e., systematic collection, transcription if necessary, keypunching, and computer manipulation. A common objective is to arrange the process so that most of the cards will be keypunched by the time the last set of data from each research project is collected. Then, a sample data set from the first batch keypunched can be used to test routines in debugging each program. As a result, the programs can be ready to run as soon as data collection is completed. This system is most efficient since several stages are in process simultaneously, thus shortening total time.

For purposes of this discussion, the assumption has been made that data collection is systematic and data types are both relevant and reliable. A further assumption is that data types have been checked for content validity, predictive validity, and/or construct (idea) validity, whichever is applicable.

The data management task is to arrange the flow of data to minimize bottlenecks and the need for side-trips to correct unanticipated problems. The following considerations are applicable whether one is designing a menu planning system or is using a "canned" program, e.g., the CAMP system. Four tasks in data management are: (a) to conceptualize data arrangement for card processing, (b) to write instructions for data collection so as to minimize errors, (c) to write instructions for keypunching so that decisions will be made in a controlled manner rather than varying over time and/or among keypunchers, and (d) to eliminate data that are unreasonable outliers or invalid due to pattern responses.

Conceptually, data is collected and arranged in some systematic manner to facilitate further processing or presentation. When manual methods are employed, data are arranged as a table; the computer equivalent is a matrix, i.e., a row by column array. Preference data are commonly arranged in a subject-by-variable matrix (Table 18.4). Recipe data are arranged in a recipe-by-vari-

TABLE 18.4

SAMPLE MATRIX—PREFERENCE DATA, SUBJECT BY VARIABLE

| | Frequency | | | | Hedonic Rating | |
| | Days/Week | | Weeks/Month | | | |
Item	S1[1]	S2	S1	S2	S1	S2
Jellied Fruit Salad	4	2	4	3	7	6
Cream-Style Corn	2	1	3	1	7	5
Lamb Roast	1	1	2	2	9	6
Green Beans	1	2	3	2	5	5
Potato Salad	1	3	3	1	7	7
Chicken Cacciatore	1	1	2	1	6	5
Cherry Pie	1	3	1	3	4	5
Roast Beef	1	1	4	4	9	9
Lasagna	1	1	2	1	6	9
Lettuce and Tomato Salad	3	1	4	1	7	2
Swiss Steak	1	1	2	1	6	6
Tomato Soup	1	1	3	1	6	6

[1] S1 = Subject 1, etc.

able matrix (Table 18.5) called the Recipe File. Ingredient information is arranged in an ingredient-by-variable matrix (Table 18.6) called the Master Ingredient File. Nutrient values for food items are arranged in a food item-by-variable nutrient matrix (Table 18.7), which may be a part of the Master Ingredient File. Nutrient values for ingredients are arranged in an ingredient-by-variable nutrient matrix (Table 18.8).

The arrangement of data for processing should be planned prior to data collection to avoid the necessity of recopying. Aside from being a waste of time,

TABLE 18.5

SAMPLE MATRIX—RECIPE FILE, RECIPE BY VARIABLE

Recipe Code	Name	No. Ingredients	Color	Texture	Shape	Kind	Acceptability	Min Frequency	Max Frequency	Total Cooked Yield (Lb)	Advance Preparation Code	Standardized Date	Standardization Code	Min Batch Size	Max Batch Size	Labor Useage Code	No. Servings	Season
32400	Beef Patty	1	5	2	10	0	2	14	5	89	0	0473	5	01	00	3	50	5
32410	Meat Loaf	8	5	2	2	0	2	21	14	124	3	1272	9	01	10	8	48	5
32411	Meat Loaf/Br. Gr	11	5	2	2	0	2	21	14	124	3	1272	9	01	10	9	48	5
32412	Stuffed Meat Loaf	16	5	2	2	0	2	28	28	248	3	0273	4	01	12	9	48	4
32413	Meat Balls/Br. Gr	11	5	2	4	0	2	21	14	124	3	0473	5	01	10	9	52	5
32414	Meat Balls/Spanish	14	2	2	2	80	1	28	28	124	3	0573	3	01	10	9	52	5
32415	Salisbury Steak	8	5	2	10	0	2	21	14	124	3	0173	9	01	10	5	48	5
32420	Beef Stew	7	5	3	1	28	2	14	7	384	5	1071	9	00	16	5	48	5
32421	Beef Ragout	9	5	3	1	28	2	14	7	384	5	0672	3	00	12	7	48	5
32430	BBQ Beef Cubes	11	2	3	1	80	3	14	7	240	0	0472	4	00	09	9	48	5
32440	Chop Suey	13	10	3	1	29	2	28	21	384	5	0771	3	01	05	9	48	5
32441	Chow Mein	13	10	3	1	29	2	28	21	384	5	0771	3	01	05	9	48	5
32450	Pot Roast of Beef	5	5	3	2	0	3	14	7	163	0	0973	8	01	08	2	50	5

TABLE 18.6

SAMPLE MATRIX—INGREDIENT FILE, INGREDIENT BY VARIABLE

Recipe Code	Food Code	Name	Nutrient Code	Quantity of Ingredients	Unit of Weight	Preparation Yield	Cooked Yield	Advance Withdrawal Code	Advance Preparation Code	Sequence Number
27040	6874	Flour, all-purpose	397	20	LB	100	100	0	00	01
27040	6821	Sugar	271	05	LB	100	100	0	00	02
27040	6707	Baking powder	403	02	OZ	100	100	0	00	03
27040	6729	Baking soda	421	01	OZ	100	100	0	00	04
27040	6724	Salt, table	416	02	OZ	100	100	0	00	05
27040	6798	Shortening, high ratio	563	02	LB	100	100	0	00	06
27040	4032	Nonfat dry milk	642	10	OZ	200	186	0	01	07
27040	6736	Vanilla	432	03	OZ	100	100	0	00	08
27040	4051	Eggs	103	02	LB	100	88	1	00	09
27040	6753	Chocolate, unsweetened	532	14	OZ	100	100	0	00	10

TABLE 18.7

SAMPLE MATRIX—FOOD ITEM BY VARIABLE (NUTRIENT)

Code	Item	CAL	PRO	FAT	CHO	Nutrients[1] CA	FE	VIT A	VIT B$_1$	VIT C
4000	Buttered Cut Green Beans	43.00	1.00	3.00	3.00	30.50	0.40	455.00	0.04	8.00
4001	Buttered Whole Green Beans	43.00	1.00	3.00	3.00	30.50	0.40	455.00	0.04	8.00
4002	Green Beans with Bacon	43.00	1.00	3.00	3.00	30.50	0.40	455.00	0.04	8.00
4003	Buttered Sliced Beets	51.00	1.00	3.00	5.00	20.50	0.05	130.00	0.02	7.00
4004	Buttered Diced Beets	51.00	1.00	3.00	5.00	20.50	0.50	130.00	0.02	7.00
4005	Baby Whole Beets	51.00	1.00	3.00	5.00	20.50	0.50	130.00	0.02	7.00
4010	Buttered Broccoli Spears	55.00	3.00	3.00	4.00	90.50	0.80	2615.00	0.09	90.00
4011	Buttered Brussels Sprouts	59.00	3.00	3.00	5.00	30.50	1.00	565.00	0.07	75.00
4012	Steamed Cabbage	47.00	1.00	3.00	4.00	35.50	0.05	195.00	0.05	37.00
4013	Buttered Carrot Rounds	51.00	0.75	3.00	5.25	23.00	0.45	7723.75	0.04	4.50

[1] Decimal fractions are carried in computations and rounded as the last step before printing.

TABLE 18.8

SAMPLE INGREDIENT-BY-VARIABLE NUTRIENT MATRIX

Code	Name[1]	ENERGY CAL	PRO G	FAT G	CHO G	CA MG	FE MG	VIT A IU	VIT B$_1$ MG	VIT C MG
1	Cheddar cheese	109	6	9	1	165	0.20	345	0.01	0
2	Cottage cheese	121	16	5	3	105	0.40	190	0.04	0
3	½ & ½	48	1	4	2	30	0.00	145	0.01	0
4	Milk, whole	165	9	9	12	285	0.10	350	0.08	2
5	Milk, nonfat	88	9	0	13	300	0.00	0	0.10	2
6	Milk-based beverages	208	8	8	26	280	0.60	300	0.09	0
7	Milk-based desserts	301	8	17	29	210	0.40	785	0.07	1
8	Cornstarch puddings	286	9	10	40	290	0.10	390	0.08	2
9	White sauce	212	5	16	12	150	0.02	610	0.06	0
10	Eggs	78	6	6	0	25	1.20	590	0.06	0
30	Asparagus	28	3	0	4	25	0.07	1055	0.19	30
31	Beans, green	16	1	0	3	30	0.40	340	0.04	8
32	Beans, lima	97	6	1	16	40	2.00	225	0.14	14
33	Broccoli	28	3	0	4	90	0.80	2500	0.09	90
34	Brussels sprouts	32	3	0	5	30	1.00	450	0.07	75
35	Cabbage	20	1	0	4	35	0.50	80	0.05	37

[1] Name was added to table for information of reader. It does not occur on printer output.

recopying increases the probability of errors and creates additional work in checking the data. When the data source is a questionnaire, its design should (a) include unambiguous instructions to the subject so that true responses are obtained, insofar as possible, and (b) assure arrangement of responses in the order in which they are to be keypunched. Data from other sources should be entered directly on forms to be used by the keypuncher. Mark-sense cards which may be read by an optical scanner and converted directly to punched cards also reduce the number of errors.

The arrangement of the data on the punch cards should be planned next. The standard punch card contains 80 columns across and 12 rows down, i.e., starting at the top of the card, 12, 11, and 0-9 (Fig. 18.3). Numeric information is

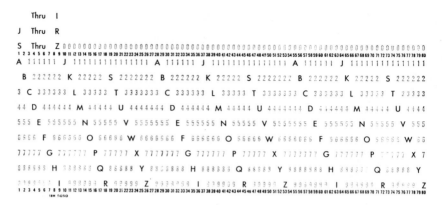

FIG. 18.3. SAMPLE 80-COLUMN PUNCH CARD SHOWING THE PUNCHES FOR
ALPHABETIC CHARACTERS

punched using 1 punch per card column, alphabetic information has 2 punches and special characters have 2 or 3 punches. Ordinarily, one *can* place the data anywhere on the card although the same type of information must be placed in the same locations on all data cards. Moreover, one usually attempts to put as many pieces of data on a card as possible. The field width, i.e., the number of columns necessary to accommodate the largest number of digits including a sign and/or a decimal point in some cases, determines the number of pieces of data that can be placed on a card. If the product of the number of variables times the field width exceeds 80 card columns, then additional cards are used to continue the data. Thus, each row of a matrix may require one or more cards to contain all of the data on a particular item or subject.

Although information may be located anywhere on a card, the computer must be instructed where to find it and when there is more than one piece of information per card, it must be instructed where one field ends and the next begins. Format statements are used for these purposes. Format statements are of three types: (a) A, alphanumeric, e.g., A5 means field of 5 alphanumeric characters, (b) I, integer, e.g., I5 means a field of 5 integer characters, and (c) F, floating point, e.g., F5.1 means a field of 5 numeric characters with a 4-digit whole number and a 1-digit fraction or F5.3 means a 2-digit whole number and a 3-digit fraction (the decimal point may be omitted from the data card since the format statement provides instructions for data storage).

When a field is to be repeated in succession, the appropriate multiple preceeds the data type indicator, e.g., 4I5 or 3F6.3, etc. Sample format statements are listed in Table 18.9 with accompanying explanation.

In order to retrieve information about a specific subject, recipe, etc., an identification code is often used. Generally, a numeric code is preferred when segments of the code are used in processing. However, an alphabetic character as the first character of a code is sometimes useful to the user, especially if it is

TABLE 18.9

PROGRAM SEGMENT SHOWING USE OF FORMAT STATEMENTS

Statements	Explanation
	This section reads Nutrient Table
DO 507 JJ = 1, 73	There are 73 cards to be read and processed
READ (1, 500) NO, (NUTV(I, JJ), I = 1, 9)	Read the number of the card and 9 nutrient values which are located on the cards as specified in statement 500
500 FORMAT (I2, 9F8.2)	Each card has a code number in the first 2 columns and then 9 nutrient values which take 8 columns each and have 2 decimal places
WRITE (3, 515) NO, (NUTV(I, JJ), I = 1, 9)	Write the number of the nutrient and 9 nutrient values according to the instructions as specified in statement 515
515 FORMAT (' ', 5x, I2, 9F8.20)	Skip a line, skip 5 spaces, write the 2 digit number, then 9 values with 8 columns each and 2 decimal places
507 CONTINUE	If this is not the 73rd card processed go back to 507 and follow the sequence again

mnemonic. Usually the digits of the code represent levels in data classification (Table 18.10). In constructing the classification, one must be sure that classes are mutually exclusive and collectively exhaustive, i.e., no item may fit in more than one class and all possible items must fit into some class. Codes are often added to indicate (a) the identity of source of information, (b) imputed values, and (c) estimates. Additional information on coding is available in the literature (Balintfy 1967; Committee to Study Data Processing 1971).

When more than one card contains information to be stored in a given row of a matrix, sequence numbers are punched in each card. This allows verification that cards are arranged in expected order, therefore intended information is stored in the various locations. Moreover, when code and sequence numbers are used, the data deck can be machine sorted to arrange cards in desired order.

Another task is to write instructions for collection of data so as to minimize errors. For example, directions on a questionnaire must unambiguously indicate methods of recording responses and whether more than one response to a question is permitted, etc. Similarly, when using other forms for data collection, these must be designed to aid the investigator in recording the data, for example by grouping data by class or point in collection.

The third task in data management is to write instructions for keypunching to reduce the number of decisions made by the keypuncher. Instructions should

TABLE 18.10

SAMPLE MASTER CODES FOR LUNCH ITEMS[1]

Code No.	Food Class
20000–3000	Lunch entrées
20000–20990	Casseroles
20000–20290	Beef casseroles
20300–20390	Pork casseroles
20400–20490	Veal and lamb casseroles
20500–20690	Chicken and turkey casseroles
20700–20790	Fish casseroles
20800–20890	Cheese casseroles
20900–20990	Vegetarian casseroles
21000–21990	Lunch sandwiches
21000–21190	Cold beef sandwiches
21200–21290	Cold pork sandwiches
21300–21390	Cold chicken and turkey sandwiches
.	
.	
.	
21500–21590	Hot beef sandwiches
.	
.	
.	
22000–22990	Lunch vegetables
.	
.	
.	
23000–23990	Lunch salads
.	
.	
.	

[1] Lunch items should be coded differently from dinner items if the portion size, garniture, price, acceptability, etc., differ. Some items are appropriate for one meal but not for the other.

state what is to be done when data are missing, when multiple responses have been made but only a single response is allowed, etc.

A number of decisions can be eliminated by proper design of forms or questionnaires. For example, numbers should be arbitrarily assigned for each response to a dichotomous variable, e.g., male = 1, female = 2; or yes = 1, no = 2. When nominal scales are used for classes of food items such as entrées, starchy food, etc., numbers are assigned for each response, e.g., dinner entrée = 15, dinner starchy food = 16, dinner vegetable = 17, etc. In both cases the numbers can be printed on the form and marked directly. This eliminates the need for the keypuncher to remember the number that represents the variable.

When all aspects of the data flow have been anticipated and planned in advance, appropriate actions are taken and data accuracy is maintained during this stage in processing. Moreover, the data are arranged to facilitate further processing.

When large amounts of data are obtained, many cards must be used. This is unhandy for the menu planner who must carry heavy boxes and it is inefficient in computer processing since the card reader is slower than other input devices. For these reasons, sequential information is stored on tape and information to be retrieved in random order is stored on disc. Standard service programs are available to transfer card information onto tape.

The fourth task is to eliminate data that are unreasonable outliers or unsuitable due to pattern responses. Special programs to screen the data are designed for this purpose. For example, if the expected range of values can be determined for each variable, then out-of-range values can be detected and an error message printed to aid in locating the erroneous data. Corrections can then be made. When a properly designed questionnaire is used, answers are expected to be distributed randomly. Therefore, any consistent pattern of responses such as all "A's" or sequences of A-B-C-C-B-A-A-B-C, etc., are unexpected and can be detected and an error message printed. In this case, however, this data set must be eliminated from further analysis.

When all of these steps have been taken one is assured of reasonably accurate data, all other things being equal. Moreover, the data is generally arranged for user and computer convenience. Other tasks may also be involved in data management such as reordering the data in a matrix or selection of various subsets of the data for special processing. While description of the actual programming is beyond the scope of this book, selected fundamental concepts are discussed to aid in (a) selection of appropriate "canned" program routines or (b) communicating with a programmer.

Data is reordered in a matrix for different purposes. For example, it may be arranged in ascending or descending order of magnitude to facilitate processing. To arrange in descending order, the first value is compared to other values until a larger value is encountered. The larger value is stored in a temporary location and the first value is inserted in its place. The process of comparing the largest value to each of the remaining values continues until a larger value is encountered and the exchange of values again takes place. This process continues until all values in the row have been compared. The largest value obtained is then stored in the first location. Then, the second value is compared to other values in the row in the same way, finally obtaining the second largest number which is stored in the second location. This process continues until all values in the row have been rearranged.

Another example is when it turns out that the data on cards are inconveniently arranged for some application. Two alternative means of reordering the data are commonly used: (a) a program can be written to read the data and punch a new data deck with the information in a new order, or (b) a routine can be added to a program to rearrange the columns or rows of a matrix. In the first case, reordering the variables in the format and punch statements will accomplish the task. In the second, a standard routine is called.

Selection of data subsets for special processing may be accomplished in many ways. A few selected examples follow. If the item code is designed so that one digit refers to the meal, a second to the meal component, and a third to the food category then the dinner entrée pork can be computer identified and sorted out from the dinner entrée beef, etc. Or, one may select items according to cost by comparing to determine whether the cost of each item is greater than or equal to some value or conversely less than or equal to some value. Or, when ingredient items are dated according to date costed, all items with a specific date can be identified by comparison; an equal comparison will trigger updating of the cost information.

The major problems in data management have been indicated and general approaches for dealing with them have been suggested. Competent systems analysts are ingenious in devising strategies for overall data management when the menu planner is articulate in describing the nature, type, and form of the data. Competent programmers can effectively rearrange data to optimize computer processing. Even so, if problems can be anticipated and avoided efficiency is greatly increased.

BIBLIOGRAPHY

ATWATER, W. O., and WOODS, C. D. 1896. The chemical composition of American food materials. USDA Bull. *28*.

BALINTFY, J. L. 1967. Computerized dietary information system, Vol. I, Data organization and collection procedures. Graduate School Business Admin., Tulane Univ. Res. Paper *14*.

BELL, B. L., OSHINSKY, N. S., and WOLFSON, J. 1965. Food acceptance and preference research: an annotated bibliography. Pioneering Res. Div. U.S. Army Materiel Command, U.S. Army Natick Labs., Natick, Mass. Tech. Rept. *EPT-5*.

BROWN, R. M. 1969. Estimating dietary labor by use of work modules. Hospitals *43*, No. 20, 103–104, 106.

Committee to Study Data Processing. 1971. Food Service Data Processing Support: Recipe Data. The American Dietetic Association, Chicago.

DAVIS, J. M. 1958. The transitivity of preferences. Behavioral Sci. *3*, 26–33.

HARRIS, R. S. 1962. Reliability of nutrient analyses and food tables. Am. J. Clin. Nutr. *11*, 377–381.

HARRIS, R. S. 1963. Role of food analyses in the solution of food and nutrition problems. Federation Proc. *22* (1, Part 1), 138–140.

IVANICKY, M. C., MASON, H. A., and VIEROW, S. C. 1969. Food preparation: labor time versus production quantity. Hospitals *43*, No. 20, 99–102.

JONES, L. V. 1954. Psychophysics and the normality assumption: an experimental report. *In* Food Acceptance Testing Methodology. D. R. Peryam, F. J. Pilgrim, and M. S. Peterson (Editors). Proc. Symp. QMFCI, Palmer House, Chicago, 8–9 Oct., 1953. Comm. Foods, Natl. Acad. Sci–Natl. Res. Council.

JONES, L. V., and THURSTONE, L. L. 1955. The psychophysics of semantics: an experimental investigation. J. Appl. Psychol. *39*, 31–36.

KAMEN, J. M. 1962A. Decision-making by users of food acceptance data. Food Technol. *16*, 48–53.

KAMEN, J. M. 1962B. Reasons for non-consumption of food in the Army. J. Am. Dietet. Assoc. *41*, 437–442.

KAZARIAN, E. A. 1969. Work Analysis and Design for Hotels, Restaurants, and Institutions. Avi Publishing Co., Westport, Conn.

MAYER, J. 1960. Food composition tables: basis, uses, and limitations. Postgrad. Med. *28*, 295–307.

MCMASTERS, V. 1963. History of food composition tables of the world. J. Am. Dietet. Assoc. *43*, 442–450.

MEISELMAN, H. L., VAN HORNE, W., HASENZAHL, B., and WEHRLY, T. 1972. The 1971 Fort Lewis Food Preference Survey. Pioneering Res. Lab., U.S. Army Natick Labs., Natick, Mass. Tech. Rept. *TR 72-43 PR*.

MOSKOWITZ, H. R., and SIDEL, J. L. 1971. Magnitude and hedonic scales of food acceptability. J. Food Sci. *36*, 677–680.

MOSKOWITZ, H. R., NICHOLS, T. L., MEISELMAN, H. L., and SIDEL, J. L. 1972. Food Preferences of Military Men, 1967. Pioneering Res. Lab., U.S. Army Natick Labs., Natick, Mass. Tech. Rept. *TR-72-70-PR*.

PERYAM, D. R., and PILGRIM, F. J. 1957. Hedonic scale method of measuring food preference. Food Technol. *11*, No. 9, Insert 9–14.

PERYAM, D. R. *et al*. 1960. Food Preferences of men in the U.S. Armed Forces. QM Food Container Inst., Chicago.

PILGRIM, F. J. 1957. The components of food acceptance and their measurement. Am. J. Clin. Nutr. *5*, 171–175.

PILGRIM, F. J. 1961. Group attitudes and behavior toward food. What foods do people accept or reject? J. Am. Dietet. Assoc. *38*, 439–443.

SCHUH, D. D., MOORE, A. N., and TUTHILL, B. H. 1967. Measuring food acceptability by frequency ratings. J. Am. Dietet. Assoc. *51*, 340–343.

SCHUTZ, H. G. 1972. Hospital patients' and employees' reactions to food-use combinations. J. Am. Dietet. Assoc. *60*, 207–212.

STOKES, J. W. 1967. How to control food costs. Cooking for Profit. Feb., 40–43, 54, 78–81.

VAWTER, H. J., and KONISHI, F. 1958. Food acceptance by soldiers under an ad libitum regimen. J. Am. Dietet. Assoc. *34*, 36–41.

WATT, B. K., and MURPHY, E. W. 1970. Tables of food composition: scope and needed research. Food Technol. *24*, 50–60.

WOOD, K. R., and PERYAM, D. R. 1953. Preliminary analysis of five army food preference surveys. Food Technol. *7*, 248–249.

CHAPTER 19

Programming Techniques and Testing Procedures

Two alternate philosophy-based strategies, linear programming and random approach, were introduced in Chap. 16. In either case, some combination of mathematical and logical statements is developed to select and test the suitability of prospective menu items for inclusion in a particular menu. Programming techniques are selected or devised to solve mini-aspects of large problems and mini-problems in ways that are consistent with the overall strategy.

LINEAR PROGRAMMING

Traditional linear programming strategies utilized by Smith and others to plan least-cost diets are based on two major concepts. One, the objective function is either to minimize cost or maximize profit. Two, attainment of the objective is restricted by conditions that must be met, i.e., constraints, and these are commonly expressed as equations or inequalities.

The linear programming model is adequate for solving problems with a small number of variables, i.e., food commodities, and a small number of generalized nutritional and/or palatability constraints. It is useful primarily for determining critical items and quantities of these items that must be provided in a food supply to provide a nutritionally adequate diet at least cost. It provides a theoretical standard for comparison. A limited concession to palatability requirements is made by selecting common foodstuffs for inclusion in the model; the effects of more liberal lists and relaxed constraints can be evaluated and utilized in policy-making decisions. However, one notes that no, or at most a small, allowance is made for accessory foods necessary to convert commodities to common food items.

The menu planning problem differs from the diet problem in that (a) menu items rather than commodities are the variables, and (b) structural requirements must be added to the list of constraints. Because available techniques were inadequate for solving the menu planning problem, Balintfy (1964, 1970) developed hybrid techniques for two general model types, the single-stage model which uses an upper bounded linear programming code and a multistage model solved by a sequence of linked multiple-choice programming problems. Both types of models are described below.

The single-stage model is used to plan a list of food items and associated quantities necessary to provide a nutritionally adequate diet for a finite number of days, e.g., the length of the menu cycle, at least-cost. It is conceptually similar to the traditional model described above. Menu items are ordered from least to most expensive, nutrient contributions for X nutrients for each menu item are standard, and nutrient constraints are explicitly defined as the product of the daily requirement and the cycle length. Although the solution is a list of items rather than a menu, menu items rather than commodities are used as variables, common structural requirements are specified in order that the solution contains items for each meal component so that menus can be planned from the lists of items, and as a concession to food preferences the maximum number of servings of individual items is specified.

Conceptually, the computer scans the array of prospective menu items and selects the items and number of servings necessary to provide for nutritional adequacy at least-cost for the entire period at one time. This subset of items is then evaluated to determine whether items have been selected for all meal components for all days in the period; if not, adjustments are made until these structural constraints are satisfied. Then the quantities of items in the solution are evaluated to determine whether any upper frequency bounds have been exceeded. If so, quantities of those items are reduced to the boundary limits and quantities of other food items are increased and/or other foods are introduced. This process continues until all constraints have been satisfied. Tables 19.1, 19.2 and Fig. 19.1 show a sample solution.

The multistage models are used to plan nutritionally adequate least-cost menus for a finite period of time; each meal or day's meals is considered as a stage and is planned independently. According to Balintfy and Blackburn (1968), input data for these models customarily include the following types: (a) food items ordered from least to greatest cost, (b) nutrient contribution of each food item in terms of X nutrients, (c) dominant food ingredients such as

TABLE 19.1

SAMPLE POOL OF BREAKFAST ITEMS TO BE USED IN
PLANNING A 500-CALORIE (475–525) BREAKFAST THAT
CONTAINS AT LEAST 20 GM PROTEIN

		Calories	Protein	RFC[1]
A[2]	Fried Eggs (1)	105	6	3
	Poached Eggs (2)	160	12	5
	Scrambled Eggs (No. 10 scoop)	175	10	8
	Grilled Ham Slice (2 oz)	215	14	20
B	Buttered Toast (2)	230	4	5
	Oatmeal with ½ c milk and sugar	190	6	7
	Toast with Peanut Butter	160	5	5
	Iced Doughnut	190	2	5
C	Cocoa (8 oz)	240	8	8
	Milk (8 oz)	160	9	10
	Skim Milk (8 oz)	90	9	10

[1] RFC = Raw Food Cost, assigned values.
[2] Select one each from component groups A, B, and C.

TABLE 19.2

SAMPLE SOLUTIONS TO A THREE-COMPONENT 500-CALORIE (475–525) MENU
THAT PROVIDES AT LEAST 20 GM PROTEIN

No.	Item Combination	Cal	Pro	Cost (¢)	Comment
1[1]	Fried Egg, Toast, Cocoa	575	18	16	Cheapest
4	Ham, Toast, Cocoa	685	26	33	High-Cal
9	Fried Egg, Toast/Peanut Butter, Cocoa	505	19	16	Cheapest
13	Fried Egg, Doughnut, Cocoa	435	16	16	Cheapest
22[2]	Poached Eggs, Oatmeal, etc., Milk	510	27	17	Optimal
23[2]	Scrambled Eggs, Oatmeal, etc., Milk	525	25	25	
25[2]	Fried Egg, Toast/Peanut Butter, Milk	525	20	18	
27[2]	Scrambled Eggs, Toast/Peanut Butter, Milk	495	24	23	
26[2]	Poached Eggs, Toast/Peanut Butter, Milk	480	26	20	
27[2]	Scrambled Eggs, Toast/Peanut Butter, Milk	495	24	23	
30[2]	Poached Eggs, Doughnut, Milk	510	23	20	
31[2]	Scrambled Eggs, Doughnut, Milk	525	21	23	
34[2]	Poached Eggs, Toast, Skim Milk	480	25	20	
35[2]	Scrambled Eggs, Toast, Skim Milk	495	23	23	
40[2]	Ham, Oatmeal, etc., Skim Milk	495	30	37	Expensive
41	Fried Egg, Toast/Peanut Butter, Skim Milk	355	20	18	Low-Cal
48[2]	Ham, Doughnut, Skim Milk	495	25	35	

[1] Key to combinations:
  No. 1–4 All eggs as ranked, Toast, Cocoa
       5–8 All eggs as ranked, Oatmeal, etc., Cocoa
       9–12 All eggs as ranked, Toast/Peanut Butter, Cocoa
       13–16 All eggs as ranked, Doughnut, Cocoa
       17–20 All eggs as ranked, Toast, Milk
       21–24 All eggs as ranked, Oatmeal, etc., Milk
       25–28 All eggs as ranked, Toast/Peanut Butter, Milk
       29–32 All eggs as ranked, Doughnut, Milk
       33–36 All eggs as ranked, Toast, Skim Milk
       37–40 All eggs as ranked, Oatmeal, etc., Skim Milk
       41–44 All eggs as ranked, Toast/Peanut Butter, Skim Milk
       45–48 All eggs as ranked, Doughnut, Skim Milk
[2] Feasible solutions.

tomatoes or green peppers, and (d) item separation ratings. In addition, constraints (Balintfy *et al.* 1967) include (a) daily nutrient requirements for X nutrients, (b) the number and kinds of variable meal components to be planned, (c) constant meal components such as bread and butter or coffee and tea, and (d) separation ratings for dominant ingredients and other compatibility factors.

Conceptually, in planning set menus using the multistage models, the computer scans the array of prospective items and selects a combination that will provide a nutritionally adequate menu at least cost. These combinations then form tentative solutions and each combination is evaluated further for feasibility. Each combination is checked to verify that it contains an item for each meal component; if not, it is eliminated. Then the computer determines when each item in the combination was last served and compares this interval with the separation rating. If shorter, this solution is eliminated for this day but is saved

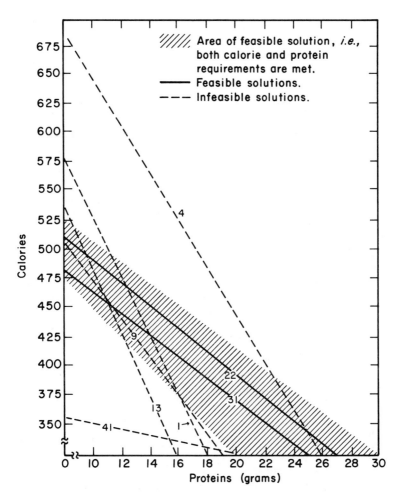

FIG. 19.1. SAMPLE LINEAR PROGRAMMING SOLUTION

for evaluation for a subsequent stage. Otherwise, evaluation continues on all additional constraints.

In the event that no solution is found using the least-cost combinations, a new subset of combinations is generated with one or more next-to-least cost items. Each combination is subjected to the same process of evaluation. If no feasible solution emerges, additional subsets of combinations with increasing cost are generated until a solution is reached that satisfies all constraints. This is the least-cost solution, given the constraints; thus it is optimal. Thus, the optimal menu is selected by a sequential process of elimination. The computer then proceeds to the next stage and reviews the tentative solutions for feasibility at this point. When a feasible solution is obtained, the computer proceeds to the next stage. This process continues until an entire cycle of menus has been planned.

The first multistage model, developed by Balintfy (1968), for planning a selective menu assumes two separate population groups with differing nutritional needs and is very similar to the model for planning set menus; structural and other requirements are the same. However, to reduce production work load, as many items as possible are common to both menus; in practice the actual meal components to have alternate items are arbitrarily predetermined.

Conceptually, having planned the set menu for the day for the first population group, the computer then selects the alternate items. Since the common items are known, subtotals for each nutrient are known and are subtracted from the requirements for the second group. The computer scans the array of items for the first meal component requiring an alternate item and selects a subset for consideration based on separation ratings. Each of the items in the subset is evaluated in terms of the adjusted set of nutritional constraints and the other constraints. The least-cost item that meets constraints is selected. Additional subsets of items for other meal components requiring alternate items are selected and evaluated similarly. In this way the selective menu is generated. Menus for additional days are planned by the same process.

The second multistage model, developed by Balintfy (Balintfy and Blackburn 1968), for planning selective menus is also similar to the model for planning set menus. It differs from the previous model in that it assumes that if base menu items are selected to meet the maximum nutritional requirements of the major population group and alternatives are provided, individuals with differing requirements can select items to fit personal needs. A further assumption is that the customary menu structure ensures approximate nutritional adequacy.

Conceptually, the basic set menu is planned with nutrient constraints for selected nutrients set for the maximum requirement, based on professional judgment. Then alternate items are selected for designated meal components without regard for their nutritional contribution. As before, a subset of items to be considered is selected subject to repetition restrictions. Items are then evaluated according to the same other constraints and the least-cost item is selected. This process continues until all alternate items have been selected. The menus for successive days are planned the same way.

The third multistage model, developed by Balintfy (Balintfy and Blackburn 1968), for planning selective menus also uses a set menu as a base. It differs from previous models in that its fundamental assumption is that alternate items for any given meal component can be selected to be nutritionally equivalent in terms of the critical nutrients, i.e., those that are likely to be insufficient in quantity, expensive to provide, or both.

Conceptually, the basic set menu is planned to meet the usual nutritional and other requirements. The nutrient contributions of the items for the meal components requiring alternate items serve as standards for comparison. For each of the designated meal components requiring alternate items, the actual nutrient contribution of the base menu item is the standard for that day. As before, a subset of items is selected subject to separation rating constraints, and each item is evaluated further. The nutrient content of each item in the subset is compared to that of the standard item. The least-cost item that is comparable and meets other constraints is selected. Other alternate items and days' meals are planned in a similar manner.

Menu planning systems based on the three linear programming models for planning selective menus that have been described above, plan a set menu as a base and then the alternate item is selected independently. A linear programming model proposed by Gue and Liggett (1967) selects the base and alternate items simultaneously. It differs in that for each meal component where selection is offered, pairs or triplets of items are prematched and treated as single items for the purpose of evaluation. The expected value, for the pair or triplet for cost, nutrient contribution, etc., is used as input data. Using historical data on consumption, probabilities of selection are computed and weighted values for cost, etc., are derived.

Conceptually, the process of selecting pairs for each meal component is identical to that used for planning a set menu. That is, the computer scans the array or pairs using separation ratings to eliminate pairs that cannot be considered for that meal or day. The subset of prospective items is then evaluated for nutrient contribution and other quality factors. The least-cost pair that satisfies constraints is selected. Additional meal components are selected according to structural requirements in sequence. Thus, a series of menus is generated.

MAN-MACHINE INTERACTIONS

The one reported menu planning system that utilizes man-machine interaction was developed by Balintfy and co-workers. Initial menu planning models developed by Balintfy planned nutritionally adequate menus at least-cost as described above. But, the menus were not well accepted by dietitians for aesthetic and other undefined reasons. To provide feedback from which to improve problem definition and model design, the man-machine interaction system was developed (Balintfy and Nebel 1966). This feature has been retained in the CAMP system as it reduces the tension resulting from dietitians' feelings of powerlessness and thus enhances acceptance and implementation. The system developed by Balintfy and co-workers (1967) is summarized below.

For purposes of explanation, the assumption is made that a series of set menus is to be planned using the general multistage model. A further assumption is that programs and required data have already been stored in the memory bank in the computer. Man-machine interactions are effected by means of typing abbreviated instructions to the computer using a terminal typewriter. A limited vocabulary with specified punctuation and grammar are used. Each word is a command that causes the computer to follow a predetermined segment of program instructions.

To initiate the menu planning process the dietitian types a key word that identifies the user to the computer monitoring system, i.e., the super-program that sequences jobs and retains information on time and charges, etc. This also calls the program and initiates actions to put into the "ready" state.

The dietitian then types information specifying choices wherever options exist or that the standard assumptions will suffice. Some of the options that may be specified include (a) number of meals per day, (b) number and name of meal components, (c) cycle length, (d) nutritional requirements—specific nutrients and levels, and (e) if carryover of nutrients is to be allowed and if so, the nutrients are specified.

With these set-up chores completed, the dietitian then indicates to the computer using a specified command word that it should proceed in planning menus. Using the prestored program and data, the computer selects a menu which is typed out for review by the dietitian.

If any item is unsatisfactory and the dietitian wishes to make a change, two alternate types of actions may be taken. The dietitian may indicate that item Q is unsatisfactory for reason X; another menu is generated which may or may not contain the same items for the other meal components since the menu must be balanced nutritionally. Or, the dietitian may elect to specify some item to replace the unacceptable one. In this case, she types a command to eliminate the unsatisfactory item and types in the code for the item to be inserted. The computer then re-evaluates the menu for nutritional adequacy. Changes in other items may be required in order to restore nutritional balance; again some item(s) may be unsatisfactory. This repetitive interactive process continues until a menu is obtained that satisfies the constraints and the dietitian.

When a satisfactory menu for the first meal is obtained it may be accepted permanently or tentatively. In the first case, it then limits choices in other meals for the day because of its cost, nutrient contribution, and other attributes. However, both dinner and supper may not both be "fixed" as permanent menus until all three meals have been planned because this might overly restrict the options in selecting items for the breakfast meal. In the case of a tentative menu, if difficulties develop in planning the remaining meal(s) for the day, it may be modified in order to obtain a solution. Also, the dietitian does have the option of accepting menus permanently that violate nutritional constraints, although the computer solution for the following day should satisfy constraints. When menus for the entire day have been planned, the nutrient content is printed.

Links among days are provided by means of carryover of nutrient excesses and control of repetition. Menus for succeeding days are planned by a separate but similar repetitive series of man-machine interactions.

TESTING PROCEDURES AND CONSTRUCTION OF TEST DECKS

Two purposes of developing testing procedures and a test deck are to provide a systematic means of determining whether (a) data errors are present or (b) all constraints function as intended. In the long run, much time and frustration are saved when this step is implemented.

The first problem is to design a system for detecting expected types of data errors that would invalidate the results. Commonly, testing procedures are developed to detect keypunch and transcription errors such as (a) outsize values, i.e., either too large or too small to be reasonable, (b) a blank when a value is expected, (c) an illegal character. Another check is usually included to determine that no data card is out of order; this check is necessary if a reading error might occur that would not terminate the run. When several cards contain information for one record, a check must be designed to determine that all cards in the group have the same code number. These checks are included in the main program, as errors of these types should be detected and processing discontinued.

It seems obvious, but individual constraints should be checked to verify that they are as effective as intended. Initially one starts with a simple constraint that is added to a simple program with a test deck constructed to test the constraint. When the results are reviewed, it often becomes obvious that some adjustment is required to control unexpected results. This happens because the conscious part of the human decision process is only the tip of the iceberg, so all aspects of the mini-problem have not been identified.

For example, Eckstein (1969) tested the effectiveness of KIND constraints utilizing meal component and overall restrictions as described in Chap. 16. A 21-day breakfast and luncheon cycle menu was used as an input test deck. The test KINDs, e.g., chocolate, green beans, tomatoes, cheese, etc., were included frequently but randomly among appropriate meal components and days of the week. The task was for the computer to select dinner menus for the 21-day period so that these KINDs were not repeated within and among days, as specified by the constraints.

In the short-run, one might interpret lack of repetition to mean that the constraints were functional. However, it is possible that ineffectiveness might be masked since the items might be eliminated for other, though unrelated, reasons. Use of a cycle menu, with a different pattern of KINDs in the history of dinner menus for each rotation, allows long-run evaluation since a long continuous menu set can be generated.

Individually, constraints may perform as intended. However, the aggregate effect may be too restrictive. An abnormally high rate of failure to find satisfactory items may result. Or, due to ordering of the constraints in the program, individual constraints may be ineffective if some other constraint inadvertently performs the screening function. These problems must be detected.

One means of detecting these problems (Eckstein 1969) is to set up a series of counters, one for each constraint or group of similar constraints. Each time a prospective item is rejected, the appropriate counter is incremented. At the end of the run, the counter totals are printed. Analysis will reveal which constraints were very active or, conversely, inactive. If it appears that a constraint was too effective it can be relaxed, and the results re-evaluated. Insofar as possible, in order to reduce processing time, constraints should be ordered in the program from most active to least active. As a result, unsuitable items are quickly eliminated. If, after several runs with the constraints arranged in various orders, any constraint has failed to cause rejection of a prospective menu item, it should be rechecked or discarded.

Another function of the testing procedure is to check the appropriateness of cutlines used for cost and nutrient control. The properly trained menu planner understands the concept of significant digits and trivial differences in value. Whereas the computer, utilizing a digit-by-digit comparison, accepts or rejects on the basis of mathematical difference rather than real differences unless specifically instructed.

For example, suppose the planned allocation for the dinner meal is 65¢ and that 36¢ is allowed for the entrée, 4¢ for the starchy food, 5¢ for the vegetable, 6¢ for the salad, 6¢ for the dessert, 3¢ for the bread item, and 5¢ for the beverage. If the cutlines for desserts are 47¢ and 60¢, and the sum of the costs for the meal components up to and including the dessert is 60.072¢, should the prospective dessert be eliminated as too expensive? No. The probability that the sum of the costs of the two remaining meal components to be selected will exactly equal 65¢ is exceedingly low. Hence, the computer should be instructed that the class limits for 65¢ extend to 65.555. . ., etc.

On the other hand, the computer should also be instructed to monitor for a consistent pattern of costs exceeding the intended value, since the cumulative and aggregate effects of such trivial costs for X-hundred thousand meals per year may be highly significant to the financial status. At the same time, one must remember that these are paper cost values and may vary from actual costs in either direction for a wide variety of reasons. Hence, it would not make sense to allow computer elimination of an otherwise excellent choice in order to "save" a trivial amount.

Or, for example, consider this pair of figures for calories: 50 and 48.3425. If a 50-calorie item is needed, an item with a computed value of 48.3425 would be rejected from further consideration. *But,* caloric values are only accurate to the nearest five calories at best! Thus, a Type II error would be made; an acceptable item would not be selected.

Selection of appropriate cutlines to control nutrient content of the menus is difficult. A compromise between two mutually exclusive goals must be reached, i.e., the nutrient limits must not be exceeded or met by (a) omitting meal components or meals or (b) excluding large numbers of items in a class, because this restricts variety. At the outset one sets tentative cutlines as the class mean ±1 standard deviation. Depending on the nutrient, the cumulative sum of the class means for each meal component may exceed the daily total allowed. Therefore, some other basis for establishing cutlines must be used. Research is now underway to develop an alternative systematic method.

BIBLIOGRAPHY

BALINTFY, J. L. 1964. Menu planning by computer. Assoc. Computing Machinery Commun., 7, 255–259.

BALINTFY, J. L. 1970. Computer Assisted Menu Planning and Food Service Management. Graduate School Business Admin., Tulane Univ., Working Paper 41.

BALINTFY, J. L., and BLACKBURN, C. R. II. 1968. Computerized Dietary Information System IV. Planning and scheduling optimum menus in multistage. Graduate School Business Admin., Tulane Univ.

BALINTFY, J. L., BLACKBURN, C. R. II, and MORRIS, K. V. 1967. Computerized Dietary Information System III. On-line terminal system. Graduate School Business Admin., Tulane Univ., Res. Paper 22.

BALINTFY, J. L., and NEBEL, E. C. 1966. Experiments with computer assisted menu planning. Hospitals 40, No. 12, 88–96.

ECKSTEIN, E. F. 1969. Menu planning by computer: the random approach to planning for consumer acceptability and nutritional needs. Ph.D. Dissertation, Kansas State Univ.

GUE, R. L., and LIGGETT, J. C. 1967. Selective menu planning by computer. Computer Sci. Center, Inst. Technol., Southern Methodist Univ. Tech. Rept. CP-67101.

CHAPTER 20

Computerizing the Menu Planning Process

The computerization process includes all of the activities that are involved in planning for, introducing, and managing the use of the computer in planning menus. The process may conveniently be divided into two phases (a) set-up and (b) implementation. Each has characteristic activities and problems. Regardless of the efficiency of the model and resultant program and/or potential benefits from its implementation, if concomitant effects on other food service subsystems are not controlled, the project may fail. In this chapter the process is examined and pitfalls are identified.

THE SET-UP PHASE

The set-up phase includes the following activities: (a) planning, (b) review of existing procedures and adjustment as necessary, (c) data collection, (d) orientation and training of personnel, and (e) debugging of test programs and off-line procedures. When the set-up phase is optimized, problems in the implementation phase are reduced.

Planning for the process of computerizing menu planning is based on a detailed analysis of (a) the relation of the menu planning subsystem to all other departmental subsystems; (b) an estimate of the type of input data requirements and availability of essential data; (c) the nature, content, format and number of reports to be generated; (d) basic strategies to be used in reviewing procedures for collecting data, orienting and training personnel, testing the program and off-line procedures, and evaluating the outcomes resulting from computerization of the process.

In general, the menu planning subsystem is related to all other food service subsystems—it determines their effectiveness to some degree and, also, feedback data from each is used in modifying input data and/or constraints in the menu planning program.

A chart depicting relationships is prepared for the individual institution. Next, the relationships between each of the other subsystems and the menu planning process are defined in detail in separate written reports. In defining relationships, data requirements and availability and/or validity problems are usually exposed. The need for various reports also becomes evident. Each document is of critical importance as it forms the basis for assumptions and hypotheses to be tested in model development and program design and testing.

In order to develop a systematic integrated approach for dealing with other aspects of the set-up phase, the basic strategies must be planned at the outset. Strategies must be selected to maximize effectiveness, given local situational variables.

220

A review of existing procedures associated with manual methods is necessary to identify need for changes. Many procedures will become obsolete and must be formally discontinued. Others will require some modification; transitional procedures may be required in some cases. Revised procedures can be implemented on a test basis during the set-up phase and unanticipated problems resolved. A positive side-effect is increased break-in time for personnel, which allows for more gradual adjustment.

Data collection is probably the most time-consuming activity of the set-up phase. Specific data needs are identified as a result of problem definition activities. Considerations and procedures related to specific data collection and validation problems were discussed separately in Chap. 18.

Planning for the reports to be generated is a task that presents many challenges. In theory, a number of standard reports, e.g., cost and nutritional analyses, are generated routinely to provide middle and top management with data summaries from which to make predictions and decisions. In practice, records often have not been prepared systematically or with regard to content validity. It is necessary to determine exactly what is wanted, in content and level of accuracy.

In planning for a computerized system one must first determine the nature of the reports to be prepared. Their nature depends on (a) planned content and (b) the data needs of the intended recipient. Two questions must be asked to justify development of a report. What is its purpose? Why is it necessary? If its purpose is to provide top management with a specific type of summary, data must be limited to pertinent information and arranged to accentuate specified portions. If its purpose (same basic data) is to provide working supervisors or dietitians with operating information summarized by category, the data must be arranged to emphasize categorical differences. "Why is it necessary" refers to the intended use of the report. Is it critical in some decision process? Is the benefit from providing the summary sufficient to justify costs of collection and processing of the data?

The content of the report is derived from its purpose. A vague statement of purpose will result in inclusion of unnecessary detail data in order to "play safe"; resultant clutter distracts and reduces clarity. A clear statement of purpose delineates the content requirements. For each type of report the content must be specified in writing as part of documentation.

The format of the report is derived from the intended recipient's need for the data and his ability to locate it with maximum efficiency. Developing the format involves (a) arrangement of data to accentuate the most important findings, (b) clear and concise labeling, and (c) spatial arrangement of the data for clarity. Various manuals with descriptive information to aid the reader in planning reports are available.

The number of reports to be generated depends on (a) the class of data to be summarized and (b) whether the various recipients require the same level of information and type of summary. When several classes of data are to be summarized for comparison, they are usually combined in one report. For example, when an X-day cycle menu is to be analyzed for nutritional adequacy, the data are summarized for the period and are compared to some standard measure. When classes of data are to be analyzed individually, separate reports are generated. For example, when the desired information is the variation in the content of nutrients Z over the X-day cycle, then totals for each of the nutrients are tabulated by day; mean, range, and standard deviation may be listed and the data may be plotted. A separate report may be generated for each nutrient.

When several levels of information or different types of summaries are necessary because of differing informational needs of the user, separate reports should be generated. Otherwise, in order to find data of use to him, each user must hunt through the entire set of data, which is time-consuming. Given time limitations, most give up and fail to use the available data. While the process of generating custom-made reports is difficult if not impossible manually, by computer it is a trivial task. Since all of the information is available, the only task is to write instructions to select and print the data according to the desired format. This is a technical task that any competent programmer can perform or one can elect to use a "canned" program.

Soft-ware programs such as Report Writer for COBOL are designed to eliminate the need for writing extensive programming statements throughout the program to control printing of reports. Input information includes a detailed description of the content and arrangement of each report (up to four). To use the program, the user then uses three verbs: (a) initiate, which sets up the Report Writer; (b) generate, which is used to control the arrangement of the content with heading; and (c) terminate, which is used to end the report (Farina 1968). Other systems for writing reports are available for use with other programming languages.

Planning for the timing of reports is also necessary. One must ascertain decision-making deadlines and work backwards allowing sufficient lead-time for data collection and processing. Until a routine is established, fairly long lead-times may be required.

Planning the basic strategies to be used in reviewing procedures for collecting data, orienting and training personnel, testing the program and off-line procedures, and evaluating outcomes of computerizing the menu planning process requires thoughtful attention to detail and dynamic interaction effects. The procedures for collecting data and testing the program and off-line procedures have been discussed in Chap. 18 and 19 respectively.

Orientation of personnel is an essential step in introducing a change of the magnitude of computerization of a subsystem. A number of alternate strategies may be used. However, all departmental employees should be given a fundamental background which includes (a) the reasons for computerization, (b) the expected benefits to customers, workers, and management, and (c) the need for accurate and precise data. The clerical personnel should also understand the expected pressures that usually result when any process is computerized.

The usual reason for computerization is to enable the department to increase its efficiency by performing tasks that would be unmanageable manually because they would take several man-years to complete, by which time the need for the information would be past and the output would be meaningless. Use of the computer allows more comprehensive and in-depth reports simultaneously.

The major benefit from computer applications usually results from the rigorous scrutiny of the manual processes and consequent removal of inefficiencies. However, while this is of benefit to management, from the employees' point of view it implies criticism and creates a threat. Hence, this benefit should be omitted from the explanation unless justified for survival. If one can eliminate routine work so as to release time for more challenging tasks and increase service to customers, *and* if one or both of these goals are valued by the employees, this point may be selected. If increased accuracy and speed increases validity and usefulness of the information, this point can be stressed. In some cases it may be possible to show that computerization will reduce the need for treating customers as mass groups, thus facilitating accommodation of individual needs and reducing impersonality.

The need for accurate and reliable data cannot be overstressed. This concept is usually accepted but may not be implemented unless carefully introduced. The employees should be shown examples of the cumulative and aggregate effects of small errors, e.g., punching a digit in a column that multiplies a cost by ten in a commodity such as flour that is used in many recipes.

When a process is computerized, clerical personnel are required to make two types of permanent adjustment. According to Myers (1967) these are (a) time discipline and (b) behavior control.

Time discipline refers to the increased requirement that segments of work be completed at specified times in order to meet data processing deadlines. Deadlines create pressure but are necessary because computer processing time is costly so it is scheduled to maximize utilization. In most situations where jobs are performed routinely and periodically, time blocks are assigned to the department to assure processing in time to meet food service needs. Deadlines are then set so that the data will be ready for processing at the planned time. In this case, if the program cannot be run at the planned time, it may not be possible to reschedule a run in time to meet departmental needs for the output (see Fig. 15.2 in Chap. 15).

Experience has shown that adjustment to time discipline is difficult for some employees and may require a long period of time. Because the number of deadlines is greatly increased and the importance of meeting them is greater because of scheduling problems, anxiety and frustration may result. Management must be understanding and supportive.

Behavior control means that systematic methods must be employed in preparing data for processing. Location of data on the card is important in most systems so it must be keypunched in specific card columns. Cards may have to be arranged in a specified order; thus, cards may have to be sorted and sequenced. But this eliminates alternate methods a clerk might use to introduce variety into the task. This job restriction may induce boredom and reduced job satisfaction (Lee 1965).

Another problem that may generate pressure is the need for accuracy of the data. The computer is commonly instructed to discontinue processing when certain types of data errors are detected. In this case, a single data error may result in termination and loss of the planned processing time block, problems in rescheduling the run with corrected data, failure to meet departmental needs for the output, and ultimately in mounting pressure. If rescheduling is required frequently, pressures from the computer center are added to departmental pressures.

The personnel problems that result from requirements imposed by computerization diminish with time. Employees who can adjust, do. These employees often seem more secure because known problems are easier to bear than unknown problems. However, thorough orientation and support are necessary during the transitionary period.

Another concept should be included in orienting employees, namely that output is not instantly available when input is completed. Although computations may only require a few minutes of processing time, output reports may not be available until the following day. Two factors are involved and should be explained. One, the job may be submitted and wait in the queue of jobs to be processed for an unknown length of time before processing begins, if there is a backlog of jobs. Two, although computations are complete, if the printer has a backlog of output reports to be printed, preceding jobs will be completed first. For these reasons, sufficient lead-time must be allowed so that output reports will reach the food service department in time for effective utilization.

THE IMPLEMENTATION PHASE

The implementation phase includes the following activities: (a) supporting personnel as they learn new procedures, (b) dealing with intermittent crises as they occur, and (c) monitoring system effectiveness in order to plan program development and refinement so as to preclude obsolescence. Each of these types of activities presents a special challenge which must be met in order to obtain quality menus on time.

The types and number of personnel problems that develop during the implementation phase are largely a function of the effectiveness of orientation and testing of procedures during the set-up phase. At the outset, a great deal of feedback and support are necessary in order to gain cooperation. Later, a somewhat reduced level may suffice in stabilizing motivation, morale, and effectiveness.

Theoretically, no crises should occur during the implementation phase. Nonetheless, various difficulties may arise. For example, an intermittant but typical situation may precipitate a crisis. Although the data is ready for processing at the specified time period, the computer is "down." No processing occurs and a backlog of jobs accumulates. This delay creates problems in purchasing, distribution of the menus, etc.

Another example of a situation that creates problems is the failure to obtain current ingredient price data. In this case routine up-dating of recipe costs is prevented; old information must be used. Therefore, the input costs in menu planning are inaccurate; the net effect may be failure to cover costs. As management personnel become conditioned to expect a high degree of cost control, they tend to overreact and problems multiply.

The interaction between the menu planning subsystem and other food service subsystems is dynamic and continuous. Monitoring and feedback systems are necessary for responsive program development and refinement. Otherwise, menus are planned using outdated premises and result in out-of-phase menus that do not meet current needs.

Moreover, as is true of other activities, rapid progress is made during the initial stages of implementation but greater effort is required for each increment of improvement in latter stages. Cost of refinement is often difficult to justify unless needed refinements are explicitly defined and substantiated. But as new techniques are discovered, they should be added if they will increase overall efficiency.

BIBLIOGRAPHY

FARINA, M. V. 1968. COBOL Simplified. Prentice-Hall, Englewood Cliffs, N.J.

LEE, H. C. 1965. Electronic data processing and employee perception of changes in work skill requirements and work characteristics. Personnel J. *44,* 365–370.

MYERS, C. A. 1967. The Impact of Computers on Management. MIT Press, Cambridge, Mass.

CHAPTER 21

Interface Interactions with Other Computerized Subsystems

The menu planning subsystem always interacts with the other food service subsystems. Input data are supplied to it from purchasing, supply, production, cost control, and patient care or other customer subsystem. In turn, the menu planning subsystem provides input data to these same subsystems. To optimize the efficiency of the food service system as a whole, a master plan is designed. Master coding systems, compatible storage and retrieval systems for common data, and facilitating mechanisms for interface interactions are developed. Some common examples of the data requirements at the interfaces are discussed below.

THE PURCHASING-MENU PLANNING INTERFACE

Since both subsystems are computerized, a linkage between them can be designed to signal cost variance or modify menu item selection. Recipes are usually costed on the basis of the last price paid for the ingredients. However, the cost of some ingredients is highly variable due to wide variation in supply and demand. The purchasing subsystem usually contains information on expected costs of these items and one may wish to recost menu items for planning purposes using these expected costs. Input to the menu planning system would be the code numbers for selected menu items with expected costs.

The menu planning subsystem might utilize this information in at least two ways. One, menus might be planned using the regular costs and the expected range in cost variation might be printed. Two, the expected costs might replace the regular cost, thus influencing the selection of menu items.

In some cases, ingredients may not be available although the cost is acceptable. The purchasing system contains this information, and input data to the menu planning subsystem would be a list of code numbers of items that cannot be selected due to lack of availability of ingredients.

THE SUPPLY-MENU PLANNING INTERFACE

It turns out that in the supply subsystem there are usually (a) some ingredients that must be "force issued" in order to use them before they deteriorate to a point where they must be discarded and (b) excessive quantities of some ingredients due to errors in forecasting requirements. Since both the supply and menu planning subsystems are computerized, a linkage can be designed to utilize selected ingredients in desired quantities. Input to the menu planning subsystem would be either (a) a list of code numbers of ingredients to be used with associated total quantities or (b) a list of code numbers of menu items using the ingredients plus the quantity used and a list of the code numbers of ingredients to be used with associated total quantities.

With input of the first type, the initial step in utilization would be to determine which menu items use the ingredients and the quantities used. These menu items might then be distributed randomly, perhaps subject to frequency and/or interval restrictions, as constants. Other items would then be selected to meet constraints. Since the input of the second type already contains the list of items to be distributed, these can be treated as constants and additional menu items can be selected to complete the menus while meeting constraints.

PRODUCTION FORECASTING-MENU PLANNING INTERFACE

Since both subsystems are computerized, a linkage between them can be designed to restrict selection of menu items in order to prevent repetition of combinations that result in production bottlenecks. The production forecasting subsystem contains information on equipment capacities, processing times, etc., as well as production records. Thus, it can provide input of two types of the menu planning subsystem: (a) for critical items, code number and maximum quantity that can be produced, and (b) sets of code numbers for combinations that cannot be produced.

The menu planning subsystem can use the information on maximum quantity limits with the expected production requirements to prevent selection of an item that cannot be produced in the quantity required. In this case the two programs interact; the production forecasting program is treated as a subroutine in the menu planning subsystem. It predicts (a) the expected patient count from historical records for the day of the week and season, and (b) the expected demand for the item from historical data on the percentage of patients selecting the item. The expected quantity requirement is then compared with the maximum quantity that can be produced. If the item can be produced, then it may be selected if it meets other criteria. Otherwise, other items will be considered for that meal component.

The menu planning subsystem can use the sets of "no-go" code numbers to prevent pairing of combinations that cannot be produced. For example, in selecting the nth entrée for the day, one of the checks can compare the code numbers for the items already selected plus the code number for the prospective item with the array of proscribed sets. In the case where the numbers match, program instructions will cause the item to be rejected from further consideration for the meal and will initiate evaluation of another item.

THE COST CONTROL-MENU PLANNING INTERFACE

Regardless of the system used in planning menus, cost constraints can only control the expected cost of the menu items. The total cost of producing and serving an item is a composite of ingredient or food item purchase cost, labor cost, plus administrative and other fixed costs that are usually prorated. Although formerly, raw food cost generally was used; and fixed cost multiplier for labor was used to estimate the expected cost. This method is no longer adequate. Many ingredients are purchased in a partially prepared state and some items are purchased ready-to-eat. In the latter cases, purchase price includes processing labor and overhead components as well as profit. However, even in these cases, some labor and fixed costs are incurred by the institution and should be assigned in determining the total cost of the item as served. For comparative purposes the sum of the exact labor cost per portion, and prorated fixed costs provide a more accurate value.

Computerized aspects of the cost control subsystem are designed to generate (a) numerous summary reports for analysis of the actual cost position and (b) graphs depicting cost relationships. Information used in preparing these reports can be made available to the menu planning subsystem to be used in correcting cost estimates. Input to the menu planning subsystem would be a list of costs to be used to reset the limits used in controlling the meal cost range, component by component. (Note: Linear programming systems usually assume the actual costs are known and are used in selecting menu items, therefore no correction should be necessary.)

THE PATIENT CARE RECORD-MENU PLANNING INTERFACE

The patient care record (Medical Record) subsystem accumulates information of various types on each individual patient and summarizes it in tabular and/or graphical reports. For example, the following types of information are available and might be used as input to the menu planning subsystem: total number of patients per day, week, month, or year and trend in patient load; age, sex, religion, etc., of patients; diagnosis; diet history; diet prescription.

Since both subsystems are computerized, a linkage between them can be designed to monitor the general patient profile and signal changes in composition that might require adjustment of some master menu planning constraints. Moreover, some of the information can be used to determine which pattern modified diets should be planned by computer; volume determines feasibility.

Since the patient care records subsystem and the menu planning subsystem are computerized, a linkage between them might also be designed so as to select menu items to meet individual needs. In general, the steps for planning an individualized menu might be as follows: (a) retrieve selected patient record data including type of diet, age, sex, religion, diet history, (if available), etc.; (b) selection of menu items from appropriate pattern menu whether general or modified; (c) print menu with some character to indicate need for special item when the pattern menu does not contain an acceptable item; (d) retrieve nutrient contribution of each of the selected menu items; (e) accumulation of total nutrient content; (f) retrieve individualized nutrient requirements or adjust the average requirements if necessary; (g) compare actual and expected nutritional contributions; and (h) print actual and expected nutrient content and discrepancy, if any.

Thus far, interface interactions where other subsystems provide data to the menu planning subsystem have been considered. The next sections will briefly indicate the use of data generated by the menu planning subsystem in preparing the various typical reports that are prepared by the other subsystems.

THE MENU PLANNING-PURCHASING INTERFACE

Since both subsystems are computerized, a linkage between them is designed so that when menu planning is complete, computation of order quantities is initiated. In this case, design of the linkage is very simple. The only input necessary to the purchasing subsystem is a list of the code numbers of all of the items for each menu for each day.

In general, the process of developing a purchase order involves the following steps for each item: (a) retrieval from the recipe file of ingredient types and quantities per number of base portions; (b) retrieval of forecasted quantity requirements for each menu item and adjustment of ingredient quantities. The next steps include (a) summation of quantities for each type of ingredient; (b) retrieval of the quantity on hand from the supply subsystem and comparison of needed and on-hand quantities for each ingredient; (c) retrieval of vendor; and (d) generation of tentative joint order by vendor for review *or* completed addressed orders to be mailed to the vendor.

THE MENU PLANNING-SUPPLY INTERFACE

Since both subsystems are computerized, a linkage between them is designed so that when menu planning is completed the process of generating daily requisitions for ingredients and food-related supplies can be initiated. Here again, the only input data necessary to the supply subsystem is a list of the code numbers of all of the menu items for each menu for each day of the menu planning period.

Separate requisitions are prepared for each day. In general, the process of compiling requisition quantities involves the following steps for each menu item: (a) retrieval of the ingredient types and quantities from the recipe file and (b) retrieval of forecasted quantity requirements for each menu item and adjustment of ingredient quantities. The next steps include (a) summation of quantities of each type of ingredient, rounding up fractions to the next whole container size as necessary; (b) comparison of needed quantities with on-hand quantities and printing of a message if supply is inadequate; and (c) printing of requisitions.

Next, each menu item for the following day(s) is checked to see if preparation is required. If so, item quantities are computed as above and are printed separately on the requisition with appropriate labeling. In the case where separate requisitions are required for each of the various food production departments, the input code numbers may be sorted if the master code indicates the department or an additional step is inserted after "b" in which the ingredient quantities are accumulated separately for each production department.

THE MENU PLANNING-PRODUCTION FORECASTING INTERFACE

Since both systems are computerized, a linkage between them is designed so that after a set of menus are planned production forecasts for each of the major items can be generated daily according to the most accurate and timely information available. The input data from the menu planning subsystem is a list of code numbers for the menu items selected for the particular day.

Usually separate reports are prepared for each production department. In general, the process of forecasting quantities involves the following steps for each menu item: (a) retrieval of information to determine whether a forecast is required; and if so, which report it should be printed on; (b) retrieval of historical data concerning the quantity produced, quantity of leftovers or run-out time, meal count, weather or other major factor, etc., for the last X times the item was served; (c) retrieval of patient count from patient care file, if applicable; (d) computation of the expected quantity required, and (e) printing the information on the appropriate report.

THE MENU PLANNING-COST CONTROL INTERFACE

Since the menu planning subsystem and some aspects of the cost control system are computerized, a linkage can be designed so that when menu planning is completed and the meals have been served, a comparison between expected and actual food costs can be provided. Several types of cost reports can be prepared using the same data by arranging it in various ways to reveal different facets of the cost picture. The input data from the menu planning subsystem is a list of code numbers for the menu items and their associated expected costs for each day.

One might compute and compare the expected and actual total food cost each day for the month and with comparable periods in previous years. In general, the process for generating this cost report involves the following steps for each day: (a) summation and printing of the expected costs from the input costs (adjusted for production forecast); (b) retrieval of the expected type and quantity of ingredients necessary for preparation and prepreparation for the forecast quantities for each day; (c) retrieval of actual useage data, both type and quantity; (d) adjustment of actual useage totals to add the costs of ingredients used in prepreparation the previous day and/or remove the costs of ingredients used in prepreparation for the following day; (e) comparison of quantities; and (f) printing of adjusted useage costs and unanticipated items with respective quantities and associated costs. Next, data from the previous years are retrieved and costs are compared and printed, showing differences.

Alternately, one might compute and compare the expected and actual food cost by class of ingredient, i.e., meats, produce, bakery items, etc. This type of report might be summarized by day, week, and/or month. Comparison with comparable periods in previous years is also possible. In general, the process for generating this cost report involves the following steps for each food item: (a) retrieval of expected type and quantity of ingredients used for preparation and prepreparation that day; (b) accumulation of expected totals by class of ingredient; (c) retrieval of useage data, both type and quantity, and sorting by class of ingredient; (d) adjustment of useage data for prepreparation as noted above; (e) comparison of quantities by class; and (f) printing of expected costs by class of ingredient and adjusted useage cost. Discrepancies, if any, should be listed for each class including items with respective quantities and associated costs. Next, data from previous years are retrieved and costs are compared and printed, showing differences by class of ingredient.

THE MENU PLANNING-PATIENT RECORD INTERFACE

Since the menu planning subsystem and the patient care record subsystem are computerized, a linkage between them can be designed so as to bill the patient directly for (a) the cost of food served and (b) the cost of planning the particular modified diet, if applicable (Holbrook 1971). The input data from the menu planning subsystem is a list of code numbers for the food items served from the master menu or the standard modified diets plus code numbers for special items added to meet individual needs. Input data records are prepared for each individual.

In general, the process of preparing an itemized statement of individual charges for dietary services to be entered in the patient care record subsystem includes the following steps: (a) retrieval and accumulation of the costs of the standard menu items served; (b) retrieval of the costs of individually prepared special items, if any; (c) retrieval of information concerning the type of diet prepared; retrieval of the special charge for modified diet planning, if applicable; and (d) entering an itemized list of charges for foods and services in the patient care record (Holbrook 1971).

EVALUATION OF EFFECTIVENESS OF COMPUTERIZED SUBSYSTEMS

The dietary information system includes both a complex of subsystems and interface mechanisms as indicated above. Both of these can be evaluated for effectiveness, though some features of each determine effectiveness of the other.

Evaluation is the process of comparing expected and obtained results according to some criteria, which are a set of predetermined and explicitly defined objectives. A number of books have been written on the subject of evaluation, but these only suggest procedures that are useful in guiding the evaluation process. Situational constraints and criteria differ for each organization. Therefore, effectiveness must be based on specific, locally-defined objectives. Information for the evaluation process should be available from the initial analysis of the system and subsequent documentation.

A complete and accurate evaluation of the effectiveness of any of the subsystems must also include statements on (a) the status of the other subsystems, (b) the effects of the other subsystems on the effectiveness of the subsystem under review, and (c) the effectiveness of the interface mechanisms. Information of these types and others are necessary in order to obtain perspective and order priorities for change, if indicated. A few examples of considerations are listed below.

The status of the other subsystems should be summarized in terms of their stated objectives and progress in achieving them. This provides a general frame of reference from which to interpret the impact of each on the subsystem under review.

The effects of each of the other subsystems on the effectiveness of the subsystem under review should be summarized in terms of the information generated as input, whether bottlenecks are created, etc. This identifies problems that must be corrected or accepted.

The effectiveness of interface mechanisms on the subsystem under review must be summarized in terms of their ability to generate timely information, facilitate programmed decision-making, etc. Here again, this information is used to identify problems that must either be accepted or corrected.

A complete and accurate evaluation of the effectiveness of any of the interface mechanisms must also include statements on (a) the requirements of each of the subsystems, (b) the amount of redundancy of data, and (c) problems in linking the various subsystems. These kinds of information and others are necessary in order to differentiate given limitations from deficiencies that must be identified and corrected. Selected examples of considerations are indicated briefly below.

The requirements of each of the subsystems must be stated in terms of data types, quantity, and quality needed as input to some subsystems and output for use in other subsystems. This information was originally used as the basis for designing specific features of the interface mechanism. Therefore, it provides appropriate criteria for judging effectiveness.

The amount of redundancy and documentation of the bases for decisions on types and quantities included in the subsystems form a foundation for review of programming strategies, etc. If a record of file use is available, one can determine whether a common file is feasible or whether separate files with some redundant information should be developed or continued.

Problems in linking the various subsystems due to arrangement of data, or whatever, may cause inefficiencies that should be identified. This may indicate a need to reorganize data files, etc.

It is possible that the stated objectives of the subsystems and interaction mechanisms will be met but the obtained results will still be unsatisfactory. In this case, retargeting is necessary. Objectives must be redefined and one must trace back to the point on the normal pathway where the deviation began. Then changes can be devised and implemented.

BIBLIOGRAPHY

HOLBROOK, F. K. 1971. A per-meal charge system. Hospitals 45, 94–97.

FOODWAYS OF AMERICAN SUBGROUP CULTURES

CHAPTER 22

Introduction

Foodways of all groups of peoples are in a constant state of change, although the rate of change varies widely among groups. For this reason, even with an adequate data base, one must monitor foodways of the population and its subgroups in order to determine differences in the type, rate, and/or direction of change.

The foodways that developed originally in the various ethnic or geographic locations were a function of (a) commodities available, (b) life style of the peoples, (c) level of technology, (d) definition of the wife-mother role, and (e) communication with outside groups (Graubard 1942A, B; Remington 1936). From the commodities available, peoples learned which foods were safe to eat in the natural state, which were consistently available, and the type of preparation that was necessary to improve each food's palatability, wholesomeness, and/or safety. Seasoning habits developed similarly. Food preferences developed from this base as people generally like what they customarily consume.

The life style of the people coupled with availability of foods originally determined food habits. In preagricultural eras, people ate the roots, leaves, seeds, berries, and nuts native to the region. Other groups living along coastal areas, streams, or lakes supplemented this diet with fish or seafood. Still other groups consumed birds, small animals, and in other cases large animals that they hunted or trapped. In early times tribes were largely nomadic, ranging over wide areas as seasons regulated the availability of various food components of the diet within the territory. The subsistence diet was generally adequate as man survived.

When man began to cultivate crops, he selected varieties from plants available that responded well and eliminated many others, some of which were nutritionally important. Nonetheless, over time as a result of trial and error, nutritional adequacy of the diet was again achieved and man survived. The need to farm plots of land, sometimes at great distance from the camp or village, as well as the discipline of agriculture had great impact on life style. Changes in food preparation methods evolved as a concomitant effect.

234

Some peoples became accustomed to eating morning and evening meals as they worked long distances from home and had no means of providing noon meals safely. Elsewhere, people learned that the working wife could prepare the evening meal easily if she put all of the ingredients into a pot with a large quantity of water to protect the food from burning. The pot was covered and left over a slow fire all day; the meal was ready when the workers returned home. Thus, some cultures became accustomed to a soup or stew as the evening meal. Inland cultures learned that meat and fish, fruits and vegetables could be preserved for later use if dried, salted, or pickled. Other customs developed similarly, according to need.

Technological developments such as ovens, metal pots, etc., have usually heavily influenced food preparation methods. In some areas, lack of or scarcity of fuel was a limiting factor restricting the variety of food preparation methods. Some cultures solved this problem by using community pits or ovens for cookery.

The definition of the wife-mother role also has had a great influence on the food habits and preferences that have developed in each area. Level of skill in food preparation has traditionally been a primary means of judging whether a woman is a good wife and mother. In most cultures the mother is expected to accommodate menus to the individual needs and desires of family members. Certain ritual foods and methods of preparation are used for the ill and elderly; the socially conscious wife-mother prepares the items in the expected manner. Certain types and/or quantities of food are an integral part of the reward system of most cultures; the wife-mother controls the distribution of rewards. Many other relationships are important. The interested reader should see other references on the subject (Fathauer 1960).

Communications with outside groups also were important in determining the strength of original foodways. When groups were isolated, narrow well-defined foodways developed. When communications networks were well developed, new customs were introduced at random intervals from the outside; the range of types and rate of change differed for these groups.

The contents of Section 4, Foodways of American Subgroup Cultures, are only intended as a guide to the characteristic foodways of each subgroup living in the United States. While some definite patterns emerge, within groups differences are also wide. These can be represented by a continuum from those of recent immigrants and/or tradition-directed individuals who follow all aspects of the subgroup foodways to those who follow them only on selected occasions such as holidays to those who totally reject the foodways of their subgroup.

New immigrants from foreign countries will often only consume the traditional diet due to general insecurity in the new situation and lack of familiarity with American fare. Orthodox Jews, Muslims and a few other groups will strictly adhere to their foodways for religious reasons. However, for other groups the critical factor is interest in the foodways of the particular subgroup and expression of concern that adequate consumption is possible.

Unless the concentration of subgroup members is high, individuals will expect to adjust to the food available. When the concentration is high, the subgroup will expect that some token efforts to accommodate their needs will be made. Usually, this means increasing the availability of staple items, e.g., rice available at one or more meals for Orientals or tortillas and beans available daily for Chicanos.

In addition, other standard items of the subgroup diet must be served at irregular intervals as an expression of concern. Such items need to be authentic and directed to the tastes of the subgroup not Americanized to appeal to the group as a whole. They should be prepared in a quantity to satisfy the cravings of members of the subgroup to which they are directed plus an allowance for others who may wish to consume the items. An alternate should be provided for the group as a whole.

Historically, some subgroups have been concentrated in localized areas of the United States in which case group pressure to retain group identity and cohesion have reduced the rate of acculturation. However, the general trend has been for foreign immigrants to attempt to adapt to American ways. Second-generation Americans have often felt a need to prove their "Americanness" and have rejected their cultural heritage, including foodways. In the late 1960's, the general climate of American society changed and became more tolerant to acceptance of differences. Accordingly, some subgroups, recognizing value in their cultural heritage as a significant factor in personal security and identity, became tradition-directed in regard to foodways and other aspects of their culture.

Moreover, a number of changes have occurred that have caused American "ethnic" foods to differ from the foods in the country of origin. German-American food is a typical example: it is quite different from contemporary German food. Adaptations to availability of essential ingredients and American culture are two factors involved. Another factor in accounting for differences results from the phenomenon of symbolism. As changes in life styles in Germany evolved to meet new conditions, foodways changed and many traditional items disappeared from the diet. As technology changed, new items were added. Whereas here in America, selected traditional items have become symbols of ethnic origin and have been preserved for this reason. Thus, in some respects, German-American cuisine is typical of German cuisine of two centuries ago.

In order to plan acceptable menus for a heterogeneous population composed of several subgroups, one must first ascertain the overall pattern of foodways of the group as a whole. Next, the pattern of differences must be mapped for each of the subgroups. Then common items can be selected as a base and alternatives that are approximately equivalent sources of the major nutrients can be paired to increase the probability of consumption of a nutritionally adequate diet. Two rules of thumb that can be applied in selecting items to appeal to subgroup needs are: (a) select only those items of diet for the menu that members of the subgroup would serve to guests—this avoids selection of items commonly served because of necessity rather than preference, and (b) avoid serving items that are associated with major feast days—items with religious significance are not usually to be shared with outsiders and other items are not for general consumption and only have meaning when accompanied by the prescribed rituals. Since within-group differences are wide, due to state of acculturation overlaid with individual differences, real alternatives must be provided for each subgroup in order to achieve nutritional goals.

The dietitian who attempts to adjust menus and/or diet instruction to the expected foodways of the individual is confronted with a number of additional practical problems (Anon. 1964). The first problem is to determine the socioeconomic, ethnic, and/or religious subgroup to which the individual belongs and his stage in acculturation. When a Guttman scale has been constructed for a particular group (Chassy *et al.* 1967) the dietitian can quickly determine the approximate list of foods consumed. This information can then be used to reduce the list of items allowed and restricted, thus simplyfying the diet instruction. The second problem is to determine the importance of foodways to the individual so that diet instruction can be adjusted, especially when economic resources are limited. A third problem is to check the validity of premises on which patient-typing is based. For example, many Protestant patients will mark "Catholic" as their religion when entering a Catholic hospital on the assumption that they will receive better care. In other cases, patients may "tell you what they think you want to hear" in regard to their eating patterns and/or food preferences. Most people have a good concept of what a balanced diet is, although for a variety of reasons they fail to consume one. A fourth problem is to convey the message of your understanding of the subgroup foodways and your acceptance of them. A supportive rapport must be established if instruction is to be effective, otherwise members of subgroups tend to see necessary dietary restrictions as an attempt to force acceptance of WASP foodways. Thus, it is clear that it is much more difficult to utilize knowledge of subgroup foodways in dealing with individuals than with groups.

The sections that follow attempt to review characteristic subgroup foods and their importance in planning menus to meet subgroup needs. A sampling of research reports and commonly available cookbooks are recommended for further reading. A cursory study of the staples and spices used by the various subgroups will reveal that most subgroups use the same basic ingredients. The distinguishing features of each cuisine are a result of differences in (a) preparation method,[1] (b) the spices and/or seasonings that are combined, and (c) size and shape of particles, i.e., some groups chop vegetables on the diagonal, others dice them uniformly, others serve them whole. The information on the following pages will enable one to make a first approximation in determining subgroup needs; a

---

[1] Due to lack of sufficient reliable information for all groups, discussion of food preparation methods and food taboos (except for major religions) were omitted from this edition.

real appreciation only develops after prolonged study of cookbooks and/or exposure through consumption of a large number of typical foods.

The food habits of Anglo-Saxons have been omitted as they form the basis of American cuisine. The foodways of various people of Africa have been omitted as the number of Africans living in the United States is small and individuals are dispersed; their needs are met on an individual basis. The cuisines of Central and South America are omitted for the same reason. With these exceptions, the foodways of the peoples of the world are discussed in the following sections.

BIBLIOGRAPHY

ANON. 1964. Food in many languages is concern in planning and teaching modified diets. Hospitals *38*, No. 7, 165–167.

CHASSY, J. P., VAN VEEN, A. G., and YOUNG, F. W. 1967. The application of social science research methods to the study of food habits and food consumption in an industrializing area. Am. J. Clin. Nutr. *20*, 56–64.

FATHAUER, G. H. 1960. Food habits—an anthropologist's view. J. Am. Dietet. Assoc. *37*, 335–338.

GRAUBARD, M. 1942A. Food habits of primitive man. I. Food and the culture pattern. Sci. Monthly *55*, 342–349.

GRAUBARD, M. 1942B. Food habits of primitive man. II. Food—biology or belief. Sci. Monthly *55*, 453–460.

REMINGTON, R. E. 1936. The social origins of dietary habits. Sci. Monthly *43*, 193–204.

TOWNSEND, C. W. 1928. Food prejudices. Sci. Monthly *27*, 65–68.

CHAPTER 23

Foodways of Blacks

Contemporary foodways of Blacks differ according to area of origin, area of residence, and socioeconomic status. However, no reliable data concerning the expected variations resulting from these factors have been published. For these reasons it is difficult to predict the needs of a particular group.

Soul Food is a popular term used to represent a common list of traditional items and a style of cooking that was typical for Blacks from the rural South prior to and during the Civil War and until the depression. What is commonly overlooked, however, is that this diet was also typical for the poor whites at that time (Cussler and DeGive 1952; Jerome 1968; Mayer 1965). It is still typical for the Black migrant worker and to some extent for others in rural areas or those in urban areas subsisting on welfare.

This diet typically included fat meat (salt pork), tripe and other variety meats, chicken, neckbones, pig's feet, ears, and tails, squirrel; starches such as cornmeal, grits, rice, and wheat flour; black-eyed peas, greens (mustard, collard, dandelion, turnip tops, kale), okra, sweet potatoes, and turnips; and molasses. Fresh vegetables grown in the garden, were eaten in season. Foods were frequently fried or boiled for long periods and hot biscuits or cornbread were prepared daily in quantities sufficient to last throughout the day (Cussler and DeGive 1952; Jerome 1968). Along the east and gulf coasts, local fish and shellfish were consumed in significant quantities when available (Mayer 1965). Other purchased items often consumed at lunch included: canned items, e.g., pork and beans, beef stew, chicken; sandwich fillings, e.g., ham spread, peanut butter, mayonnaise and jelly; crackers, cookies, soft drinks (Delgado *et al.* 1961).

Payton *et al.* (1960) reported the following meal patterns for pregnant southern Black women:

(A) Breakfast—meat (bacon or sausage), eggs, bread item, and beverage; or cereal product, meat, eggs, bread item, and beverage.

(B) Lunch—sandwich, dessert or fruit (optional) and/or beverages; or leftovers from a dinner meal.

(C) Dinner—meat or fish, starchy food, vegetable, bread item, and for some, dessert and/or beverage. Since the wife-mother prepared the meals, this pattern is probably typical for families as a whole.

Since the 1940's large numbers of Blacks migrated from the rural south to the industrial east, north and west. Changes in food habits were a necessary part of the adjustment to a new urban industrial life style. A study by Jerome (1968) outlines changes observed in one midwest city. Significant points are:

(A) Traditional meal patterns were retained to the extent possible, i.e., the name of the meal and the time the meal was consumed were changed and some items were shifted from one meal to another but all items were retained though served less frequently.

(B) The traditional breakfast was modified from assorted fried meats, rice, grits, biscuits, gravy, fried potatoes (sweet or white), coffee, and milk to eggs (with or without bacon and sausage), hot biscuits, bread, and coffee.

(C) A lunch meal was added at noon to replace the heavy boiled dinner. This meal consisted of soup, sandwich, fruit and fruit-drink—the meal commonly consumed by industrial workers.

(D) The warmed-over dinner meal was replaced by a new, heavier dinner meal—the week divided between boiling and frying days. On boiling days dinner might consist of a main dish of boiled vegetables or legumes seasoned with some type of meat, sweet or white potatoes, cornbread, a sweet beverage or milk, and possibly a dessert of fruit. On frying days the traditional breakfast, noted above, is served for dinner.

One review paper (Mayer 1965) indicated that northern-born Blacks consume a diet that is the same as that of their socioeconomic peers. However, the point was also made that southern-born Blacks living in the north often spend their limited food money for traditional southern foods such as fat-backs and grits in special neighborhood stores that cater to their needs. Institutions serving such groups would need to provide traditional foods in order to meet their needs. To date no studies for groups of southern-born Blacks living on the east or west coasts have been reported.

Moreover, since the 1940's the south has become increasingly industrialized. As the economic level of southern Blacks has increased, so has their access to standard American foods. While traditional items and methods of preparation are used more frequently than they would be by WASP groups in the same community, their diet is otherwise the same (Mayer 1965).

However, Bauer et al. (1968) report that although Blacks have generally accepted the values of middle-class WASP culture, the majority do not have the economic basis for purchasing the goods used as symbols of these values.

Alexander (1968) found that during the 1950's urban Blacks in New York City tended to maintain traditional food preferences except those associated with poverty. He inferred that processed foods were purchased as symbols of social status. Generally, frozen dinners were not well-accepted; they were purchased by a large number of Blacks but infrequently. Dehydrated soups were neither well-liked nor purchased frequently.

More recent information reported by Coltrin and Bradfield (1970) indicates that Blacks buy (a) somewhat less frozen juices and frozen desserts; (b) more pork, chicken, greens, baking supplies, and other foods associated with southern cookery; (c) soft drinks, candy, and other snack items. A number of items are less expensive substitutes for fresh products; others are expensive and are purchased as status symbols.

Black Muslim groups follow the traditional proscription of the Muslim diet. These are discussed in the section Foodways of the Middle East.

A study by Sanjur and Scoma (1971) showed that the low-income Black child's eating habits were influenced by the mother's familiarity or like-dislike response to various foods. This study indicates that foods liked (50% of sample or more) include:

(A) Meat, fish, poultry, and eggs—baked liver, chili con carne; fish sticks; stewed chicken.

(B) Dairy products—American cheese, buttermilk (mother's), chocolate milk, cottage cheese (mother's), evaporated milk, ice cream, milk, skim milk.

(C) Cereal products—biscuits, doughnuts, noodles, oatmeal, rice, white bread.

(D) Fruits and vegetables—collard greens, orange juice, prune juice, raw tomato, spinach, sweet potatoes.

This study also indicates that the following items are relatively disliked (less than 50% of sample):

(A) Meat, fish, poultry, and eggs—none indicated.

(B) Dairy products—buttermilk and cottage cheese (children), skim milk.

(C) Cereals—none indicated.

(D) Vegetables—broccoli, pumpkin, squash, (green pepper and raw cabbage are marginal).

On the west coast, Blacks consume a diet that is essentially the same as that of WASPs of the same economic level. Although most of the Blacks migrated to the west after World War II, they have not retained their former eating habits due to new life styles, i.e., working hours that do not permit preparation of heavy breakfasts, a heavy noon meal, etc. Moreover, ingredients used in their former life style are not as readily available and prices of them are higher in the west than locally-produced items.

Meal Pattern and Food Consumed

Three meals plus snacks is the most common meal pattern. The traditional breakfast may be consumed on weekends; on weekdays the fare is coffee and toast or cereal and milk. Lunch usually consists of a sandwich and milk or soft drink. A housewife at home usually eats leftovers. Dinner is usually a fried meal. Few recipes are used, but the cooking style is distinctive and a fairly uniform quality is achieved.

(A) Spices and seasonings—sugar frequently added to vegetables; fat meat such as salt pork, ham ends, ham hocks, bacon ends or bacon drippings essential in cooking foods such as dried or green beans, cabbage, greens; hot chili peppers, onion, garlic, salt, and pepper are also added to foods.

(B) Staples—the same basic ingredients available to them as to others in the surrounding area; convenience foods used as the budget allows.

(C) Meat, fish, poultry, and eggs—beef, pork, chicken, and fish of all kinds;

veal and lamb not accepted; eggs eaten often, primarily at breakfast; "soul foods" (e.g., tripe, neck) consumed in limited quantities.

(D) Dairy products—milk (in limited quantities); cheddar cheese but not others; ice cream.

(E) Cereal products—biscuits (often canned); breads, corn bread (mix); hominy grits with butter; macaroni; rice.

(F) Fruits—all are consumed to some degree depending upon season and price.

(G) Vegetables—all are consumed but in variable quantities; favorites are: beets, broccoli, collard greens, corn, English peas, green beans, greens (mixture of mustard and turnip leaves), sweet potatoes, and yams.

(H) Other—legumes: black-eyed peas, chili beans, pinto beans, pork and beans, red beans; peanut butter; solid shortenings for frying; standard snack foods.

BIBLIOGRAPHY

ALEXANDER, M. 1968. The significance of ethnic groups in marketing. *In* Perspectives in Consumer Behavior. H. H. Kassarjian, and T. S. Robertson (Editors). Scott, Foresman & Co., Glenview, Ill.

BAUER, R. A., CUNNINGHAM, S. M., and WORTZEL, L. H. 1968. The marketing dilemma of Negroes. *In* Perspectives in Consumer Behavior. H. H. Kassarjian, and T. S. Robertson (Editors). Scott, Foresman & Co., Glenview, Ill.

BRADFIELD, R. B., and COLTRIN, D. 1970. Some characteristics of the health and nutrition status of California Negroes. Am. J. Clin. Nutr. *23*, 420–426.

COLTRIN, D. M., and BRADFIELD, R. B. 1970. Food buying practices of urban low-income consumers—a review. J. Nutr. Educ. *1*, 16–17.

CUSSLER, M. T., and DEGIVE, M. L. 1952. 'Twixt the Cup and the Lip. Twayne Publishers, New York.

DELGADO, G., BRUMBACK, C. L., and DEAVER, M. B. 1961. Eating patterns among migrant families. U.S. Public Health Rept. *76*, 349–355.

DICKINS, D. 1929. Negro food habits in the Yazoo Mississippi Delta. J. Home Econ. *18*, 523–525.

GRANT, F. W., and GROOM, D. 1959. A dietary study among a group of southern Negroes. J. Am. Dietet. Assoc. *35*, 910–918.

JEROME, N. W. 1968. Changing meal patterns among southern-born Negroes in a midwestern city. Nutr. News *31*, 9, 12.

JEROME, N. W. 1969. Northern urbanization and food consumption patterns of southern-born Negroes. Am. J. Clin. Nutr. *22*, 1667–1669.

MAYER, J. 1965. The nutritional status of American Negroes. Nutr. Rev. *23*, 161–164.

PAYTON, E., CRUMP, E. P., and HORTON, C. P. 1960. Dietary habits of 571 pregnant southern Negro women. J. Am. Dietet. Assoc. *37*, 129–136.

SANJUR, D., and SCOMA, D. 1971. Food habits of low-income children in Northern New York. J. Nutr. Educ. *2*, 85–95.

SCHUCK, C., and TARTT, J. B. 1973. Food consumption of low-income, rural Negro households in Mississippi. J. Am. Dietet. Assoc. *62*, 151–155.

WILSON, M. T. 1964. Peaceful integration: the owner's adoption of his slaves' food. J. Negro History *49*, 116–127.

CHAPTER 24

Foodways of Chicanos

Properly, the term "Chicano" refers to Central Americans as well as Mexicans. Here, it is used in the popular sense of referring to Mexican-Americans.

The diet of Chicanos, although commonly portrayed as invariate, differs from one locale to another; although some items are consumed in common, the Chicano diet is influenced by local availability of ingredients and the attraction of alternate items of diet. Thus, the diet of Chicanos living in Texas, New Mexico, Arizona, California, Michigan, and New York will differ, all other things being equal. Little scientific information is available about the diet of Chicanos in California (Bradfield and Brun 1970). This is probably true in other states as well.

Economic status also causes variability in the Chicano diet. Migrant workers' diet will differ from that of upper-class Chicanos quantitatively, qualitatively, and in the amount of variety.

Area of origin and sociocultural status in Mexico also are determining factors in the composition of the diet. The majority of Mexicans who have immigrated to the United States are from the northern states of Mexico. Many are poor rural "mestizos" so their traditional diet is similar to that described for the Native American gardeners and gatherers of the Southwest.

The basic diet in Mexico is a composite influenced by the major population subgroups, namely Indians, Spaniards, and Negroes. This base is overlaid with food habits acquired from people who have settled there from all over the world. For this reason, Chicanos from the urban upper classes are as cosmopolitan in their food habits as urban upper class Americans.

FOOD HABITS OF MIGRANT WORKERS

Migrant workers' diets are usually at the subsistence level for economic reasons. Moreover, many Chicano migrant workers speak little English, if any, and combined with their economic constraints this restricts their access to standard American food. The children have some exposure, when they attend school as most receive free lunches. However, many American foods are rejected in favor of traditional Chicano foods (Bruhn and Pangborn 1971). Typical Chicano foods include:

(A) Meat, fish, poultry, and eggs—albondigas, burritos, carne adobada, carne seca, chili con carne, chorizo, enchiladas, meat empanandas, picadillo, posole, tacos, tamales, tostadas, huevos rancheros; red snapper, crab, mullet, prawns, shrimp; eggs.

(B) Dairy products—flan or baked custard, mild cheese, milk (evaporated, fresh).

(C) Cereal products—bread pudding, buñuelos, cornmeal masa, rice, rice puddings, sopapaillas, tortillas (cornmeal or wheat flour).

(D) Fruits—nopales (cactus), mango, all others commonly available in the United States.

(E) Vegetables—chilis (many varieties, mild to hot), corn, greens, potatoes, tomatoes, wild greens, and all others commonly available in the United States.

(F) Beverages—carbonated beverages, coffee, hot chocolate, pinole, pulque.

(G) Other—cooking fat (lard), legumes (calico, garbanzo, kidney, pinto).

They also consume some American foods such as hamburgers, hot dogs, macaroni and cheese, ice cream, cookies, doughnuts, and cake. For additional information see Cravioto et al. (1945), Czajkowski (1969), Kight et al. (1969), McGuire (1954), Pangborn and Bruhn (1971), Zelayeta (1944).

According to Bruhn and Pangborn (1971) the meal pattern for Chicano migrant workers is (a) breakfast (consumed at 9:00 a.m. break in the field)— eggs, tortillas, fried beans, cereal, and beverage; (b) lunch (between 12:00 and 2:00 p.m. consumed in the field)—beans and/or tortillas, meat or stew, beverage; and (c) supper (about 6:00 p.m.)—beans and/or meat, rice or potatoes, tortillas, and sometimes a vegetable, beverage. Cookies, doughnuts, etc., are eaten in between at coffee breaks.

Since this group of Chicanos has limited exposure to American foods, traditional Chicano foods must be prepared in an acceptable manner on a continuous basis if adequate consumption is to be assured. If an objective is to increase exposure to standard American foods, such items should be provided in addition to, rather than in lieu of, traditional items. Otherwise, nutritional goals cannot be met.

FOODWAYS OF LOWER CLASS CHICANOS

Lower-class Chicanos have more exposure to standard American foods and values than do migrant workers. Much of the exposure is through schools. While they frequently consume traditional items in their homes more frequently than would other members of the same community, there is some evidence (Hacker et al. 1954) that beans are increasingly rejected in favor of meat, especially beef. In order to meet the needs of this group, so as to assure consumption, traditional Chicano foods should be provided systematically as an alternative to standard American foods.

FOODWAYS OF MIDDLE- AND UPPER-CLASS CHICANOS

A study by Clark (1959) indicated that middle- and upper-class Chicanos are dispersed in suburbia and frequently have been assimilated into the general American culture. In their homes, some may serve traditional items somewhat more frequently than other members of the same community but otherwise the foodways are the same.

This group appreciates the concern expressed by a food service that makes an effort to prepare authentic foods at irregular intervals. However, no special effort in adapting menus is necessary on a continuing basis.

BIBLIOGRAPHY

BOOHER, M. 1937. A study of the dietary habits of Mexican-American families in Tucson, Arizona. MA Thesis. Univ. Arizona. (Unpublished)

BRADFIELD, R. B., and BRUN, T. 1970. Nutritional status of California Mexican-Americans. Am. J. Clin. Nutr. 23, 798–806.

BRUHN, C. M., and PANGBORN, R. M. 1971. Food habits of migrant farm workers in California. Comparisons between Mexican-Americans and "Anglos." J. Am. Dietet. Assoc. 59, 347–355.

CLARK, M. 1959. Health in the Mexican-American Culture. Univ. of Calif. Press, Berkeley.

CRAVIOTO, R. et al. 1945. Composition of typical Mexican foods. J. Nutr. 29, 317–329.

CZAJKOWSKI, J. M. 1969. Mexican Foods and Traditions. Univ. Conn. Coop. Ext. Serv. Bull. 64-64.

HACKER, D. B. et al. 1954. A study of food habits in New Mexico (1949–1952). New Mexico Agr. Expt. Sta. Bull. 384.

HACKER, D. B., and MILLER, E. D. 1959. Food patterns of the Southwest. Am. J. Clin. Nutr. 7, 224–229.

KIGHT, M. A. et al. 1969. Nutritional influences of Mexican-American foods in Arizona. J. Am. Dietet. Assoc. 55, 557–561.

MCGUIRE, L. M. 1954. "Mexico" in Old World Foods for New World Families. Dolphin Books, Doubleday & Co., Garden City, N.Y.

ORTIZ, E. L. 1967. The Complete Book of Mexican Cooking. Bantam Books, New York.

PANGBORN, R. B., and BRUHN, C. M. 1971. Concepts of food habits of "other" ethnic groups. J. Nutr. Educ. 2, 106–110.

TAYLOR, B. H. 1969. Mexico: Her Daily and Festive Breads. Creative Press, Claremont, Calif.

WOLFE, L. (Editor). 1960. McCall's Introduction to Mexican Cooking. McCall Publishing Co., New York.

ZELAYETA, E. 1944. Elena's Famous Mexican and Spanish Recipes. Dettners Printing House, San Francisco.

CHAPTER 25

Foodways of Native Americans

A large number of the common ingredients, methods of cooking, and dishes consumed in this country originated with one of the groups of Native Americans and were adopted by the early settlers. Ingredients learned from the Native Americans include corn, squashes, tomatoes, peppers, beans, avocadoes, white and sweet potatoes, pumpkins, and various nuts and berries. Preparation methods that have been adopted include cooking in earthenware pits, curing of country hams, barbecueing of salmon, clambakes. Native American dishes that have been adopted include roast turkey, baked beans, corn chowder, corn bread, chili con carne, jerky, persimmon pudding.

The foodways of Native Americans living in urban areas are highly variable and depend on such factors as (a) original cultural group and food native to the area, (b) stage in acculturation, and (c) socioeconomic status. In order to plan acceptable menus one must have a basic understanding of cultural differences among groups of Native Americans and whether or not the particular group is tradition-directed.

The majority of studies available refer to (a) traditional diets of specific cultural groups living on reservations and/or (b) adaptations of traditional diets to food scarcity problems and subsequent government-sponsored food and/or nutrition programs.

The urban Native American living in a community with many ethnic groups will not usually expect that typical foods will be prepared for him; he probably consumes the standard American diet. However, on reservations and in communities with concentrations of Native Americans, the menu should list typical local items of diet (Anon. 1964).

Moreover, as Fathauer (1960), an anthropologist, has pointed out, although Native Americans speak English and often wear standard clothing and work at varied occupations, they usually have retained their traditional values and beliefs. Some of these have weakened; others have grown stronger. Religion has grown stronger and ancient rites have been revived. Similarly, there has been a revival of traditional, almost lost, foodways among some groups of Native Americans. Other groups have kept their traditional diets and foodways since early times.

There are wide tribal differences in food habits, preferences, and other aspects of foodways. However, discussions of Native American foodways are commonly divided according to geographic region as follows: (a) the gardeners and gatherers of the Southwest, (b) the fishermen of the Pacific Northwest, (c) the wandering hunters of the plains, (d) the planters of the South, and (e) the woodsmen of the East (Kimball and Anderson 1965; Bosley 1959). Discussion of the foodways of each group follow. A discussion of Eskimo foodways will conclude this section.

THE FISHERMEN OF THE PACIFIC NORTHWEST (COOK 1941; KIMBALL AND ANDERSON 1965)

The foods consumed by this group of Native Americans characteristically include:

(A) Meat, fish, poultry, and eggs—bear, deer, elk, groundhog, jack rabbit, porcupine, otter, wild goat; candle fish, clams, cod, crab, flounder, halibut, herring, mussels, oysters, red snapper, salmon, seal, smelts, sole, whale; duck, goose, lark, pelican, plover, sage hens, sea gull; bird eggs.

(B) Cereal products—acorn meal, biscuit-root, breadroot, Indian potatoes, nut grass, seed meal, sego lily, trimble weed, tule potatoes, wild potatoes.

(C) Fruits—apples, grapes, wild berries including black hawthorne, blueberries, chokecherries, currants, elderberries, salal, skunk berries.

(D) Vegetables—beets, carrots, greens (cat-tail, clover, cow-parsnips, ferns, Indian lettuce, sunflower leaves, wild celery), mushrooms, potatoes, squashes.

(E) Beverages—teas (peyote, Russet Buffalo Berries, three-lobed sumac, white sage, wild rose, yerba buena).

(F) Other—ant pudding, buckeyes, honey, kelp, mosses, nuts (pine nuts and hazelnuts), salt, seaweed, seeds of wild grasses.

(G) Spices and herbs—anise, garlic, mustard, onions, peppermint, sage, spearmint, torweed.

Vegetables are traditionally cooked in a unique way. They are brought to the boil in woven baskets by dropping enough hot stones into the water until it bubbles. The baskets would burn if hung over a fire so this ingenious way of heating the water is used (Kimball and Anderson 1965). Meat and fish are broiled over an open fire on a spit. The meal pattern is two meals per day.

The Adapted Diet

At present, Native Americans on reservations still consume customary foods prepared in traditional ways, to the extent possible. However, exposure to other cultural groups has introduced many standard American foods. Government commodities are also consumed by a significant proportion of the group. The present diet includes, but is not limited to:

(A) Meat, fish, poultry, and eggs—beef, luncheon meats, pork; canned fish; chicken; eggs.

(B) Dairy products—some milk and cheese.

(C) Cereal products—dry breakfast cereals, farina, oatmeal.

(D) Fruits—native fruits as above, apples, bananas, fruit cocktail, oranges, canned peaches, pears, pineapple.

(E) Vegetables—native vegetables as above, celery, green peas, lettuce, tomatoes.

(F) Beverages—coffee, soft drinks.

(G) Other—jams, jellies, sugar; cooking fat (lard).

THE WANDERING HUNTERS OF THE PLAINS

The characteristic traditional food of this group of Native Americans includes:

(A) Meat, fish, poultry, and eggs—antelope, buffalo, deer, elk, frogs, pemican, rabbit; brook trout, grouse, pheasant; bird eggs.

(B) Cereal products—wild rice.

(C) Fruits—buffalo berries, chokecherries, rose hips.

(D) Vegetables—beans, beets, carrots, corn, mushrooms, potatoes, squashes, tomatoes, turnips, watercress.

(E) Other—honey, nasturtium petals, wild herbs.

Meats were roasted on a spit or cooked in outside pits lined with hot stones and skins. Some items were boiled in pots over an open fire.

The Adapted Diet

Today the traditional hunting grounds of these tribes are farms and ranches. So the Native American who lives on a reservation obtains his foods from the trading post. Those in cities and towns purchase their foods at grocery stores and/or obtain government commodities. The present diet includes, but is not limited to, the following items:

(A) Meat, fish, poultry, and eggs—beef (ground and stew, unless they raise their own), luncheon meats, pork, variety meats (heart, kidney, liver); canned fish; chicken; eggs.

(B) Dairy products—some milk and cheese.

(C) Cereal products—bread, cornmeal, dry breakfast cereals, farina, macaroni, noodles, oatmeal, rice, wheat flour.

(D) Fruits—native fruits as above, apples, bananas, oranges, watermelon; canned peaches, pears, fruit cocktail.

(F) Beverages—coffee, soft drinks.

(G) Other—jams, jellies, preserves; cooking fats (lard, fat back), sugar.

THE PLANTERS OF THE SOUTH

Foods commonly consumed by this group of Native Americans include:

(A) Meats, fish, poultry, and eggs—bear, deer, possum, rabbit, racoon, squirrel; crabs, flounder, oysters, red snapper, shrimp, trout, white fish; cranes, osprey, pheasant, plover, quail, turkey.

(B) Cereal products—cornbread, corn meal, dressing, wild rice.

(C) Fruits—crab apples, grapes, oranges, persimmons, plums, wild berries.

(D) Vegetables—beans, corn, Jerusalem artichokes, mushrooms, okra, pumpkins, squashes, sweet potatoes, wild greens.

(E) Other—hickory nuts, honey, peanuts, pecans, walnuts, wild herbs.

Food preparation methods are varied. Meats are steamed, diced for soups or stews, roasted. Cornbread and other items are baked on hot stones.

THE GARDENERS AND GATHERERS OF THE SOUTHWEST

The characteristic and traditional foods of this group of Native Americans includes (Carpenter and Steggerda 1939; Darby et al. 1956A, B; Kimball and Anderson 1965; Steggerda and Eskardt 1941):

(A) Meat, fish, poultry and eggs—beef, goat, horsemeat, lamb, pork (salt pork, bacon, ham, etc.), wild game; canned luncheon meats; chicken; eggs.

(B) Dairy products—evaporated milk, goat's milk.

(C) Cereal products—acorn meal, atole (a corn gruel), corn meal mush, fry bread, hominy, piki (a paper-thin, blue-green bread that is rolled), rice, white bread.

(D) Fruits—apples, apricots, cactus stems and buds (prickly pears and others), chokecherries, dried yucca, ground cherries, muskmelon, oranges, peaches, wild berries, watermelon; canned fruits.

(E) Vegetables—beans (green, pinto), chiles and other peppers, green corn, green peas, onions, potatoes, squashes, tomatoes, wild carrots, wild celery, wild potatoes, pumpkin.

(F) Beverages—coffee with milk and sugar, soft drinks, tea with sugar.

(G) Other—cooking fat (lard), honey, nuts (acorns, pinon, seeds of wild grass, squash seeds), wild herbs (Darby *et al.* 1956B).

A large number of Mexican foods are commonly consumed such as chili con carne, guacamole, refried beans, tamales, tortillas, tostadas.

Corn is the staple and white, yellow, red, and blue varieties are grown. White corn is used to make cornmeal and hominy. Yellow (sweet corn) is roasted and eaten fresh, roasted and dried, dried, or made into cornmeal. Red and blue corn are made into cornmeal for use in making piki, blue marbles, and other dishes. Ashes are used to create the alkaline pH necessary for maintenance of the blue color.

In recent years as the exposure of the Native Americans to the standard American culture has increased there has been a definite shift in eating habits (Cook 1941; Darby *et al.* 1956A, B). In addition to the traditional foods the following are consumed:

(A) Meat, fish, poultry, and eggs—canned corned beef, canned hash, cold cuts, sardines and other canned fish such as salmon and tuna; heart, kidney, liver.

(B) Dairy products—evaporated milk, fresh milk, goat cheese but not cheddar.

(C) Cereal products—biscuits, cooked and dry cereals of most kinds, cornbread, popovers, white bread.

(D) Vegetables—white potatoes.

(E) Beverages—coffee, soft drinks.

(F) Other—cakes, cookies, peanut butter, pies.

THE WOODSMEN OF THE EAST

The typical foods consumed by this group of Native Americans include:

(A) Meat, fish, poultry, and eggs—bear, beaver, :deer, muskrat, rabbit, squirrel; bass, catfish, clams, eel, halibut, lobster, oysters, perch, trout; duck, goose.

(B) Cereal products—corn meal, Indian pudding, wild rice.

(C) Fruits—apples, cranberries and other wild berries, cherries, grapes, plums.

(D) Vegetables—baked beans, corn, mushrooms, potatoes, pumpkin, squashes, tomatoes, wild greens (milkweed, kalsa, fern sprouts).

(E) Others—hazelnuts, hickory nuts, honey, maple syrup, wild herbs.

The traditional meal pattern consists of one main meal per day—a brunch in the middle of the morning with snacks available throughout the rest of the day (Kimball and Anderson 1965).

The Adapted Diet

Most of these Indians live in farming or urban areas and purchase most of their foods. However, a number rely on government commodities. Their present diet includes, but is not limited to:

(A) Meat, fish, poultry, and eggs—beef (ground or stew), canned meats, luncheon meats, variety meats (heart, kidneys, liver), fish as above, chicken, eggs.

(B) Dairy products—cheese, evaporated milk.

(C) Cereal products—coffee cake, cornmeal, dry breakfast cereals, flour, fried bread, macaroni, oatmeal, pancakes, spaghetti, white bread, wild rice.

(D) Fruits—native fruits as above; canned peaches.

(E) Vegetables—native vegetables as above; asparagus, beets, cabbage, carrots, green beans, lettuce, peas.

(F) Beverages—canned fruit juices, coffee, soft drinks.

(G) Other—native items as above; cooking fats (butter, lard, margarine), sugar.

FOODWAYS OF ESKIMOS AND NATIVE AMERICANS OF ALASKA

The foodways of Eskimos and Native Americans of Alaska have been changing in recent years due to increased exposure to American foods through the school lunch program, hospitals, company cafeterias, and National Guard. Procurement has been facilitated by increased income and the establishment of trading posts in the villages (Heller and Scott 1967).

The Traditional Diet

The aboriginal diet of the Eskimos and Native Americans of Alaska was carnivorous, i.e., largely based on meat and/or fish. It varied with geographic location as described below.

Northern and Northwestern Groups.—The traditional diet is based on sea mammals including: oogruk, polar bear, seals, walrus, whale. All parts are consumed—raw, dried, or frozen (Stefansson 1937).

Southern Groups.—The traditional diet is based on fish including: Blackfish, herring, pike, salmon, shellfish, smelts, sticklefish, tomcod, trout, white fish (ICNND 1959).

Interior Groups.—The basis for this diet is land mammals primarily caribou. Moose, beaver, muskrat are also consumed (ICNND 1959; Stefansson 1937).

In addition, the Eskimos and Indians eat birds (auklet, cormorant, duck, goose, murre, ptarmigan, puffin, sea pigeons), bird eggs, hares, porcupines, mink and other small animals, berries, roots, seaweed and green plants in season (Cremeans 1930; ICNND 1959). However, these are consumed in small portions.

Staples.—The Alaska Basic Five Food Groups list the following items, which are generally available:

(A) Meat, fish, poultry, and eggs—bear, beaver, carabou, moose, muskrat, porcupine, rabbit, reindeer, seal (oogruk, etc.), walrus, whale; blackfish, grayling, halibut, herring, needlefish, salmon, sheefish, smelt, tomcod, trout, whitefish; badarki, clams, cockles, crab, mussels; duck, goose, grouse, ptarmigan, spruce hen; eggs (bird, duck, fish, goose, hen).

(B) Dairy products—evaporated milk, nonfat dry milk.

(C) Cereal products—biscuits, black lily flour, cornmeal, farina, fry bread, hotcakes, macaroni, oatmeal, pilot crackers, rice, spaghetti, white and wheat bread.

(D) Fruits—blackberries, blueberries, cloudberries, cranberries, crowberries, currants, Pacific serviceberry, red raspberries, rose hips, salmonberries, strawberries (beach), western crabapple; apricots (canned), orange juice (canned), peaches (canned), tomatoes or juice (canned).

(E) Vegetables[1]—beach asparagus, beach greens (sea chickweed, seabeach sandwort, sea purslane), brake, brook saxifrage, cabbage, carrots, cattails, coltsfoot, cow parsnip, cowslip leaves and roots, dandelion leaves, Eskimo potato, felty-leafed willow, fireweed shoots, goose grass, green beans, leaves of Siberia sprig beauty, mouse nuts, nettles, pallas buttercup, parsnip wallflower root, pinkplume leaves and roots, potato plant, pumpkin, riverweed leaves, rock cress,

---

[1] Heller (1953) has compiled a list of plants that are consumed in season. These are important but form a small part of the year-round dietary. These items have been merged with the list from the Basic Five.

roseroot leaves and roots, scurvy grass, seashore plantain leaves, seaside plantain, seaweed, sourdock, sour grass, spiked saxifrage, spinach, spreading woodfern, strawberry spinach, turnip greens, turnips, water sedge, wild celery, wild chives, wild cucumber shoots and berries, wild rhubarb, wild spinach (i.e., pigweed or lambsquarters), wild sweet potatoes, willow greens, willow leaves and shoots, winter cress, wooly lousewort.

(F) Beverages—coffee, Labrador tea, tea.

(G) Other—cooking fats and oils (bacon, caribou fat, fish oil, lard, moose fat, muktuk, margarine, salad oils, seal oil, shortening, other land and sea animal fats).

The Current Diet

The meal pattern is three meals a day with the main meal in the evening, especially during the school year. Breakfast is cooked or raw frozen fish or meat. Dinner meats may be steamed or fried; a meat or fish soup is common with rice or macaroni, salt, curry powder, and perhaps a canned meat or soup added.

The traditional diet is still followed by Eskimos and Native Americans from outlying villages. However, it has been supplemented by imported common staples including dry cereals, oatmeal, rice, cornmeal, coffee, crackers, butter, margarine, flour, canned fruits and juices, shortening, condensed and evaporated milk, sugar, vegetables (potatoes, onions, rutabagas), peanut butter, and condiments such as catsup, pickles, etc. (Heller and Scott 1967).

BIBLIOGRAPHY

ANON. 1964. Food in many languages is concern in planning and teaching modified diets. Hospitals *38*, No. 7, 165–167.

ANON. 1969. Arizona Diet Manual for Nursing Homes and Small Hospitals, 2nd Edition. Arizona Dietetic Assoc.

ANON. 1970. Alaska Basic Five Food Groups. Nutr. Dietet. Branch, Alaska Area Native Health Serv., Univ. Alaska, College, Alaska.

BENSON, E. M., PETERS, J. M., EDWARDS, M. A., and HOGAN, L. A. 1973. Wild edible plants of the Pacific Northwest. Nutritive values. J. Am. Dietet. Assoc. *62*, 143–147.

BOSLEY, B. 1959. Nutrition in the Indian health program. J. Am. Dietet. Assoc. *35*, 905–909.

CARPENTER, T. M., and STEGGERDA, M. 1939. Food of the present-day Navajo Indians of New Mexico and Arizona. J. Nutr. *18*, 297–305.

CARR, L. G. 1943. Survival foods of the American aborigines. J. Am. Dietet. Assoc. *19*, 845–847.

COOK, S. F. 1941. The mechanism and extent of dietary adaptation among certain groups of California and Nevada Indians. Ibero-Americana *18*, Univ. Calif. Press, Berkeley.

CREMEANS, L. M. 1930. Food habits of the Eskimo people of St. Lawrence Island as ascertained by the Bunnell-Geist expedition. J. Home Econ. *22*, 263–269.

DARBY, W. J. *et al.* 1956A. A study of the dietary background and nutriture of the Navajo Indians. II Dietary pattern. J. Nutr. *60* (Suppl. 2), 19–34.

DARBY, W. J. *et al.* 1956B. A study of the dietary background and nutriture of the Navajo Indian. I. Background and food production. J. Nutr. *60* (Suppl. 2), 1–18.

DRAPER, H. H., and BELL, R. R. 1972. The changing Eskimo diet. Illinois Res. *14*, No. 4, 14–15.

DRUCKER, P. 1955. Indians of the Northwest Coast. McGraw-Hill Book Co., New York.

FATHAUER, G. H. 1960. Food habits—an anthropologist's view. J. Am. Dietet. Assoc. *37*, 335–338.

HACKER, D. B. *et al.* 1954. A study of food habits in New Mexico (1949–1952). New Mexico Agr. Expt. Sta. Bull. *384.*

HELLER, C. A. 1953. Wild, edible and poisonous plants of Alaska. Univ. Alaska Coop. Ext. Serv. Bull. *40.*

HELLER, C. A., and SCOTT, E. M. 1967. The Alaska dietary survey 1956–1961. U.S. Dept. Health, Educ., Welfare, U.S. Public Health Serv. Publ. *999-AH-2.*

ICNND 1959. Alaska An Appraisal of the Health and Nutritional Status of the Eskimo. Interdepartmental Comm. Nutr. Natl. Defense, Washington, D.C.

KIMBALL, Y., and ANDERSON, J. 1965. The Art of American Indian Cooking. Doubleday & Co., New York.

KROEBER, A. L. 1904. Types of Indian culture in California. Am. Archaeol. Ethnology *2*, No. 3, 81–103.

MURPHY, E. V. A. 1959. Indian Uses of Native Plants. Desert Printers, Palm Desert, Calif.

SCULLY, V. 1970. A Treasury of American Indian Herbs, Their Lore and Their Use for Food, Drugs, and Medicine. Crown Publishers, New York.

STEFANSSON, V. 1937. Food of the ancient and modern stone age man. J. Am. Dietet. Assoc. *13*, 102–119.

STEGGERDA, M., and ESKARDT. R. B. 1941. Navajo foods and their preparation. J. Am. Dietet. Assoc. *19*, 217–221.

TATE, J. L. 1971. Cactus Cook Book. Cactus Succulent Soc. Riverside, Calif.

TSCHOPIK, H. 1952. Indians of North America. Am. Museum Nat. Hist., New York.

UNDERHILL, R. M. 1953. Red Man's America. Univ. Chicago Press, Chicago.

U. S. Dept. of Health, Education and Welfare. 1957. Cultural characteristics. *In* Health Services for American Indians. U.S. Public Health Publ. *531.*

WEATHERWAX, P. 1954. Indian Corn in Old America. Macmillan Co., New York.

CHAPTER 26

Foodways of Puerto Ricans and Cubans Living in the United States

The basic foods consumed by Puerto Ricans and Cubans are derived from three cultures, namely native Indian Caribs, Spanish, and Negro. The resultant blend has been established for centuries but is overlaid with imported foods from other cultures.

In the United States both Puerto Rican and Cuban-Americans tend to cluster together, especially on the east coast, and preserve their traditional culture including foodways. Nutritionists working with these groups have encouraged some dietary changes and have been partially successful. For example, since many of their preferred fruits and vegetables are tropical, and, hence, imported and therefore expensive, use of standard American fruits and vegetables has been encouraged. Consumption of cereals such as farina, oatmeal, cornflakes, etc., has also become customary. Substitution of vegetable oil in place of lard and use of nonfat dry milk have been partially effective.

TRADITIONAL DIET

Meal Pattern

Fernandez *et al.* (1971) reported that three meals are commonly consumed. Breakfast patterns of three types were reported: (a) coffee with milk, bread; (b) coffee with milk, eggs, bread; and (c) coffee with milk, cereal, fruit, eggs. Two alternate lunch menus were also observed: rural families consumed starchy vegetables with codfish and urban families consumed rice and beans with meat. Supper consisted of beans and rice with meat, milk and vegetable added when income allowed.

Spicing and Seasoning

Foods are distinctively spiced. Common spices include: albaranilla (a type of onion), anise, annato, basil, bay leaf, bergamot, capers, cayenne, chocolate, cilantro (coriander), cinnamon, cloves, coffee, garlic, ginger, lemon juice, marjoram, mint, nutmeg, olive oil, oregano, paprika, parsley, pepper (black, cayenne, sweet), pimento, rue, rum, vanilla, vinegar, watercress, wine.

Staples

The traditional diet as consumed in Puerto Rico includes, but is not limited to, the following items:

(A) Meat, fish, poultry and eggs—beef (fresh, canned, dried), brains, kid, pork (blood sausage, chops, empanadas, fresh and smoked hams, meatballs, pig's feet, roasts), rabbit, tongue, tripe, veal; barracuda, bonito, butterfish, crab, dolphin, dried codfish, gar, grouper, grunts, mullet, porgie, robalas, salmon, snapper, Spanish mackerel, tarpon, tripletails, yellowtail; chicken, guinea fowl, pigeon, turkey; eggs (hen).

(B) Dairy products—imported cheeses (American, cheddar, Edam, Parmesan), milk (evaporated, fresh, nonfat dry).

(C) Cereal products—cornmeal, crackers, flour, French bread, hominy, macaroni, noodles, oatmeal, plantains, rice, rice meal, rolls, spaghetti, vermicelli, yuca.

(D) Fruits—acerola cherry, avocado, banana, breadfruit, caimeto, cassava, citron, cocoplum, custard apple, genipap, gooseberries, grapefruit, guama, guanabana (soursop), guava, guinep, hevi, Jamaica plum, kumquats, lemon, lime, mamey, mango, orange, papaya, pineapple, plantain, pomarrosa, pomegranate, Puerto Rican cherry, raisins, raspberries, roselle, sea grape, sapodilla, star apple, sugar apple, tamarind, tangerine, yautia, yellow mombin; canned peaches and pears.

(E) Vegetables—artichokes, arracacha (celery plant), arrowroot (water chestnut), banana (green), beets, black-eyed peas, breadfruit, broccoli, cabbage chayote, corn, cucumbers, dasheen, eggplant, green beans, greens (beet tops, turnip tops), leren, lettuce, lima beans, okra, onions, palmillo, red and green peppers, pimento, plantain, potatoes, pumpkins, radish, spinach, squashes (several kinds), sweet potato, Swiss chard, tomatoes, yams (several varieties— yellow, purple, white), yautía (taro), yuca.

(F) Beverages—black beer, chocolate, coffee, cold fruit drinks, soft drinks.

(G) Other—legumes (black-eyed peas or cowpeas, garbanzos, kidney beans, lima beans, pigeon peas, white navy beans), nuts (annato, almonds, cashews, coconut, peanuts, sesame seeds), olives.

THE ADAPTED DIET

According to Alexander (1968), who conducted a consumer survey in New York City, Puerto Ricans continue to consume the traditional diet but accept convenience foods as supplements. Thus, frozen dinners, frozen meat, frozen pies, instant coffee, cake mixes, and dehydrated soups—the model foods used in the survey—were well-accepted. These foods are apparently purchased for the sake of convenience and are used as frequently as the budget will allow. Thus, Puerto Ricans appear to accept new foods relatively easily.

The Puerto Rican and Cuban Americans prefer their customary foods prepared in the traditional manner. They will not accept Americanized versions. They are particular about the texture of rice; it must not be mushy.

Typical staples of diet and meal patterns for Puerto Ricans have recently been reported by Fernandez et al. (1971). However, as Sanjur et al. (1971) point out, relatively little dietary information is available on those who have immigrated to the United States.

BIBLIOGRAPHY

ALEXANDER, M. 1968. The significance of ethnic groups in marketing. *In* Perspectives in Consumer Behavior. H. H. Kassarjian, and T. S. Robertson (Editors). Scott Foresman, & Co., Glenview, Ill.

CABANILLAS, B., and GINORIO, C. 1956. Puerto-Rican Dishes. Waverly Press, Baltimore.

CZAJKOWSKI, J. M. 1971. Puerto Rican Foods and Traditions. Univ. Conn., Coop. Ext. Serv. Bull. *70-17.*

DOOLY, E. B. K. 1948. Puerto Rican Cook Book. Dietz Press, Richmond, Virginia.

FERNANDEZ, N. A., BURGOS, J. C., ASENJO, C. F., and ROSA, I. 1971. Nutritional status of the Puerto Rican population: master sample survey. Am. J. Clin. Nutr. *24,* 952–965.

MARTIN, E. A. 1971. Nutrition in Action, 3rd Edition. Holt, Rinehart, & Winston, New York.

ROBERTS, L. J., and STEFANI, R. L. 1949. Patterns of Living in Puerto Rican Families. Univ. Puerto Rico, Rio Piedras, Puerto Rico.

SANJUR, D. 1970. Puerto Rican food habits: a socio-cultural approach. N.Y. State Coll. Human Ecology, Dept. Human Nutr. Food.

SANJUR, D., ROMERO, E., and KIRA, M. 1971. Milk consumption patterns of Puerto Rican preschool children in rural New York. Am. J. Clin. Nutr. *24,* 1320–1326.

TORRES, R. M. 1959. Dietary pattern of the Puerto Rican people. Am. J. Clin. Nutr. *7,* 349–355.

CHAPTER 27

Foodways of Jews

The foodways of American Jews are basically determined by two factors (a) religious sect, i.e., Orthodox, Conservative, or Reform, and (b) geographic and/or ethnic area of origin, i.e., Ashkenzai (Eastern European), Sephardim (Spain, Portugal, and northern Africa), or Oriental. Most American Jews are Ashkenazic (84%); Sephardic and Oriental Jews comprise 16% of the Jewish population according to a recent article in Time magazine (Anon. 1972). The following discussion of Jewish foodways will be divided into (a) religious aspects, (b) geographic/ethnic differençes and (c) general comments.

ORTHODOX DIETARY RULES (KOSHER OR KASHRUTH)

The purpose of the religious laws relating to food preparation and consumption are to provide a framework for controlling the drive for food by means of a system of discipline the observance of which leads to moral and spiritual freedom (Sadow 1928). In general, foods are classified into three groups. (A) Those that are permitted or kosher, i.e., fruits, vegetables, grains, tea, and coffee. (These may be consumed with either dairy products or meat.) (B) Those that are permitted if processed according to prescribed methods to make them kosher, i.e., specified meats, poultry, fish. (C) Those that are not permitted, i.e., pork products, shellfish, birds of prey, insects except locusts, reptiles, amphibians, cartilaginous fishes. Furthermore, four additional proscriptions apply to the use of dairy products: (a) dairy products and meats may not be cooked together, (b) foods containing a mixture of dairy products and meat may not be consumed, (c) the same utensils, dishes, and cutlery may not be used for preparation and/or service of meat and dairy products, and (d) milk products may not be consumed within 1, 3, or 6 hr (the length of time varies with the interpretation by a particular sect) after consuming the meat.

Moreover, even flesh of animals normally permitted may be proscribed for a number of specified reasons. For a complete discussion, see Levin and Boyden (1941).

In general, except in institutions equipped with a kosher kitchen, the orthodox dietary laws cannot be observed. Kosher convenience foods provide a feasible solution; these should be sealed and served to the patient in the sealed container (Anon. 1970). The Union of Orthodox Jewish Congregations certifies genuine Kosher products which bear their official insignia. Other items may be permitted but labels must be carefully checked. Hospitals and nursing homes should expect to serve kosher meals intermittently. Other institutions are not usually obligated to provide kosher meals.

REFORM JUDAISM

The reform movement in Judaism resulted in almost total elimination of ritual law including dietary laws. Hence for the majority, eating habits and preferences are typical of the American culture. However, the Kosher laws are observed by approximately 8% and approximately 25% do not eat pork (Anon. 1972). Other proscriptions are observed, if at all, only on religious holidays. These include:

(A) Avoidance of serving dairy and animal products at the same meal.

(B) Never serving two vegetables of the same botanical family at the same meal.

(C) Use of chicken or vegetable oil rather than lard or tallow.

(D) Reworking leftovers to produce an entirely new dish rather than reheating or reserving the item.

Food is a significant part of the ritual observance of several religious holidays on which Kosher foods and preparation methods may be used. These include, but are not limited to:

(A) Rosh Hashanah (New Year) in September or October.

(B) Yom Kippur (Day of Atonement) in September or October.

(C) Channukah (Festival of Lights) in December.

(D) Pesach (Passover) in April.

The dietitian who wishes to serve traditional foods to the consumer on one of these holidays should consult one of the cookbooks listed.

GEOGRAPHIC AND ETHNIC AREA OF ORIGIN

Jews have long been dispersed throughout the world and by necessity have become adept in adjusting their life style and foodways to local conditions (Masson 1971). Generally, within the proscriptions of the dietary laws, during the process of centuries of acculturation they accepted the foodways of the particular locale (Kaufman 1957). Thus, Jews emmigrating to the United States have brought a variety of foodways with them. Jews emmigrating from Europe have brought foodways of all groups, e.g., French, German, Italian, Hungarian, etc.; see appropriate sections for treatment of ethnic foodways. Those originating in the Middle East or Africa brought customs typical of those areas. When living in areas of the United States with concentrations of gentiles of the same geographic or ethnic background they will generally consume the typical ethnic foods.

Furthermore, in the United States, because Jews of varying origin have often lived in the same community, intermingling has resulted in a large pool of foods of varying ethnic origin that are consumed by most Jews. When available, these items are preferred.

GENERAL COMMENTS

The majority of Jews living in the United States consume a standard diet, at least when they are away from home. However, Alexander (1968) found that second generation Jewish housewives purchase fresh rather than canned or frozen foods whenever possible and tend to serve traditional items frequently. Moreover, he found that as a group Jews are slower to accept convenience foods than are some other ethnic groups.

Staples

(A) Appetizers—anchovies, assorted pickled vegetables, assorted raw vegetables, brisling, dips, liver sausage, rollmops, salads, sausage, and cream cheese.

(B) Meat, fish, poultry, and eggs—beef, lamb, mutton, sausages (many varieties), veal; anchovies, bass, bream, carp, cod, halibut, herring, pike, red snapper, salmon, shad, smoked salmon, St. Peter's fish, trout, tuna, whitefish; chicken, duck, goose; eggs.

(C) Dairy products—cream cheese, milk, sour cream, whipping cream, yogurt.

(D) Cereal products—bagels, barley, buckwheat groats, bulgar, challah, cornmeal, cornstarch, doughnuts, farina, graham flour, matzo, noodles, potato starch, rice, vermicelli, wheat flour, whole wheat flour.

(E) Fruits—apples, avocados, black cherries, cantaloupe, currants, dates, dried apricots, green grapes, kumquats, lemon, olives, oranges, peaches, pears, plums, prickly pears, prunes, raisins, raspberries, strawberries.

(F) Vegetables—asparagus, beets, broccoli (green or purple), Brussels sprouts, cabbage, carrots, cauliflower, celeriac, celery, clokes, eggplant, green beans, green pepper, Jerusalem artichokes, leeks, mushrooms, okra, onions, parsnip, peas, potatoes, sauerkraut, sorrel, spinach, tomatoes, turnips.

(G) Other—cooking fats (butter, chicken fat, corn oil, margarine, olive oil, soy bean oil, suet), lentils (black beans, chick peas, harricot beans, split peas), nuts (almonds, pecans, walnuts), poppy seeds, sesame seeds.

(H) Spices and seasonings—allspice, basil, bay leaf, capers, cardamom, caraway, chili pepper, cinnamon, cloves, coriander, cumin, curry, fennel, fenugreek seeds, garlic, ginger, horseradish, mace, mint, nutmeg, paprika, parsley, pepper (black and red), rosemary, saffron, shallots, tarragon, thyme, agar-agar, alcoholic beverage, beer, chives, chocolate, cordials, fruit jams and jellies, gelatin, gherkins, honey, lemon juice, oak or cherry leaves, rosewater, soya mayonnaise, vanilla, vinegar, wine.

BIBLIOGRAPHY

ALEXANDER, M. 1968. The significance of ethnic groups in marketing. *In* Perspectives in Consumer Behavior. H. H. Kassarjian, and T. S. Robertson (Editors). Scott, Foresman & Co., Glenview, Ill.
ANON. 1970. Kosher foods described. J. Am. Dietet. Assoc. *57*, 328.
ANON. 1972. The Jews: next year in Jerusalem? Time Mag. Apr. 10.
BAR-DAVID, M. L. 1965. Jewish Cooking for Pleasure. Paul Hamlyn, London.
BELLIN, M. G. 1952. Modern Jewish Meals. Block Publishing Co., New York. Encyclopaedia Judaica. 1971. Dietary laws. Vol. *6*.
KAUFMAN, M. 1957. Adapting therapeutic diets to Jewish food customs. Am. J. Clin. Nutr. *5*, 676–681.

KORFF, S. I. 1966. The Jewish dietary code. Food Technol. *20*, 926.

LEVIN, S. I., and BOYDEN, E. A. 1941. The Kosher Code of the Orthodox Jew. Herman Press, New York.

MASSON, M. 1971. The International Wine and Food Society's Guide to Jewish Cookery. Drake Publishers, New York.

SADOW, S. E. 1928. Jewish ceremonials and food customs. J. Am. Dietet. Assoc. *4*, 91–98.

SARNOFF, S., and MILLER, J. 1952. Like Mama Used to Make: a Collection of Favorite and Traditional Jewish Dishes. Ann Arbor chapter of Hadassah, Ann Arbor, Mich.

Toronto Nutrition Committee. 1967. Jewish Food Customs. Toronto Nutr. Comm., Toronto, Ontario, Canada.

CHAPTER 28

Foodways of Vegetarians and Fruitarians

Some types of vegetarian diet is the typical diet consumed in many parts of the world and by various religious groups. According to Simoons (1961) many reasons have been given as the rationale for avoidance of flesh foods. However, incorporation of the taboo by a religious leader into the religious beliefs, rituals, and sanctions offers the most plausible explanation. In a particular group, when the taboo against flesh becomes a symbol of group identity, it acts as a cohesive force binding group members; it also identifies out-groups. As long as it serves these purposes, the taboo against consumption of flesh foods is perpetuated.

Moreover, throughout history there have been groups of vegetarians and periods when vegetarianism has been common. When meat is scarce, i.e., unavailable or expensive, vegetarianism increases (Hardinge and Crooks 1964A). This pattern is true for the United States as well.

Lists of permitted and prohibited foods differ for each group of vegetarians. Some groups permit consumption of tea, cereal products, fruits, and vegetables. Others allow eggs and/or dairy products (Table 28.1). The specific requirements of a particular individual or group must be ascertained.

RELIGIOUS AVOIDANCE OF MEAT

In the United States, the most enduring group of conscientious vegetarians are Seventh Day Adventists, even though avoidance of meat is a voluntary individual expression of faith. The lacto-ovo vegetarian (milk, eggs, vegetables) diet is recommended.

The diet consumed by this group can be balanced nutritionally by proper selection of items, including supplementation of the cereal protein with milk and egg protein (Foote and Eppright 1940; Hardinge and Crooks, 1964B, C). Because the diet is low in saturated fats, several studies have been conducted using members of this group for comparative purposes in studying the relationship of quantity of fat and degree of saturation to heart disease (Hardinge and Stare 1954A, B; Mirone 1954; West and Hays 1968). These reports include some description of the diet.

A number of meat analogs prepared from a legume and/or nut base are commercially available. Some products resemble meatballs, meat patties, and sausages. They are flavored and sauced in the same way as the meat items they resemble. Textured vegetable protein products that resemble sliced beef, chicken, ham, bacon, etc., are also available.

Concepts from Oriental philosophy, religion, and medicine provide the rationale for avoidance of meat by another set of vegetarians in the United States. Basically, the objective of dietary restrictions is to set up a physiological

TABLE 28.1

FOOD PATTERNS OF VEGETARIANS AND FRUITARIANS

Subgroup	Food Pattern
Religious	
Buddhists	Practices variable depending upon sect.
Seventh-Day Adventists	Practice voluntary abstension from flesh foods; abstain from alcohol. Lacto-ovo vegetarian (milk, eggs, vegetables) is recommended diet.
Catholic Trappist Monks	Are lacto-vegetarians.
Jains	
Hare Krishnas	Consume lacto-vegetarian diet.
Macrobiotics	Food pattern is variable. Ranges from strict vegetarian to consumption of fowl, fish, eggs, and dairy products as well as cereals and vegetables.
Food Faddists	
Nonviolence philosophy	Practices nonviolence and kindness to animals and health. Abstension from flesh foods is intermittent, variable in duration, type, and degree of abstinence.
Lacto-ovo vegetarians	Consume milk, eggs, and vegetables. Abstain from meat only.
Moderate vegetarians	Abstain from animal flesh and animal products as such. But may consume made dishes that contain milk, eggs, etc., such as cake and puddings.
Strict vegetarians (vegans)	Will eat no animal products in any form. Do not eat cooked foods, refined or processed foods.
Moderate fruitarians	Eat mostly fruits and nuts. But may consume small quantities of vegetables, cereals and/or dairy products.
Strict fruitarians	Eat only fruits and nuts.
Economic	
Financially and geographically motivated	This group consumes animal flesh and animal products when they are available and when they can afford them.

state that frees the mind by means of balancing the forces of yin (good) and yan(g) (evil). All foods are classified as being yin or yan(g). Selections are made to achieve balance according to religious precepts, as interpreted by the individual and his particular needs. Oriental ingredients, spicing, and preparation methods are used to assure goal attainment. Soy bean curd, lumps of gluten, and legumes are major protein sources in entrées.

A highly visible subgroup are the Hare Krishnas who are lacto-vegetarians. Indian ingredients, spicing, and preparation methods are used to prepare foods that are high in spiritual value, according to religious precepts.

AVOIDANCE OF MEAT FOR OTHER REASONS

In addition to those who avoid flesh foods for religious reasons, there have always been individuals and groups who are labeled food cultists. Their consumption of some type of vegetarian diet has usually been considered a form of socially deviant behavior.

Individuals often appear to embrace some form of vegetarianism in the hope of finding a cure for a real or imagined illness. However, it turns out that according to New and Priest (1967), these persons often are searching for peace of mind. Hence, they will select the "in" food item in the hope that it will provide the cure. Thus, specific items are emphasized, even eaten to excess, for their curative virtues while other items are rejected for being suspected of causing physical harm, e.g., processed foods.

Groups tend to embrace a particular form of vegetarianism for philosophical, often quasi-religious, reasons. Hence, food items are emphasized that are compatible with and/or reinforce philosophical positions. For example, several forms are related to Oriental philosophies and rely on balancing yin and yan(g) in the diet. Others build on natural fear of the unknown, i.e., chemicals are incomprehensible and therefore bad, so only organically-grown foods may be consumed. Moreover, adherence to the diet by members of these groups is quite strict.

The impact of vegetarians on the menu planning process varies in intensity among the various types of institutions depending on whether the consumer group is captive or not. Its impact on a particular institution is also related to the concentration of vegetarians.

HOSPITALS

To date, the number of patients requiring vegetarian diets in most hospitals has been very small. Few hospitals include vegetarian entrées as alternate items on a regular basis. Vegetarians are treated as special cases and their needs are met on an individual basis.

COLLEGES AND UNIVERSITIES

Currently, so many students are following vegetarian diets, at least part of the time, that some college and university food service units have been obliged to provide vegetarian meals as an alternative to the regular fare. In general, cookbooks for Middle Eastern and/or Oriental peoples provide suitable recipes for entrées based on rice, corn, bulgar, buckwheat groats, and legumes such as lentils, chick peas, split peas, and various beans. Many traditional items from these areas are suitable since many subgroups in these areas have long been vegetarians for religious reasons.

While in many cases the ingredients are relatively inexpensive, the majority of these recipes require a great deal of expensive preparation labor. Moreover, some colleges and universities have found that their costs are increased because the policy of unlimited seconds allows the student-consumer to select several entrées as a result of a combination of enthusiasm and ignorance of composition. Also, as many of these entrées are low in satiety value, a larger quantity is consumed than is either necessary or desirable. Thus, the menu-planning challenges are to select a combination of items that are (a) acceptable to most vegetarians, (b) producible, (c) not too expensive, and (d) filling.

RESTAURANTS

In urban areas, particularly surrounding colleges and universities, the population of vegetarians is of sufficient size that restaurants featuring organic foods and vegetarian entrées are profitable. The points regarding recipe sources and labor costs, noted above, are pertinent. On the other hand, a set menu or a selective menu can be used to advantage. Portion size is preplanned and is controlled by the cook or chef; serving price is set accordingly.

BIBLIOGRAPHY

BLACK, P. H., and CAREY, R. L. 1971. Vegetarian Cookery Series: Book 1, Appetizers/ Salads/Beverages; Book 2, Breads/Soups/Sandwiches; Book 3, Main Dishes/Vegetables; Book 4, Pies/Cakes/Cookies/Desserts; Book 5, Exotic Foods/Candies/Cooking for a Crowd. Pacific Press Publishers Assoc., Mountain View, Calif.

FOOTE, R., and EPPRIGHT, E. S. 1940. A dietary study of boys and girls on a lacto-ovo vegetarian diet. J. Am. Dietet. Assoc. *16*, 222–229.

HARDINGE, M. G., and CROOKS, H. 1964A. Non-flesh dietaries. 1. Historical background. J. Am. Dietet. Assoc. *43*, 545–549.

HARDINGE, M. G., and CROOKS, H. 1964B. Non-flesh dietaries. 2. Scientific literature. J. Am. Dietet. Assoc. *43*, 550–558.

HARDINGE, M. G., and CROOKS, H. 1964C. Non-flesh dietaries. 3. Adequate and inadequate. J. Am. Dietet. Assoc. *43*, 537–541.

HARDINGE, M. G., and STARE, F. J. 1954A. Nutritional studies of vegetarians. 1. Nutritional, physical and laboratory studies. Am. J. Clin. Nutr. *2*, 73–82.

HARDINGE, M. G., and STARE, F. J. 1954B. Nutritional studies of vegetarians. 2. Dietary and serum levels of cholesterol. Am. J. Clin. Nutr. *2*, 83–88.

JAFFA, M. E. 1901. Nutrition investigations among fruitarians and Chinese. USDA Office Expt. Sta. Bull. *107*.

JAFFA, M. E. 1903. Further investigations among fruitarians. USDA Office Expt. Sta. Bull. *132*.

MIRONE, L. 1954. Nutrient intake and blood findings of men on a diet devoid of meat. Am. J. Clin. Nutr. *2*, 246–251.

NEW, P. K. M., and PRIEST, R. P. 1967. Food and thought: a sociologic study of food cultists. J. Am. Dietet. Assoc. *51*, 13–18.

REGISTER, U. D., and SONNENBERG, L. M. 1973. The vegetarian diet. J. Am. Dietet. Assoc. *62*, 253–261.

SIMOONS, F. J. 1961. Eat Not This Flesh: Food Avoidances in the Old World. Univ. Wisc. Press, Madison.

WEST, R. O., and HAYS, O. B. 1968. Diet and serum cholesterol levels: comparison between vegetarians and non vegetarians in a Seventh Day Adventist Group. Am. J. Clin. Nutr. *21*, 853–862.

CHAPTER 29

Foodways of Central European-Americans (Dutch, French, German)

French and Germanic influences dominate the cuisines of the western European countries. Each are discussed below.

DUTCH

Dutch food is solid and simple. It is similar to German food because of common heritage.

Indonesia was long a colony of Holland. During this period many Dutchmen lived in Indonesia. As a result, many spices and Indonesian cuisine became part of Dutch cuisine. For a discussion of Indonesian cuisine see section of Foodways of Other Orientals Living in the United States.

The cuisines of Belgium and Luxembourg are similar to the Dutch cuisine. They have been omitted, since the countries are small and few have immigrated to the United States from these countries.

Meal Pattern

The customary meal pattern is three main meals and two smaller between-meal feedings. Breakfast is usually tea (with sugar and milk), bread (with butter and jam), cheese, cold meat, egg. Morning coffee break is usually coffee and cookies. Lunch commonly consists of bread, sausage, cheese, luncheon dish, fruit, coffee. Afternoon break is tea and biscuits. Dinner typically includes soup, meat or fish entrée, potatoes, dessert, beer.

Spices and Seasonings

Spices and seasonings commonly used to add interest to dishes include, but are not limited to: bay leaf, black pepper, capers, chervil, cinnamon, cloves, curry powder, leeks, mace, marjoram, mustard, nutmeg, oregano, paprika, parsley, vanilla; chocolate, currant jelly, pickles, soy sauce, vinegar, wine, Worcestershire sauce.

Staples

(A) Meat, fish, poultry, and eggs—beef, lamb, pork, rabbit, veal, variety meats, frankfurters; cod, haddock, herring, oysters, pike, shrimp, sole; chicken, duck, goose, partridge, pheasant.

(B) Dairy products—buttermilk, cheeses (Edam, Gouda, Leiden—with cumin).

(C) Cereal products—breads including black, rolls, rye, whole wheat, white, zwieback; macaroni, vermicelli.

(D) Fruits—apples, dried apricots, pears, raspberries, raisins.

(E) Vegetables—asparagus, beets, Belgian endive, Brussels sprouts, cabbage (red and white), carrots, cauliflower, celery, celery root, cucumber, kale, lettuce, mushrooms, onions, peas, potatoes, radishes, rhubarb, sorrel, spinach, tomatoes.

(F) Beverages—coffee (with sugar and milk), Dutch gin, hot chocolate and cocoa, tea.

(G) Other—legumes (split peas, lentils); nuts (almonds, chestnuts).

FRENCH

Food is a very important part of the life-style in France. Meals are eaten leisurely and with enjoyment. Meal preparation is a major production expressing love and artistic accomplishment. Because of the care with which the food is prepared, the diner is culturally conditioned to seriously evaluate the merit of food commenting favorably and/or presenting direct constructive criticism (Garvin 1958).

Meal Pattern

Breakfast is the typical continental breakfast consisting of brioche and butter or jam, coffee with milk. Lunch or supper commonly includes soup, omelet, vegetable, bread and butter, fruit, milk. Dinner is more elaborate, consisting of appetizer, fish course, meat with sauce, potato or other vegetable, salad, bread and butter, dessert (cheese and fruit or sweet dessert), black coffee. While the two main meals are heavy, between-meal snacking is uncommon so all nutritional needs have to be met in the two meals.

Spices and Seasonings

French cuisine is famous for use of herbs and spices in various sauces. Spices and seasonings commonly used include, but are not limited to: angelica, bay leaf, bouquet garni, capers, chives, chocolate, cinnamon, cloves, coffee, cognac, Dijon mustard, dry mustard, fennel seeds, fine herbs, garlic, gherkins, ginger, horseradish, juniper, kirsch, leeks, lemon juice, lemon peel, lemon rind, mace, mustard, nutmeg, onions, orange blossoms, orange peel, orange rind, paprika, parsley, pepper (black, cayenne, white), prepared mustard, rosemary, rum, saffron, shallots, sweet basil, tarragon, thyme, vanilla, wines.

Staples

A wide variety of staples are available in France. In addition to domestic items, many items are imported. Staples commonly used include, but are not limited to:

(A) Meat, fish, poultry, and eggs—beef, frog legs, horsemeat, mutton, ox tongue, pork (bacon, Canadian bacon, ham—several varieties, roasts, sausages, etc.), rabbit, snails, variety meats (brains, kidneys, liver, sweetbreads, tripe), venison; anchovies, bass, carp, cod, haddock, herring, mackerel, mullet, perch, pike, red gurnet, salmon, sardines, sea bream, shad, skate, sole, sturgeon, trout, turbot, whiting; Coquilles St. Jaques (sea scallops), crab, crayfish, lobster, mussels, oysters, rock lobster, shrimp; chicken, duck, goose, partridge, pheasant, pigeon, quail, thrush, turkey; egg (hen, caviar).

(B) Dairy products—cheese (Beaufort, Bleu cheese, Brie, Camembert, Cantal, Carre Demi-Sel, Comte, Coulommiers, Fondue cheese, grape seed cheese, Gruyere, Livarot, Munster, Neufchatel, Parmesan, Petit Suisse, Pont-L'Eveque, Reblochon, Roquefort, Saint-Paulin, salami cheese, Triple Creme Aromatise); cream, heavy cream, sour cream.

(C) Cereal products—arrowroot starch, barley, buckwheat, canneloni, cornstarch, gnocchi, macaroni, noodles, rice, rye, spaghetti, tapioca, vermicelli, wheat flour, wheat starch; French bread.

(D) Fruits—apples, apricots, bananas, cherries, currants, gooseberries, grapefruit, grapes (many varieties), lemons, olives, oranges, peaches, pears, pineapples, plums, prunes, raspberries, rhubarb, strawberries.

(E) Vegetables—artichokes, asparagus, beets, Brussels sprouts, cabbage (red, white, sauerkraut), carrots, cauliflower, celery, cucumbers, eggplant, green beans, green peppers, greens (celery leaves, corn-salad, curly chicory, dandelion, endive, romaine), Jerusalem artichokes, leeks, lettuce, mushrooms, peas, potatoes, pumpkin, radishes, salsify, scallions, sorrel, spinach, tomatoes, turnips, truffles, watercress.

(F) Beverages—beer, black tea, cider, coffee, coffee with milk, hot chocolate, liqueurs, red and white wines, tisanes (anise, bergamot, borage, camomille, lime, linden, mint, verbena).

(G) Other—cooking fats (butter, lard, margarine, marrow, olive oil, salad oil, salt pork), legumes (kidney beans, lentils, lima beans), nuts (almonds, chestnuts, filberts, walnuts), white beans.

GERMAN

Although Germany is a small country, its climate and terrain are varied creating different styles of cuisine in its various states. Moreover, Germany like many other European nations is an aggregate of numerous local fiefdoms. This increased the diversity of regional cuisines. Beer, wurst, apples, caraway, sauerkraut, and dumplings are part of the sterotyped image of German foods; however, many other items are consumed as indicated below.

Germanic influence in cooking is seen in the cuisines of neighboring countries. Swiss cooking has been influenced by French cuisine as well, and has been omitted. Austrian cooking has also been influenced by the cuisines of the slavic countries to the east. Austrian cuisine has also been omitted from the discussion.

Meal Pattern

Breakfast usually consists of bread and butter, and coffee with milk; a soft cooked egg is optional. A sandwich with beer or wine is consumed at the morning break. Lunch is meat and potatoes in rural areas; soup-sandwich or casserole in the cities. Sausages and beer are traditionally consumed at the afternoon break. Dinner, which is served at about 7 p.m. consists of a cold cheese and meat platter, bread, dessert and a beverage or soup and dessert are served in the cities. The midnight snack usually consists of sausages and cheese, a sandwich, dessert, and coffee (Sheraton 1966).

Spices and Seasonings

Sweet-sour combinations are popular and fruit is often served with the meat. Commonly-used spices include: allspice, anise, basil, bay leaves, borage, capers, caraway, cardamom, chervil, chives, cinnamon, cloves, curry powder, dill, garlic, ginger, juniper, lemon—juice and rind, lovage, mace, marjoram, mustard, paprika, parsley, pepper—black and white, poppy seeds, rosemary, rose water, sage, savory —summer and winter, tarragon, thyme, woodruff. Seasonings include: almond paste, apples, arrack, beer, candied fruit, chocolate, coffee, horseradish, jams and jellies, pumpernickel crumbs, rum, vanilla, vinegar, wine.

Staples

The following items are commonly consumed. Basic ingredients include, but are not limited to:

(A) Meat, fish, poultry, and eggs—beef, blood, boar, hare, lamb, pork (bacon, fresh ham, pig's feet, tail, etc.), sausages, variety meats (e.g., brain, kidneys, liver, tongue, etc.), veal, venison; snails; carp, flounder, haddock, halibut, herring, mackerel, perch, pike, salmon, shark, sturgeon, trout; crab, eel, lobster, oysters, shrimp, turtle; chicken, Cornish hen, duck, goose, grouse, partridge, pheasant, squab, turkey; eggs (hen).

(B) Dairy products—buttermilk, cheese spreads, domestic cheeses (Allgauer, Cheshire, Ementhaler, Handkase, Kummelkase, Limberger, Munster, Quark, Romadour, Tilsiter), imported cheeses (Gorganzola, Parmesan, Roqueforte, Swiss), milk, sour cream.

(D) Fruits—apples, apricots, bing cherries, blackberries, blueberries, currants, dried apricots, elderberries, gooseberries, grapes, lemons, nectarines, oranges, peaches, pears, plums, quinces, raisins, raspberries, rhubarb, strawberries.

(E) Vegetables—artichokes, asparagus, beets, broccoli, Brussels sprouts, cabbage (red, Savoy, sauerkraut, white), carrots, cauliflower, celery, celery roots, chestnuts, cucumbers, endive, eggplant, green beans, green peppers, kale, kohlrabi, leeks, lettuce, mushrooms, onions, parsley root, parsnips, peas, potatoes, radishes, salsify, spinach, Swiss chard, tomatoes, turnips, zucchini.

(F) Beverages—beer, coffee, fruit brandies, herbal teas, schnaps, wine.

(G) Other—cooking fats (bacon, butter, lard), legumes (kidney beans, lentils, navy beans, split peas—green and yellow), nuts (almonds, hazelnuts, pecans, walnuts).

BIBLIOGRAPHY

CZAJKOWSKI, J. M.   1971.   French Foods and Traditions.   Univ. Conn. Coop. Ext. Serv. Bull. *57-16*.

GARVIN, F.   1958.   The Art of French Cooking.   Bantam Books, New York.

LIMBURG STIRUM, C. COUNTESS VAN.   1961.   The Art of Dutch Cooking.   Doubleday & Co., Garden City, N.Y.

SHERATON, M.   1966.   The German Cookbook.   A Complete Guide to Mastering Authentic German Cooking.   Random House, New York.

TANTE MARIE.   1972.   Real Family Cooking.   The Oldest and Best French Cuisine. Editions A. Taride, Paris. (French)

MITCHELL, H. S., and JOFFE, N. F.   1944.   Food patterns of some European countries: background for study programs and guidance of relief workers. J. Am. Dietet. Assoc. *20*, 676–687.

CHAPTER 30

Foodways of Eastern European-Americans
(Hungarian and Polish)

Prior to World War II, a small number of Eastern Europeans immigrated to the United States each year. During World War II a fairly large number of refugees immigrated and settled primarily in the east and midwest. Typically in these countries, the diets of the urban aristocrats and village peasants were quite different. While recent immigrants maintain their native customs to some degree, the American-born generations consume the standard American fare except that traditional items are prepared for social events such as weddings and festivals. The cuisines of Czechoslovakia, Bulgaria, and Rumania are similar so they are omitted.

HUNGARIAN

Food is very important to Hungarians. Lack of refrigeration in this country lead to preserving fruits by drying and vegetables by pickling. Fruits soups are served frequently as desserts. Pastries are also common.

Meal Pattern

The meal pattern is typical of that of Eastern European countries. Breakfast is usually a porridge and some fruit and coffee. Lunch is sausage.

Spices and Seasonings

Paprika is the seasoning used most frequently; it is a distinguishing characteristic of Hungarian food. However, others are also used. These include, but are not limited to: allspice, basil, bay leaf, capers, caraway, chocolate, cinnamon, cloves, coffee, curry powder, dill weed, garlic, horseradish, lemon juice, mace, marjoram, mint, mustard, nutmeg, onions, parsley, pepper (black, white), pimiento, poppyseeds, poultry seasoning, sage, tarragon, thyme, vanilla; beer, gingersnaps, vinegar, wine.

Staples

The basic diet in Hungary is somewhat more varied than that of other Eastern European countries due to local availability of a greater number of staples. The diet commonly includes, but is not limited to:

(A) Meat, fish, poultry, and eggs—bacon, beef, corned beef, frog legs, lamb, liver, mutton, pork (ham, sausages), rabbit, variety meats (brains, kidneys, liver, lungs, sweetbreads, tongue, tripe), veal, venison; carp, cod, crab, finnan haddie, flounder, haddock, halibut, herring, lobster, oysters, perch, pickerel, pike, salmon, sardines, scallops, shad, shrimp, smelts, trout; chicken, duck, goose, grouse, guinea hens, partridge, pheasant, pigeon, quail, turkey, woodcock; eggs.

(B) Dairy products—cottage cheese, cream cheese, evaporated milk, pot cheese, sour cream, whipping cream.

(C) Cereal products—barley, cakes, cookies, cornmeal, doughnuts, dumplings, farina, matzo balls, noodles, pancakes, pearl tapioca, pumpernickel, rice, tartes, turnovers.

(D) Fruits—apples, apricots, blueberries, red sour pitted cherries, cranberries, currants, dates, grapefruit, grapes, lemons, olives, oranges, peaches, pears, plums, prunes, quince, raisins, raspberries, rhubarb, strawberries.

(E) Vegetables—artichokes, asparagus, beets, broccoli, Brussels Sprouts, cabbage (white, red, sauerkraut), carrots, cauliflower, celeriac, celery, corn, cucumbers, eggplant, green beans, green peppers, kale, mushrooms, onions, peas, potatoes, sorrel, spinach, squash, tomatoes, turnips, watercress.

(F) Beverages—coffee, coffee Imperial (laced with an alcoholic beverage), cocoa, eggnogs, fruit punches, malted milk, milk punch, tea, wine.

(G) Other—cooking fats (butter, chicken fat, goose fat, lard, olive oil, suet, sour cream), gelatin, honey, legumes (lentils, lima beans, split peas), maple syrup, molasses, nuts (almonds, chestnuts, filberts, walnuts).

POLISH

Historically, Poles were primarily dairy farmers who also grew potatoes and grains such as barley, oats, and rye. Game and fish were also readily available. In the 16th Century the aristocracy introduced vegetables from Italy and later fancy desserts were developed.

Meal Pattern

Four to five meals were customary in Poland. In the United States breakfast consists of cereal and milk, fruit, and coffee or bacon and eggs, toast, and coffee. Lunch is often soup, sausage and bread, fruit. Dinner is a stew or casserole, potatoes and/or creamed vegetable, fruit, and coffee.

Spices and Seasonings

Polish food is simply prepared except for spicing of sausages and a few spices used in desserts. Spices commonly used include, but are not limited to: anise, bay leaves, bitter almonds, black pepper, caraway seeds, chocolate, cloves, coriander, dill weed, garlic, horseradish, juniper, marjoram, nutmeg, onion, paprika, parsley, pepper, poppy seeds (fillings for pastries), sage, shallots, thyme, vinegar.

Staples

The traditional diet of the Polish peasant was based on (Morzkowska and McLaughlin 1928; Ochorowicz-Monatowa 1958):

(A) Meat, fish, poultry, and eggs—beef, bigos (i.e., blood sausage), brain, hare, liver, pork (mostly as sausage), rabbit, tripe, veal, venison; carp, crayfish, eel, frog legs, herring, perch, pike, salmon, snails, sole, trout; chicken, duck, goose, grouse, partridge, peacock, squab, turkey, wood thrush; eggs.

(B) Dairy products—cheese of various kinds, milk, sour cream.

(C) Cereal products—barley, buckwheat, corn, dumplings, millet, noodles, oats, pirogen, potato starch, rye bread, wheat breads and rolls, wheat grits, cakes, cremepits, pastries.

(D) Fruits—apples, apricots, blackberries, dates, grapes, hawthorne berries, plums, prunes, raisins, raspberries, strawberries; candied fruits.

(E) Vegetables—beets, Brussels sprouts, cabbage, carrots, cauliflower, celery root, chard, eggplant, kohlrabi, French beans, onion, peas, potatoes, pumpkin, sorrel, tomato, turnip, wax beans, wild mushrooms.

(F) Beverages—black coffee, milk, tea.

(G) Other—cold fruit soups (apricot, berry, plum), honey, legumes (kidney beans, lentils, split peas), nuts (almonds, chestnuts, walnuts); cooking fats are salt pork and flaxseed oil.

BIBLIOGRAPHY

GREEN, R. 1938. Hungarian-American Cook Book. Tudor Publishing Co.. New York.

MITCHELL, H. S., and JOFFE, N. F. 1944. Food patterns of some European countries: background for study programs and guidance of relief workers. J. Am. Dietet. Assoc. 20, 676–687.

MORZKOWSKA, M., and MCLAUGHLIN, L. 1928. Polish food habits. J. Am. Dietet. Assoc. 4, 142–148.

OCHOROWICZ-MONATOWA, M. 1958. Polish Cookery. (Translated by J. Karsavina.) Crown Publishers, New York.

CHAPTER 31

Foodways of Northern European-Americans (Danes, Finns, Norwegians, Swedes)

The smorgasbord or a similar equivalent is served in each of these Northern European countries. A wide assortment of items is available in buffet fashion to allow the diner choice in selecting items or an opportunity to sample all. Although there are differences in food habits among the four ethnic groups, their food is basically similar.

Meal Pattern

Breakfast—tea and pastry or coffee and bread and butter; laborers add cereal or eggs, meat, fish or cheese and potatoes. Lunch—open face sandwich and coffee or open face sandwich, meat or fish entrée, vegetables, dessert, and coffee. Dinner—soup, entrée, vegetable, dessert, coffee.

Spices and Seasonings

Many rich spiced sauces are used. Common spices and seasonings include, but are not limited to: allspice, bay leaf, beer, capers, cardamom, chervil, chocolate, cinnamon, cloves, curry powder, dill, garlic, ginger, horseradish, lemon juice, lemon and orange peel, mace, marjoram, mustard, mustard seed, nutmeg, paprika, parsley, pepper (black, cayenne, white), rose hips, saffron, salt, sour pickles, tarragon, thyme, vanilla, vinegar, wine, Worcestershire sauce, molasses.

Staples

Scandinavians use many dairy products in cooking and consume a great deal of fish. Foods are rich but not highly spiced. Staples include, but are not limited to:

(A) Meat, fish, poultry, and eggs—beef, goat, lamb, hare, pork (bacon, ham, sausages), reindeer, veal, venison; bass, carp, cod, crab, crayfish, eel, finnan haddie, flounder, grayling, haddock, halibut, herring, lobster, mackerel, mussels, oyster, perch, pike, roche, salmon, sardines, shrimp, sprat, turbot, trout, white fish; chicken, goose, grouse, partridge, pheasant, quail, turkey; eggs; blood pancakes.

(B) Dairy products—cheese with anise, caraway or fennel seeds, clabbered milk, milk (cow, reindeer), sour cream, yogurt, butter, cream.

(C) Cereal products—barley, cornstarch, dumplings, flat bread, hardtack, macaroni, noodles, oats, pancakes, potato starch, pumpernickle, rice, rusk, rye, tapioca, wheat.

(D) Fruits—apples, apricots, blueberries, cherries, cloudberries, currants, lingonberries, oranges, pears, pineapple, plums, prunes, raisins, rhubarb, strawberries.

(E) Vegetables—asparagus, beets, cabbage (red and white), carrots, cauliflower, celery, celery root, cucumbers, green beans, green pepper, greens (nettles), Jerusalem artichokes, kohlrabi, leeks, mangels, mushrooms, onions, parsnips, peas, potatoes, radishes, spinach, tomatoes, yellow and white turnips.

(F) Beverages—coffee with cardamom, hot chocolate, tea; ale, aquavit, beer, wine.

(G) Other—fruit soups—hot and cold, served frequently; honey, molasses; legumes (split peas, lima beans, brown beans); nuts (almonds, chestnuts, walnuts); cooking fats (butter, margarine, salt pork).

BIBLIOGRAPHY

BROBECK, F., and KJELLBERG, M. 1948. Scandinavian Cookery for Americans. Little, Brown & Co., Boston.

CZAJKOWSKI, J. M. 1963. Finnish Foods and Traditions. Univ. Conn. Coop. Ext. Serv. Bull. 56-40.

CZAJKOWSKI, J. M. 1971. Swedish Foods and Traditions. Univ. Conn. Coop. Ext. Serv. Bull. 71-28.

MITCHELL, H. S., and JOFFE, N. F. 1944. Food patterns of some European countries: background for study programs and guidance of relief workers. J. Am. Dietet. Assoc. 20, 676-687.

CHAPTER 32

Foodways of Southern European-Americans (Italian, Greek, Spanish)

Peoples from these countries have long been seafarers trading with nations in Africa, the Middle East, then Asia and the Americas. Consequently, their cuisines have assimilated spices, fruits and other less perishable imported items.

ITALIAN-AMERICANS

Italy is a nation built from a large number of independent states with varying customs including foodways (Cantoni 1958; Blair 1972). The greatest variations in food habits are based on differences in availability of basic foods; the north-south difference is greatest. For example, northerners use butter as a cooking fat and consume fresh pasta, rice, polenta, green sauces, etc.; southerners use olive oil in cooking and consume dry pasta (commercially prepared), spicy red sauces, etc. (Blair 1972). These differences are reflected in the food habits of Italian-Americans from the various areas.

Meal Pattern

Generally three meals are consumed with dinner the heaviest. Breakfast usually consists of bread and coffee with milk. Typically, the large dinner meal consists of (a) the aperitif, (b) antipasto, (c) minestra (light soup) or Riestti (rice dish) or Pasta Arciutta (needle-type dough with sauce), (d) Prime Patto (main meat course) and Canterno (vegetable, salad, and/or potato), (e) dolee (dessert of cakes or cookies), (f) fruitta and (g) beverage (LaSasso 1958). The light noon meal which may be served as supper in some areas usually consists of minestrone or pastafasioli (bean) soup, cheese or cold cuts, salad, and beverage (Cantoni 1958; Czajkowski 1971). Coffee is imbibed between meals.

Spices and Seasonings

Italian-Americans use a wide variety of spices in almost every traditional dish prepared; each requires the use of specific spices. Anise, basil, bay leaf, capers, cinnamon, cloves, dill, garlic, marjoram, mint, mustard, nutmeg, onion, oregano, parsley, red pepper, rosemary, saffron, sage, and thyme are commonly used.

Staples

The following list is necessarily abbreviated but includes the typical items:
(A) Antipasto—anchovy fillets, artichoke hearts, capocollo, celery hearts, cheeses, eggs, fennel, herring roe, green or black olives, pimiento, prosciutto, radishes, salami.

(B) Meat, fish, poultry, and eggs—bacon, capocollo (highly seasoned pork butt), lamb, pork, proscuitto, variety meats (brains, liver, sweetbreads), veal; flounder; eggs frequently.

(C) Dairy products—bel paise, caciocavallo, fontina, gorgonzola, incanestrato, mozzarella, parmesan, parmiagiano, pecorino, provolone, ricotta, romano, scamozza.

(D) Cereal products—acini, fusilli, gnocchi, Italian bread, lasagna, linguini, macaroni, mostaccioli, perciatelli, polenta (cornmeal porridge), ravioli, rigatoni, vermicelli.

(E) Fruits—apples, apricots, bananas, cherries, dates, figs, grapes, lemons, melons, oranges, peaches, pears, plums, pomegranates, quinces, tangerines.

(F) Vegetables—artichokes, asparagus, broccoli, cabbage, celery, chicory, eggplant, escarole, endive, fava beans, fennel, green beans, green lima beans, green peppers, lettuce, mushrooms, mustard greens, peas, potatoes, romaine, Swiss chard, tomatoes, zucchini.

(G) Beverages—coffee, espresso, soft drinks, tea; wines—mild burgundy, chablis, chianti, claret, Rhine wine, sauterne, dry white port, vermouth, etc.

(H) Other—cooking fats (butter, olive oil), honey, legumes (chick peas, white beans), nuts (pinenuts).

Attitudes to Consider

Two attitudes have great impact on foodways. First, Italian-Americans enjoy their food and resent permanent changes in diet. This has implications for dealing with them as patients. They have great respect for the physicians and will follow the diet as long as there is pain. As they recover, they tend to find it difficult to understand the need to continue the diet, hence they become increasingly less cooperative (Cantoni 1958).

Second, adult Italian-Americans do not drink milk; they drink wine with meals (Lolli *et al.* 1958). Cheese provides calcium in the diet.

Findings from Consumer Studies.—Alexander (1968) reports that second generation Italian-Americans still prefer fresh vegetables and meat. Therefore, they have been reluctant to accept convenience foods; however, this is changing.

GREEK-AMERICANS

Greece is a nation composed of numerous states, each with its own foodways. Moreover, Greek foods in the villages are very plain and monotonous except on feast days whereas food in Athens and other major cities is elegant and cosmopolitan (Kopulos and Jones 1966). See also Chap. 38 for information on Eastern Orthodox feasts and fasts.

Meal Pattern

Generally, two substantial meals are consumed. A light breakfast; lunch of soup, cheese, egg, green onions, pastry; dinner of soup, meat, cheeses, egg, green onions, pastry.

Spices and Seasonings

These are used extensively in cooking; use of lemon juice and olive oil is characteristic. Those used frequently include; anise, basil, bay leaves, capers, cheese, cinnamon, cloves, cumin, dill, garlic, honey (various flavors), lemon juice and rind, mahlepe, marjoram, masteka, mint, mustard, nutmeg, olive oil, onion, oregano, parsley, pepper (black and red), rosemary, sesame seeds, tansy, thyme, wine, vinegar, sage, scallions, vanilla.

Staples

The following list is abbreviated but indicative of typical diet components:

(A) Mezedakia (appetizers)—caviar; cheese; cheese, meat, or spinach triangles; chicken livers; hot meatballs; lamb; marinated vegetables, nuts (walnuts and almonds); olives; squid.

(B) Meat, fish, poultry, and eggs—beef, lamb (most popular), pork, rabbit, veal; cod, crayfish, cuttlefish, mullet, mussles, octopus, prawns, red snapper, rockfish, shrimp, smelts, squid; chicken, duck, partridge, pigeon; egg frequently.

(C) Dairy products—feta cheese, kasseri (rich white cheese), kyatolyri (used grated), milk (goat's), yogurt.

(D) Cereal products—frantzola (like French bread), kouloura (rich round ring bread), macaroni, noodles, psome (round bread with sesame), rice, farina, cornstarch.

(E) Fruits—(fresh accepted, canned not well-accepted) apples, apricots, cantaloupe, cherries, dates, figs, grapes, lemons, limes, oranges, pears, plums, strawberries, tangerines, watermelon.

(F) Vegetables—artichokes, asparagus, beets, cabbage, carrots, cauliflower, celery, cucumbers, eggplant, grape leaves, green beans, green peppers, greens (chicory, dandelions, endive, escarole), leeks, lettuce, mushrooms, okra, peas, potatoes, spinach, tomatoes, zucchini.

(G) Beverages—coffee (like Turkish coffee), various red and white wines, ouzo.

(H) Other—soups (using lamb or chicken stock): bean, egg and lemon, fish, lentil, mint broth, noodle soups, vegetable; desserts: bland puddings, cookies, deep fried sweets, custards, fresh fruit, pastries with honey glazes, powdered sugar, nuts and fruit toppings; olives; legumes (beans, chick peas, lentils); cooking fat is olive oil; nuts (pine nuts, almonds, walnuts, pistachios).

SPANISH-AMERICAN

Regional cookery is distinctive in Spain and reflects differences in local availability of foods. Seafoods predominate in coastal diets, mutton in the Basque regions, and pork in southern regions. The effect of Moorish domination for several centuries can be noted in use of rice and various spices.

Meal Pattern

Three meals are consumed daily. Breakfast is commonly toast and coffee or hot chocolate. Lunch is served at about 2:30 p.m. and dinner between 10 p.m.

and midnight. The main dish is usually a stew (meat or fish, potatoes and chick peas), bread, dessert, and wine (Hillgarth 1970; McGuire 1954).

Spices and Seasonings

Extensive use is made of various seasonings and some are essential in preparing a regional specialty although each cook prepares her own variation using selected spices. Typical seasonings include: bay leaf, black pepper, cayenne pepper, chervil, cinnamon, cloves, coriander, cumin, fennel, garlic, leeks, lemon juice, marjoram, mint, mustard, nutmeg, parsley, saffron, sage, tarragon, thyme, vinegar, and wine. Chocolate (unsweetened) is used in seasoning meat and fish dishes.

Staples

The following abbreviated list indicates traditional items.

(A) Tapas—almonds, cheeses, fish purées, ham, olives, stuffed eggs.

(B) Meat, fish, poultry, and eggs—beef, goat, hare, horsemeat, mutton, pork (ham, sausages, all variety meats), veal; bream, haddock, halibut, herring, mullet, salmon, shellfish (barnacles, clams, crab, lobster, mussels, scallops, shrimp), trout, tuna, turbot, whiting; dried cod, octopus, squid; chicken, duck, goose, partridge, pigeon, turkey, woodcock; eggs (hen).

(C) Dairy products—cheese (Ampurdan, Idiazabal, Mahones), milk (cow, goat, sheep).

(D) Cereal products—cakes, cornstarch, pasta from Italy (many varieties), pastry, rice, wheat bread.

(E) Fruit—apples, apricots, bananas, dates, figs, grapefruit, grapes, lemons, medlars, peaches, oranges, raisins, Seville oranges (for marmalade).

(F) Vegetables—artichokes, asparagus, cauliflower, cucumbers, eggplant, green peppers, lettuce, mushrooms, onions, parsnips, peas, pimientos, potatoes, shallots, spinach, Swiss chard, tomatoes, turnips, zucchini.

(G) Beverages—coffee, hot chocolate, "malta"—a coffee substitute, wine.

(H) Other—honey, legumes (broad beans, chick peas, kidney beans, lentils, white beans), nuts (almonds, hazelnuts, pine nuts, walnuts), olives.

BIBLIOGRAPHY

ALEXANDER, M. 1968. The significance of ethnic groups in marketing. *In* Perspectives in Consumer Behavior. H. H. Kassarjian, and T. S. Robertson (Editors). Scott, Foresman & Co., Glenview, Ill.
ANON. 1969. Understanding Food Patterns in the U.S.A. Am. Dietet. Assoc., Chicago.
BLAIR, E. C. 1972. Northern Italian cuisine. Institutions/VF *71*, No. 3, 34-37.
CANTONI, M. 1958. Adapting therapeutic diets to the eating patterns of Italian Americans. Am. J. Clin. Nutr. *6*, 548-555.
CZAJKOWSKI, J. M. 1971. Italian foods and traditions. Univ. Conn. Coop. Ext. Serv. Bull. *71-69*.
HILLGARTH, M. 1970. Spanish Cookery. International Wine & Food Publishing Co., David & Charles, London.

KOPULOS, S., and JONES, D. P. 1966. Adventures in Greek Cookery. World Publishing Co., Cleveland.

LA PINTO, M. 1955. The Art of Italian Cooking. Doubleday & Co., New York.

LASASSO, W. R. 1958. The All-Italian Cookbook. Macmillian Co., New York.

LOLLI, G., SERIANNI, E., GOLDER, G. M., and LUZZATTO-FEGIZ, P. 1958. Alcohol in Italian Culture. Food and Wine in Relation to Sobriety among Italian and Italian-Americans. Free Press, Glencoe, Ill.

MCGUIRE, L. M. 1954. Old World Foods for New World Families. Dolphin Books, Doubleday & Co., Garden City, N.Y.

MITCHELL, H. S., and JOFFE, N. F. 1944. Food patterns of some European countries: background for study and guidance of relief workers. J. Am. Dietet. Assoc. 20, 676-687.

MUDGE, G. G. 1923. Italian dietary adjustments. J. Home Econ. 15, 181-185.

CHAPTER 33

Foodways of the Middle East
(Armenia, Egypt, Iran, Iraq, Lebanon & Syria, Turkey)

The cuisines of each of these countries is similar although each has some unique dishes and distinctive combinations of seasonings. Climate has controlled availability of basic staples but as these countries have long been trading nations, spices and seasonings from the Orient and Occident are used frequently. Historic influences of Greek and Roman domination have had their impact. The Muslim and Eastern Orthodox religions practiced by the people in each of these countries have contributed their proscriptions which influenced the kinds of foods selected and/or combined.

Thousands of people from Middle Eastern countries live in the United States. Unstable political situations in these countries have caused individuals to emigrate. The Armenian-Americans are one such group. Moreover, there are also many students and professional people from these countries. In general, the latter groups are largely from affluent families and are quite cosmopolitan in their food habits. Therefore, aside from possible need to plan for religious proscriptions, standard foods can be served to these groups.

ARMENIAN-AMERICAN

Although Armenia no longer exists as a nation since parts have been divided between Iran and Turkey, Armenians who immigrated to the United States have settled in groups and have preserved much of their culture including their food-ways. The traditional diet is described below. It is followed by comments on current adaptations to American culture.

Meal Pattern

In general, three meals are consumed. Breakfast consists of bread, yogurt, fruit, and coffee for adults. Lunch is usually a stew with bread and yogurt plus salad and fruit. Dinner includes the following meal components: salad, soup, meat and/or fish, pilaf, fried or baked vegetable, and fruit. A pastry is served for dessert when feasting.

Spices and Seasonings

Characteristically, meat and vegetables are cooked together. Meats often contain garlic, cinnamon, mint, lemon juice, and tomatoes in the sauce. Commonly-used spices include: allspice, anise, cardamom, cloves, coriander, cumin, fenugreek seed, garlic, green pepper, lemon juice, mint, muhlab, onion, parsley, pepper (black and red), saffron, sumak, tarragon; honey and wine (for non-Muslims).

280

Staples

The typical diet is based on the following staples:

(A) Meat, fish, poultry, and eggs—beef, camel, lamb; chicken, duck, goose; eggs.

(B) Dairy products—milk (cow, camel, goat), salted cheese, string cheese, yogurt (madzoon).

(C) Cereal products—baklava, breads (Armenian thin bread, milk and honey bread, sesame rings, turnovers, unleavened bread, yeast rolls), bulgar, cakes, cookies, cornstarch, noodles, oatmeal, rice.

(D) Fruits—apricots, currants, dates, figs, grapes, melons, olives, pears, plums, pomegranates, quinces, raisins.

(E) Vegetables—artichokes, cabbage, cucumbers, eggplant, endive, grape leaves, green pepper, leeks, lettuce, okra, onions, potatoes, spinach, squash, Swiss chard, tomatoes, turnip, zucchini.

(F) Beverages—Arabic coffee, Armenian tea, madzoon beverage, sweet mint tea.

(G) Other—cooking fats (clarified butter, olive oil, tallow), legumes (black beans, chick peas, horse beans, lentils), nuts (almonds, filberts, pine nuts, pistachios, pumpkin seeds, sesame seeds, walnuts).

EGYPT

The diet of Egyptians varies with economic class and religion. The poor people eat a monotonous diet based on Arabic bread with small quantities of other items; the affluent classes consume a varied cosmopolitan diet. Most of the population are Muslims and observe the proscriptions. However, there is a sizeable group of Coptic Christians with different food habits.

Meal Pattern

Two alternate breakfast patterns are common (a) dates, oranges, sweet biscuit, and coffee or (b) beans, olives, cheese, eggs, and tea. Lunch appears to have the same meal components as breakfast. Dinner consists of pea soup, meat, salad, vegetable, coffee, and dessert of pastry or fruit.

Spices and Seasonings

Spices and seasonings used in Egypt are those used frequently in other Middle Eastern countries. These include, but are not limited to: allspice, black pepper, cayenne pepper, coriander, cumin, curry powder, garlic, lemon juice, mint, nutmeg, parsley, pepper, red pepper, rose water, sesame seeds.

Staples

Common staples in the Egyptian diet include:

(A) Meat, fish, poultry, and eggs—beef, lamb; porgy; chicken, pigeon; eggs.

(B) Dairy products—milk (buffalo, cow's), sheep's milk cheese, whipping cream.

(C) Cereal products—Arabic bread, barley, bulgar, farina, rice (long-grain), rice flour, wheat.

(D) Fruits—apricots, currants, dates, figs, lemons, olives, oranges, pomegranates, raisins.

(E) Vegetables—broad beans, cabbage, cauliflower, celery, eggplant, green beans, okra, Romaine lettuce.

(F) Beverages—coffee (Arabic and with cardamom), Erkesous (licorice flavored), Shair (from barley), Soubya (fermented rice liquor), Tambarhandi (date palm juice).

(G) Other—cooking fat (sesame oil, olive oil), honey, legumes (chick peas, lentils, navy beans, red beans), nuts (pine nuts, peanuts, pistachios, sesame seeds, walnuts).

IRAN, LEBANON, AND SYRIA

Food is an important aspect of culture in these countries. As in other Middle Eastern countries the diet of the lower and upper classes differ widely. Although information on food habits of Lebanese is meager, clinical observations indicated that the cereal-legume diet is inadequate as a number of nutritional deficiencies are common among the peasants who live in abject poverty (Cowan *et al.* 1964). On the other hand, the superrich consume a varied diet with many imported delicacies.

Meal Pattern

Three meals a day are consumed in these countries. Breakfast is bread with boiled milk or pancakes or eggs, white cheese, grapes, figs or other fresh fruit, and coffee. Lunch is pilaf and 1 to 10 other dishes depending on family circumstances (e.g., bread, yogurt, pickles, a hot dish, and perhaps a vegetable, dessert, and coffee). Dinner is usually a stew with a small amount of meat or a salad, bread, cheese, and coffee. Snacks of bread and jam or cheese or fruits are consumed ad libitum.

Spices and Seasonings

The spices and seasonings used here are typical of the Middle East in general. For centuries caravans carrying spices crossed these countries so a large number from India and the Spice Islands are used commonly. They include, but are not limited to: allspice, anise, basil, bay leaf, caraway, cardamom, celery seeds, cinnamon, cloves, coriander, cumin, dill, fennel, fenugreek seeds, garlic, ginger, lemon juice, mahleb, marjoram, mint, mustard seeds, nutmeg, orange blossoms, oregano, paprika, parsley, pepper (red and black), rosemary, rose water, saffron, scallions, sumak, tarragon, thyme, turmeric, vanilla, vinegar, wine. Gum arabic is used as a thickener; gum mastic, beet sugar.

Staples

The native diet is supplemented with many imported items. However, the basic list includes:

(A) Maza (appetizers)—Arabic bread, black olives, garlic eggplant, flaming apples, meat pies, pickled turnips, spinach pies.

(B) Meat, fish, poultry, and eggs—beef, kid, lamb, mutton, preserved spiced mutton, rabbit, variety meats (brains, kidney, liver, tongue, tripe, etc.), veal; bass, cod, flounder, halibut, mackerel, salmon, sardines, Sultan Ibrahim; anchovies, clams, crab, crayfish, frog legs, mussels, lobster, oysters, redfish, mullet, scallops, shrimp; chicken, duck, goose, larks, pheasant, pigeon, quail, sparrow, turkey; eggs.

(C) Dairy products—cream cheese, cheeses (Joban, Kashsawan, Laban dahareej, yogurt cheese), milk (cow's, goat's, sheep's), yogurt (called laban in Lebanon).

(D) Cereal products—Arabic flat bread, barley, bulgar, cornstarch, farina, noodles, orzo (vermicelli), rice (long-grain), shredded wheat biscuits, spaghetti.

(E) Fruit—apples, apricots, avocado, dates, figs, grapes, lemons, melons (cantaloupe, Persian), mulberries, oranges, olives, peaches, pears, pomegranates, quince, raisins, rhubarb, sour cherries, strawberries, coconut and pineapples.

(F) Vegetables—artichokes, asparagus, baby lima beans, beets, broad beans, broccoli, cabbage, carrots, cauliflower, celery, cucumbers, dandelions, eggplant, grape leaves, green beans, green onions, green pepper, lettuce, mushrooms, okra, onions, potatoes, radishes, Romaine lettuce, scallions, spinach, squashes, Swiss chard, tomatoes, truffles, turnips, zucchini; avocados and Belgian endive are imported. Various leaves of local plants are consumed in rural areas.

(G) Beverages—anise tea, Arabic coffee (Turkish), arak (anise flavored liqueur), cinnamon tea, shraab (a blend of several fruit juices).

(H) Other—cooking fats (clarified butter, olive oil, sesame oil), honey, legumes (black beans, chick peas, fava beans, kidney beans, lentils, split peas, white beans), nuts (almonds, cashews, pine nuts, pistachios, poppy seeds, pumpkin seeds, sesame seeds, walnuts), halava, baklava.

IRAQ

Food in Iraq resembles that of other Middle Eastern countries. Here again, the diet of the lower and upper classes is very different. The peasants live in abject poverty on a subsistence diet. Conspicuous consumption of imported delicacies, etc., characterizes the diet of the superrich.

Meal Pattern

Breakfast usually consists of tea or coffee, bread, cream, date syrup, honey. Lunch and dinner patterns are similar to those of other countries of the Middle East.

Spices and Seasonings

A number of spices from India and the Spice Islands were introduced centuries ago and have become essential in preparation of many dishes. The following abbreviated list of spices are used commonly in Iraqi cookery: cardamom, cinnamon, chives, cloves, cumin, curry powder, dill, fennel, garlic, ginger, lemon juice, manna, marjoram, mint, orange blossoms, parsley, pepper (black and red), rose water, rosemary, saffron, sage, thyme, turmeric.

Staples

The staples forming the basis of the diet in Iraq are typical. They include, but are not limited to:

(A) Appetizers—Kleichu, Sanbusak, and a yogurt dip with nuts, herbs, or cucumbers.

(B) Meat, fish, poultry, and eggs—lamb; biz; bunni, catfish, dhakar, shabbat; bustard, chicken, chuker, duck, goose, partridge, pigeon, quail, sandgrouse, snipe, turkey, woodcock; eggs.

(C) Dairy products—lebenia cheese, milk (buffalo), yogurt.

(D) Cereal products—Arabic bread, arrowroot starch, bulgar, cornstarch, farina, macaroni, rice.

(E) Fruit—apricots, currants, dates, lemons, oranges, pomegranates, raisins.

(F) Vegetables—cabbage, cauliflower, celery, cucumber, eggplant, green pepper, lettuce, mushrooms, onion, parsley, potatoes, pumpkin, spinach, squashes, tomatoes, truffles, zucchini.

(G) Beverages—coffee, herb teas (camellia, lime, mint), sharbat, tea.

(H) Other—cooking fats (butter, mutton fat, olive oil), legumes (beans, chick peas, lentils, peas), nuts (almonds, chestnuts, hazelnuts, melon seeds, pine nuts).

TURKEY

Traditionally, Turks spend a large proportion of their income on food. The traditional dishes are prepared using the highest quality ingredients whatever the cost (Orga 1958). Situated close to both Europe and Asia, features of both can be noted in the cuisine.

Spices and Seasonings

Turkish food is heavily spiced. Typical spices include, but are not limited to: allspice, anise, basil, bay leaf, caraway seed, chervil, chives, chocolate, cinnamon, coriander, dill, fennel, garlic, ginger, lavendar, lemon juice, linden blossoms, mace, marjoram, mint, mustard, nasturtium flowers, nutmeg, oregano, paprika, parsley, pepper (black, cayenne, red), rose petals, rosemary, saffron, sage, savory (summer and winter), sorrel, tarragon, thyme, vinegar; raki.

Staples

The Turkish diet is somewhat more varied than that of its Middle Eastern neighbors. The list of staples is more extensive and includes:

(A) Meat, fish, poultry, and eggs—beef, ham, hare, lamb, mutton, ox tongue, rabbit, sausage, variety meats (liver), veal; bass, carp, flounder, haddock, mackerel, perch, sardines, swordfish, whiting; caviar, crab, lobster, mussels, oysters, prawns, shrimp; chicken, duck, goose, pigeon, turkey; eggs. *seafood*

(B) Dairy products—kosher cheese, tulum (sheep's milk cheese), whipped cream, yogurt.

(C) Cereal products—barley, bulgar, corn meal, farina, macaroni, puff pastes, rice (long-grain), rice flour, shredded wheat biscuits, spaghetti, wheat flour; Arabic bread.

(D) Fruit—apples, apricots, black bing cherries, currants, dates, figs, grapes, lemons, olives, oranges, peaches, plums, pomegranates, raisins, raspberries, strawberries.

(E) Vegetables—artichokes, asparagus, beets, broad beans, broccoli, Brussels sprouts, cabbage, carrots, celeriac, celery, cucumbers, eggplant, French beans, green pepper, leeks, lettuce, mushrooms, okra, onions, peas, pimientos, potatoes, pumpkin, tomatoes, zucchini.

(F) Beverages—arrack, mint tea, Turkish coffee.

(G) Other—cooking fats (butter, olive oil, vegetable shortening), gherkins, honey, legumes (assorted beans, chick peas, lentils, split peas), nuts (almonds, chestnuts, hazelnuts, pine nuts, pistachios, walnuts).

MUSLIM DIETARY LAWS

Muslims may not eat pork in any form or meat that has been slaughtered without mentioning God's name or by an atheist; and may not drink alcoholic beverages or eat foods flavored with an alcohol diluent. On the other hand, Muslims are exhorted to eat foods necessary for development of strong bodies. In this regard, a number of foods are specifically recommended such as honey, milk, dates, meat, seafood, sweets, and vegetable oil (Sakr 1971).

About two million Muslims live in the United States (Sakr 1971). In order to meet their dietary needs Kosher gelatin, shortening, meats, poultry, and seafood should be served. Otherwise, the devout Muslim will refuse such foods rather than risk offending Allah.

BIBLIOGRAPHY

ADOLPH, W. H. 1954. Nutrition in the Near East. J. Am. Dietet. Assoc. *30*, 753–755.
BABOIAN, R. 1971. The Art of Armenian Cooking. Doubleday & Co., Garden City, N.Y.
COREY, H. 1962. The Art of Syrian Cookery. A culinary trip to the land of Bible history —Syria and Lebanon. Doubleday & Co., Garden City, N.Y.
CORNFELD, L. 1962. Israeli Cookery. Avi Publishing Co., Westport, Conn.
COWAN, J. W., CHOPRA, S., and HOURY, G. 1964. Dietary survey in rural Lebanon. J. Am. Dietet. Assoc. *45*, 130–132.
ICNND. 1962. Nutrition Survey—Republic of Lebanon. Interdepartmental Comm. Nutr. Natl. Defense, Washington, D.C.

KHAYAT, M. K., and KEATINGE, M. C. 1959. Food from the Arab World. Kjatats, Beirut.

MAY, J. M. 1961. The Ecology of Malnutrition in the Far and Near East: Food Resources, Habits and Deficiencies, Hafner Publishing Co., New York.

MCGUIRE, L. M. 1954. Old World Foods for New World Families. Dolphin Books. Doubleday & Co., Garden City, N.Y.

ORGA, I. 1958. Turkish Cooking. Andre Deutsch, London.

ROWLAND, J. 1950. Good Food From the Near East. M. Barrow & Co., New York.

SAKR, A. H. 1971. Dietary regulations and food habits of Muslims. J. Am. Dietet. Assoc. *58*, 123–126.

SERANNE, A., and GADEN, E. 1964. The Best of Near Eastern Cookery. Favorite Dishes from the Balkans, Turkey, Israel, Jordan, Saudi Arabia, and Other Countries of the Arabian Peninsula. Doubleday & Co., Garden City, N.Y.

SHEHATA, N. A. 1966. Nutrition education project to emphasize the importance of a Daily Food Guide for Egyptian farm people. M.S. Thesis, Oklahoma State Univ.

SIMOONS, F. J. 1961. Eat Not This Flesh: Food Avoidance of the Old World. Univ. Wisc. Press, Madison.

CHAPTER 34

Foodways of Chinese-Americans

The foodways of the Chinese-Americans depend on the region of origin in China, economic status, region of settlement in the United States, and stage in acculturation. Discussion of the foodways of Chinese-Americans is divided into two sections (a) the traditional diet and (b) the adapted diet.

THE TRADITIONAL DIET

Food is even more of an obsession with the Chinese than the French (Feng 1954; Howe 1969). Each food is prepared and arranged as an artistic creation. The Chinese equivalent to chef is Daai See Fooh or "Grand Maestro of the Culinary Arts" according to Feng (1954). Quality is indicated in several ways. If a meat has skin, it should be crisp. Vegetables are stir-fried to retain color, texture, and flavor. Natural gravy on meats and vegetables is thickened slightly with rice flour or cornstarch.

Traditionally, each of the four main regions of China have had their own cuisines. The Peking region, in the North, is more cosmopolitan than some other areas and wheat is the staple. Therefore, steamed bread, noodles, dumplings, and pancakes are basic items of diet. Other features include wine sauces, meat pastries, and hot-pot dishes. The Shanghai region, in the East, is noted for use of heavily thickened sauces heavily flavored with soy sauce served over braised foods. Many items are sweetened with white sugar but garlic is disliked. Rice is the main staple and fish is the main source of protein. The cuisine of the Szechwan region, in the West, is spicy with hot pepper, garlic, ginger and green onions. Rice is the basis of each meal. Ham is a favorite meat and many fungi are used in cooking. Noodle dishes are used as snacks. Food from the Canton region, in the South, includes rice, fish, roast pork, plum sauce, many vegetables, and frequent use of herbs. Most foods including entrées are steamed, and lightly seasoned in order to emphasize the original flavor of the food. Many sweet and sour dishes are featured. Dim-sum (appetizers) such as chicken livers, dumplings, meatballs, and pastries originated in Canton (Howe 1969). Most Chinese food served in restaurants in the United States provide items that are reasonable facsimiles of Cantonese food.

Spices and Seasonings

As indicated above, the use of spices and seasonings varies with the region of origin. Typical spices and seasonings include, but are not limited to: anise-pepper, anise seed, cinnamon, cloves, cumin, curry powder, chwen fa jioo or "five spices" (fennel, star anise, anise pepper, cloves, cinnamon), fennel, garlic, ginger, golden needles (lily flowers), green onions, mace, monosodium glutamate, mustard seed, nutmeg, parsley, pepper (black, chili, red and Szechwan pepper), red dates, sesame seeds (black and white), star anise, tangerine skin, turmeric; black bean sauce, bean paste, catsup, oyster sauce, red soy sauce, rice vinegar, rice wine, shrimp paste, soy sauce, tobacco.

The Chinese Communist Revolution has had a leveling effect on the foodways of the mainland Chinese. The same staples and spices are available everywhere (special items are purchased on the Black Market). However, regional differences have tended to disappear under the impact of an ideology that discourages differences. For these reasons, the foodways of recent immigrants from mainland China differ from those of the 1940's, 1950's, and 1960's. Immigrants from Taiwan are of mixed background from all areas on the mainland; however, they are likely to consume the typical Northern Chinese diet. Moreover, they have tended to preserve their traditional cuisines as one means of strengthening cultural identity.

Staples

The staples of diet vary with the region of origin but in general these include, but are not limited to:

(A) Meat, fish, poultry, and eggs—field mice, lamb, lizards, oxtails, pork (bacon, ham, roasts, pig's feet, smoked ham, smoked pork sausage, etc.), tree beetles, variety meats from beef, lamb, pork (brains, heart, kidneys, liver, tongue, tripe); blue gill, carp, catfish, cod, fish tripe, fishcake, herring, king fish, mandarin fish, minnows, mullet, perch, red snapper, salmon, salted fish, sea bream, sea perch, sea bass, river bass, shad, sole, sturgeon, tuna, turbot; abalone, clams, crab, jellyfish, lobster, mussels, oysters, prawns, scallops, sea cucumbers (sea slugs), shark's fin, shrimp, squid; snails; chicken, duck, quail, rice birds, squab; eggs (hen's, duck, quail, pigeon), salted eggs, tea eggs, "thousand year old eggs."

(B) Dairy products—almost none except for infants when the mother is unable to nurse the child; soy bean milk is used instead.

(C) Cereal products—arrowhead, barley, bow, chestnut flour, green vermicelli, Job's tears, lily seed bow, millet, mung bean starch, noodles, pea starch jelly, rice (short-grain, glutinous), rice crackers, rice flour, rice porridge, scented flour, seaweed vermicelli, steamed sponge cake and sugar cake, tapioca flour, vermicelli, wheat flour, wonton.

(D) Fruit—apples, bananas, custard apples, dates, dragon's eyes, figs, golden melon, grapes, lily seed, lime, lychee, mango, muskmelon, oranges, papaya, passion fruit, peaches, persimmons, pee par, pineapple, plums, pomegranates, pummel, tangerines, watermelon.

(E) Vegetables—amarantus (in-tsai), asparagus, bamboo shoots, banana squash, bitter melon, carrot tops, cauliflower, celery, chayote, Chinese cabbage (Pe-tsai, gai-choi, bok choi), Chinese long bean, Chinese mustard (choi-toi), Chinese parsley, Chinese pea pods, Chinese preserving melon (Zit-kua), corn, cucumbers, eggplant, flat beans, fuzze melon, ginger root, green limas, green pepper, hang-shoon, leeks, lettuce, lily blossoms, lily root, lotus roots and stems, mung bean sprouts, mushrooms (dried and fresh, many varieties), mustard root, okra, parsnips, peas, pea sprouts, pumpkin, spinach, squashes (bitter squash or La-kua, hairy squash or Sing-kua, water squash or Sua-kua), swamp cabbage, tea melon, tomatoes, turnips, vegetable sponge, water chestnuts, water cress, wax beans, winter melon, yams, yam beans.

(F) Beverages—black tea (many varieties), cane sugar juice, dew wine, green tea (many varieties), Jasmine tea, oolong tea, tisanes (camellia, chrysanthemum, lychee, rose); wines: shao hsingfu—everyday yellow rice wine, shantung—yellow rice wine from Peking, five companies—spicy yellow rice wine from Canton, kaoliang—white wine from kaoliang grain; fruit wines: quince, rose petal, pear, and orange.

(G) Other—agar-agar (agar-based water gels, e.g., almond curd), bean curd, cooking fats (bacon, butter, lard, peanut oil, sesame oil, soya bean oil, suet), fermented soy beans, legumes (cowpeas, horse beans, red kidney beans, soya beans, split peas, white beans), nuts (almonds, apricot kernels, areca nuts, betel nuts, chestnuts, peanuts, watermelon seeds), pickled mixed vegetables such as carrots, cucumbers, turnips, onions, and ginger root; birds' nest, seafood paste, sesame paste, soy bean cheese, soybean milk, fungi (cloud ear, wood ear), sweeteners (brown sugar, honey, white sugar), meats eaten infrequently due to cost or availability (cat, dog, cockroaches, rice worms, snake, locusts, raw monkey brains; octopus, frog's legs).

THE ADAPTED DIET

In major cities such as Boston, Chicago, Los Angeles, New York, San Francisco, and Seattle with concentrations of Chinese immigrants, customary staples are available. So the recent immigrant and the Chinese-American often continue the traditional diet. Reports by Blasdale (1899) and Jaffa (1901) indicated that traditional staples were produced locally or were imported and thus were available in the San Francisco area. Bailey (1894) reported a list of Chinese vegetables that were available in the Boston and New York areas.

Jaffa (1901) showed that urban Chinese-Americans consumed some standard American foods in addition to the traditional Chinese diet whereas truck farmers tended to accept only traditional foods. Moreover, the diets were varied; 35 staples were reported in the diet of laundrymen and 22 staples in the diet of truck farmers.

Despite the embargo on trade with Communist China in recent years, many of the traditional Chinese ingredients have continued to be available in major urban areas. Restaurants feature Northern Chinese cuisine as well as Cantonese and traditional foods are prepared in the homes, at least part of the time.

In suburbia, or in other areas of the United States, the Chinese-American usually consumes the standard American diet most of the time. This is largely due to difficulty in procuring the necessary ingredients, which must be ordered special from a major city. When necessary ingredients can be obtained, traditional items are prepared at irregular intervals and/or at festive occasions such as Chinese New Year, weddings, anniversaries, etc. Even so, the number of items are limited. As a result, skill in preparation of traditional items is gradually lost. Instead, commonly available items are prepared in quasi Chinese style, e.g., any vegetable is cut into bite-size pieces and is cooked by the stir-fry method, any fish is marinated in soy sauce, long-grain rice is substituted for glutinous rice.

BIBLIOGRAPHY

BAILEY, L. H. 1894. Some recent Chinese Vegetables. N.Y. Agr. Expt. Sta., Bull. *67*.

BLASDALE, W. C. 1899. A description of some Chinese vegetable food materials. USDA Office Expt. Sta. Bull. *68*.

CHAN, S. L., and KENNEDY, B. M. 1960. Sodium in Chinese vegetables. J. Am. Dietet. Assoc. *37*, 573–576.

CHANG, C. D. 1969. Full Color Chinese Cooking. Shufunotomo Co., Tokyo.

CZAJKOWSKI, J. M. 1967. Chinese Food and Traditions. Univ. Conn., Coop. Ext. Serv. Bull. *67-64*.

FENG, C. D. 1954. The Joy of Chinese Cooking. Grosset & Dunlap, New York.

HARRIS, R. S. *et al.* 1949. The composition of Chinese foods. J. Am. Dietet. Assoc. *25*, 28–36.

HAWKS, J. E. 1936. Preparation and composition of foods served in Chinese homes. J. Am. Dietet. Assoc. *12*, 136–140.

HOH, P. W., WILLIAMS, J. C., and PEASE, C. S. 1933. Possible sources of calcium and phosphorus in the Chinese diet. The determination of calcium and phosphorus in a typical Chinese dish containing meat and bone. J. Nutr. *7*, 535–546.

HOWE, R. 1969. China. *In* The International Wine and Food Society's Guide to Far Eastern Cookery. Drake Publishers, New York.

JAFFA, M. E. 1901. Nutrition investigations among fruitarians and Chinese. USDA Office Expt. Sta. Bull. *107*.

LEUNG, W. T. W. 1961. Some native foods in East and Southeast Asia. . . . How nutritious are they? Interdepartmental Comm. Nutr. Nat'l. Defense, Office Intern. Res. Nat'l. Health, Bethesda, Maryland.

MA, N. C. 1960. Mrs. Ma's Chinese Cookbook. Charles E. Tuttle Co., Rutland, Vermont.

CHAPTER 35

Foodways of Japanese-Americans

Japanese immigrants to the United States have settled mainly in Hawaii and on the West Coast. As a result of relocation during World War II there are concentrations in some of the inland areas as well.

THE TRADITIONAL DIET

The traditional Japanese diet is consumed by recent immigrants and in some cases by Issei (first generation Japanese-Americans). In order to meet the nutritional needs of this group, traditional foods must be provided and prepared in a variety of customary ways. Japanese foods are prepared in a number of ways. Recipes are commonly classified under the following groupings: (a) suimono—clear soups, (b) yakimono—broiled foods, (c) nimono—boiled foods, (d) mushimono—steamed foods, (e) agimono—fried foods (f) sashimi—sliced raw fish, (g) namasu—pickled raw fish and vegetables, (h) hitashimono—boiled greens in shoyu, (i) tsukemono—pickles, and (j) suki-yaki—chafing dish cookery. Various periods in Japanese history are associated with specific developments in food preparation and presentation methods (Table 35.1). However, Oiso and Suzue (1970) report that even in Japan a westernized diet is consumed increasingly, with bread and butter becoming a staple and rising consumption of milk.

Characteristically, ingredients are arranged artistically for service. Dishes are selected as a frame for the food. Some items are served whole, others are cut into uniform bite-size pieces that will cook rapidly. Food is only

TABLE 35.1

HISTORICAL INFLUENCES ON JAPANESE DIET

Period	Contribution to the Diet
Nara Period (710–784)	Buddhism established and vegetarianism began; development of Yushiki Ryori (Court Dishes).
Heian Period (784–1185)	Introduced sashimi (raw fish), yakimono (broiled fish and fowl), nimono (broiled fish and fowl with vegetables), shirumono (soups), mushimono (steamed fish, fowl and eggs), sushi (rice cakes), somen (vermicelli), mochi (rice flour), malt, honey, dried persimmon powder, amazura.
Ashikaga Period (1332–1568)	Tea ceremony developed; roasting of fowl whole and on skewers developed.
Edo Period (1603–1867)	Tea ceremony perfected in present form. Increasing use of fish and introduction of Western cookery.
Meiji and Taisho (1912–1926)	Introduction of concept of rationalizing cooking procedures in a scientific manner.

served in-season, at its peak of perfection and the season is emphasized as part of the presentation.

Meal Pattern

According to Tezuka (1936), the traditional meal pattern consists of three meals. Breakfast consists of three basic items: rice, soup, pickled vegetables plus other variable items. Lunch consists of rice, entrée, vegetables, miso-paste, pickles, green tea, fresh fruit. Dinner consists of rice, clear soup, sashimi, sukiyaki, tempura, steamed egg custard and boiled vegetables, pickles, tea. Morning and evening snacks are also customary.

Spices and Seasonings

The fundamental seasonings are shoyu and wasabi (green horseradish). According to several reports (Fukushima 1968; Howe 1969; Kato 1968; Makihara 1968; Ohyama 1969; Suzuka 1968; Yashiroda 1968), others include: alum, anemone, anise seeds, caraway seeds, chives, cortwing, curry powder, dashi (fish stock), garlic, ginger, Japanese mint, Japanese thyme, mioga ginger, miso, mitsuba (chervil), monosodium glutamate, dry mustard, prickly ash (flowers, fruit, leaves), purple perilla, red pepper, saké, sansho, sea urchin paste, "shimichi" or seven spices (black, and white sesame, green laver, hempseed, perilla seed, prickly-ash seed, red pepper), shiso leaves and berries, shoyu, smartweed, sweet coltsfoot, mirin or sweet saké, uzu—fruit and flowers, tiger lily bulb, vinegar, voilet, water dropwort, welsh onion, and wood nettle.

Staples

The traditional Japanese diet has many basic ingredients. Common staples include, but are not limited to:

(A) Meat, fish, poultry, and eggs—beef, deer, dog flesh, lamb, pork (fresh, hams), rabbit, veal, wild boar; blowfish, bream, carp, cod, cuttle fish, eel, flounder, herring, mackerel, octopus, red snapper, salmon, sardines, shark, sillago, snipefish, swordfish, trout, tuna, turbot, whale; abalone, clams, earshell, lobster, mussels, oysters, scallops, shrimp; capon, chicken, duck, goose, partridge, pheasant, quail, thrush, turkey; eggs (hen, duck, quail).

(B) Dairy products—butter, milk.

(C) Cereal products—arrowroot starch, green noodles (buckwheat and green tea), many individual cakes, konnyaku (root starch), millet, panic grass, potato starch, rice cakes, rice crackers, shiretake (vermicelli), short grain glutinous rice, soba (buckwheat noodles), soybean, sweet potato starch, udon (macaroni), wheat.

(D) Fruits—apples, apricots, bananas, dates, figs, grapefruit (yuzu), grapes, lemons, loquats, melons, oranges, peaches, pears, pear-apples, persimmons, plums, pineapples, strawberries, summer mandarin.

(E) Vegetables—artichokes, aster, aster leaves, bamboo shoots, bean sprouts, beets, bofu leaf, bracken fern, broccoli, Brussels sprouts, burdock root, burnet, cabbage (Chinese, white), carrots, catbrier, chickweed, Chinese onion, crysan-themum, cinnamon fern, corn, cucumber, daikon, eggplant, green onions, green pepper, green perilla, horsetail, Japanese angelica, Japanese mugwort, knot-weed, lamb's quarters, leeks, lettuce, lotus root, meadow-rue, meadowsweet, "mountain vegetables" (plumed thistles, sweet coltsfoot, tasselflower, worm-wood), mushroom (mastsutake), okra, ostrich fern, mustard cabbage, peas, plantain lily, radishes, rhubarb, sorrel, spinach, squash, sweet coltsfoot leaves, taro, tomatoes, trefoil (greens with three leaves), turnip, udo or Japanese asparagus, watercress, water-dropwort, water-shield, yams.

(F) Beverages—carbonated beverages, coffee, tea (black and green), saké.

(G) Other—agar-agar, amazura, cooking fats (butter, olive oil, peanut oil, sesame oil, vegetable oil, suet), dashi (fish bouillon), honey, legumes (red bean curd—tofu, lima beans, black beans), nuts (chestnuts, gingko-nuts, peanuts, walnuts), seaweed (hijiki, kombu, nori, wakame), poppy seeds, sesame seeds (black and white).

THE ADAPTED DIET

Food habits of Japanese-Americans in Hawaii have undergone progressive modifications in the past half century. However, according to Wenkam and Wolff (1970), there are three distinct stages of acculturation coexisting today: (a) tradition-directed, (b) partially adapted, many typically Japanese foods are consumed although less frequently; and (c) assimilated, westernized foods are consumed and the traditional diet is rejected. Moreover, these authors reported that observed dietary changes could be attributed to the cumulative and aggregate effects of (a) desire for the status associated with consumption of American food, (b) disintegration of the traditional family control over foodways, (c) acceptance of Hawaii as home and reallocation of funds with an increase in the food budget, (d) increased exposure to foods consumed by other ethnic groups with gradual acceptance of some of these items, and (e) the impact of a deliberate effort by the educational system to inculcate various aspects of the American culture, including foodways.

Generally, Japanese-Americans living on the west coast can be classified according to the same three stages of acculturation as those in Hawaii. And, dietary changes can probably be attributed to a similar complex of factors.

In general, Nisei (second-generation Japanese-Americans) are westernized in their eating habits. Although they consume rice and use shoyu more frequently than their WASP neighbors in a community, they usually eat standard American food. Traditional items are prepared at irregular intervals and at special festivals. Special ingredients are available in the major cities on the west coast.

Ho *et al.* (1966) reported that Japanese students at American universities, who are usually from urban areas with previous exposure to American food, made no attempt to obtain traditional Japanese foods. Thus, it would seem that American food is generally acceptable.

BIBLIOGRAPHY

ABIAKA, M. H. 1973. Japanese-American food equivalents for calculating exchange diet. J. Am. Dietet. Assoc. *62*, 173–180.

BAZORE, K. 1949. Hawaiian and Pacific Foods. M. Barrows & Co., New York.

EGAMI, T. 1959. Typical Japanese Cooking. Shibata Publishing Co., Tokyo.

FUKUSHIMA, K. 1968. Kyoto's traditional "Shichimi" spices. Plants Gardens *24*, No. 2, 16–17.

GRIFFIN, S. 1956. Japanese Food and Cooking. Chas. E. Tuttle Co., Rutland, Vermont.

HAMADA, S. 1968. Some of our favorite home-grown herbs. Plants Gardens *24*, No. 2, 20–22.

HO, G. P., NOLAN, F. L., and DODDS, M. L. 1966. Adaptation to American dietary patterns by students from Oriental countries. J. Home Econ. *58*, 277–280.

HOWE, R. 1969. Japan. *In* Far Eastern Cookery. Drake Publishers, New York.

Japan Trade Center. 1960. Japanese Recipes. Japan Food Corp., San Francisco.

KATO, N. 1968. Herbs used today in northern Japan. Plants Gardens *24*, No. 2, 18–19.

MAKIHARA, N. 1968. Spices and herbs used in Japanese cooking. Plants Gardens *24*, No. 2, 14–15.

OHYAMA, I. 1968. Akita-buki, giant sweet coltsfoot. Plants Gardens *24*, No. 2, 20–22.

OISO, T., and SUZUE, R. 1970. Topics of nutrition in Japan. Am. J. Clin. Nutr. *23*, 1096–1098.

ORR, K. J. and GASCON, H. C. 1967. About Japanese foods. Univ. Hawaii, Coop. Ext. Serv., Home Econ. Circ. *340*.

STANDAL, B. R. 1963. Nutritional values of proteins of Oriental soybean foods. J. Nutr. *81*, 279–285.

SUZUKA, O. 1968. Japanese culinary and medicinal herbs. Plants Gardens *24*, No. 2, 4–13.

TEZUKA, K. 1936. Japanese Food. Maruzen Co., Tokyo.

UEDA, K. 1968. Some notes on cooking chrysanthemums. Plants Gardens *24*, No. 2, 23–24.

WENKAM, N. S., and WOLFF, R. J. 1970. A half century of changing food habits among Japanese in Hawaii. J. Am. Dietet. Assoc. *57*, 29–32.

YASHIRODA, K. 1968. A dictionary of popular Japanese herbs and their uses today. Plants Gardens *24*, No. 2, 44–58.

CHAPTER 36

Foodways of Polynesians[1]

INTRODUCTION

Polynesian foodways are a blend of the foods and customs of (a) native island peoples (varying from place to place), (b) Chinese (a major influence), (c) Japanese (from immigration waves in 1886-1906), (d) Filipino (from immigration waves in 1906-1922, 1940-1944), (e) Spanish and Portuguese, and (f) American (Abel 1954).

Prior to World War II, few Americans, were interested in Polynesian foodways. Anthropologists studied the cultures as examples of primitive societies but their findings were not widely known. However, World War II destroyed and/or resulted in the establishment of new modified foodways on most of the islands. Much research resulted. Moreover, as a result of military exposure interest in Polynesian foodways was greatly increased in the continental United States.

The Hawaiian Islands are usually taken as class representatives for Polynesia. The diet includes, but is not limited to:

(A) Meat, fish, poultry and eggs—beef, beef jerky, corned beef, kupee, lamb, mutton, pipipi, pork, pupu; ahi, bagoong, fish cake, mahimahi, mullet, octopus, opihi, canned salmon, sardines, sea cucumbers, sea urchins, shrimp, squid, swordfish, trout, turtle, whale; chicken, duck, squab, turkey; eggs (hen, duck).

(B) Cereal products—cornstarch, noodles (rice flour, soy bean, wheat flour), poi, Portuguese bread (Pao Doc), rice, rice flour.

(C) Fruits—apricots, avocados, ascerola cherries, bananas, breadfruit, cantaloupe, carambola, carrisa, figs, grapefruit, grapes, guavas, Java plums, ketambilla, kumquats, lemons, limes, loquat, lychees, mango, mountain apples, black mulberry, oheloberry, oranges, papaya, passion fruit, peaches, pears, persimmon, pineapple, plantain, methley plums, poha, prunes, raisins, roselle, soursop, strawberry, surinam cherry, tamarind, tangerine, watermelon.

(D) Vegetables—beans (hyacinth, soy, winged), bean sprouts, bitter melon, burdock root, cabbage (white, Chinese), carrots, cauliflower, daikon, eggplant, ferns, green pepper, horseradish, jute, kohlrabi, leeks, lettuce, lotus root, hiolabor, nightshade, mustard greens, green onions, parsley, Chinese peas, poi, pumpkin, purslane, spinach, squashes, swamp cabbage, sweet potato tops, sweet potatoes, taro, tomatoes, toro (dasheen), taro leaves, turnip greens, watercress, water chestnuts.

---

[1]This section differs from previous sections in that it also is intended as a guide for planning special menus.

(E) Beverages—coffee, okolehao (from ti root), tea.

(F) Other—bean curd, coconut milk, cooking fats (butter, coconut oil, margarine, peanut oil, sesame oil) chutney, legumes, (cowpeas, French beans, hyacinth beans, lentils, long beans, navy beans, pigeon peas, sword beans, winged beans), nuts (coconut, lychee, macadamia, peanuts), pickle relish, seaweeds (limu eleeli, limu kohu, limu lipoa).

Spices and Seasonings

Black pepper, celery seed, curry powder, garlic, ginger root, green onion, mint, monosodium glutamate, paprika, soy sauce.

An earlier book reports the basic diets of various peoples migrating to Hawaii and their stage of acculturation in the 1940's (Bazore 1949). Principle groups that have migrated to Hawaii include Samoan, Chinese, Japanese, Korean, Portuguese, Puerto Ricans and Filipinos according to Bazore (1949). The Samoans have not been fully integrated with other peoples of Hawaii so their foods have not been assimilated into the general culture. By contrast, Chinese food is commonly consumed. It is discussed under the section of foodways of Chinese-Americans. Japanese from southern Japan have also contributed many foods to island cuisine; while the older people continue their traditional foodways, the younger generations have been assimilated. The South Koreans who emigrated to Hawaii were largely from urban areas; their diet had little impact on the overall cuisines of the Islands. Filipinos were the last group to immigrate to Hawaii; they tend to live by themselves and their diet has not become a part of the general Island cuisine.

Masuoka (1945) reported that Japanese immigrating to Hawaii continue to consume rice and fish but that the quantity of rice consumed decreases over time. Rice is replaced with white flour, macaroni, crackers, breads, and other standard American foods. Abel (1954) reported that the schools exerted a tremendous influence on children in Westernizing them including teaching them to eat the standard American diet.

More recently, Haseba and Brown (1968) reported that students living in the residence halls were more likely to consume a standard American breakfast than those with other living arrangements. Moreover, those who did not consume breakfast, were likely to consume a snack rather than a regular breakfast on the occasions when they did consume a meal. Thus, if the standard meal is provided it is likely to be consumed.

Wenkam (1973) recently discussed current food habits of Hawaiians. Breakfast and lunch are the common types of Western fare. Dinner is often the only meal that shows Polynesian influence. The distinctive feature of Hawaiian home-cooked dinners is the common practice of serving several entrées at a meal, each of which may represent a different ethnic cuisine. For example, one might serve a Japanese beef dish, a Chinese chicken dish, and a Filipino pork dish.

POPULARIZED CUISINE

During the 1950's Polynesian cuisine was popularized by Victor Bergeron (Trader Vic) of Trader Vic's restaurants. Elegent specialties from various islands, and traditional Japanese and Chinese cookery are featured. In addition, a large number of pseudo-Polynesian items have been created. Other Polynesian restaurants generally offer similar menus.

During the same period luaus and Hawaiian hospitality became popular as a party style. A sample menu is shown in Table 36.1. Recipes can be obtained from cookbooks such as The Hawaii Dietetic Association (1956).

TABLE 36.1

SAMPLE MENU FOR A HAWAIIAN-STYLE PARTY

Beef, Green Pepper, and Tomato Kabob   Shrimp and Bacon Kabob
Pickled Vegetables

Roast Suckling Pig

Polynesian Chicken   Baked Fish, Oriental Style
Baked Sweet Potatoes   Steamed Rice
Steamed Greens   Baked Bananas
Fresh Pineapple Spears   Coconut Milk Pudding
Guava Nectar   Passion Fruit Juice
Coffee   Tea

Source: Hawaii Dietetic Association (1956).

BIBLIOGRAPHY

ABEL, M. G. 1954. Teaching nutrition in the melting pot of the pacific. J. Am. Dietet. Assoc. *30*, 148.

BAZORE, K. 1949. Hawaiian and Pacific Foods. M. Barrows & Co., New York.

CZAJKOWSKI, J. M. 1971. Hawaiian Foods and Traditions. Univ. Conn. Coop. Ext. Serv. Bull. *60-25.*

HASEBA, J., and BROWN, M. L. 1968. Breakfast habits of college students in Hawaii. J. Am. Dietet. Assoc. *53*, 334-335.

Hawaii Dietetic Association. 1956. The Hawaii Hostess Cookbook. Favorite Recipes for Fifty. Pacific Publishing Co., Honolulu, Hawaii.

HO, G. P., NOLAN, F. L., and DODDS, M. L. 1966. Adaptation to American dietary patterns by students from oriental countries. J. Am. Home Econ. Assoc. *58*, 277-280.

HOAR, J. W. (Not Dated) South Pacific Cookery Book. South Pacific Public Health Serv. Nutr. Sect., Suva, Fiji.

MARETZKI, A. N., and CHUNG, C. 1971. An evaluation of the school lunch program of five high schools in Honolulu, Hawaii. I. Attitudes of high school students toward their school lunch program. II. Beyond the federal regulations for the Type A school lunch: Nutrients and plate waste. Monograph, Univ. Hawaii.

MASSAL, E., and BARRAU, J. (Not Dated) Food plants of the South Sea Islands. South Pacific Comm. Tech. Paper *94*.

MASUOKA, J. 1945. Changing food habits of Japanese in Hawaii. Sociol. Rev. *10*, 759-765.

MILLER, C. D., and BRANTHOOVER, B. 1957. Nutritive values of some Hawaii foods. Hawaii Agr. Expt. Sta. Circ. *52*.

MILLER, C. D., BAZORE, K., and BARTOW, M. 1965. Fruits of Hawaii. Univ. Hawaii
    Press, Honolulu.
MURAI, M., PEN, F., and MILLER, C. D. 1958. Some tropical South Pacific Island foods.
    Description, history, use, composition, and nutritive value. Univ. Hawaii Press, Honolulu.
SIA, M. 1956. Mary Sia's Chinese Cookbook. Univ. Hawaii Press, Honolulu.
WENKAM, N. S. 1967. Sodium and potassium content of Hawaiian foods. Hawaii Agr.
    Expt. Sta., Honolulu.
WENKAM, N. S. 1973. Personal communication. Univ. Hawaii, Honolulu.

CHAPTER 37

Foodways of Indians and Other Orientals Living in the United States

This chapter discusses the foodways of the foreign nationals from India and other Oriental nations who reside in the United States. In general, the majority of these peoples are from affluent families in their respective countries. They often came as students and decided to remain. Because of their economic background, their food habits are not typical for their countries. They are more cosmopolitan and usually learn to accept the American diet. Some exceptions, that may be expected, are listed below.

INDIANS

India is a large subcontinent with a high population density and many people living at the subsistence level. It also has many climates, numerous religions, and cultural subgroups. Accordingly, it is difficult to generalize about the Indian diet. However, a few points emerge: (a) rice is the staple of eastern areas, wheat the staple of the west; (b) southern food is highly spiced but northern food is somewhat milder; (c) many Indians are vegetarians who follow strict religious rituals in selection, preparation, and service of food; (d) beef is not eaten by the Hindus and pork is not eaten by the Muslims.

Indians living in the United States are usually from the upper classes in India, they are dispersed throughout the country, and their customary diets vary according to religion, etc. For these reasons, they generally expect to adapt to the American diet. However, single women, couples, and/or families often attempt to maintain the traditional dietary pattern, especially if they expect to return to India or if dietary restrictions are related to religious beliefs. If the customary ingredients are readily available at reasonable prices, the diet may remain nutritionally adequate. Otherwise, difficulties develop as necessary adaptations may not be readily accepted.

The single Indian male usually adapts his diet to what is available. Ho *et al.* (1966) reported that less than half the Indian college students surveyed followed their traditional diet. The others either followed dietary restrictions to some degree or made no attempt to follow them. As most Indian males have little experience in food preparation, they purchase convenience foods and/or eat meals in restaurants. Neither alternative is conducive to maintenance of customary dietary patterns or good nutrition.

KOREANS

As a result of the Korean War, an increased number of Koreans have immigrated to the United States. Moreover, a small number of Korean students are usually found at major universities.

The traditional Korean diet, heavily influenced by Chinese and Japanese cookery, is continued in the United States, to the extent possible. According to Ho *et al.* (1966), milk is the only consistent addition.

Spices and Seasonings

Pickled vegetables (kimchee) and heavy use of garlic, chili pepper, and hot peppers are distinguishing characteristics of Korean food. Spices and seasonings used commonly include, but are not limited to: cinnamon, garlic, ginger root, green onions, monosodium glutamate, red chili pepper, sesame seeds, soy sauce; vinegar; crude sea salt.

Staples

The basis of the diet is rice. Small quantities of numerous other foods are eaten to add interest. According to Bazore (1949), Howe (1971), and Morris (1959) staples in the Korean diet include, but are not limited to:

(A) Meat, fish, poultry, and eggs—beef, variety meats (heart, kidney, liver), oxtail, pork; codfish, mackerel, mullet, perch; abalone, clams, jelly fish, lobster, oysters, shrimp; chicken, pheasant; eggs.

(B) Cereal products—barley, rice (glutinous), rice crackers, wheat or buckwheat flour, vermicelli.

(C) Fruits—apples, cherries, dates, grapes, melons, pears, persimmons, plums.

(D) Vegetables—bean sprouts, beets, cabbage (celery, white), celery, cucumbers, eggplant, fern, green beans, green onions, green peppers, leaf lettuce, leeks, lotus root, mushrooms, onions, peas, potatoes, spinach, sweet potatoes, turnips, water chestnuts, watercress, white radishes (daikon).

(E) Beverages—coffee, fruit drinks, green tea, honey-water, Jasmine tea, magnolia flower drink, rice tea, rice water, rice wine, tisanes (ginseng, cinnamon, ginger tea), wines (talsju, yakju, soju).

(F) Other—cooking fats (salad oil, sesame oil), honey, legumes (lima beans, homemade bean pastes, mung beans, red beans, soy beans, soy bean mush, soy bean milk, soy bean curd), nuts (chestnuts, gingko nuts, hazelnuts, pine nuts, pistachios, sesame seeds, walnuts), seaweed (kin, miyck, t'uikok), soy bean noodles.

CAMBODIANS AND VIETNAMESE

The war in Southeast Asia has introduced many American men to these cuisines and has resulted in an influx of immigrants from these countries. Their traditional cuisines were influenced by Chinese cuisines centuries ago and by the French cuisine in recent colonial times.

Meal Patterns

Two basic meals are commonly consumed. Nibbling throughout the day is customary. Breakfast usually consists of rice or noodle soup, coffee with milk. Lunch and dinner consist of rice and a stew with a small quantity of meat or fish and several vegetables.

Spices and Seasonings

Fish sauces rather than spices and seasonings are used to flavor foods. The basic list includes, but is not limited to: allspice, alum, bindweed, black pepper, borax, cayenne pepper, Chinese parsley, chives, coconut milk, coriander, curry powder, fennel, garlic, ginger root, hot chili, lemon grass, lemon juice, lily flowers, lotus seed, mint, monosodium glutamate, paprika, saffron, star anise, stick cinnamon, tamarind juice, and vinegar.

Staples

The basis of the diet is rice of which there are many varieties. Many sauces and other special items are consumed with the rice to add interest to the diet. Staples include but are not limited to:

(A) Meat, fish, poultry, and eggs—beef, buffalo, pork (Chinese sausages, pig's feet, head, hams, etc.), variety meats (liver, kidneys, tripe); anchovies, carp, crab, crayfish, cuttlefish, dried shrimp, ladyfish, prawns, rock oyster, salt cod, sardines, sea-urchins, squid, swordfish, tuna; chicken (also heart and gizzards), duck, pigeon, sparrow; eggs (fish roe, hen's).

(B) Dairy products—not used by Vietnamese.

(C) Cereal products—arrowroot, Chinese rice sticks, cornstarch, bean thread, French bread, glutinous rice, Japanese somen, rice, rice crackers, rice cakes, rice noodles, rice vermicelli, tapioca, toasted rice.

(D) Fruits—bananas, custard apples, grapefruit, green grapes, guavas, lychees, mangos, mangosteens, mountain apples, papayas, pineapples, rambuttons, star gooseberries, star apples, tamarinds.

(E) Vegetables—asparagus, bamboo shoots, banana leaves, bitter melon, cabbage, carrots, cauliflower, Chinese cabbage, Chinese peas, Chinese yams, chives, cucumbers, eggplant, green beans, green papaya, green peppers, kohlrabi, leeks, lotus root, mushrooms (straw and dried), mustard cabbages, pumpkin, spinach, squashes, sweet potatoes, taro, tomatoes, turnip, water chestnuts, watercress, winter melon, various leaves (guava, lemon, lime, ti), yams.

(F) Beverages—coffee with milk, tea.

(G) Other—cooking fats (bacon, lard, onion flavored oil, shortening), legumes (lentils, mungo beans), nuts (coconut, peanuts), pickles of many kinds, sauces (nguoc-nam–soy sauce and fish paste, bean sauce, fish sauce, shrimp sauce), sweeteners (brown sugar, caramelized sugar, sugar cane), tree fungus.

FILIPINOS

Filipinos have immigrated to the United States in sizeable numbers in recent years. West Coast cities such as San Diego, Long Beach, San Francisco, and Seattle have Filipino communities as many of the men are in the U.S. Navy. Filipino students are dispersed throughout the United States.

The Filipino diet is a composite with elements of Spanish, Chinese, and American cuisine added to the native diet.

The variety of food consumed by each household depends on its economic level. Low-income groups usually eat mostly dried or fresh fish, rice, leafy vegetables and fruit in season. Middle- and high-income groups eat meat at most meals. Most people eat three meals per day. Rice is usually eaten at lunch and dinner. A native bread "pande sal" is eaten at breakfast. Midmorning and mid-afternoon snacks called "marienda" are common. These usually consist of puddings or cakes made with sweet rice and coconut milk or rice noodles sautéed with vegetables and some meat.

A typical breakfast might include the following: (a) dried fish or meat (native pork sausage, fried flank steak, or imported Vienna sausage, Gouda cheese or Australian cheddar cheese, Chinese cured ham), (b) rice—either boiled or fried, (c) bread and imported butter or local margarine, and (d) hot chocolate or coffee. Lunch or supper might consist of: (a) fresh vegetable salad (marinated), (b) meat or fish sautéed with leafy vegetables, (c) rice—either boiled or fried, and (d) dessert—a pudding, cake, or fruit in season.

Spices and Seasonings

Food is spicy but the variety of spices used is limited. It includes: bagoong, garlic, hot pepper, lemon grass (tanglad), pandan mabango, turmeric; vinegar; salty fish sauce.

Staples

A wide variety of items are basic in the Filipino diet. Staples include, but are not limited to:

(A) Meat, fish, poultry, and eggs—beef, blood, deer, goat, lamb, pork, rabbit, talaba, tulya, variety meats (beef knuckles, liver, tail); abalone, bangus, barra-cuda, bonito, cardinal fish, crab (alimango, alimasag), croaker, dapa (sole), fish paste, grouper, grunt, herring, mackerel, marbled sting ray, moray eel, mullet, mussels, octopus, oysters, pampano, parrot fish, perch, porgy, prawns, red snap-per, rock bass (lapu-lapu), sardines, sea bass, sea catfish, shark, shrimp, squid, swordfish, tarpon, threadfin, trepang, tuna, white bait, whiting; frog, tortise; chicken, duck, goose, Moor hen, pigeon, turkey, wild duck; eggs: ant, balut (duck eggs with partially-formed ducklings—eaten raw), hen, lizard, tortise.

(B) Dairy products—evaporated milk, milk (water buffalo, also called carabao, cow, goat), native cheese. Milk is not consumed to any extent.

(C) Cereal products—bihon, bread, corn, farina, gabi, kanote, macaroni, mesuwa, mike, mongo starch, mung bean starch, noodles, pan de Sal, pinipig (young rice), rice (glutinous), rice flour, rice noodles, spaghetti, tapioca flour, toasted rice, ubi, wheat flour, wheat noodles.

(D) Fruits—anones, apples, avocados, kalabaw (Phillipine mango), bananas (100 varieties), banana blossoms, breadfruit, cahil, calamansi star fruit (bilimbing), chicos, Curacao apples, custard apples or sweet sop (atis), dubot, grapes, guava, honeydew melon, kamatsili, kasuy fruit, langka, lanzones pomelo (suhi), lemon (kalamansi), lime (dayap), lychees, makopa (Java apple), Malay apple, mango, mangosteen, melons, Mindanao grapefruit, narangita (tangerine), oranges, papaya, pears, pineapples, plums (black, govenor, Java—dukat, Spanish), pomegranates, pomelo, rhubarb, roselle, sahas (cooking bananas), sampalok, santol, sapodilla, sapote, siniguwelas, soursop (guwayabano), star apple (kaimito), strawberries, sugar apple, tamarind, tskio, watermelon.

(E) Vegetables—alugbati, ampolaya fruit, Baguios spinach, bamboo shoots (lagoong), banana inflorescence, beets, Betel nut, bittermelon, cabbage, carrots, cashew nut leaves, cassava, cauliflower, celery, Chinese celery, coconut heart, eggplant, endive, garlic, green beans (abitsuwelas), green papaya, green peppers, Himbabao flowers, horseradish leaves, hyacinth bean (batao), kamote tops, kamote tuber, kangkong leaves, leeks, lettuce, long green beans (sitaw), malunggay leaves, mango leaves, mungo, mushrooms, nettles, New Zealand spinach, okra, onions, pacu (a type of leaf fern), palmetto heart, parsley, payaap, pechoy (lettuce-celery), pigeon peas, pitsay, potatoes, pumpkins, purslane, radish, safflower, sesben flower, sinkamas (Chinese turnips), sitao, snow peas, spineless amaranth, sponge gourd, squash blossoms, squash lima beans, squash tops, squashes (bottle gourd upo, butternut, chayote, cucumbers, patola, summer, yellow), sugar palm shoot, swamp cabbage, sweet potato, talbos (tips of various squash and bean vines), taro, taro leaves, taro root (gabi), tomatoes, turpeth root, ubi (a yam), water chestnut, watercress, wax gourd, winged beans (sequidillas), yams.

(F) Beverages—chocolate milk, cocoa, coffee with milk.

(G) Other—brown sugar, coconut honey, coconut jam, cooking fats (coconut oil, vegetable oil), legumes (black beans, chick peas, cowpeas, lentils, limas, mung beans, mungo, pigeon peas, white kidney beans), nuts (cashew—kasuy, coconut, peanuts, pili nuts), seaweed (gamet).

INDONESIAN

Indonesian food has been influenced by religious and ethnic groups. Javanese are largely Muslim (see the section on Foodways of the Middle East for the dietary laws) and eat no pork and use no wine. Buddhists and Hindus are vegetarian. Portuguese and Dutch customs were introduced during colonial periods. Chinese influences were introduced earlier.

Meal Pattern

The traditional breakfast of cassava, rice or steamed bananas is common though the Dutch breakfast of coffee, eggs, and bread is consumed. Other meals are based on rice accompanied by an assortment or spicy meat and/or vegetable dishes.

Spices and Seasonings

A large number of spices are native to the Islands of Indonesia. Spices used commonly include, but are not limited to: allspice, bay leaf, black pepper, caraway seeds, chilis, cinnamon, cloves, coconut milk, coriander seeds, garlic, ginger root, lemon grass, lemon peel, lemon verbena, lemon juice, lime juice, nutmeg, orange peel, tumeric.

Staples

The staples of the Indonesian diet vary with the island and the religious group. An abbreviated list follows:

(A) Meat, fish, poultry, and eggs—buffalo, pork; anchovies, mackerel, sardines, tuna; prawns; chicken, pigeon; eggs.

(B) Dairy products—not used in quantity.

(C) Cereal products—cassava, corn, noodles, rice, shrimp crisps, tapioca, wheat.

(D) Fruits—avocados, bananas, breadfruit, durians, grapes, jackfruit, lemons, limes, mangos, oranges, papaya, pineapple, pomegranates, raisins, rambuttans, tamarinds, tangerines.

(E) Vegetables—bean sprouts, cabbage, celery, corn, cucumbers, eggplant, green beans, green pepper, green onion, mushrooms, onions, potatoes, scallions, spinach, sweet potatoes, tomatoes.

(F) Beverages—coffee, hot chocolate, tea.

(G) Other—cooking oil (butter, peanut oil), chutneys, ketchups, nuts (almonds, cashews, coconuts, peanuts), pickles, shrimp paste, blachan (fermented fish paste), soy sauce, sweeteners (brown sugar, honey, molasses), vinegar, wine.

BIBLIOGRAPHY

ANON. 1967. What does the average middle-class Indian family eat? Participant 2, No. 2, 26.

BAZORE, K. 1949. Hawaiian and Pacific Foods. M. Barrows & Co., New York.

HO, G. P., NOLAND, F. L., and DODDS, M. L. 1966. Adaptation to American dietary patterns by students from Oriental countries. J. Home Econ. 58, 277-280.

HOWE, R. 1971. Far Eastern Cookery, Drake Publishers, New York.

ICNND. 1957. Nutrition survey of the Armed Forces—Korea. Interdepartmental Comm. Nutr. Natl. Defense, Washington, D.C.

JONES, G. T. 1966. The influence of income and family structure on the family diet in India. Farm Economist 10, 485-496.

MORRIS, H. 1959. The Art of Korean Cooking. Charles E. Tuttle Co., Rutland, Vermont.

PIL, N. K. 1955. Land of plentiful. J. Am. Dietet, Assoc. *31,* 1030-1032.

RAO, K. V. 1967. Patterns and trends in food consumption in India. J. Nutr. Dietet., India *4,* No. 2, 79-87.

SIMOONS, F. J. 1961. Eat not This Flesh. Food Avoidance in the Old World. Univ. Wisconsin Press, Madison.

STEWART, G. 1958. Manila Cookbook. Evening News, Manila.

CHAPTER 38

Foodways of Russian-Americans

The traditional foodways of Russians were determined by a combination of three major factors (a) socioeconomic, (b) ethnic, and (c) religious. The typical diet of aristocrats in precommunist times was varied and preparation was similar to French cuisine in elegance. The peasant diet was based on cereals and root vegetables. Thus, socioeconomic factors largely controlled availability of ingredients and, hence, variety.

Ethnic background was a major factor determining style of cuisine. Russians are the eastern branch of the Slavonic ethnic groups of Indo-Europeans who inhabit the European subcontinent. The Russians can be divided into four main groups: (A) The Great Russians are the largest and most dominant group who occupy central and northern Russia, Moscow, and Leningrad, respectively. The food habits of this group are used as class representatives for Russian cookery. (B) The Little Russians (Ukrainian) are from southeastern areas such as Kiev and Kharkov. (C) The White Russians (Western Russia centered around Minsk). (D) The Carpatho-Russians (Galician) which, prior to World War I, were part of the Austro-Hungarian Empire (now Czechoslovakia and Poland).

Other peoples of non-Slavic origin who are part of the population of the Soviet Union are Balts (Estonians, Latvians, and Lithuanians), Jews, Armenians, Georgians, Mongols (Tartars, Uzbeks, Turkmen, Kirghiz, Calmuks, etc.), Germans, and Finns.

The major religion of Russia was Eastern Orthodox. Special foods and/or fast periods are associated with specified religious observances. These are followed by members of the Eastern Orthodox Church living outside of Russia.

Easter, or Holy Pascha, is the feast of feasts and the greatest holiday celebrated by members of the Eastern Orthodox Church. The date for Easter is not fixed; it is always celebrated on the first Sunday after the full moon following the spring equinox according to the solar calendar. Moreover, it is always after the Hebrew Passover, never before or on the same day. For this reason, its date sometimes differs from the Western Easter.

The traditional foods served on Easter include (a) Pascha which is a dessert in the form of a pyramid containing cheese, cream, butter, eggs, sugar, and candied fruits, (b) Kulich which is a very rich sweet yeast dough baked in a tall cylindrical can, (c) colored or hand-decorated eggs, (d) sausages, (e) smoked fish, (f) eggplant and caviar, and (g) a cold vegetable salad called vinaigrette. All foods are served cold as no cooking is done on this day.

In addition to Easter, there are twelve other major feasts. These are listed in Table 38.1. Major fasts are listed in Table 38.2. On fast days, no animal products are consumed, including milk, cheese, butter, and eggs.

TABLE 38.1

MAJOR FEAST DAYS OF THE EASTERN ORTHODOX CHURCH[1]

Gregorian Calendar Date (New Style)	Julian Calendar Date (Old Style)	Feast Day	Food
Dec. 25	Jan 7	Christmas Eve (Nativity of Our Lord)	12 different dishes; e.g., dry mushroom soup, bread, sauerkraut and peas, beans, potatoes, fish (stuffed, baked, or fish balls), pickled herrings, stuffed cabbage, dried fruit compote or sweetened cereal desserts. "Kutya," a fasting food served made of boiled wheat, honey, nuts, poppy seeds, and fruit.
		Christmas Day	For Russians: roast pork and turkey. For Greeks, Serbians, and Syrians: roast lamb and various sweet yeast dough desserts.
Jan 6	Jan. 19	Theophany (12 days after Christmas)	
Febr. 2	Febr. 15	Presentation of Our Lord into the Temple	
Mar. 25	Apr. 7	The Annunciation	
Sunday before Easter		Palm Sunday	(A fast day)
40 days after Easter		The Ascension	
50 days after Easter		Pentecost (Trinity) Sunday	Kulich, saved from Easter.
Aug. 6	Aug. 19	The Transfiguration	(Blessing of fruit)
Aug. 15	Aug. 28	The Dormition of the Holy Theotokos	
Sept. 8	Sept. 21	The Nativity of the Holy Theotokas	
Sept. 14	Sept. 27	Elevation of the Holy Cross	(A strict fast day)
Nov. 21	Dec. 4	The Presentation of the Holy Theotokos	

[1] Note: Russians and most other Slavic Orthodox still follow the Julian calendar, which in the 20th Century is 13 days behind the Gregorian calendar. Thus, dates of the stationary feasts differ according to the calendar used. Frequently, a feast day is a heavy meal that includes meat, milk, butter and/or cheese for the first time in days or weeks.

Since the communist revolution, universal availability of selected ingredients in controlled quantities in conjunction with an ideology that discourages differences has resulted in a more-or-less uniform diet. Thus, the effects of socioeconomic status, ethnic background, and religion have been minimized. Moreover, as cooking facilities in the home are limited, Russian adults frequently consume all of their meals in their industrial plant cafeteria. Children consume their meals at the day-care center or school.

THE TRADITIONAL DIET

The traditional diet of aristocrats in precommunist times was varied and the style of cuisine was similar to the French cuisine. Because of the lack of adequate transportation and consequent seasonal restrictions on availability coupled with the lack of refrigeration, the Russians developed other methods for pre-

TABLE 38.2

FAST DAYS[1] OF THE EASTERN ORTHODOX CHURCH

Fast Days[2]

Wednesdays and Fridays of the year except for fast-free weeks:
    Week following Christmas to Eve of Theophany
    Bright Week, week following Easter
    Trinity Week, week following Trinity Sunday
Eve of Theophany (Jan. 6 or Jan. 18)
Beheading of John the Baptist (Aug. 29 or Sept. 11)
The Elevation of the Holy Cross (Sept. 14 or 27)

Fasting Periods[2]

Nativity Fast (Advent) (Nov. 15 or Nov. 28 to Dec. 24 or Jan. 6)
Great Lent and Holy Week (seven weeks prior to Easter)
    The week before Lent is Carnival Week or Cheese-Fare Week where no meat is eaten but
    only dairy products. Among the Russians it is the time when *blini* are eaten (pancakes
    made with a yeast batter and served with melted sweet butter, smoked salmon or caviar,
    and sour cream).
Fast of the Apostles (St. Peter and St. Paul)
    (May 23 or June 5 to June 16 or June 29)
Fast of the Dormition of the Holy Theotokos
    (Aug. 1 or Aug. 14 to Aug. 15 or Aug. 28)

---

[1] Exact dates depend upon whether the Julian or the Gregorian calendar is followed.
[2] No meat or animal products such as milk, butter or cheese, nor fish can be eaten. Some
Greeks also abstain from olive oil.

TABLE 38.3

HISTORICAL INFLUENCES ON RUSSIAN COOKERY

Orthodox Christianity (988 A.D.)
    An elaborate church calendar of fast days and feast days was devised.
New meatless dishes and formalized revelry were introduced.
Mongols (Tartars) 13th to 15th Century (conquest and subjegation by Tartars)
    Mare's milk dishes (kumis), sour milk, broiled meats, curd cheese from soured or fermented
    milk, cabbage preserved in brine, tea drinking.
16th Century during reign of Ivan the Terrible
    Italian influence of architects imported from Italy to build the Kremlin, St. Basil's Church,
    etc.: salami, noodles, macaroni, fancy pastries.
17th Century during reign of Peter the Great
    German influence: sausages, schnitzel, fruit soups.
    Dutch influence: vegetable dishes and spiced cakes.
18th Century during reign of Catherine the Great
    Influence of French aristocracy cuisine from the beginning of the 18th Century up to the
    1917 Russian Revolution: sauces, pastries, cream soups.
Other influences
    From Caucasus and Middle East: small pieces of meat on skewers (shashlik), ground meat
    in vine leaves (dalma), rice dishes (plan) or pilaf. (Turks introduced rice from Persia.)

serving foods. For example, milk is preserved by souring, vegetables are salted or pickled, fruits are dried or made into preserves, meats are dried, fish are salted, pickled, or smoked. Historical influences on Russian cookery are shown in Table 38.3.

Peasants usually consumed a very meager diet. It consisted mainly of beets, cabbage, potatoes, onion, black bread, a small amount of meat and wild fruits in season.

The U.S.S.R. covers a wide area with many climatic and geographic zones. In area, it covers $1/6$ of the inhabited area of the globe. And, more than $3/4$ of the area is north of the 50th parallel. A rich, heavy diet is consumed in order to compensate for the cold. Moreover, plumpness is considered desirable.

The boundaries of the U.S.S.R. have changed from time to time during history. For these reasons, ingredients and food preparation methods tend to be variable, reflecting various influences. For example, Russians from the east consumed a diet similar to the Chinese; those from the southwest consumed one similar to that typical of the Middle East. Those from the northwest consumed one typical of Eastern Europeans.

Spices and Seasonings

A number of spices and seasonings are traditional ingredients in Russian cooking. These include, but are not limited to: caraway, dillweed, horseradish, half-sour cucumbers, nutmeg, parsley, poppyseeds, saffron, sunflower seeds.

Staples

Although the basic staples in the diet of the peasants were very limited, other classes consumed a wide variety of items. These included but are not limited to:

(A) Meat, fish, poultry, and eggs—beef, boar, hare, lamb, mutton cooked on a spit, pork, veal; more than 80 kinds of sausages were common; bream, carp, crayfish, herring, kilki (sardines), perch, pike, salmon (fresh and smoked), sturgeon; chicken, duck, goose, partridge, pheasant, quail, woodcock; eggs (hen's, caviar).

(B) Dairy products—cheese (tvorog), sour cream (smatana), sour milk; butter (unsalted preferred); cheese with caraway or fennel, cottage cheese.

(C) Cereal products—blini (similar to a pancake), buckwheat, corn, fried pies, millet, noodles and dumplings of many kinds, piroshki (similar to ravioli), potato starch, rice, rye bread, wheat; honey and walnut cakes, Kulich, baked products including cakes made with yeast doughs.

(D) Fruits—apples, apricots, cherries, cranberries, gooseberries, lemons, melons, oranges, peaches, pears, plums, quinces, strawberries.

(E) Vegetables—beets, Brussels sprouts, cabbage (red and white), carrots, cucumbers, eggplant, green beans, lettuce, mushrooms, onions, parsnips, peas, green peppers, potatoes, radishes, spinach, tomatoes, turnips.

(F) Beverages—coffee with hot milk, tea, vodka, wines, kuas (fermented leftover rye bread).

(G) Other—nuts (walnuts).

THE RUSSIAN-AMERICAN DIET

Migrations of Russians to the United States have occurred in four major waves. The earliest migration was between 1880 and 1910. Russian Jews and Carpatho-Russians from Austro-Hungry who settled in Pennsylvania, Ohio, Michigan, and Minnesota came at that time. Between 1910 and 1914 White Russians and Ukrainians of peasant stock arrived and settled in New York, New Jersey, and New England. Between 1918 and 1930 the first large postrevolutionary immigration occurred. Great Russians and other classes besides peasants, including aristocratic farmers, middle class intellectuals and professionals arrived in the United States from the east via Europe and from the west through Siberia. The last wave of immigrants was the post World War II migration that began in 1946. These were displaced persons, mainly Great Russians who had settled in the Balkans, Poland, Germany, and China who were uprooted by political pressures in those areas.

The largest colony of Russians in the United States is located in San Francisco. Customs are retained more in that community than in others in the United States due to availability of ingredients and social opportunities. In San Francisco is found the most representative examples of Great Russians and numerous food stores and restaurants.

In general, Russians have easily adopted the American diet. However, the following habits and patterns may still be followed or preferred: (a) continental breakfast, (b) soups eaten frequently accompanied by black bread, (c) salads—usually tomatoes and cucumbers, (d) liberal use of sour cream, (e) use of sweet butter, (f) heavy consumption of fish, and (g) preference for rich pastries.

BIBLIOGRAPHY

ANAN'EV, A. A. 1966. "Culinary" (Kulinaria). Zkonomika, Moscow. (Russian)
ANON, 1966. 1000 Tasty Dishes. Translated from the Lithuanian into Russian by Lithuanian Political & Scientific Literature. Vilnius.
FROLON, W. 1947. Katish, our Russian Cook. Farrar, Straus & Co., New York.
Holy Trinity Cathedral Parish in San Francisco. 1972. Personal communication with parish members.
HOWE, R. 1964. Russian Cooking. Roy Publishers, New York.
KENGIS, R. P. 1966. Home Preparations. Pichevaia Promychaennosty, Moscow. (Russian)
KROPATKIN, A. 1947. How to Cook and Eat in Russian. G. P. Putnam's Sons, New York.
MCGUIRE, L. M. 1954. Russia. In Old World Foods for New World Families. Dolphin Books, Doubleday & Co., Garden City, N.Y.
PAPASHNILY, H., PAPASHNILY, G., and Editors of Time-Life Books. 1969. Russian Cooking. Time-Life Books, New York.
SAPER, M. 1961. Cooking the Russian Way. Spring Books, London, England.
SOULSBY, T. 1972. Russian-American food patterns. J. Nutr. Educ. 4, No. 4, 170–172.

Appendix

TRADE MAGAZINES AND JOURNALS

American Chef, American Institute of Chefs, Columbus, Ohio

Bar Management, Schwartz Publications, 6 West 57 St., New York, N.Y. 10022

Catering Executive, Executive Business Media, Inc., Box 788, Lynbrook, N.Y. 11563

Chef, Culinary Review, Inc., 866 United Nations Plaza, Rm. 428, New York, N.Y. 10017

Chef Magazine, Culinary Federation, Inc., New York, N.Y.

Commercial Kitchen and Dining Room, U.S. Industrial Publications, Inc., 209 Dunn Ave., Stamford, Conn. 06905

Cooking for Profit, Gas Magazines, Inc., 1202 S. Park St., Madison, Wisc. 53715.

Dining: The Leisure Restaurant Magazine, 144 East 44th St., New York, N.Y. 10017.

Drive-In & Carry-Out, Clissold Publishing Co., 401 N. Wabash, Chicago, Ill. 60611.

Drive-In Management, Ojibway Press, Inc., Duluth, Minn. 55802

Fast Food, Fast Food Service, Inc., 144 E. 44th St., New York, N.Y. 10017.

Food and Lodging Hospitality, Patterson Publishing Co., 5 S. Wabash, Chicago, Ill. 60603

Food Executive, Food Service Executives Assoc., Alexandria, Va.

Hospitality, Patterson Publishing Co. 614 Superior Ave. West, Cleveland, Ohio 44113.

Hospitality Magazines Restaurant Combination, Patterson Publishing Co., 5 S. Wabash, Chicago, Ill. 60603

Institutional Distribution, 144 E. 44th St., New York, N.Y. 10017

Institutions/Volume Feeding, Cahners Publishing Co., Chicago Div., 5 S. Wabash, Chicago, Ill. 60603

Metropolitan Restaurant News, New York State Restaurant Assoc., 1225 Broadway, New York, N.Y. 10001.

Nation's Restaurant News, Lebhar-Friedman Publications, Inc., 2 Park Ave., New York, N.Y. 10016.

Pacific Coast Record, Pacific Coast Record, Inc., 1011 S. Los Angeles St., Los Angeles, Calif. 90015.

Restaurant News and Hotel Magazine of Washington State, Restaurant Assoc. of the State of Washington, 220 Securities Bldg., Seattle, Washington 98101.

Restaurant Profit Ideas, National Research Bureau, Inc., 221 N. LaSalle St., Chicago, Ill. 60601.

Vend, Billboard Publishing Co., Cincinnati, Ohio.

AMERICANIZED ETHNIC COOKBOOKS

AARON, J., and SALOM, G. G. 1965. The Art of Mexican Cooking. Doubleday & Co., New York.

AMUNATEGUI, F., and ORTIZ, E. 1971. Masterpieces of French Cuisine. Macmillan Co., New York.

BABOIAN, R. 1971. The Art of Armenian Cooking. Doubleday & Co., New York.

BENNETT, P. P., and CLARK, V. R. 1954. The Art of Hungarian Cooking. Doubleday & Co., New York.

BONI, A. 1950. Talisman Italian Cook Book. Crown Publishers, New York.

CALEVA, H. 1956. Italian Cookbook for Quantity Service. Ahrens Publishing Co., New York.

CALEVA, H. 1958. Chinese Cookbook for Quantity Service. Ahrens Publishing Co., New York.

CALEVA, H. 1958. Mexican Cookbook for Quantity Service, Ahrens Publishing Co., New York.

The CHAMBERLAINS. 1965. The Flavor of Italy. Hastings House Publishers, New York.

CHANG, W. W., CHANG, I. B., KUTSCHER, H. W., and KUTSCHER, A. H. 1970. An Encyclopedia of Chinese Food and Cooking. Crown Publishers, New York.

CHOY, J. 1964. The Art of Oriental Cooking. Doubleday & Co., New York.

CORNFELD, L. 1962. Israeli Cookery. Avi Publishing Co., Westport, Conn.

DULL, S. R. 1968. Southern Cooking. Grosset & Dunlap, New York.

FREDRIKSON, J. 1967. The Great Scandinavian Cookbook. Crown Publishers, New York.

GARCIA, C. 1970. Clarita's Cocina Cook Book. Doubleday & Co., New York.

HAZELTON, N. S. 1964. The Art of Danish Cooking. Doubleday & Co., Garden City, N.Y.

HESS, O., and HESS, A. 1967. Viennese Cooking. Crown Publishers, New York.

HONG, W. Y. 1952. The Chinese Cook Book. Crown Publishers, New York.

KRAUS, B. 1970. The Cookbook of the United Nations. Simon & Schuster, New York.

LEONARD, L. W. 1963. Jewish Cookery. Crown Publishers, New York.

LEONE, G. 1967. Leone's Italian Cookbook. Harper & Row Publishers, Scranton, Pa.

LAPINTO, M. 1948. The Art of Italian Cooking. Doubleday & Co., New York.

MITCHELL, J.   1956.   Luchow's German Cookbook.   Doubleday & Co., New York.

SHERIDAN, M. 1965. The Art of Irish Cooking. Doubleday & Co., New York.

EDITORS OF SUNSET BOOKS.   1970.   Sunset Oriental Cook Book.   Lane Magazine and Book Co., Menlo Park, Calif.

WASON, B.   1967.   The Art of German Cooking.   Doubleday & Co., Garden City, N.Y.

WASON, B. 1963. The Art of Spanish Cooking. Doubleday & Co., New York.

WEISS, E. 1970. Hungarian Cookery, Paprikas Weise, New York.

Index